# Marketing for Congregations

"This is the most comprehensive and helpful book on church management and marketing I've read. It's worth the price of ten books. It's indispensible for ministry in the 1990s."

Rick Warren
Saddleback Valley Community Church

# Marketing for Congregations

## Choosing to Serve People More Effectively

Norman Shawchuck, Ph.D.
Philip Kotler, Ph.D.
Bruce Wrenn, Ph.D.
Gustave Rath, Ph.D.

Abingdon Press
Nashville

MARKETING FOR CONGREGATIONS
CHOOSING TO SERVE PEOPLE MORE EFFECTIVELY

2.54.5
M345

**Library of Congress Cataloging-in-Publication Data**

Marketing for congregations : choosing to serve people more
    effectively / Norman Shawchuck . . . [et al.].
        p.    cm.
    Includes bibliographical references and index.
    ISBN 0-687-23579-0 (alk. paper)
    1. Church management.    I. Shawchuck, Norman, 1935-
    BV652.M37    1992                                    92-12748
    254.4—dc20                                           CIP

The authors gratefully acknowledge the following for permission to reprint:

American Management Association for excerpts from *The Frugal Marketer* by J. Donald Weinrauch and Nancy Croft Baker. Copyright © 1989 by J. Donald Weinrauch and Nancy Croft Baker. Published by AMACOM, a division of American Management Association. All rights reserved.

Associated Press for excerpts from the article "Young Adults Lean to 'Megachurches.'" Copyright © 1991 by Associated Press.

*The Chicago Tribune* for excerpts from the article "Marketing Becomes a Tool in the Business of Religion" by Michael Hirsley. Copyright © 1990 by Chicago Tribune Company. All rights reserved.

*Christianity Today* for excerpts from "Admen for Heaven," by David Neff. Copyright © 1987 by CHRISTIANITY TODAY.

HarperCollins for charts from *The Clustering of America* by Michael J. Weiss. Copyright © 1988 by Michael Weiss.

Macmillan Publishing Co. for excerpts from *The Practice of Marketing Management* by William A. Cohen. Copyright © 1988 by Macmillan.

New American Library, a division of Penguin Books USA Inc., for the adaptation of *The Service Edge* by Ron Zemke and Dick Schaaf. Copyright © 1989 by Ron Zemke and Dick Schaaf.

*Public Relations Quarterly* for excerpts from the article "Do's and Don'ts for Religious Advertisers," by Ben Ramsey. Copyright © 1977 by *Public Relations Quarterly*.

*U.S. News and World Report* for excerpts from the article "Spreading God's Word: Five Success Stories." Copyright © 1984 by *U.S. News and World Report*.

Scripture quotations are from the New Revised Standard Version Bible, copyright © 1989, by the Division of Christian Education of the National Council of the Churches of Christ in the United States of America. Used by permission.

# Contents

**Chapter 9**

**Chapter 10**

# List of Exhibits

# Marketing for Congregations

# Acknowledgments

This book was inspired by Philip Kotler's book *Marketing for Non-profit Organizations* (New York: Prentice-Hall, 2nd ed., 1982; 3rd ed. written with Alan Andreasen, 1987), which describes and applies marketing needs, concepts, tools, and practices to a variety of nonprofit organizations. There is much, however, that is special and distinctive about religious organizations, and a new book was needed that specifically addressed the problems and opportunities of churches and synagogues. This book, while using some of Professor Kotler's material, adds substantial reformulations and new material of interest to churches and synagogues.

Many of our colleagues and students contributed to gathering information for this book. They include Dr. Ric Olson of the Iowa Annual Conference and previously of the Indiana Conference of The United Methodist Church; Professor Roger Heuser of Southern California College; the Rev. Bruce Ough, Council Director; and the Rev. Nancy Allen, Program Consultant of the Council of Ministries, Iowa Conference of The United Methodist Church. Each contributed significant information and facilitated interviews with pastors. The Rev. Gene Koth of the Walnut Hill Methodist Church, Des Moines, Iowa; the Rev. Ron Blix of Christ Community United Methodist Church, Cedar Rapids, Iowa; the Rev. Bill Poland of Salem United Methodist Church, Council Bluffs, Iowa.

We also want to thank Rabbi Edelheiht, of Emanuel Congregation of Chicago, who has heightened our awareness of Jewish sensitivity and has offered us many valuable comments; Father Leo Bartel of the Rockford Dioceses of the Roman Catholic Church; the Rev. Jon Pyne, Hennepin Avenue United Methodist Church, Minneapolis; Jim Anderson, council member of First Baptist Church, Belvidere, Illinois; the Rev. Mark Erickson of the Assembly of God Church in Elgin, North Dakota; Dr. Wayne Purintun of the Presbytery of Cincinnati, Ohio; the Rev. Roger Fritts of First Unitarian Church of Evanston, Illinois; the Rev. Larry X. Peers, staff member of the Unitarian-Universalist Association; Ms. Robin Chaddock of Second Presbyterian Church in Indianapolis, Indiana; and the Rev. John Roberts, pastor of the United Methodist Church, Blaine, Minnesota.

15

The production of the materials was facilitated by the help of many persons, including Sharon Robinson of Northwestern University and Winston Lees and Henry Chang, Northwestern University seniors.

A special thanks for editorial suggestions and support goes to Paul Franklyn, Linda Allen, and the Abingdon Press staff.

The authors accept full responsibility for the book and its opinions, which may at times differ from those of all the persons who have assisted in this project.

# Preface

The following article appeared on the front page of the Chicago Tribune, November 6, 1990.

---

### Marketing Becomes a Tool in the Business of Religion

*By Michael Hirsley, Religion Writer,*

Facing an audience of fellow Roman Catholics here for a national symposium on regenerating Catholicism among young adults, Patrick Flynn talked turkey.

More literally, he talked hamburger.

Flynn, executive vice president of McDonald's Corp., told the recent gathering of nearly 300 Catholic leaders in the Midland hotel that the fast-food chain tries to "reach out generically with advertising, but then reach out at a local level—trying to live what we advertise."

After the conference, Flynn acknowledged, "There were probably some attendees who were asking why we were talking about McDonald's. I didn't try to draw any parallels to the Church."

But discussion groups afterward did.

"Pat Flynn's advice to 'Think like a brand; act like a retailer' is perfectly applicable to churches," said symposium organizer John Fontana, who directs a center at Chicago's Old St. Patrick's Church that tries to connect parishioners with their faith.

Religious professionals long have held an "anti-business bias," Fontana said. "They want to keep a business/church dichotomy, as opposed to finding similarities and learning from successful marketing strategies."

Words such as "consumer," "market" and "shopping around," which have become commonplace in American secular usage, are being heard increasingly in religious circles, a segment of society that used to shun such terms.

Religion in the United States faces new opportunities and new dilemmas, experts on church growth agree. They say many unchurched Americans particularly among the 75 million in the Baby Boom generation, now ages 28 to 43, are looking for organized faith.

---

17

However, the Boomers are not blindly loyal to the denominations in which they were raised, and they are not hesitant about testing different churches, the experts say.

In other words, many unchurched Americans must be viewed as a market of educated consumers who are shopping around.

"A church should not be run like a used car lot," says Ron Sellers, project director for the Barna Research Group of Glendale, California. But once you pay a pastor's salary, pay building and maintenance costs, buy insurance . . . it is a business."

"And there is a market out there to whom you sell yourself in terms of how to affect those people's lives," said Sellers.

"Denominational loyalty is a thing of the past," said Rev. Lyle Schaller of Naperville, a United Methodist minister and a church growth researcher with the Yokefellow Institute of Richmond, IN.

"It evokes hostility among many religious leaders when you talk about competition," he said. "But churchgoers today go shopping for pastors and programs. What the church scene is today is a market."

Who survives in this new marketplace? There is no simple answer. Witness three growing churches in the Chicago area.

At non-denominational Willow Creek, 14,600 members can avail themselves of 90 ministries, including personal finances, single parenting and car repair. Rev. Bill Hybels polled the neighborhood needs for a church before beginning his ministry 15 years ago.

At Old St. Patrick's Catholic Church, 700 W. Adams St., 1,200 members often fill pews at services that drew only a few dozen worshipers seven years ago; Rev. Jack Wall's outreach to a target community filled with single people and young childless couples includes a "world's largest block party" every summer.

At Grace United Methodist Church, whose 2,500 members represent a growth of one-third since 1983 in highly mobile suburban Naperville, Rev. Arthur Landwehr said the first step was simply encouraging members to invite their neighbors to church.

Those successes cross denominational lines, and the growth at Grace United Methodist Church goes counter to an overall drop in membership among Methodists. In all three cases, members say they were attracted by a welcoming attitude, access to smaller group services within the larger church, and sermons that address real-life problems.

It all boils down to a change from 25 years ago, when churches took it for granted that people would come, researchers said.

"Back then, new churches' three factors for success were location, location, location," Schaller said. "Today, the three factors
are pastor, pastor, pastor."

Times have changed when a major newspaper will feature the topic
of religion and marketing on its front page!

Times *have* changed. There are now more persons in America
who are either not associated with any religion whatsoever or who
are connected to a religious tradition other than the traditional
Catholic, Orthodox, Protestant, and Jewish faiths. The advent of the
baby-boom generation provides us with the first generation of
Americans who have not simply "bought" the faith and ecclesiastical
traditions of their parents.

In this milieu congregations and religious organizations are striving to be faithful and successful in the context of new competitors—
sports, drugs, Eastern philosophies, and so on. Some of these religious organizations are turning to the discipline of marketing as a
means of doing the job more effectively.

As an organized theory, marketing is a new kid on the block, having matured as a science and an art in the last thirty years. However,
in many ways the world's great religious movements arose out of the
work of founders who innately utilized the concepts and methods
that have today come to be known as marketing, and by these means
attracted disciples in great numbers, who in turn carried the Word
around the globe.

When John Wesley founded the Methodist movement, he
quickly recognized the need to go where the unchurched were
and to communicate in their terms so that they might respond. This
decision caused him to begin preaching outdoors, because the
churches would not allow the poor and uneducated to attend their
services. This was no easy change of method for Wesley. "I must
become more vile," he said, as he laid aside the pleasing and
"accepted" methods of the Church of England to begin his field
preaching, which carried him 250,000 miles on horseback from

cemeteries (where he preached standing on a tombstone), to coal mines, to hills outside of Bristol. He lived in a day when a favorite form of fellowship among family and friends, at home and in the tavern, was group singing, and he utilized this as a means of communicating his message to the listeners. His brother Charles wrote over 6,000 hymns, most of them set to the familiar folk music of the day, which the Wesleys taught to their mostly illiterate listeners. As his movement grew, he stressed upon his laypreachers that they needed to discover and respond to the pain and problems of those they hoped to reach. "Go to those who need you. Go to those who need you most," was his constant plea.

Had the *Tribune* article been written in 1750, John Wesley probably would have been featured as a prime example of a religious leader who was adopting marketing theory. We have interviewed many leaders of congregations and other religious organizations who are utilizing sound marketing methods. Yet when we visited with them, they disavowed knowing anything about marketing. A more formal learning of marketing principles could perhaps have made many of them even more effective.

For all religious organizations, a marketing perspective can provide rich insights into more effectively conducting a number of major activities, including:

1. Starting a new congregation;
2. Targeting prospective members;
3. Attracting first-time visitors;
4. Building membership involvement and commitment;
5. Attracting and managing volunteers;
6. Keeping members;
7. Involving members in measuring the importance and performance of the organization's ministries and services;
8. Attracting funds and other resources.

In addition, marketing raises the question of how religious organizations should go about judging their success. Is the measure of success size and growth? Member satisfaction? The level of member participation? Marketing feedback mechanisms allow leaders of religious organizations to evaluate the success of their programs and to assess the extent to which ministry objectives have been achieved.

This book will explore the many uses of marketing theory and practice to understand how leaders of religious institutions can build a more viable organization—one that better captures the opportunities for ministering to the needs of its members, and eliciting from them the levels of faith, support, and participation that are essential for living a spiritually rich life.

This book will not tout marketing as the coming of the kingdom or a cure for all ills. Marketing is not an *end* for the religious organization; rather, it is a tool—a *means* to more effectively carry out the mission and ministry of the religious organization.

Marketing is, however, the next management discipline to be seriously considered and adapted by the religious community. Marketing is not a fad—a novelty to play with for a while. Rather, marketing is a more effective response to the rapidly changing, turbulent environment in which religious organizations find themselves today.

At the same time, marketing is not a substitute for the essential place of spirituality and vision in the life of the religious leader and his or her organization. Spirituality and vision grow out of one's relationship with God and as a result of a disciplined life, nurtured by God as one gives oneself to the means of grace God has provided God's people.

The people of God have always believed God speaks to them, if they listen. This discernment of the leading of the Lord comes through reflection, prayer, and faithfulness to the disciplines and paths God sets before the leader and the people.

Marketing is no substitute for this. However, there is nothing about marketing that is against this. Further, there is a great deal about marketing that can support and inform one's praying, listening, discerning, and doing of ministry.

It is the intent of the authors of this book to be humble about the place of marketing in the list of the religious priorities, but also to be bullish about the role it can play in making almost any ministry or minister more effective. In this book, there is at least one good idea for every religious leader or worker. Basically, the book presents a new way of conceptualizing, planning, and implementing ministry. The book will take nothing away from what you already know about management and ministry. Rather, it will clarify, augment, and support what is already known. Marketing is simply another step toward more effective ministry.

What is marketing? Marketing is a process for making concrete decisions about what the religious organization can do, and not do, to achieve its mission. Marketing is not selling, advertising, or promotion—though it may include all of these. *Marketing is the analysis, planning, implementation, and control of carefully formulated programs to bring about voluntary "exchanges" with specifically targeted groups for the purpose of achieving the organization's missional objectives.* In other words, marketing can help a religious organization accomplish its desired ends through its interactions with various groups. Most of all, marketing is a process for building *responsiveness* into a religious organization—responsiveness to those myriad groups whose needs must be satisfied if the organization is to be successful in its ministry endeavors.

This book will equip you with theory and tools to more productively use available resources in order to better achieve religious objectives by becoming more responsive to those whom the organization exists to serve. You will gain concepts and tools for determining mission; discovering needs that may be converted into ministry opportunities; analyzing, segmenting, and targeting groups or concerns, both internal and external; planning responsive programs; and evaluating results of the effort.

# How Marketing Can Help Religious Organizations Achieve Their Objectives

## Introduction to Part One

Part One opens the discussion of marketing for religious organizations by attempting to define the mission, role, and limits of marketing for religious institutions (chap. 1). From this discussion we begin to deal more specifically with how a "market orientation" for a religious organization may be manifested (chap. 2). Such a discussion involves something of a paradigm shift for many religious leaders who are not accustomed to thinking of their institutions as needing to become market oriented to achieve their objectives. Indeed, many may even question the advisability of adopting such an orientation by a spiritually based institution. We have struggled through these philosophical debates ourselves and believe we have some insights and answers for skeptics. Chapter 3 details what it means for religious organizations to be responsive to their environment, to their members, and to their calling. The differences between being unresponsive or casually, highly, or fully responsive are very real and, we believe, very important for religious organizations.

If, as we hope, you desire to become a leader of a fully responsive organization, we must address the issue of how that end can be achieved. Chapter 4 specifies the essential marketing concepts for responsive religious organizations. Some of these concepts have a familiar sound to them (mission, publics); some sound familiar but may take on new meanings when viewed from a marketing perspective (image, exchange, satisfaction); and some may be relatively new to you (segmentation, targeting, positioning). These concepts constitute the building blocks of marketing and provide the foundation for the planning and "doing" of marketing, which is the focus of Parts Two and Three of this book.

# 1

# Facing Change and Crisis in Congregations:

## The Role of Marketing

We believe that religious leaders and congregations can benefit greatly from incorporating market-oriented thinking, planning, and action into their everyday activities. Our purpose is not to ask clergy and lay leaders to become marketers. Rather, our purpose is to help them think systemically and insightfully about the market of people who currently or potentially have unmet needs for spirituality, meaning and purpose in life; and to think about what their congregation can offer to meet those needs.

Religious institutions are unique in society. They are the only social institution formally set up to provide spiritual and moral nourishment to the citizens. Other institutions to which we belong or interact with—business firms, schools, unions, hospitals, government agencies, community organizations, reform groups, etc.—do not address the spiritual and moral issues facing us as individuals and families. It is the unique mission of religious organizations to raise our sights above the mundane tasks of "getting and spending" to address the larger questions of personal purpose, service to others, what it means to be a fulfilled human being, and the mysteries of the cosmos.

If religious organizations were thriving and fulfilling this purpose of satisfying our needs for spiritual and moral nourishment, this book would not have to be written. The sad fact is, however, that religious organizations seem to be growing more irrelevant over time to the majority of Americans. Most of the 300,000 churches in America are not satisfying their congregations and more people are becoming unchurched citizens. We firmly believe it is not the message that is obsolete, but the way it is delivered, and to whom it is delivered, and what is included. In a word, many churches and synagogues have lost

25

touch with their constituents. They continue to preach about what people should do rather than listen to what is on people's minds and help them, individually and collectively, to find their way.

This book is not written to help clergy and lay leaders become marketers. It is to help them become market-oriented and opportunity-focused. The shortest definition of marketing is *meeting needs profitably.* In the context of religious organizations, this means creating "spiritual profit" for both the provider and the receiver through transactions and relationships taking place in religious organizations.

In the course of preparing this book, we asked many religious leaders to list the main questions on their mind concerning the purpose and role of marketing in religious organizations. The main questions are listed below. The remainder of the chapter will address, and hopefully answer these questions:

1. Why is marketing important for religious organizations?
2. Can marketing be used by religious organizations of all sizes and types?
3. What characterizes successful congregations?
4. How can the major criticisms of marketing be addressed?
5. What are the distinctive characteristics of religious organization marketing?

## Why Is Marketing Important for Religious Organizations?

### Contemporary Challenges Facing Religious Organizations

Religious organizations in America are facing a crisis. The percentage of persons not connected to a church or synagogue in virtually every county of the United States is greater than ever before in the history of our country. For the first time in history there are more nonChristians than Christians in America, making ours a "functionally atheistic" society. This would seem to imply that every congregation—whether in a rural, suburban, or urban area—has greater opportunities to expand its ministries than ever before. Yet the work of the ministry remains (or grows) difficult. This is true in part because of the following contemporary challenges facing religious organizations.

**Secularization.** The secularization of American society points to non-religious values and institutions (wealth, power, independence, etc.) displacing religious values and institutions as the motivating factors of persons' attitudes, values, and behavior.

As society becomes more secularized, there arises a compensatory need for persons to experience the transcendent and spiritual. The issue is whether current religious dogmas and practices can supply the form of spiritual and transcendent experience that people are seeking in an overly secularized world.

In the late 1960s and early 1970s, young people fed their spiritual hunger through human potential offerings, rather than established religious programs. It is revealing to note that when, in the 1980s, people were surveyed as to what they did for relief of depression or discouragement, 77 percent of the people polled said they would spend more time with a hobby, watching TV, or listening to music. Only 48 percent said they would spend more time in prayer, meditation, or reading the Bible.[1]

**Anomie.** People find themselves increasingly fragmented and dissociated from others. This is manifested in the decline of family life: escalating divorce rates, more children in single-parent households, broken homes. *Gemeinschaft* (community) is disappearing. As a result, persons are experiencing a growing need for meaningful association with others, for fellowship. A 1988 survey showed that 94 percent of the people would like to see more emphasis on traditional family ties in the years ahead.[2] Congregations are in a most opportune position to meet the growing hunger for fellowship and to strengthen traditional family ties.

**Erosion of ideology.** People are losing faith in the things they formerly believed in—such as the American Dream, money, and success—as an answer to all of our problems. When asked whether they would like to see less emphasis on money in the coming years, 67 percent of those polled said they would welcome such a change.[3] Likewise, when asked if they were satisfied or dissatisfied with the honesty and standards of persons in the United States today, 63 percent said they were dissatisfied.[4] Congregations can meet the need for a more positive structure of beliefs and values to guide one's life.

**Changing demographics.** The 1980s, and now the 1990s, have witnessed a growth of nontraditional groups, such as gays, cohabitors, singles by choice, and childless couples. There have also been ethnic shifts within cities and neighborhoods. In most large cities there are areas where the number of churches has remained constant, but the turnover rate within the constituents has been high. The large number of old-line church closings in some areas has been matched by an equal number of new ethnic churches, often in the same denomination.

Population shifts have also occurred regionally. As people moved south, they often changed their denomination to the popular one in their new location. A United Methodist family from the North moves South and joins a Southern Baptist church. To this extent, some of the growth of certain denominations is a function of geographical movement, not doctrinal shifts.[5]

**Intensifying competition.** Religious organizations face stiff competition from many sectors: secular activities (movies, sports, travel), religious activities (local congregations, TV ministries, Eastern religions), and human potential offerings (humanism, new age movement, etc.). For example, a 1988 poll found that 49 percent of the surveyed adults felt that religion was losing influence on American life, while only 36 percent felt that it was increasing in influence. Two years earlier, in 1986, these figures were approximately the reverse of the 1988 findings.[6]

Many religious leaders see the competition as coming from other churches (i.e., mainline church vs. evangelical vs. independent). There is some competition here, but not so much as one might think. With an ever-increasing percentage of Americans claiming no religious affiliation, the prospect pool is large enough to fill every church in town. The more substantial competition are the habits that millions of Americans have developed for their Sunday morning routine—the Sunday paper, a warm cup of coffee, a comfortable chair, a TV set, a nice boat on a beautiful lake, a golf course. These alternatives are the competition the church faces when it tries to fill its sanctuary on Sunday morning. In Chicago, the Chicago Bears and Lake Michigan are greater competition to the United Methodist congregations than are the Presbyterians a couple of blocks down the street.

**Rising costs of operations.** Religious organizations do their spiritual labor with their feet planted in material and economic realities. Virtually every mainline denomination is struggling (some are reeling) with the rising costs of pensions and insurance for their clergy. During the fuel crisis of the early 1970s, many congregations had to close down because they were unable to shoulder the fuel bills. One estimate was that 40 percent of the churches in America would have had to close had fuel costs continued at such high levels.

**Recent scandals on the religious scene.** Jim and Tammy Bakker, Jimmy Swaggart, and other public religious personalities have led many people to question whether highly visible religious leaders are exploiting their followers for personal gain. A 1987 survey found that 53 percent of adults believed television evangelists to be dishonest, 51 percent felt they were insincere, 56 percent that the TV evangelist did not have a special relationship with God, and 63 percent believed the evangelists were not trustworthy with money.[7]

**A la carte religion.** Many young people are not inheriting the religion of their parents but are delaying commitment to a church or synagogue until some nodal event (e.g., the birth of a child) precipitates religious "shopping" behavior. The individual or couple then "samples" congregations until finding one that fits the preferred lifestyle. Increasingly, loyalty to a particular denomination fails to accompany a family when it changes its residence.

**Privatization of faith.** People no longer believe church or synagogue attendance is essential to their faith. Surveys in 1988 revealed that nationally 76 percent of American adults felt a person could be a good Christian or Jew without attending church or synagogue. This percentage was even higher among those aged 25-29 (84 percent) or in those living in the West (83 percent). Also, 42 percent of the people said that there has been a period of two years or more when they did not attend church or synagogue apart from weddings, funerals, or special holidays such as Christmas, Easter, or Yom Kippur.[8]

Thus we see that there are several factors accounting for the decline of attendance and loyalty to organized religion.

Yet, ironically, most community residents still want the "meeting house on the corner." Fewer, however, are interested in being regular participants in the programs. Rather, they want the church or synagogue, and the clergy, to be there for the special occasions in their lives and for a few high holy days—weddings, funerals, serious illness, Yom Kippur, Christmas, Easter, Bar Mitzvahs.

In a conversation with the authors, Father Robert Doherty, S.J., professor at Pope John XXIII National College, described the increasing tendency to view churches as "religious museums." "Everyone," he said, "wants to have museums in their community. But no one visits the museum every week, and few expect to be involved. Rather, the museum is a place where people go two or three times a year—to look and enjoy."

Not all churches or synagogues are exhibiting signs of becoming religious museums. Rather, many are growing in number and expanding in ministry. But—and this is important—those that are realizing greater success in ministry are moving toward becoming *community centers* that offer a variety of worship, learning, social, educational, and leisure opportunities for their members and participants—without losing sight of their mission and *raison d'être*. The idea of congregations becoming "community centers" causes a congregation to rethink its concept of purpose and ministry.

## The Entrepreneurial Concept of a Religious Organization

Should a church or synagogue operate only as a house of worship or should it provide a broader set of services to its members and communities? Dr. Gary Tobin, Professor of Modern Jewish Studies at Brandeis University, calls upon religious organizations to be entrepreneurial and broad in their mission and ministries. He sees an entrepreneurial church or synagogue as offering not one but six products to its members. The religious organization would be:

1. *A worship center,* in ministering to the spiritual, moral, and religious needs of the community.
2. *A community center,* in building a community of kindred spirits pursuing common goals and sharing a common ethos.
3. *An education center,* in providing religious instruction to children and continuous education programs for adult members.
4. *A human services center,* in providing assistance to members who need psychological, social, medical, or financial help.
5. *A community service center,* in carrying out social action to improve the quality of life of everyone in the society.

6. *A family substitute center,* in providing a larger family sense to members whose families have broken up or are not functioning fully.

These various roles of the congregation do not depend on its size. The religious organization need not be a megachurch or synagogue.[9] All of these opportunities can be provided to members and the community if the needs are there.

For the religious organization to function in this way, it needs a set of committees or task forces. Dr. Tobin suggests the following committees:

1. Mission committee
2. Leadership development committee
3. Interagency planning and programs committee
4. Financial resources committee
5. Membership committee
6. Communication and marketing committee
7. Special events and projects committee
8. Community development committee
9. Human services committee
10. Adult and family education committee
11. Interfaith program committee
12. Personal touch committee

Dr. Tobin believes that churches and synagogues must move toward professionalizing their staffs to achieve entrepreneurial objectives. It is not enough to be run by a board, a clerical staff, and a few volunteers. Without becoming entrepreneurial and more professional, churches and synagogues are in danger of becoming "religious museums."[10]

The good news is that every church and synagogue, large and small, might make itself more appealing, relevant, and sensitive to its constituents and its environment without compromising its mission. Marketing can assist these congregations, large and small, to accomplish that goal. Marketing can be a "tool" in the hands of the faithful minister.

At the same time, the role of marketing is not simply to produce *church growth* or *financial growth.* It is important to distinguish marketing's role from the roles played by the church growth movement (spearheaded by the Church Growth Institute at Fuller Theological Seminary) and the activities given to *financial growth*—to increase the contribution base. While both church growth and financial growth have important roles to play in the church or synagogue, marketing is neither.

*Marketing is a discipline intended to address the development of quality congregations and ministries.* Religious marketing is committed to the idea that it is better to conduct one ministry with excellence than to conduct many ministries of marginal worth or relevance to the people they are intended to serve. Developing quality congregations usually will lead to church growth and financial growth, but as a by-product rather than as the essential goal.

## Can Marketing Be Used by Religious Organizations of All Sizes and Types?

Here we will present three stories—one of a very small congregation, another of a medium-sized congregation, and the third of a very large congregation—to illustrate the quality development of congregations and their ministries, rather than the pursuit of growth and expansion for the sake of growth and expansion.

The first story concerns a tiny congregation of 13 members.

Prior to becoming the pastor of the Guthrie, Oklahoma, Church of the Nazarene, Ed Morres operated an oilfield service business in west Texas. Then in 1986, at the age of 34, Ed felt a call to ministry. He had no prior theological training.

When Ed arrived in Guthrie in 1986, 13 willing church members waited to greet him. That was it, 13 members. The congregation was then 66 years old. Ed knew that in order for the congregation to become vital it would have to reach out to serve its community. On the other hand, 13 people were certainly not able to serve many needs. He decided, therefore, that the congregation would identify one group in the community that demonstrated great need, and that the congregation of 13 people might serve.

Within a couple of months, Ed was able to identify just such a group. The group consisted of uneducated, economically distressed families, most of whom had children and young people in the household. The congregation then focused on the basic needs of this group; responding with clothing, food, educational assistance, tutoring, employment assistance, and, occasionally, shelter.

The congregation's efforts to serve this group gained the attention of social service and civic organizations in Guthrie, as well as those who were now being served by the congregation. A year and a half later, the average Sunday service attendance stood at 197. This was not the same congregation it was 2 years earlier. Now the emphasis was on serving the needs of others with excellence, not on attracting greater numbers.

The second story concerns a church with under 100 members.

McGrawsville, Indiana, is located 15 miles from Peru and 18 miles from Kokomo, Indiana. It is a small town with 20 houses, a grain elevator, and a United Methodist church. In the late 1970s, attendance at the church hovered around 65. The congregation was served by a part-time pastor, since it could not afford to pay the salary of a full-time pastor. The congregation did have strong lay leadership, both men and women with a desire and vision of becoming a strong and growing congregation. This vision began to move toward reality in the early 1980s as several steps were taken by the congregation: The group committed itself to a strong mission outreach and began a series of significant budget increases for mission projects; a Kids Klub was started, which they called the Joybunch; several spiritual renewal efforts were undertaken, including two Lay Witness Missions and home fellowship groups; and the congregation worked to have more vital and satisfying worship services.

The congregation's efforts proved fruitful, and by 1985 the group had grown large enough to hire its first full-time pastor. with the taking of this significant step, the congregation experienced an even deeper commitment to serve its community and to witness to their neighbors. Over the decade of the 1980s, several new ministries were undertaken by the members, including a commitment to word-of-mouth witness and inviting neighbors to become a part of the congregation; lay visits to the home of first-time visitors to take gifts of home-baked goods and to thank them for visiting the church; home visitation to persons in need; the installation of large, attractive church signs at the two main highways leading to McGrawsville; and response ministries to families in crisis, such as farm help projects, roofing, painting and maintenance, food and prepared meals, utility payments, and the like.

Along the way the original Kids Klub grew to an average attendance of 70 children, and a Junior Joybunch was started, which now has 25 3- to 5-year-old kids. The church's Sunday attendance averages 250 worshipers.[11]

The next story will demonstrate how market-oriented thinking can produce results in a large congregation.

Willow Creek Community Church conducted its first worship service on October 12, 1975, in a rented movie house located in Palatine, a northwest suburb of Chicago. About 125 persons attended. Now located in Barrington, the weekend service attendance is in excess of 15,000.

The origin of the Willow Creek Community Church has been built up in a rich oral tradition. New members hear the story during their process of membership instruction. Each year its founder and senior pastor, Bill Hybels, preaches a message describing the congregation's mission, its doctrine, and the meaning of membership.

When Pastor Hybels and three colleagues decided to start a church, they began by conducting door-to-door interviews. At each house they asked, "Do you actively attend a local church?" If the person answered in the affirmative, they would say, "Good, keep it up. Have a nice day." If the person said no, they asked, "Why not? What is there about church that makes it difficult for you to attend?" These people gave several reasons, the five most often ones being:

1. "It is irrelevant to my life. They use words I don't understand. They talk about things I don't know anything

about or have no interest in. The church and the Bible
have no practical application in my everyday life."
2. "It is boring. Everything they do is a dull, predictable
routine. I'm turned off by their liturgy and symbolism."
3. All they want is my money. They don't care about me.
All they care about is what they can get out of me."
4. "I always leave feeling depressed or guilty."
5. "They invade my privacy and embarrass me. They
want me to stand up or sign a book or wear a tag."

To conclude the interview, Pastor Hybels and his colleagues
would ask a hypothetical question, "If such a church existed that
was not like this, would you be interested in attending? If we start
such a church, may we call you?" From the results, they concluded that if an unchurched person is going to attend church, it is
going to be on Sunday morning. And if the service is to have any
appeal for the unchurched, it must:

1. Provide anonymity, so that the person is not singled out
or embarrassed;
2. Present the message at an introductory level;
3. Be free of pressure on the person to decide anything
until she or he feels ready;
4. Be excellent in programming and presentation.

With this in mind they designed Christianity 101, a service
specifically for first-time visitors who have little or no positive
experience with what to expect in a church service. The design
worked; attendance reached over 1,000 in the first year. Each
week Christianity 101 is planned with Unchurched Harry in mind.
Every member knows him and can tell you about him. Unchurched
Harry is any male between the ages of 25 and 50 who sees himself as self-reliant, who dislikes tradition, and feels little or no
need for religion.

The founders of Willow Creek decided to target Unchurched
Harry, reasoning that if the male head of the household could be
attracted to church, other persons would come along—spouse,
children, associates. Later the concept of Unchurched Mary was
added, but the emphasis is still on Harry. Unchurched Mary is a
female with similar demographics as those stated for Harry.

As persons become more active in the church and are ready to move beyond Christianity 101, they are introduced to Christianity 201. Christianity 201 is the Wednesday and Thursday evening services, called New Community. The leaders know that the people who are more committed will come together at a time other than Sunday morning. New Community started in 1975 with a group of 30 people. Presently, weekly attendance is in excess of 5,000.

The congregation has age diversity. Persons come dressed casually and comfortably. On Wednesday and Thursday evenings, people wear everything from blue jeans and sneakers to suits and ties. Very few people are seen carrying Bibles on weekends. However, the midweek congregation comes with Bible and spiral notebook.

The music in both services is excellent. There are no hymnbooks for the congregation; rather words are projected onto overhead screens. New Community has a great deal of singing to assist the congregation into a worshiping mood. On weekends, however, there is little congregational singing because they have found that Unchurched Harry does not like to sing.

For some years no Sunday offerings were taken. Persons who wanted to support the church financially could drop their gifts in boxes inconspicuously located at the rear of the auditorium. Audience pressure finally convinced the leaders to include an offering time in Christianity 101. As a part of the offering, however, the leader asks nonmembers not to give, since they are there as guests and the church does not need their money.

The church has a well-defined and clearly articulated mission and philosophy of ministry, which are known and used by staff and members alike to introduce strangers and new members to the congregation. The mission is reviewed annually in a special Wednesday worship service to remind the congregation who they are as a church and what is expected of each member. They state their reasons of existence as four E's:

1. Exaltation: to encourage persons to worship God in the New Community, and in small groups and privately.
2. Edification: to build up each other, and share one another's troubles.
3. Evangelism: to commission each believer to reach the nonchurched.
4. Extension (Social Action): to arrest social decay.

Over 90 different ministries are available to members. Short courses of 6 to 8 sessions are offered, covering topics such as parenting skills, marriage, and divorce. All members are strongly urged to participate in a cell structure of 8-10 persons who meet weekly for prayer, Bible study, and fellowship.

It is not easy to become a member. Anyone who is over the age of 12 and desires to become a member must first be an affiliate member for one year and be baptized as a believer. During the year of preparation, these persons are taught the history, doctrine, mission, and expectations of the church. They are interviewed by an elder regarding their spiritual journey and stage of commitment. Every member is expected to be in a volunteer ministry position.

Though it is not easy to become a member, it is easy to drop membership. Every member is asked to renew his or her member commitment annually. Every member is sent a commitment card rehearsing the expectations for membership. Anyone failing to sign the commitment card for the coming year is simply dropped from the membership list. At Willow Creek there are no inactives. No one is pressured to remain a member, since this would go against the church's commitment not to apply pressure or embarrass anyone.

## What Are the Common Characteristics of Successful Congregations?

There are some congregations of every size and in every ecclesiastical body that are characterized by growth and expanding ministries. What characterizes those congregations who have successfully met their challenges? One study discovered four things held in common by successful contemporary churches and synagogues, whether large or small.[12]

1. *They know why they're in business.* They have a clear sense of their mission.[13] They clearly see the role they play in the spiritual lives of their constituents and in serving human need in the community.

2. *They are person-oriented rather than program-oriented.* They make a concerted effort to discover, understand, and minister to the needs of their constituents and others whom they have chosen to serve.

3. *They involve their members in developing and carrying out their ministries.* Members are given a variety of opportunities to get involved with programs and ministries inside and outside the four walls of their building.

4. *If large, the congregation is able to maintain an intimacy by being honeycombed with small groups dedicated to serving the differing needs of the members and those segments of the community they have chosen to target in their outreach ministries.*

In a nutshell, successful congregations are *responsive* religious organizations—they have structured themselves to be responsive to the needs of their current constituents, and to the needs felt by a well-defined segment of society. They are responsive by understanding what those needs are, how they might function to satisfy certain needs, the process by which persons choose a congregation to satisfy their needs, how to develop ministries and communicate the need-satisfying ability of those ministries to a specific segment, and how to ensure that all this will take place within the context of a well-defined mission for the congregation. This responsiveness to internal and external needs epitomizes the essence of what a marketing orientation can contribute to religious organizations.

Despite the appeal of marketing as we have described it, marketing still has its share of doubters. The next section looks at some of the criticisms leveled at marketing.

### The Major Criticisms Against Marketing

Modern marketing carries negative connotations in the minds of many people, tracing back to ancient times. Plato, Aristotle, Aquinas, and other early philosophers thought of merchants as unproductive and acquisitive. Merchants were seen as taking advantage of helpless customers through buying cheap and selling dear. In modern times, marketers are accused of getting people to buy what they do not want or need. Customers are seen as victims of high-pressure, and sometimes deceptive, selling.[14]

Until recently, several professions—medicine, law, accounting—banned their licensed members from engaging in explicit marketing activities. Their codes of professional ethics proscribed direct client solicitation, advertising, and sharp price cutting. In this way the practitioners could feel they were above "selling" their services. They were simply available to those who needed them.

The truth is that these professionals were carrying on marketing at a less obvious level. They made it their business to get around, to be in the right places, to meet the right people, to deliver speeches, and to write articles—all of which would bring attention and, they hoped, produce new clients.

Recently, the United States Supreme Court decided that the formal bans in the canons of professional ethics had the effect of reducing competition through depriving firms of the right to inform potential clients about their services, as well as depriving potential clients of useful information about the firms. As a result, advertising and certain other marketing practices are now allowed in several professions.

Many religious organizations come close to the professions in their negative attitude toward marketing. Administrators of religious organizations feel that they must proceed cautiously with marketing activity lest their publics criticize them.

Five types of criticisms are anticipated.

## 1. Marketing Wastes Money Given to God

A frequent criticism of marketing activities is that they are too expensive. Advertising, market research, and fund raising all cost money. Among administrators of religious organizations it is commonly understood that some independent religious relief programs report spending 70-90 percent of all monies raised on their own fund raising and administration, leaving very little to be used for the purposes set forth in their fund raising efforts.

Religious organizations, of course, should not spend money on activities that do not contribute to the organization's mission and ministry. They should be careful to choose effective, low-cost approaches to marketing research, communications, and the like. Help is available from books that describe low-cost marketing strategies (see Appendix A).

Religious organizations owe their publics an explanation of the benefits they are seeking to achieve through their marketing expenditures. They should not overspend, and they should not under-spend. At the present time, religious organizations are more prone to underspend than to overspend on marketing. Religious leaders should, however, be concerned about the "return" on their market-ing expenditures.

## 2. Marketing Activity Is Intrusive

A second objection to marketing is that it often intrudes upon people's personal lives. Marketing researchers or salespeople go into persons' homes or phone them in an attempt to make a sale or to ask them about their likes and dislikes, beliefs, attitudes, incomes, and other personal matters. For example, a team of Jehovah's Witness workers appear on the doorstep on Saturday morning, the only day the family has to clean the house, and attempts to prolong the con-versation, to give unwanted literature, to acquire a reluctant com-mitment.

Ironically, marketing research must be carried on to learn the needs and wants of people and their attitude toward the congregation's cur-rent offerings so that it can deliver greater satisfaction to its target publics. At the same time, congregations, and other religious organi-zations, must show a sensitivity to the public's desire for privacy.[15]

## 3. Marketing Is Manipulative

A third criticism is that organizations will use marketing to unduly influence a person's behavior. Many smokers resent the anti-smoking ads put out by the American Cancer Society as trying to control them through fear appeals. Many people resent the attempts of the Roman Catholic Church to use legal and persua-sive means to enforce their views regarding birth control or abor-tion.

Religious leaders should be sensitive to the possible charge of exercising improper influence when they implement marketing pro-grams. In the majority of cases, the religious organization is seeking a public good for which there is widespread consensus, and it is using proper means.

## 4. Marketing Militates Against the Spirit of Leadership

If one interprets marketing to be that of "responding to the needs and interests of one's congregation," this would seem to put the religious leader in a response mode, rather than a leadership mode. What if the pastor or rabbi wants to "fire up" the congregation about an issue, say a church elementary school or AIDS? If they don't respond, should the pastor or rabbi keep harping on it? What if the clergy's preoccupation with a cause drives some members to quit the congregation? Is this being responsive to *their* needs and interests? Is this tantamount to serving *them?*

Ironically, marketing in the popular mind is "selling" rather than "responding." The religious leader who keeps pushing a favorite cause is trying to *sell* the congregation on embracing that issue. This is not necessarily "bad" marketing. A congregation cannot serve everyone and every interest. "Good" marketing would suggest, however, that the clergy should recognize differences among members in the congregation and aim to generate support for the cause among those who are most predisposed. Instead of making his or her issue a congregation-wide issue, with all the guilt feelings and resistance that this could generate, the pastor or rabbi might organize an interest group and "fire" them up about the cause. This would amount to more effective leadership than turning off a large segment of the congregation with a personal cause he or she espouses. One needs only review the history and trends of some of the denominations from the 1960s until today to understand that this is correct.

Marketing does not mean the death of leadership, but rather outlines, through its ideas on segmentation and targeting, a more effective way to create a motivated cause constituency without alienating others in the congregation. Marketing, rightly done, is an ally of leadership and ministry.

## 5. Marketing Desacrilizes Religion

The field of marketing is believed by many to be synonymous with selling or advertising. While this definition is somewhat myopic in scope, it does tend to cause the term *marketing* to leave a bad taste in one's mouth as one contemplates the typical complaints made against these activities: "Advertising is deceptive, causes the price of goods to increase unjustifiably, and is often vulgar and annoying." "Pushy salespeople cause people to buy things they don't really need or want, and frequently can't afford." "Advertising causes people to become materialistically oriented, prompting them to be avaricious and acquisitive, instead of concerned with higher spiritual or social goals."

These charges are particularly offensive to those in the religious community who recall many Bible verses warning of the dangers inherent to a materialistically centered life, which marketing systems seem to promote (see Pss. 20:7-8; 49:5-6).

These are serious accusations against a management discipline, and if they accurately describe the entire focus and intent of marketing, there is good reason to question the legitimacy of its use by a religious organization. The use of such a method would tend to desacrilize the religious offering to which it is applied.

In marketing's defense, stigmatizing the entire marketing discipline as being synonymous with objectionable practices is a gross overgeneralization. Levy refers to this as the synecdochic mechanism:

> All group prejudice is a form of over generalizing, or fallacy of composition. To identify it here, the way a part of marketing is taken for the whole is called the Synecdochic Mechanism. A synecdoche is a rhetorical device wherein the singular is substituted for the plural: here the disapproved marketer is being used to define the category, substituted for those others who strive to make a fine product, offer an excellent service, price fairly, sell helpfully, and communicate honestly.[16]

Why does marketing stand out among management disciplines as more suspect and base in its motivations? Levy says:

> Marketing is stigmatized because it is associated with the many frustrations of wanting and giving—with material things and guilt over the desire for them, with money and its deflection of direct interest in providing goods and services—leading to the projection of these frustrations on marketing and marketers, and to the synecdochic equation of the whole field with its worst manifestations.[17]

Metaphorically, a lack of understanding as to the true nature of marketing can be likened to the individual who has seen a hammer being used only as a tool of *destruction* and who, upon being handed a hammer when asking for a tool to use in *construction*, wonders if the other person has taken leave of his senses. In the same way, if marketing has been perceived as only deceptive advertising by dishonest salespersons and as efforts to manipulate demand (tool of destruction), it will be dismissed by individuals or religious institutions when faced with problems that it might help them solve.

It is necessary, therefore, to distinguish marketing as a process (facilitating exchange of values) from the sometimes objectionable *use* of that process. As we shall see in the following chapters, the Bible is replete with examples of the use of marketing techniques by individuals pursuing honorable ends. When viewed as an exchange-facilitating mechanism, rather than viewing the worst manifestations of its implementation, there is nothing inherent in marketing that would desacrilize religion.

We are not implying, however, that good marketing is all that is needed to generate religious exchanges. We are aware of the Divine admonition that success comes "not by might, nor by power, but by my spirit, says the LORD of hosts" (Zech. 4:6). We do, however, think of these types of biblical examples when we contemplate Zechariah's message:

> The LORD said to Moses, "Send men to spy out the land of Canaan, which I am giving to the Israelites." . . . Moses sent them to spy out the land of Canaan, and said to them, "Go up there into the Negeb, and go up into the hill country, and see what the land is like, and whether the people who live in it are strong or weak, whether they are few or many, and whether the land they live in is good or bad, and whether the towns that they live in are unwalled or fortified, and whether the land is rich or poor, and whether there are trees in it or not."
>
> (Numbers 13:1-2, 17-20)

While God might have revealed this information to the Israelites in a dream, He chose to have them use their own powers of observation, analysis, and planning to obtain and use this data. Therefore, there is to be a joining of divine inspiration with human action if a religious leader is to be successful in achieving the organization's objectives. Marketing can, when used appropriately, contribute to the effects of human action, but it cannot be a substitute for God's guidance. Marketing is a means to the desired ends, it is not the desired end.

## The Distinctive Characteristics of Marketing for Congregations and Other Religious Organizations

Since the phrase "religious organization marketing" is not one that automatically engenders positive thoughts in the minds of many people, we will now explain what we mean by "marketing" and why we believe it to be of practical necessity for congregations that are striving to be faithful and successful in today's socioreligious context.

### What Does "Marketing" Mean?

When this question was put to 300 educational administrators whose colleges were in trouble because of declining enrollments, spiraling costs, and rising tuition, 61 percent said that they saw marketing as a combination of selling, advertising, and public relations.[18] Another 28 percent said that it was only one of these three activities. Only a small number thought marketing had something to do with needs assessment, marketing research, product development, pricing, and distribution.

Like these educators, most people think of marketing as synonymous with selling and promotion. Indeed, selling and promotion have been the historical use of marketing as it has been utilized by religious institutions. Every great religion had a charismatic founder who attracted and equipped disciples to act as a sales force. Evangelization, as done in many Christian churches today, is a form of marketing in the selling sense. Many congregations have a doctrine that they want to persuade others to accept. This is sales-driven marketing. The product exists. It will not be altered in any fundamental way to meet the needs of the customers. Rather, the customers' needs will be bent toward the existing product.

It is not surprising that most people think of marketing as selling. Americans are bombarded with television commercials, junk mail, newspaper ads, telephone sales calls made by a computer, and mass retailing. Someone (or some computer) is always trying to sell something. Therefore, it may surprise you to hear that the essential component of marketing is not selling! Selling is only the tip of the marketing iceberg. It is only one of several functions that marketers perform, and often not the most important one. In fact, if the appropriate ministries and services are offered and pricing, distributing, and promoting them is done effectively, these ministries and services will be supported and utilized without selling.

Willow Creek Community Church, for example, does not gain its constituents by selling so much as by listening and responding. With an operating budget in excess of $1.6 million, only about $10,000 is allocated to advertising.

Peter Drucker, one of the leading management theorists, says, "The aim of marketing is to make selling superfluous."[19] Marketing is not a peripheral activity of modern organizations, but one that grows out of the essential quest to effectively serve some area of human need. To survive and succeed, organizations must know their markets, attract sufficient resources, convert these resources into appropriate products, services, and ideas, and effectively distribute them to various consuming publics. These tasks are carried on in a framework of voluntary action by all the parties. The market-oriented organization does not utilize force to attract resources. Nor does it beg for resources or distribute them carelessly. The market-oriented organization relies mainly on creating, offering, and exchanging values with other parties in order to elicit their cooperation. In short, marketing organizations rely on exchange mechanisms, rather than threat systems, on the one hand, or love systems on the other, to achieve their goals.[20]

Marketing is a process for making concrete decisions about what the congregation is going to do, and not do, to achieve its mission. Marketing is not selling, advertising, or promotion—though it may include all of these. It is the analysis, planning, implementation, and control of carefully formulated programs to bring about voluntary exchange and relationships with specifically targeted markets for the purpose of achieving the organization's missional objectives.

Several things should be noted about this definition of marketing. First, marketing is defined as a managerial process involving analysis, planning, implementation, and control. Marketing can also be looked at as a social process in which the needs of a society are identified, expanded, and served by a set of institutions.[21] However, we will not use the social process view of marketing in this book. That view is appropriate for those interested in social values and public policy, but less relevant to religious organizations facing very practical marketing problems.

Second, marketing manifests itself in carefully formulated programs (not just random actions) to achieve desired responses. If a group of volunteers is asked to go out and collect money, this is not a program and is likely to produce disappointing results. The volunteers are without direction as to whom to call on, what to say about the organization and its ministries, or how much money to ask for. Their effort is more akin to selling than marketing. Marketing must take place before any selling begins, and it must manifest itself in carefully formulated plans and programs. The apparatuses used in most congregation-wide pledge campaigns are not marketing.

Third, marketing seeks to bring about voluntary, mutually beneficial responses. Persons employing marketing seek a response from another party, but it is not a response to be obtained by any means or at any price. Marketing is the philosophical alternative to force, guilt, or fear. When marketing, the congregation seeks to formulate a bundle of benefits for the target market (the persons whom the congregation wishes to serve) of sufficient attractiveness to produce a voluntary relationship of value to both parties.

Fourth, marketing means the selection of target markets, rather than a quixotic attempt to be all things to all people. On the surface this may seem to be contrary to the calling some Christian churches take seriously to go "into all the world" with their message (Matt. 28:19). We are not saying that some groups should be served while others are ignored. Rather, we are suggesting that the most efficient use of scarce resources demands that each targeted group's needs, perceptions, preferences, and behaviors be researched and addressed so that the message communicated to that group will be fulfilling and favorably received. It may also be necessary to prioritize the order in which groups are targeted to most effectively generate new resources to use in reaching out to other groups more difficult to persuade. The result of trying to be all things to all people generally will result in being nothing to anyone. Local congregations are more likely to be successful if they target specific population groups with specific needs and set about planning programs that will satisfy those needs. When Ed Morres targeted the uneducated, distressed families of Guthrie, Oklahoma, and focused the resources of the congregation to address the needs of this group—the congregation experienced new life.

Fifth, the purpose of marketing is to help organizations ensure survival and continued health through serving their markets more effectively. In the business sector, the major objective is profit-making, while in the nonbusiness sector other objectives prevail: a park district wants to expand the recreational services and opportunities available to the community; the National Safety Council wants to lower the death and accident rates in the nation; a synagogue desires to enrich the spiritual life of its members and to meet human needs outside of its own constituency. Effective marketing planning requires that an organization be very specific about its objectives and in choosing its target groups.

Sixth, marketing relies on designing the organization's "offering" in terms of the target market's needs and desires, rather than in terms of the seller's personal tastes. Marketing is a democratic, rather than an elitist, technology. It holds that efforts that try to impose a product on a market are likely to fail if the market perceives that the product, service, or idea is not matched to its needs or wants.

In the commercial world, companies that design products they feel are good for the market without consulting the market beforehand are often disappointed. Few customers beat a path to their door. In the noncommercial sector, the same thing holds true. Local governments that design playgrounds or toll roads without studying public needs and attitudes often find the subsequent use level to be disappointing.

Effective marketing is user-oriented, not seller-oriented. This does not imply, however, that one's theology is adjusted to meet a market's demand. It does mean that the process by which a congregation presents its core doctrines, ministries, and programs should be developed by considering the prospective user's perspective, rather than the seller's perspective, of what constitutes value in the offering. Marketing in congregations requires that those in charge put themselves in the "shoes" and mind of the person they want to serve. It requires "outside-in" thinking (the information for planning a ministry comes from the persons the ministry is intended to serve), not "inside-out" thinking (the planners decide they know better what the persons "out there" need). Wrong thinking consists of planning the ministry—and then trying to convince the target group that it really is best for them.

Seventh, marketing utilizes and blends a set of tools called the marketing mix—product design, pricing, communication, and distribution. Too often persons equate marketing with only one of the tools, such as advertising. But marketing is oriented toward producing results—and this requires a broad conception of all the factors influencing buying behavior. A congregation, for example, may do no advertising and yet attract a large following because of other elements appealing to the target public's needs.

At the same time, the use of marketing by religious organizations is sufficiently different from business and other nonbusiness marketing to justify separate consideration. Several important distinctions between religious and other types of marketing are made below.[22]

## The Nature of the Product

Lovelock and Weinberg classify products or market offerings in three broad categories: physical goods, services, and social behavior. Marketers of physical goods produce a product that can be inventoried and consumed as a means of providing a need satisfaction. In services marketing, the product cannot be inventoried, since it is created by the interaction between the service provider and the consumer. Benefits may be immediate (as in airline transportation) or delayed (as in surgery), but in either case the marketer is seeking to persuade the consumer to engage in a service exchange with the provider. A substantial part of religious organization offerings is in the nature of services, of course.

Social behavior products are ways of thinking, feeling, and behaving. Congregations offer an assortment of social behavior products (a sense of community, a sense of purpose to life, hope in the future). These social behavior products often require a person to give up some tangible, short-term, satisfying, but more or less harmful, behavior. Consequently, when marketing principles are applied to the marketing of religion, these principles may require fresh thought about the nature of the "product."

## The Dominance of Nonfinancial Objectives

Churches and synagogues, in common with other nonprofit organizations, do not seek a profit, but give priority to nonfinancial objectives. What is the objective of the congregation and its leaders? Some congregations want to maximize their membership size. This is the church-growth thesis. Perhaps some congregations *should* try to attract 25,000 members, as some have, but the marketing perspective does not dictate any one objective for all congregations. Rather, marketing is a management system for achieving an appropriate and feasible objective.

Setting nonfinancial or nonnumerical objectives makes it difficult to evaluate performance against those objectives. Yet, performance evaluation is an important management task. Appendix B discusses performance evaluation in greater detail.

## The Need for Resource Attraction

Unlike business firms, which pay for the resources they need, religious organizations often seek to attract resources without payment (volunteer labor, services in kind, donated facilities, tax exemptions). Therefore, they must market themselves to resource providers as well as to consumers of their services. Marketing expertise is needed to attract resources to be used in pursuit of the religious organization's mission and objectives.

## Multiple Constituencies (Publics)

The religious organization must market itself to several constituencies, or publics. For example, Garrett Evangelical Theological Seminary has identified 18 publics to which the school must be marketed (see Exhibit 1-1).

Balancing the needs and expectations of these various publics can be a difficult undertaking. Marketing is the management function that manages the exchanges with these internal and external publics. Few business organizations face the number of multiple constituency exchanges as do churches and synagogues.

**Exhibit 1-1**

**THE GARRETT-EVANGELICAL THEOLOGICAL SEMINARY AND ITS PUBLICS**

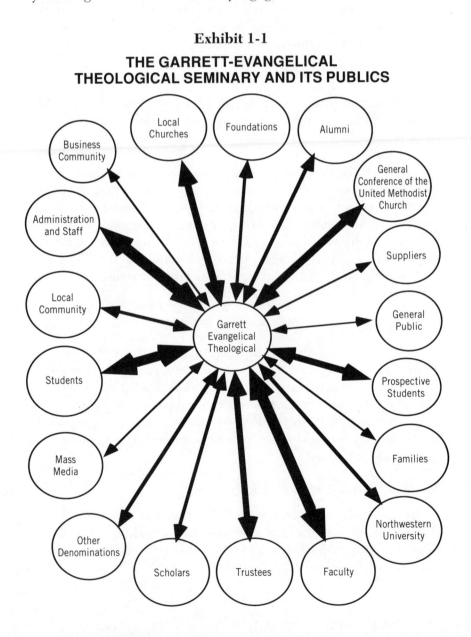

## The Tension Between Mission and Customer Satisfaction

The *marketing concept,* as typically applied to business marketing, means finding what needs exist among a target market and designing products and/or services that will satisfy those needs at a competitive advantage over other offerings. Such customer sovereignty is alien to the fulfillment of the mission of a church or synagogue to enrich the spiritual lives of its members by sharing theological truths. Truths do not come in adjustable forms to fit the believer. Moreover, the mission of the congregation is decidedly long-term in its scope, and it does not include pandering to current popular tastes. However, it is also endemic to the mission of a congregation to bring structure and meaning to the lives of its members; to promulgate a sense of community; to provide a source of joy, inspiration, and awe; to foster a sense of mutual obligation for each other's welfare; to be an antidote for loneliness; and to give hope and peace to the seeker. Therefore, the tension exists between offering a non-adjustable theology and delivering customer satisfaction by satisfying the very real and important needs of individuals.

Marketing does not require that a religious body alter its theology, doctrines, or mission to meet market demands. Rather, marketing helps to communicate and persuade people of the worth of religious experience, and to demonstrate the value of religion in their lives and of the beneficial consequences of their active involvement with an organized religious institution. That may mean that the programs and processes used by the organization to achieve its mission are developed using strategic marketing principles. Therefore, while most readers would agree that the "product" should not be altered to fit popular tastes, they would probably also agree that the religious organization's mission requires that there be "consumers" of the service that is being offered.

While the concept of "altering a product to fit the need" may not apply to religion, marketing is an appropriate means to develop programs and consummate exchanges consistent with the mission and objectives of the church or synagogue.

## Public Scrutiny

Few private or public agencies of comparable size find themselves subject to the kind of public scrutiny that religious institutions undergo. The scandals of several TV evangelists, Vatican edicts on many subjects, and other denominational stands on women's ordination, abortion, gay rights, or other issues, are subjected to intense scrutiny in the media. Locally, the fund-raising activities of a congregation are usually highly visible, and large gifts may be widely publicized.

## The Ability to Obtain Free or Inexpensive Support

One advantage of religious and other nonprofit organizations, which to some degree offsets their disadvantages when compared to business firm, is the possibility of drawing on donated labor and services to help stretch meager resources. We say "possibility" because, as is well known to experienced church persons, it is far from assured that such responses will be forthcoming with calls for help. Turning such a possibility into a reality may require marketing planning. Likewise, managing these donated resources when they are made available requires varied management skills, including *internal marketing*—that is, marketing to motivate those within the organization.

## Management in Duplicate or Triplicate

A final factor distinguishing the development of religious marketing programs from those of private sector firms concerns the number of groups involved in making decisions. As has been noted by a former executive director of Girl Scouts U.S.A.: "In many nonprofit enterprises, boards assume management responsibilities and volunteers occupy places in the management hierarchy. Seldom do they have a direct reporting relationship with the paid administrative staff."[23]

Most pastors deal with a local church board as well as with directives from the denomination's hierarchy, sometimes at a myriad of levels. Persuasion, more often than power legitimized by position, is frequently the key to successfully dealing with management in duplicate or triplicate. Developing a coherent marketing program for the church under such circumstances may be particularly trying.

## Summary

Religious organizations are unique in society in that they are the only social institutions formally set up to provide spiritual and moral nourishment and guidance to the citizens. Yet the sad fact is that religious organizations seem to be growing more irrelevant over time to many Americans. We believe that religious organizations have not lost their way so much as they have, in many cases, failed to establish transformational exchange relationships between the organization and the people it sees its mission to serve. We believe marketing, in some small part, may provide answers to questions on the minds of religious leaders seeking to make their institutions more relevant in the lives of their constituents. We have sought in this first chapter to provide answers to some of these early questions: Why is marketing important for religious organizations? Can marketing be used by religious organizations of all sizes and types? What characterizes successful congregations? How can the major criticisms of marketing be addressed? What are the distinctive characteristics of religious organization marketing?

We have taken a stand that, while religious marketing may be substantially different from the marketing done by for-profit companies, marketing does have a legitimate place in the management of religious organizations. We proceed, in chapter 2, to a discussion of what is involved in moving a religious organization toward a marketing orientation, and how a marketing orientation differs from the more traditional "production" and "selling" approaches used by religious organizations.

# 2

# *Approaching People in the Right Spirit:*

## **The Societal Marketing Concept**

Religious leaders are beginning to consider marketing as a possible tool for increasing their ability to understand and respond to the changing American religious scene.

A computer search of articles written on religious marketing from 1949–1989 will reveal dozens of articles written on the subject, including: "The Marketing of Pastoral Care and Counseling, Chaplaincy, and Clinical Pastoral Education"; "Marketing Pastoral Counseling"; "Applying Marketing Principles to Outreach Programs"; "What Churches Can Learn from Marketing"; "Marketing the Church's Ministry"; "Effective Evangelism: A Matter of Marketing"; "Religion as a Marketing Problem and How Research Can Help"; "Marketing the Church"; "True Marketing Concept Is Based Upon the Biblical Philosophy of Life."[1]

Also, several books have been published on religious marketing.[2] While the appropriateness of marketing for congregations remains somewhat controversial, there is evidence that the majority of pastors and rabbis feel marketing techniques are appropriate for their ministry.[3] Nevertheless, as Thomas Huxley said, "Skepticism is the highest of duties, blind faith the one unpardonable sin."

Marketing is a disciplined approach to keeping a congregation's ministry on target with the needs of its inside and outside publics. When these publics are satisfied that the church or synagogue is offering something of genuine value, they will gladly and willingly enter into meaningful "exchanges" that will benefit themselves—and the congregation.

But the question still stands: Why do we have to do this?

Into the mid-1970s the students enrolling in most mainline church seminaries were predominantly unmarried white males, fresh out of college. There were only a few ethnic students and a small, but growing, number of females.

The main marketing strategy for most of these schools was to visit college campuses to talk to graduating seniors about choosing a career in ministry, and considering their school as the school of choice. By way of advertising materials, the schools prepared introductory brochures, which were mailed to pastors and denominational officials urging them to recruit interested young people to the school. For decades this had been an effective approach—and would have remained effective had things stayed the same.

But things didn't stay the same. By the mid-1980s, less than 25 percent of the students enrolling in many mainline seminaries were young white males. For many of these schools the entering classes were predominantly female. The percentage of ethnic students had increased greatly, and 50 percent or more of the entering students were second or third career persons—older, more experienced, married.

These changes in student demographics prompted many mainline seminaries to drop the old recruitment methods in favor of totally new approaches. Some installed offices of marketing and recruitment. Former inexpensive and low-key promotional materials were replaced by completely new (and in some cases strikingly beautiful) school catalogs and recruitment materials. Curricula, teaching styles, and class schedules were reviewed with an eye toward meeting students where they "are"—they are no longer a collection of young, inexperienced recent college graduates. They are now older, experienced professionals answering God's call to a new (but perhaps not first) career.

The recruitment problems facing a seminary in this new mix are enormous! Prospective students are no longer clustered on college campuses or participating in a local congregation's youth group where the pastor may observe and visit with them regarding their career choices. Now the prospective students are scattered everywhere. They are "hidden" in the offices and institutions of corporate America. They are men and women of many ethnic cultures, reflecting the rainbowing of America. They are better educated, more experienced, more mature.

Indeed, for the seminary, local congregations, denominational agencies, and for all religious organizations—things are different.[4] To continue doing the same things in the same way will almost certainly lead to regret. In times of rapid and radical environmental change, new approaches must be found for ministry, or the organization will drift toward anomie and irrelevance, simply because the world around it (its publics, competition, societal characteristics, needs, and interests) is changing while it is not.

When new approaches to ministry are required, marketing offers the best theories and tools currently available. Marketing is based on systems theory, which has grown out of the need to understand and proactively respond to new and changing environments. Marketing, coupled with the best of "faith-full" listening and discernment practices, can help any religious organization achieve greater effectiveness in ministry, and avoid wasting scarce resources—or outright failure.

## Basic Approaches to Ministry

There are 3 basic approaches to ministry in American religion today. They are production, sales, and marketing. The marketing approach may be applied to persons only, or to societal concerns as well as persons. This orientation toward society as well as individuals is known as the societal marketing orientation. We shall describe these approaches in this chapter.

### The Production Approach

In the production approach we produce a product—over and over again—with no change, unless forced to do so.

The production approach to ministry is based on the idea that things aren't changing, that people inside and outside the congregation think and act as they always have. Based on this assumption, it makes sense to "produce" a ministry product that does not change. Since persons and societies do not change all that much, the clergy and congregation can get by well enough by producing an unchanging "product." Furthermore, they will get better and better at producing it. Lloyd Perry, retired professor of Trinity Evangelical Divinity School, told his students about churches whose guiding principle was "Come weal or come woe, our status is quo." This is a production approach to ministry.

When the environment changes to the extent that the ministry or its "packaging" becomes valueless, the "production" ministry spirals into decline.

Yet, making changes in a production-oriented congregation is never easy. When the Roman Catholic Church moved from the Latin mass to the vernacular mass in the language of the people, it caused tremendous wrenching among the ranks. Many priests could not imagine having to relearn the mass in another language. Many older Catholics could not imagine a mass in any language but Latin. The same is true of many Protestant leaders today who still believe the King James Version of the Bible is the only one of value. So they continue the public Scripture readings in archaic English, never stopping to consider that there aren't many people out there still using the "begats," and "thous" in their conversations.

We are not saying that members of a religious body should not love their "product." In fact, if they don't strongly believe in their faith and tradition they will be poor advocates of it. However, there is a difference between being in love with the *production* of religion and being in love with the *essence* of what the religion represents—

> A production orientation holds that the major task of an organization is to pursue efficiency in production and distribution of a product that it thinks would be good for the public.

so in love, in fact, that the greatest joy is seeing the effects that the product's "consumption" can make in the life of a new "consumer." In this case, the love is for the successful marketing of the product (i.e., a mutually beneficial "exchange") rather than in a rigid and possibly outdated method of producing the product. A production orientation consists of an unchanging devotion to the *production* of the product, rather than a commitment to the mission the product is intended to support.

## The Sales Approach

Whereas a production approach to ministry focuses on producing and distributing a product that the producer thinks is best for its publics, a sales approach focuses on the organization's ability to sell its publics on a product (idea, program, method). The product itself is not as important as the effectiveness of the sales effort.

The sales approach does not aim to maximize information about a product. In fact, it may conceal information, because sales do not depend on informing the public on all aspects of the product. It works to "hype" the product. For the salesperson, selling often becomes an exercise in persuasion, rather than an exchange of values or benefits.

The sales approach, like the production mode, is common to religious organizations. A pastor will "sell" the congregation on a new day school or the need for a building program. The denominational official will "sell" a pastor on accepting a certain appointment.

A sales orientation to ministry differs from the production approach in one significant way. Whereas the production approach will produce a product and attempt to defend it against any change, the sales approach will pick and choose a form of ministry it thinks it can sell. If it doesn't sell, the sales approach will discard it for something else that might produce better sales. The production approach to ministry doesn't want to pay attention to the users' tastes and interests at all. The sales approach, on the other hand, pays attention, but only to change the tastes and interests of potential users, not to respond to them.

The sales approach to ministry often takes form around one main actor who leads the congregation or organization in directions he or she wants it to go. This person (the salesperson) decides the style and focus of ministry and sells it by the strength of his or her charisma and persuasion. Consequently, when the main actor is removed from the scene, the ministry often folds. There are many current examples of this in the American church scene, especially in the scandal-ridden world of televised evangelism.

Some organizations believe they can substantially increase the size of their market by increasing their selling effort. Rather than change their products to make them more relevant to a changing environment, these organizations will increase the budget for advertising, personal selling, sales promotion, and other demand-stimulating activities. Thus the pastor reacts to a decline in attendance, or membership, by turning to promotion. This tactic may have an immediate effect of stimulating curiosity and subsequent attendance, but it fails to address more long-term problems.

Selling in religious organizations has an important place. For example, if the leader-as-salesperson is educating the people to see higher values and to "buy" them as their own, selling is achieving a good purpose. When there are programs that are good and valid, and the people should support (buy) them, a strong sales effort may be called for. On the other hand, selling falls short when the salesperson is not so much interested in the value of the product, as in his or her ability to sell it. Perhaps the worst example of selling is when the salesperson is attempting to sell a value that isn't there, or to make up for a product's deficiency by a strong sales effort.

> A sales orientation holds that the main task of the organization is to stimulate the interest of potential consumers in the organization's chosen products and services.

It is a cardinal rule that you cannot sell what you haven't got. Sooner or later the "buyer" will catch on.

## The Marketing Approach

The marketing approach to ministry embraces a guiding principle that the ministry exists to serve the needs and interests of persons. Since people and environments change, the religious organization must adapt and customize its specific "products" and "packaging," while remaining faithful to its doctrine.

Thus the religious organization remains vital in its environment. When the main actors leave, it survives, because it is not based on a product or a person, but on a commitment to religiously relevant needs and interests of its people and community.

The best examples of ministries based on the marketing approach are perhaps being carried on by persons who have not studied marketing, and who would be surprised if we suggested they are utilizing marketing concepts. These are pastors of both large and small churches, rabbis of synagogues, evangelists, seminary administrators—men and women who are succeeding in renewing their organizations by implicit or explicit marketing.

When Tom Wilson became the pastor of First Nazarene Church in Salem, Oregon, he spent about three months studying the community, its people, and their predominant needs. He rode with police on their rounds, with paramedics responding to emergency calls, talked to social service workers, and to people on the street.

He also studied his Sunday and Wednesday congregations to see who *wasn't* there.

He discovered that there was a large gap in the ministries of Salem's churches in meeting the needs of two large and growing groups: the divorced and the singles by choice. Having reached this conclusion, he encouraged the church's ministry team to develop programs and services targeted to the needs and interests of these two groups.

He reviewed the church's newspaper, radio, and television advertising from the point of view of what singles and divorced persons would listen to and read. He designed the church's weekly newspaper advertising to accentuate programs for single and divorced persons. He placed the ads not in the religious section, but in the sports and entertainment sections. He reasoned that few singles and divorced persons were sitting around reading the religious section of the newspaper.

As Easter Sunday approached, the congregation rented the city's largest coliseum for their Easter worship services, reasoning that the unchurched would be more willing to attend Easter worship if the services were conducted on more "neutral" territory than the church's sanctuary.

This was not an easy decision for the congregation to make; they loved their church and its building. However, they were more interested in reaching the city's unchurched than they were in enjoying the beauty and solace of their beloved sanctuary. The church launched a heavy media campaign to welcome the unchurched to worship with them in the coliseum. On Easter Sunday, 6,000 people filled the coliseum to capacity. An estimated 3,000 people were turned away. The congregation's largest Easter attendance prior to this was 2,500.

The results of these adjustments in their ministries and "packaging" were that over the next year, some 1,000 singles, divorced persons, and young married couples joined the congregation.

The ministry team's focus on the needs of singles and divorced persons constituted a marketing approach. The team started with understanding the needs of a targeted group, not with what they wanted to produce or sell to an audience. Yet in talking to the authors of this book, Pastor Wilson and others on the team disavowed knowing anything about marketing. They said they only knew how to "find a need and fill it." "And," they said, "whenever the church succeeds in doing this, people will come to the church on their own."

Some congregations have discovered the value of focusing their attention not on production, products, or sales, but on meeting persons' changing needs and interests. They recognize that without satisfied customers, the organizations will soon find themselves customerless and tailspin into oblivion. A true market orientation exists only when the focus of satisfying needs pervades all areas of the organization, rather then being adopted only by its leader.

The marketing approach requires that the congregation systematically study needs, wants, perceptions, preferences, and satisfaction of its members and others whom it is trying to reach. The planners must then act on this information to meet those needs more effectively.

---

In the basement of Second Baptist Church, Houston, Texas, is an area set aside for the night custodians to prepare themselves for their work, have lunch, and so on. After an evening service, one of the authors wandered into this area, only to find the night custodians readying themselves for work. He was warmly greeted and invited in. A most stimulating conversation followed.

"Can you tell me what this church is all about?" the visitor asked. The custodians told him of the mission and program of the church, much as he had heard the senior pastor describe it earlier in the day.

"What is it like to have to work all night in this huge building, when everyone else is home sleeping?" the visitor inquired.

"It's wonderful," the custodians replied. "As we clean each room, we pray for the people who used it that day and for

> those who will use it tomorrow. This isn't just a job. It's our ministry."
>
> "But how do you know what's going on in these rooms when you are here only at night?"
>
> "We know," they replied, "because the pastor meets with us each week and tells us about what happened here the week before, and what will be happening here in the coming week." The visitor went away, knowing that here was a place where a sense of mission and ministry pervades the work of everyone—from the senior pastor to the night custodians.

The user orientation that Pastor Ed Young has built into the mentality of Second Baptist Church (known as The Fellowship of Excitement) expresses itself in the manner in which the custodians approach their task, in the friendliness with which the receptionist answers the telephone, and in the helpfulness of various church employees in solving parishioners' and visitors' problems. The employees and volunteers in a market-oriented congregation will work as a team to meet the needs of the specific target markets that are to be served.

It is clear that different organizations within the same industry will vary in the degree to which they truly work for the present or potential users of their product. Consider a service industry such as airlines. A British guidebook publisher decided to rate the quality of 14 different airlines as an aid to travelers.[5] The staff boarded 43 transatlantic flights armed with tape recorders and evaluated each trip on such factors as check-in service, baggage delivery, food, cleanliness, friendliness, and response to special stress situations, such as asking for aspirin, and so on. The scores were combined in a weighted index with a maximum score of 100. The results showed a great variation, with Delta topping the list at 77 and the worst airline scoring only 36.

Churches, like airlines, can demonstrate considerable difference in the degrees to which their operations reflect a sensitive and

> *A market orientation holds that the main task of the organization is to determine the needs and wants of target markets and to satisfy them through the design, communication, cost, and delivery of appropriate and competitively viable products and services.*

caring attitude toward their members and others they are seeking to serve.

## A Societal Market Orientation

A market-oriented congregation faces two problems in committing itself to satisfying needs and wants of its members and others whom it wishes to serve. First, persons may have wants that are not proper to satisfy, either because they go against society's interest (such as buying handguns) or against the consumers' long-term interests (such as cigarette smoking). Second, persons may have needs of which they are not aware (such as the need for a personal relationship with God). In this instance the congregation may want to offer help to the person for his or her good, even though it may be costly to do so.

There is a growing awareness on the part of religious leaders that the congregation is called to minister to society as well as to persons. Society may function either as a competitor or an ally in the congregation's efforts to produce a "transformed person." A market orientation that carries concern also for society takes four factors into account in making marketing decisions: the person's interests, society's interests, and the short-term and long-term consequences of satisfying those interests. This orientation can be called a "societal" market orientation.

> *A societal market orientation holds that the main task of the organization is to determine the needs, wants, and interests of target markets and to adapt the organization to delivering satisfactions that preserve or enhance the consumer's and society's well-being on a long-term as well as short-term basis.*

Adherence to a societal market orientation is consistent with the biblical "Golden Rule" of concern for the long-term welfare of others. If profit and nonprofit organizations alike were to practice a societal marketing concept, it is likely that our quality of life would improve. The "quality of life" includes the quality, quantity, availability, and cost of goods; the quality of the cultural environment; the quality of our spiritual lives and how that affects our relationship with God and with each other. People judge marketing systems not just by the amount of direct consumer satisfaction that is created, but also by the impact of marketing on the quality of the physical, cultural, and spiritual environment. In fact, research has shown that both devotional (private) and participatory (public) aspects of religion have a positive relationship with life satisfaction.[6]

Thus a societal market orientation, as difficult as it may be to adopt, can be accepted as a way for religious organizations to pursue their mission. If the term "market orientation" still makes some of our readers a bit uneasy, they can substitute "responsive" or "outreach" or "development" for "market" orientation. The key, as we shall see in chapter 3, is to utilize the suggested approach to help achieve the objectives of the religious organization, while satisfying the needs of its targeted groups.

Congregations will more and more need to consider modern marketing practices, because religion is an increasingly "tough sell." Comfortable life-styles among the affluent, general cynicism and ennui among the middle class, and basic survival concerns among the disadvantaged distract many from listening to what churches and synagogues have to say about the need for God in our lives. Rabbi Harold Kushner, in his book *Who Needs God?*[7] makes a persuasive argument that religion is a fundamental need of the human condition, but many seem skeptical of the role of organized religion in their lives. It is frequently difficult to get "trial use" among prospective users. This is nothing new. The path to God is intentionally narrow, steep, and rock strewn. While everyone may need religion, to many persons it is far from obvious that a product so difficult to obtain is desirable and satisfying.

Moreover, true religion faces strong competition from other sources, such as the New Age movement, secular humanism, and materialism. Marketing, when practiced according to the societal marketing concept, is of value to all religious leaders because it offers a means by which to achieve their objectives—to improve the quality of life of all to whom they minister. The societal marketing concept focuses on the long-term welfare of people through satisfaction of "healthy" needs that ultimately benefit society as well as the individual. This indeed is a worthy objective for organized religion as well.

## *Summary*

When properly understood, a marketing orientation can be seen to adhere to scriptural principles of concern for others' needs more than the production and selling orientations which exemplify the approaches taken by many religious organizations in dealing with their "markets." Nevertheless, some very successful religious leaders have been leading their congregations in what could be described as a societal marketing orientation without knowing about marketing principles. A societal marketing orientation holds that the main task of the organization is to determine the needs, wants, and interests of target markets and to adapt the organization to delivering satisfaction that preserves or enhances the consumer's and society's well-being on a long-term as well as short-term basis. Such an orientation results in an improved quality of life for those affected by the implementation of such an approach to fulfilling a religious organization's mission.

Our purpose thus far has been to help you learn what marketing is and to decide whether it is appropriate for your organization. The next chapter will discuss ways by which marketing can contribute to making the religious organization a more responsive institution.

# 3

# *Serving People Effectively:*

# *The Responsive Congregation*

In Brooklyn, New York, there is a sterling example of a congregation whose responsiveness led the founders to a very different approach from that utilized by many congregations under similar circumstances.

The church was founded by first-generation Norwegian immigrants to this nation's eastern shores. All services were conducted in the Norwegian language. The congregation flourished, and a beautiful church building was constructed to house the congregation. But by the second and third generations many of the children could no longer speak Norwegian. The older folk were now confronted with a tough decision—whether to force their children and grandchildren to attend Norwegian worship services and classes, and to risk losing them altogether, or to discontinue Norwegian services and thereby constrict the older generation, who could not speak English, to services they could not understand.

Their response was to build another edifice identical to the first and to connect the two by a common entrance and foyer. In the old building, Norwegian would remain the spoken language. The new building would house English-speaking services and programs. Thus everyone would enter the church through a common entry, but once inside one could choose the language of one's choice.

Time passed, and with it the older Norwegian-speaking congregation. Changes were also coming to the community. Now instead of being an entirely English-speaking populace, there were a great many residents whose native language was Spanish.

The English-speaking congregation decided to launch a Hispanic congregation in the building that had previously served the Norwegian-speaking congregation. The Hispanic congregation flourished. Later persons from India moved into the area and were welcomed to use the facilities.

> Today Hispanics, Anglos, and Indians enter by the same door and, once inside, are free to choose the services of their choice. By this means, the congregation has continued to renew itself in response to the needs and interests of its community.

Perhaps none of the founders of the Norwegian congregation ever took a course or read a book on marketing. But they were market-oriented in the best sense of the word. They were responsive to environmental shifts, and were willing to translate their ministry through the new opportunities the changes in their community offered.

## The Responsive Congregation

The result is that the people who come in contact with these responsive congregations report high personal satisfaction. "This is the best church I ever belonged to." "This synagogue really cares about people." "This church enriches the spiritual life of all its members." These recipients (consumers) of the congregation's ministry become the best advertisement for that church or synagogue. Their goodwill and favorable word-of-mouth recommendation reach other ears and make it easy for the congregation to attract and serve more people. The congregation is effective because it is responsive.

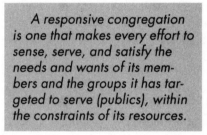

*A responsive congregation is one that makes every effort to sense, serve, and satisfy the needs and wants of its members and the groups it has targeted to serve (publics), within the constraints of its resources.*

There is an ambiance about a responsive congregation that is quite unmistakable. These congregations have managed to imbue their paid and volunteer workers with a spirit of service to members and strangers alike. Ushers, custodians, and secretaries go out of their way to answer questions, smile, and be helpful. The ministry team and lay boards continuously ask persons what they think of the worship services, church school, music, outside signs, indoor signs, bulletins, attitude of custodians, office staff, and so on. Based on the responses, the leaders constantly work to improve the overall experience that members and strangers have when coming into contact with the congregation and its buildings, staff, and ministries.

## Levels of Congregational Responsiveness

Congregations fall into one of four levels of responsiveness: the unresponsive, the casually responsive, the highly responsive, and the fully responsive congregation. The four levels of responsiveness are shown in Exhibit 3-1, "Four Levels of Consumer-Responsive Organizations."

### Exhibit 3-1

**FOUR LEVELS OF CONSUMER-RESPONSE ORGANIZATIONS**

|  | Unresponsive | Casually Responsive | Highly Responsive | Fully Responsive |
|---|---|---|---|---|
| Complaint system | No | Yes | Yes | Yes |
| Surveys of satisfaction | No | Yes | Yes | Yes |
| Surveys of needs and preferences | No | No | Yes | Yes |
| Customer-oriented personnel | No | No | Yes | Yes |
| Empowered customers | No | No | No | Yes |

### The Unresponsive Congregation

An unresponsive congregation is at one extreme. Its main characteristics are: (1) It does not encourage inquiries, complaints, suggestions, or opinions from its members or participants. (2) It does not measure current member or participant satisfaction or needs. (3) It does not train its staff to be member- or participant-minded.

The unresponsive organization is typically characterized by a bureaucratic mentality. Bureaucracy is the tendency of organizations to make routine their operations, to replace personal judgment with impersonal policies, to specialize the job of every employee, to create a rigid hierarchy of command, and to convert the organization into an efficient machine.[1] Bureaucrats are not concerned with innovation, with problems outside their specific authority, or with considering human responses and needs. They will serve people as long as their problems fall within their jurisdiction. People's problems are defined in terms of how the bureaucratic organization is set up, rather than structuring the organization to respond to people's problems. Questions of structure dominate questions of substance; means dominate ends.

## Congregations Intentionally Acting Unresponsive

The most extreme type of unresponsive congregations are those that intentionally decide to be unresponsive to the publics they claim to want to serve. Here is an example:

A congregation in a community of about 100,000 people had a membership of 1,700 in 1964. By 1984 the membership had declined to slightly more than 1,000. The congregation is located in the downtown area, which for a short time was the scene of racial unrest in the 1960s. No racial disturbances have occurred since that time. Relationships between the white and black communities are quite satisfactory.

At the time of the racial unrest in the 1960s, electronic locks were placed on all the church doors, and mirrors were installed so that anyone standing at the only door providing access during weekday office hours could be observed by the office staff before the door was unlocked by a buzzer in the office. During the 1960s, and continuing, the entire residential area surrounding the church migrated from white to black.

By the 1980s, many myths and fears had grown around the dangers of letting a black person in the building. Yet the congregation had declared that a part of its missional understanding was to reach the community surrounding the downtown area. Members would at times lament the unresponsiveness of the black community to its programs.

Unresponsive congregations tend to be unresponsive in all their relations. Selective unresponsiveness is hardly possible. Along the way the church decided not only to be unresponsive to its community, but also to be unresponsive to its members.

The once-beautiful chapel, adjacent to the sanctuary, was now a combination storage and meeting room. Upon entering the office, one confronted a 4-foot high plexiglass barrier, which separated the visitor from the workers cloistered behind the barrier. One had to lean over the barrier to converse with a secretary. Wall paneling on the office walls hung loose. There were no chairs to sit in while waiting to see a pastor or office worker. One could sit in the church parlor, but it was not heated during winter months.

The offset printer was located in the office area. When it was running, conversation was nearly impossible. The printer also sputtered, so that the office carpet was besmeared with ink. The worship bulletins and monthly newspaper coming off the aged press looked like the office floor.

Curtains in Sunday school rooms were rotting. Ushers sat in the parlor, drinking coffee during worship services, or stood in the back of the sanctuary, visiting so loudly that persons sitting near them complained that they were distracted from worship.

The congregation employed a financial secretary. Nonetheless, members' quarterly statements of giving were often late and consistently inaccurate.

The outdoor sign, lawns, and garden were unattended. No interior signs pointed the way to the church offices or rest rooms.

---

This example demonstrates that when a congregation is unresponsive, it tends to be unresponsive all over. Unresponsiveness is migratory—it creeps into every nook and cranny of the organization. By being unresponsive to the outside community, the leaders set in motion attitudes that move the entire organization toward being unresponsive to the needs and interests of its own members. Whether to be responsive is among the most crucial missional decisions a religious organization will ever make.

An unresponsive organization assumes either that it knows what its publics need, or that their needs do not matter. It sees no reason to consult with those it attempts to serve. Unfortunately, many congregations today fit this description—the leaders assume they know what the members and participants need—or they don't care.

Such an unresponsive congregation brings about a host of undesirable consequences. The programs and ministries are usually poorly done or irrelevant. Members and participants grow frustrated and dissatisfied. Their dissatisfaction leads to conflict, withdrawal, apathy, decline, and may ultimately doom the congregation.

There are varying degrees of unresponsiveness within congregations. The example above portrays the most extreme. Other unresponsive organizations may be grouped under two types; those preferring to concentrate on others things, and those lacking the resources to be responsive.

## CONGREGATIONS PREFERRING TO CONCENTRATE ON OTHER THINGS

One type of unresponsive congregation prefers to concentrate on things rather than on member or nonmember satisfaction.

> In a Midwest congregation of about 1,500 members, all weddings and social functions had to be scheduled with the custodian (weddings at least 6 months in advance) before being scheduled with the pastor or church office. In this church the pastor and members were expected to bend their schedules to fit the custodian's calendar. Once the custodian had scheduled a wedding, the pastor was expected to do whatever necessary to accommodate that schedule, since the custodian, having once set a date for the wedding would refuse to offer another.

This church was unresponsive to its staff, its members, and others who wished to make use of the church's services. However, no definite decision was made to be unresponsive. Rather, wanting peace at all costs, the congregation drifted into a situation where the janitor ran the show, and no one challenged his demands.

## CONGREGATIONS LACKING THE WILL OR THE RESOURCES TO BE RESPONSIVE

Yet another type of unresponsive congregation is those that would like to be more responsive, but lack the will, or the resources, to motivate paid and volunteer staff to higher standards of responsiveness. Or they see so much human need and opportunities that they are paralyzed. They do not know where to begin, or they lack resources to meet all the human needs they see surrounding them.

We recently visited with the pastor of a congregation located in one of America's largest cities. The church building is strategically located and very unique.

The pastor sees so much opportunity, but meanwhile the congregation is declining. During our visit, he said, "To the east of us is a large area of expensive high-rise condominiums with about 15,000 affluent executive type people living there; to the north is a growing community of over 30,000 yuppies; just west of us is a complex of about 15,000 lower-income workers; and south of us there are thousands of poor and affluent mixed together."

We asked what he planned to do. With worry etched into his brow, he said, "I think I'll start a ministry for the homeless." It turns out that this was a successful ministry for him in a former parish. When we asked how a homeless ministry would be an apt response to the local opportunity, it became apparent that the opportunities were overwhelming him. He could think only of retreating to a comfort zone of a successful former ministry that he thought he could do again.

When resources are meager or opportunities are overwhelming, the responsive church must segment its possibilities and target the groups it will seek to minister to—*today.* No matter how meager the resources, any congregation can serve the needs of at least one outside group, while also meeting its own member needs.

## The Casually Responsive Congregation

The casually responsive congregation differs from unresponsive congregations in two ways: (1) It encourages members and others to submit inquiries, complaints, suggestions, and opinions; (2) It undertakes periodic studies of members' and participants' satisfaction.

Often, but not always, casually responsive congregations are unresponsive congregations who see "the handwriting on the wall." Other casually responsive congregations simply reflect the results of a former highly responsive institution drifting into indifference.

As many seminaries began to experience a decline in student applications in the early 1970s, they began to pay more attention to their students and publics. Administrators who once were oriented toward problems of hiring faculty, scheduling classes, and running efficient administrative services—the earmarks of the bureaucratic mentality—now began to listen more to the students. They left their doors open, made occasional surprise appearances in the student lounge, encouraged suggestions from students, created student life committees, and began to elect a student or two to the board of trustees. These steps moved the seminaries toward being casually responsive. The result was to create a greater sense of satisfaction among the students (and, sometimes, among faculty and donors).

This is a first step in building a partnership between the served and the serving. Whether the increased sense of satisfaction continues depends on whether the seminary merely makes a show of listening or actually undertakes to do something about what it hears. It may merely offer a semblance of openness and interest without intending to use the results in any way. If so, sooner or later it will become apparent to the students that this is a public relations ploy. This will lead to even greater strain than previously existed because the students now have higher expectations than when the seminary was completely unresponsive. If their voices fall on deaf ears, they resent the school and its leaders—and may very well try to force the organization into greater responsiveness.

What has been said regarding seminaries can also be said about many religious organizations.

## The Highly Responsive Congregation

A highly responsive congregation differs from a casually responsive congregation in two additional ways: (1) It not only surveys current member and participant satisfaction, but also researches their unmet needs and preferences to discover ways to improve its services. (2) It selects and trains its paid and volunteer workers to view the members, participants, and strangers as the *raison d'être* of their work.

Many religious organizations fall short of being highly responsive. Churches and synagogues rarely take formal surveys of their members' and participants' real needs and desires, nor do they sensitize and train their paid and volunteer workers to be member- or participant-minded.

Recently a small liberal arts college recognized this failing and developed the following philosophy to guide its faculty and staff.
The students are:
* the most important people on the campus; without them there would be no need for the institution;
* not cold enrollment statistics, but flesh-and-blood human beings with feelings and emotions like our own;
* not dependent on us; rather, we are dependent on them;
* not an interruption of our work, but the purpose of it; we are not doing them a favor by serving them—they are doing us a favor by giving us the opportunity to do so.

If this attitude could be successfully implanted in the paid and volunteer staffs, and in the volunteer administrative committees, of a congregation, it would have moved a long way toward being highly responsive.

Earlier we gave an example of an unresponsive congregation. Happily, the story of this church does not end there.

In 1984 the congregation decided to become responsive to its community. The locks, buzzers, and mirrors were removed to allow its members, and visitors, ready access to the building during office hours and during the hours of public services.

Within a few months an African-American congregation requested space to conduct its worship services and Sunday school. The request was granted. A short while later, a predominantly black Girl Scout troop was invited to use the facilities for its meetings. Three years later, the congregation received an African-American pastor onto its ministry staff.

Within a few weeks of the congregation's decision to be more responsive to its neighbors, members began to notice how totally uninviting was the main office. Two members approached the trustees with a blank check to pay for remodeling the area. Even as the remodeling was proceeding, another member asked the trustees to restore the chapel area to its original condition. This request was also accompanied by a blank check for the costs.

> Less than two years later the congregation launched a complete restoration of the entire building, with specific instructions to the trustees and architect to pay attention to the needs of physically handicapped persons.

Even as unresponsiveness tends to permeate an entire institution, so does the decision to become responsive. The first step toward responsiveness attracts attention and causes many persons to sense the need for change in other areas of the organization.

## The Fully Responsive Congregation

The highly responsive congregation is free to accept or reject complaints and suggestions from its members and participants, based on what it thinks is important and what it is willing to do.

A fully responsive congregation, however, moves beyond being highly responsive to overcome any sense of the "we-they" mentality that lingers in the highly responsive congregation. The fully responsive church or synagogue blurs the "we-they" distinction by accepting all whom it serves as equals with its members.

Among examples of fully responsive organizations, at least in principle, are local town democracies, democratic nation-states, and rapidly growing churches. The organization is seen as existing for and serving the interests of the citizen members. There is no question of the organization's going off on its own course to pursue goals that are not in the interest of its members. The organization shows an extreme interest in measuring the will of the members and responding to their wishes and needs.

When these principles are fulfilled, the expectation is that the citizen members will be highly involved, enthusiastic, and satisfied. Recently, a Canadian university was searching for ways to build a more active alumni association. Just sending out newsletters about the school no longer sustained alumni pride or interest. So it developed the idea of conferring membership status on its alumni, with privileges and voting rights on certain issues. Suddenly, the alumni became alive with interest in the school. This gesture proved very meaningful to the alumni, who had hitherto felt that the university was simply using them for their money.

The characteristics of a fully responsive congregation are: (1) It encourages all who share in its ministries and programs to participate actively in the affairs of the congregation. (2) It responds to the wishes of its members and participants as expressed through the ballot box or other means of less formal communication.

First United Methodist Church, Marietta, Georgia, is an example of a fully responsive congregation. This church has over 4,500 members and is constantly growing. We have visited the church several times to observe it in action. In a late-night conversation with Pastor Charles Sineath, we asked about the attention paid to the exterior gardens, lawns, and parking lot. He said, "We believe every blade of grass is an evangelist. People see the lawn before they see the sanctuary. The first contact persons have with the church is when they turn off the street onto our grounds. Friendliness begins in the parking lot. We train our parking lot attendants to be responsive to every question and to spot people who need help before they ask for it."

When we asked a lay staff member about her views of the church's success, her first response was "This church is what it is because we have so many people who really care."

We asked for an example. She said, "We have a custodian here who takes his job as a true ministry. A few weeks ago we had a wedding at which the wedding director did not show up. As soon as Rick [the custodian] heard about it, he took over. There he was at the back of the sanctuary, sending the wedding party in at the correct times. He fixed the pillow for the rings and helped the bride get over her nervousness. The wedding came off without a hitch." We asked whether Rick had ever been trained for this work. She said he had not, but that every worker is trained to put people above their work assignments. Whenever Rick sees anyone in trouble in the building, he goes immediately to her or his assistance.

The full-time ministry team is composed of clergy and laypersons, but one cannot know who is which simply by observing them in staff meetings or by watching their work. Virtually no distinction is made between persons on the staff. To an amazing

> degree, this is true even of the senior pastor, Charles Sineath. We were introduced to the ministry team in one of their staff meetings. We could not guess who the senior pastor was. Finally we asked.

The distinctions between unresponsive, casually, highly, and fully responsive congregations are real. Any religious organization fits somewhere on this continuum. Your degree of responsiveness can be determined by interviewing members and participants, and by observing the responses of the leadership and ministry units to specific situations or persons.

The understanding and application of some of the basic concepts of marketing will almost certainly make any ministry more responsive, effective, and satisfying—both for the minister and for those who receive the ministry.

## Summary

Religious organizations that are responsive to the needs of their constituents and to an ever-changing social environment are characterized by the high personal satisfaction felt by the people who come into contact with these organizations. However, being a highly responsive organization does not come naturally or easily to most congregations. Being a fully responsive congregation means measuring the will of the members and responding to their wishes and needs. It means encouraging all who share in its ministries and programs to participate actively in the affairs of the congregation. But it does not mean abandoning your calling to run after the latest social fashion. The first three chapters of this book have tried to argue the case that congregational leaders can become fully responsive to the needs of their members by adopting a societal marketing orientation without ever compromising their calling or the mission of their institution. Indeed, we believe that it is marketing's role to more effectively and efficiently allow that mission to be fulfilled.

In the next chapter, we will discuss the key marketing concepts that go to the heart of making a church or synagogue fully responsive to its members and all others who come within the reach of the congregation's life and ministry.

# 4

## Traveling the Marketing Trail:

### Fundamental Marketing Concepts

---

**Saddleback Valley Community Church**

Pastor Rick Warren has long been in training for his job. He is a fourth-generation Baptist minister. His great-grandfather was converted under the ministry of Charles Spurgeon in London, England, and came to the United States as a circuit rider.

While in seminary, Rick developed an intense interest in the dynamics of large congregations. From this study, he prepared a set of guidelines he would use to guide his work upon graduation. The questions he asked in his study were:

1. What are the common denominators of large and growing churches?
2. Why do some churches "explode" with growth?
3. Why do some churches, though committed, never grow?

Rick discovered that almost universally large congregations have been served by a long-tenured pastor. Before graduation, Rick asked God to honor this covenant, "I will go anywhere you want me to go; only let me invest my entire life in one location."

Upon graduation in 1979, Rick spent the summer months praying for guidance—and studying the census data of the four fastest growing areas of the West Coast. He discovered that Saddleback Valley was the fastest growing area in the fastest growing county in the United States. Here he decided to start a new church, where he expects to spend the rest of his ministry.

Saddleback Valley Community Church was founded in January 1980, in the home of Pastor Rick Warren. Seven persons were present: Pastor Warren, his wife and daughter, the real estate agent who had sold Rick the condo (only one week earlier), his wife, their daughter, and another person whom the real estate agent had invited. From this humble beginning in Laguna Hills, California, the congregation has grown to an average Sunday attendance of 6,000.

At the same time, the congregation has founded 20 other "daughter" congregations. The daughter congregations are independent. However, the pastors meet monthly with Rick Warren as a study and spiritual support group.

The congregation has never had a building of its own, choosing rather to rent a facility until they have outgrown it, and then move on to a larger rented space. The congregation has met in 53 locations. A part of the congregation's ethos has been the statement: "We are a people on the move. We are not settlers, but pioneers."

Now the congregation and its programs require more space than is available to them. They have recently purchased 74 acres and are making plans to construct a permanent campus.

During the first 12 weeks of 1980, Rick spent his time conducting a marketing study of Saddleback Valley. He began with a door-to-door survey in the neighborhood of his condo, during which he visited with more than 500 residents. His questions were:

1. Are you an active member of a local church? (If the person answered yes, Rick said, "Great! I won't bother you with anymore questions." If the person answered no, Rick said, "Fantastic! You are the kind of person I want to talk to. I am not going to try to covert you, but I would like to ask you a couple of other questions.")
2. What is the greatest need in the Saddleback Valley?[1]
3. Why do you think most people don't attend church?
4. If you were looking for a church, what kind of things would you be looking for?
5. What advice would you give me as a pastor of a new church?
6. What could I do for you?

The responses most given to question 3 were:

a. The sermons are boring.
b. Church members are unfriendly to visitors. It feels like a clique.

c. Most churches are more interested in your money than they are in you as a person. They say, "Give us your time, your money, and help us do our thing."
d. Young couples in Saddleback want the highest quality care for their children.[2]

From the results of his market study, Rick and his small congregation developed a "philosophy of ministry" for their church. See Exhibit 4-1 for an outline of the strategy of ministry.

At the heart of the philosophy was that: (1) Saddleback Church would be a church for people who didn't like to go to church. They would focus their ministries and services to meeting the needs and interests of the baby boomers who are interested in spiritual values, but believe the church has little or nothing to say about spiritual things.[3] (2) The operating style of the church would be open, friendly, unstructured, and nonbureaucratic. (3) The services would be informal, in keeping with the southern California life-style.

Based on this philosophy, Rick wrote an open letter, listing the four reasons people don't like to go to church (from his door-to-door survey) and stating how this new church would deal with each issue.[4] The letter then announced that the first service of the new church would be held in the Laguna Hills High School, on Easter Sunday.

The congregation hand-addressed and hand-stamped 15,000 letters to homes in the neighborhood. The letters were dropped 10 days previous to Easter Sunday. The first public service of Saddleback Valley Community Church, Easter Sunday 1980, attracted 205 people.[5] Twelve years later, on Easter Sunday 1992, more than 14,000 attended.

Once the philosophy of ministry was in place, Rick Warren and his small group designed a strategy of ministry to ensure that everything about the church's operation fit with the culture of southern California and the baby boomers who live there. During the work week the entire staff dresses casually;[6] all persons are addressed by their first names; friendly hospitality is the hallmark of the office operations. Pastor Warren often wears a Hawaiian shirt on Sunday mornings, and he never wears a coat on Sunday mornings. Many in the congregation arrive in jeans and sneakers.

## SADDLEBACK'S STRATEGY

### S *EEKER SENSITIVE SERVICES*
1 Cor. 9:22-23 (LB) ". . . Whatever a person is like, I try to find common ground with him so he will let me tell him about Christ and let Christ save him. I do this to get the Gospel to them."

### A *FFINITY GROUPS*
Acts 5:24 (GN) *"Every day in the temple, and in people's homes they continued to teach and preach the Good News."*

### D *RIVEN BY PURPOSE*
Matt. 22:36-40 & 28:19-20 Purposes from the Great Commandment & Great Commission

### D *EMONSTRATE ACCEPTANCE*
Rom. 15:7 *"Accept one another, then, just as Christ accepted you."*

### L *IFE DEVELOPMENT PROCESS*
Phil. 1:6 (Ph) *"I am confident of this: that the One who has begun his good work in you will go on developing it until the day of Jesus Christ."*

### E *VERY MEMBER A MINISTER*
Rom. 12:5-6 *"In Christ we who are many form one body, and each member belongs to all the others. We have different gifts according to the grace given us."*

### B *EHAVIORAL PREACHING*
James 1:22 *"Do not merely listen to the Word, and so deceive yourselves. Do what it says."*

### A *UTHENTIC LEADERSHIP*
Heb. 13:7 *"Remember your leaders, who spoke the word of God to you. Consider the outcome of their way of life, and imitate their faith."*
Eph. 4:11-12 *"(God) has given . . . pastors and teachers to prepare God's people for works of ministry, so the body of Christ may be built up."*

### C *IRCLES OF COMMITMENT*
Eph. 4:13-15 (Ph) ". . . *We arrive at real maturity—that measure of development which is meant by 'the fullness of Christ.' We are not meant to remain as children . . . but to grow up in every way into Christ."*

### K *EEP THE STRUCTURE SIMPLE*
Luke 5:37 *"You can't pour new wine in old wineskins."*
Heb. 8:13 (Ph) *"When a thing grows weak and out of date it is obviously soon going to disappear."*

## Exhibit 4-1

The Sunday morning service is designed for "Saddleback Sam," the unchurched and/or uncommitted person. The Wednesday night service is designed for the members, at whatever stage they are in their growth and commitment.[7]

The church's leadership has identified the following five constituencies that comprise the congregation (see Exhibit 4-2).

1. The core ministry group, approximately 1,000 people;
2. Committed (committed to maturity; accumulative) 1,900;
3. Congregation (committed to membership; accumulative) 2,400;
4. Crowd (committed to attendance; accumulative) 4,500–7,000 on a given Sunday;
5. Community (uncommitted occasional attenders; accumulative) 16,000.

The church's assimilation plan calls for moving each member through an intentional growth program called C.L.A.S.S., Christian Life And Services Seminars (see Exhibit 4-3). Exhibits 4-2 and 4-3, together, describe how the leaders plan to move people from one constituency to another.

Every member is part of a small "cell" group within the church. The purpose of the small groups is to provide a personal experience for every individual, within the context of the large congregation.[8] The groups' agendas include sharing prayer requests, personal needs, support, and the like.

Saddleback Valley Community Church is an example of a fully responsive religious organization. While remaining faithful to his Baptist theology and teachings, Pastor Rick Warren has succeeded in making the church fully responsive to the culture, interests, and needs of those whom the congregation is attempting to reach and serve.

**THE FIVE CONSTITUENCIES WHICH COMPRISE
THE SADDLEBACK CONGREGATION**

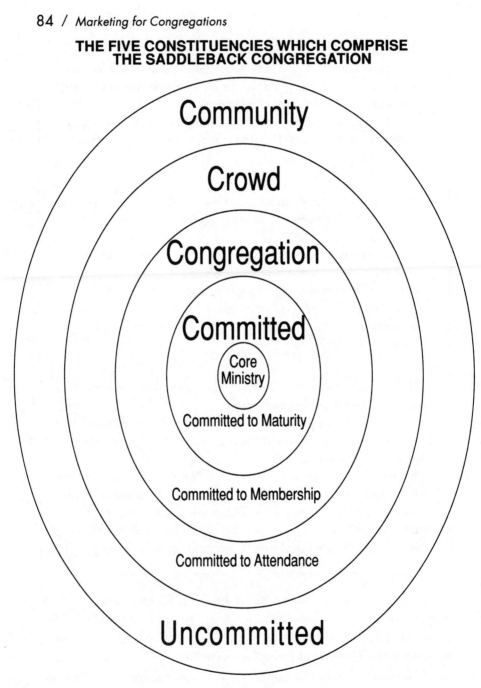

Community

Crowd

Congregation

Committed

Core
Ministry

Committed to Maturity

Committed to Membership

Committed to Attendance

Uncommitted

**Exhibit 4-2**

## SADDLEBACK'S PROGRAM TO HELP YOU GROW THROUGH CHRISTIAN LIFE AND SERVICE SEMINARS

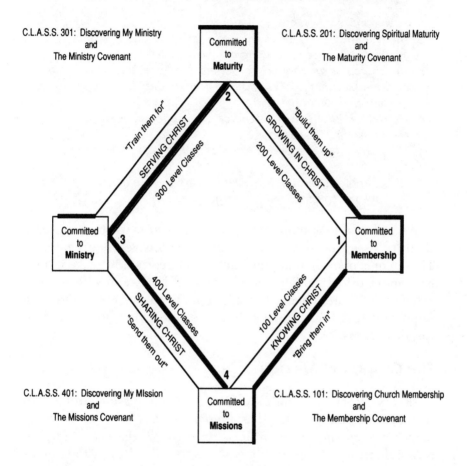

C.L.A.S.S. 301: Discovering My Ministry
and
The Ministry Covenant

C.L.A.S.S. 201: Discovering Spiritual Maturity
and
The Maturity Covenant

Committed to **Maturity**

Committed to **Ministry**

Committed to **Membership**

Committed to **Missions**

C.L.A.S.S. 401: Discovering My Mission
and
The Missions Covenant

C.L.A.S.S. 101: Discovering Church Membership
and
The Membership Covenant

"Train them for" SERVING CHRIST 300 Level Classes

"Build them up" GROWING IN CHRIST 200 Level Classes

"Send them out" SHARING CHRIST 400 Level Classes

"Bring them in" KNOWING CHRIST 100 Level Classes

| An Overview of C.L.A.S.S. | |
|---|---|
| 100 Level Seminars: | To lead people to Christ and Membership at Saddleback |
| 200 Level Seminars: | To grow people to spiritual maturity |
| 300 Level Seminars: | To equip people with the skills they need for ministry |
| 400 Level Seminars: | To enlist people to the worldwide mission of sharing Christ |

**Exhibit 4-3**

Essential Marketing Concepts

1. Each congregation has a mission.
2. The church or synagogue will undertake exchanges with a large number of publics in carrying out the mission.
3. The church or synagogue will segment the populace into groupings, and target those it will serve from among the great many publics in its environment.
4. To perform its mission, the church or synagogue needs to attract resources through exchange.
5. The publics will respond in terms of their image of the congregation.
6. The congregation and its ministry team can take concrete steps to improve the satisfaction of its target publics.

We will now look more closely at the set of marketing concepts that are essential for building fully responsive congregations. These concepts, when applied, are almost certain to make a ministry more effective. They are described here, and will be used extensively in later chapters of this book. Each concept serves as an important tool for understanding and improving organizational responsiveness.

## The Concept of Mission

Every effective organization starts with a mission. In fact, an organization can be defined as a *human collectivity that is structured to perform a specific mission through the use of largely rational means.* Its specific mission is usually clear at the beginning. However, unless it is continually being clarified in response to the changes going on within the organization and its environment, the organization's mission will soon become forgotten, irrelevant, or banal. Pastor Rick Warren and his new congregation of 7 persons began their church with a mission: "We will be a church for unchurched 'Saddleback Sam.'" In support of this mission, they prepared a profile of "Saddleback Sam," listened to the reasons "Sam" wasn't interested in going to church, and then designed their entire program in response to what they had learned about "Sam."

The congregation's mission should be thought of as that to which God is calling it to *be* and *do* at this particular time, in its particular place. A clear understanding of a congregation's mission requires that the people discover the relationship among four distinct concerns:

1. What does Scripture and our own faith tradition tell us about our mission?
2. What unique and specific needs and interests do our members want the congregation and its programs to satisfy?
3. What specific needs in our community can and should we address?
4. What specific needs in society and the world can and should we address?[9]

It is in the interrelationship of these four concerns that a congregation comes to understand its mission. Unfortunately, some religious traditions tend to focus only on item 1 in seeking to understand their mission, while others tend to focus more on items 2, 3, and 4. But all 4 must be held in tension if the congregation is to correctly understand its mission.

An example of a congregation broadening its missional understanding may be found in one of the churches we discussed earlier. The original mission of the Salem First Church of the Nazarene was to deepen religious faith among believers through offering worship, religious training, and fellowship. With Tom Wilson as its pastor, the church added another dimension to its mission: that of meeting the needs and interests of singles, divorced persons, and children of single-parent households. It is no longer so easy to distinguish between the church's core mission and its peripheral missions. Is the church basically a religious center, a social center, or a mental health center? The church's growing responsiveness to other needs is changing its character and its membership composition.

Every church and synagogue that wants to be responsive must answer two questions: *responsive to whom and to what?* No congregation can serve everyone and every need. If it tries to serve everyone, it will serve no one well. From time to time, each congregation must reexamine its mission to see whether it is still on target with the needs of its members and the expectations of those it is trying to reach.

Exhibit 4-4 depicts the components of a congregation's mission statement as stemming from two contexts, the eternal and the timely.[10]

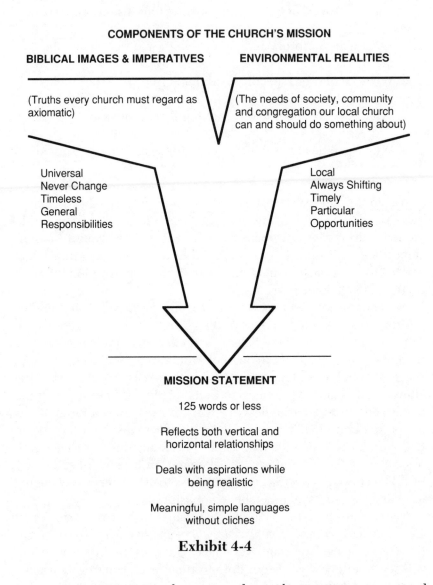

**COMPONENTS OF THE CHURCH'S MISSION**

**BIBLICAL IMAGES & IMPERATIVES**     **ENVIRONMENTAL REALITIES**

(Truths every church must regard as axiomatic)

(The needs of society, community and congregation our local church can and should do something about)

Universal
Never Change
Timeless
General
Responsibilities

Local
Always Shifting
Timely
Particular
Opportunities

**MISSION STATEMENT**

125 words or less

Reflects both vertical and horizontal relationships

Deals with aspirations while being realistic

Meaningful, simple languages without cliches

**Exhibit 4-4**

Years ago, Peter Drucker pointed out that organizations need to answer the following questions: (1) What is our business (mission)? (2) Who is the customer? (3) What is of value to the customer? (4) What will our business be? (5) What should our business be?[11] Although the first question ("What is our business?") sounds simple, it is actually the most profound question an organization can ask itself. The "business" of a religious organization is defined as its mission.

A religious organization should not define its mission by listing the particular services it offers. Rather, it should identify the group(s) it wants to serve and the needs and interests of the group(s) that the organization will try to satisfy.

Ultimately, the religious organization must decide what its mission is, so as not to lose sight of its targeted publics or confuse its ministries with a host of intermediate goals and services that it might provide. An example of this is found in Willow Creek Community Church, which holds as its focus to target Unchurched Harry for its Sunday services, so they include in their mission statement exaltation, edification, evangelism, and extension, all of which are actions in concert with whom they want to be and whom they want to reach.

Clarifying the congregation's mission is a soul-searching and time-consuming process. Different members will have different views of what the church or synagogue should be about. It is not uncommon for a searching congregation to hold numerous meetings over a 1- or 2-year period before membership consensus is developed regarding the mission.

A helpful approach to defining mission is to establish the congregation's scope along 3 dimensions. The first is its *customer groups*—namely, *who* is to be served and satisfied. The second is its *customer needs*—namely, *what* is to be satisfied. The third is *alternative technologies*—namely, *how* persons' needs are to be satisfied.[12] For example, consider a synagogue serving mainly senior citizens who want only a simple weekly worship service. (This synagogue's mission scope is represented by the small cube in Exhibit 4-5A.) Now consider the mission of Salem First Church of the Nazarene (Exhibit 4-5B). This church serves all age groups, meets at least 4 strong needs, and provides services through the chapel, meeting rooms, and outings.

# THE MISSION SCOPE OF TWO CONGREGATIONS

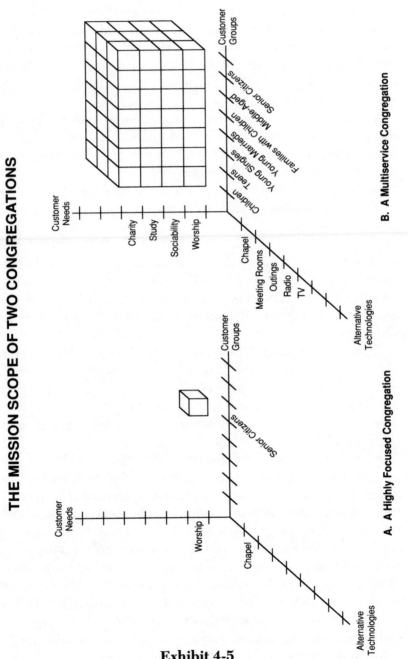

A. A Highly Focused Congregation

B. A Multiservice Congregation

**Exhibit 4-5**

Still other congregations will have a different mission scope. A campus church will serve primarily students of a particular religious faith and meet a wide variety of needs (for belief, sociability, counseling, and so on) within the four walls of a religious house. On the other hand, the church pastored by Robert Schuller, Garden Grove Community Church, Garden Grove, California, meets a wide variety of needs of 12,000 members, and serves them through such modern technologies as radio, television, and cassettes, in addition to its $16 million Crystal Cathedral.[13]

A congregation should strive for a mission that is *feasible, distinctive,* and *motivational.* In terms of being feasible, the organization should avoid a "mission impossible." Pastor Robert Schuller wants his church to grow to 25,000 members. While this may be feasible for Garden Grove Community Church, it would likely prove infeasible for most congregations. To accomplish this mission, Schuller's followers must believe in the feasibility of this goal if they are to lend their support. An institution should always reach high, but not so high as to produce incredulity in its publics.

A mission serves best when it is distinctive. A well-stated mission allows persons to make differential comparisons, allowing members and seekers to see how and why this church is different from the other churches in the community, thus helping persons to decide whether this is the church for them. The mission identifies the church's uniqueness, sets it apart from other churches, strengthens its boundaries, and helps members know "who we are."

If all churches were carbon copies of one another, there would be little basis for pride in one's particular church. People take pride in belonging to an institution that "does it differently" or "does it better." By cultivating a distinctive mission and personality, an organization stands out more and attracts a more loyal group of members.

The mission should also be motivational. Those working for the organization should feel that they are worthwhile members of a worthwhile endeavor. A congregation whose mission includes helping the poor is likely to inspire more support than one whose mission is meeting the social, cultural, and athletic needs of its current members. The mission should be something that enriches people's lives.

## *The Concept of Publics*

Every organization has to address at least one public in order to carry out its mission. An organization may have only 1 public, but growth or expansion will almost always cause the organization to relate to more than 1. Publics may be "internal"—that is, inside the organization—or "external"—outside the formal structures of the organization.

When Rick Warren decided to target "Saddleback Sam," the unchurched yuppie living in Saddleback Valley, he identified an external public with which he would seek to affect certain exchanges of value, and to whom he would communicate a particular message: "Saddleback Church is a church for those who don't like going to church."

But even before this he recruited the real estate agent and his wife and daughter, plus his own family to be the first members of the new church. These persons became an internal public—they were on the "inside" of the organization. To this public, Rick can be expected to communicate a different message and seek to affect different exchanges from those he is seeking to establish with the unchurched yuppie, "Saddleback Sam."

At the first public worship service, 205 persons came together to form yet another public. Rick would relate to this public also, but not in the same way as with the members nor as with the unchurched yuppies.

Since each public has a different relationship with the church, they have different expectations and are experiencing different needs and interests. Therefore, the church leaders must communicate differently and hold different expectations of each group.

The concept of "publics" may be new to many readers. To illustrate this concept, an example from a familiar organization, McDonald's, is used to clarify 2 familiar terms, *customers* and *consumers*.

McDonald's is a franchise corporation. As such, the persons who purchase a franchise and open a McDonald's restaurant are the corporation's customers—they have purchased something from McDonald's and will continue to purchase many items from the company. However, the owners of McDonald's restaurants do not consume the many products on the menu. Here, then, is another of McDonald's Corporation's publics—the persons who buy and eat (consume) the products.

These 2 distinct groups constitute 2 publics of the McDonald's Corporation: its customers and its consumers. The 2 publics experience differing needs and interests, which McDonald's Corporation seeks to satisfy, and by so doing hopes to receive in exchange certain values for the corporation.

The company must communicate differently to each public, even though it is talking about the same thing—hamburgers. To its customers, the company communicates profits, while to its consumers, it communicates taste. This is necessary because the customer has different interests and needs from those of the consumer—even though both are interested in the hamburger.

The Ronald McDonald House offers another illustration. Each McDonald's franchise owner is expected to contribute a certain percentage of sales to support the house. In order to keep its restaurant owners feeling good about this, the company must convince them that this is an exchange of value, and so the company emphasizes high publicity, consumer good-will, and increased sales. But to the consumer, the company communicates "the house that love built."

In our interviews with the leaders of Willow Creek Community Church, Saddleback Valley Community Church, and the Crystal Cathedral, we found many similarities of thinking and operation. One is that each church is very clear as to who is its "customer" and its "consumer." The leaders do not try to communicate a one-size-fits-all message. Rather, they communicate specific messages to specific publics.

Both Willow Creek and Saddleback devote the entire weekend program to communicating with their *consumers*—the unchurched and the as of yet uncommitted.

Also, both churches devote the entire midweek services to communicating with their *customers*—those who have bought into the church's philosophy and are committed to growth and maturity in their religious journey.

Undoubtedly, the ability to distinguish between their "customers" and "consumers," and to interact with each appropriately, is one of the success secrets of these churches.

Even a small congregation faces many publics, often more than a local business firm. A local congregation has many internal and external publics whom the leaders must seek to satisfy—and *each public can only be satisfied in terms of its own unique needs and interests.*

It is fairly easy to identify the key publics that surround a particular congregation. Exhibit 4-6 shows several major publics with which a local church relates. The diagram is intended to illustrate that a congregation generally has its *internal publics* and its *external publics.* Marketing must take place *within* the congregation and also *outside* its own organizational structures—through its interactions with those publics it is trying to reach or serve beyond its own membership groups.

> A public is a distinct group of people or organizations that have an actual or potential interest or impact on an organization.

## THE CONGREGATION AND ITS PUBLICS

**Exhibit 4-6**

Not all publics are equally active or important to a religious organization. Publics come about because the organization's activities and policies can draw support or criticism from inside and outside groups. A *welcome public* is one that likes the organization and whose support the organization welcomes. A *sought public* is one whose support the organization wants, but which is currently indifferent or negative toward it. An *unwelcome public* is one that is negatively disposed toward the organization and that is trying to impose constraints, pressures, or controls on it.

Publics can also be classified by their functional relation to the organization. Exhibit 4-7 presents such a classification. An organization is viewed as a resource-conversion machine in which certain *input publics* supply resources that are converted by *internal publics* into useful goods and services that are carried by *intermediary publics* to designated *consuming publics* and influenced by various external publics. We will look at the various publics more closely.

## THE MAIN PUBLICS OF A CHURCH OR RELIGIOUS ORGANIZATION

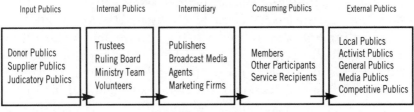

| Input Publics | Internal Publics | Intermidiary | Consuming Publics | External Publics |
|---|---|---|---|---|
| Donor Publics<br>Supplier Publics<br>Judicatory Publics | Trustees<br>Ruling Board<br>Ministry Team<br>Volunteers | Publishers<br>Broadcast Media<br>Agents<br>Marketing Firms | Members<br>Other Participants<br>Service Recipients | Local Publics<br>Activist Publics<br>General Publics<br>Media Publics<br>Competitive Publics |

**Exhibit 4-7**

## Input Publics

**Input publics** mainly supply original resources and constraints to the organization, such as donors, suppliers, and judicatory agencies.

**Donor publics** are those who make gifts of money and other assets to the organization. A synagogue's donors consist of constituents, friends of the synagogue, foundations, and Jewish religious organizations.

**Supplier publics** are those organizations that sell needed goods and services to the organization. Religious organizations often try to obtain price concessions or even donations of goods and services, but don't always succeed.

**Judicatory publics** are agencies that impose rules of conduct upon the congregation. The **regulatory publics** of a church or synagogue include federal, state, and local government agencies, ecclesiastical hierarchies, and various academic accreditation associations for schools. The church or synagogue must keep in close contact with these ecclesiastical and regulatory organizations and be ready to argue against regulations that will harm its ability to provide high-quality programs and ministries to its members and external publics.

## Internal Publics

The various inputs are managed by the organization's internal publics to accomplish its mission. The internal publics of a congregation consist of several groups, including trustees, ruling boards, ministry teams, volunteer leaders and workers, paid staff, and the congregation as a whole. In keeping with the illustration of McDonald's Corp., these comprise the customers of the congregation—they prepare and serve the congregation's *product*—its services and ministries.

**Trustees** are a legal entity charged with the responsibility of managing the organization's financial and real assets within the constitution of the state, the ecclesiastical hierarchy, and the local body.

**The ruling board** is charged with the management of the organization's goals, programs, and ministries. Further, the board is charged with the public trust of the organization and its external publics. When members do not trust the leadership and their decisions, the board is responsible. In addition, the board establishes the policies by which the programs and ministries will be administered.

**The ministry team** is composed of the paid and volunteer leaders and workers who share responsibility for carrying out the congregation's ministries and programs. The lead pastor or rabbi is generally charged with the administrative oversight of the congregation's paid and volunteer personnel, which is carried out within the policies established by the ruling board and the congregation.

**Volunteer leaders and workers.** In almost any religious organization, volunteer workers constitute a major part of the ministry's work force and, as such, are a highly important public. In this group are persons who are often more experienced in program planning and management, financial management, personnel supervision, and the like than are the clergy and other paid staff. Adequately marketing to this public is of prime importance to the success of the religious organization.[14]

## Intermediary Publics

Marketing intermediaries assist the organization in promoting and distributing its goods and services to the final consumers. They are described below.

**Publishers.** Most congregations depend on local newspapers, the yellow pages, and similar services to announce themselves to the public.

**Radio and television media.** Many congregations also utilize the airwaves to carry their announcements and entire services to the public.

**Agents.** Congregations and national-level religious organizations depend on parachurch agencies to assist in missions projects. For example, many congregations rely on such organizations as World Vision, Compassion, Young Life, Campus Crusade for Christ, Prison Fellowship, and InterVarsity to assist in carrying out their mission projects.

**Facilitators.** These are organizations—such as transportation companies, real estate firms, and media firms—that assist in the distribution of products, services, and messages, but do not take title to or negotiate purchases. Thus the congregation will use the telephone company and the post office to send messages and materials. These facilitators are paid a normal rate for their transportation, communication, and storage services.

**Marketing firms.** These are organizations—such as advertising agencies, marketing research firms, and marketing consulting firms—that assist in identifying and promoting the organization's products and services to the right markets. The congregation may hire the services of these marketing firms to investigate and promote to new member markets.

## Consuming Publics

Various groups consume the outputs of a church or synagogue. They are described below.

**Members.** The members are those who are committed to the organization and its mission and who carry responsibility for its overall success. They *are* the organization. In a local church or synagogue, however, the members are also a major consuming public. They receive and utilize a great amount of the congregation's ministry.

**Other participants in the congregation's ministries and programs.** These include those who attend its services, who participate in its programs, and who may even contribute financially to those programs in which they hold greatest interest.

**Recipients of services.** These people benefit from the congregation's ministries, often without attending any of its religious services or feeling a part of the congregation. These include patients at a free clinic, the guests of a soup kitchen, and the person asking for financial help.

The internal publics and the consuming publics represent the religious organization's primary publics, its *raison d'être*. Drucker insists that the only valid definition of a business is to create a customer (a public that the organization might serve).[15] He says that hospitals exist to serve patients, colleges to serve students, opera companies to serve opera lovers, and social agencies to serve the needy.

Various names are used to describe consumers, such as clients, buyers, constituents, patients, and members. In some cases the appropriate term is elusive. Clearly, an organization can have multiple sets of customers and consumers, and one of the management tasks is to distinguish these groups and their relative importance to the organization.

Consider this issue in relation to a church or synagogue. Who is its primary consumer? The current members who pay for and "consume much of the product"? Inactive members, whom the leaders might desire to bring back "into the fold"? Prospective new members whom the church is attempting to interest in joining the congregation? People in the local community who benefit from the social service ministries of the congregation?

In formulating it services and policies, a congregation must take into account the interest of all of these groups. At times, the congregation will aim to increase its service to one group more than to another. At times, membership growth may be a top priority, and so resources are shifted to carry the message to prospective new members. At other times the goal may be to involve more current members in the religious organization's program, to increase the congregation's sense of community, as well as to broaden shared responsibilities.

## External Publics

**Local publics.** Every congregation is physically located somewhere and comes in contact with local publics, such as neighborhood residents and community organizations. These groups may take an active or passive interest in the congregation's activities. Thus community residents often get concerned about traffic congestion and other things that go along with living near a church or synagogue.

However, many local congregations are not responsive to the community's situation. Rather, they expect the community to accord it a favored status because it is a religious organization. Yet the church or synagogue that targets one or more local publics and wholeheartedly serves their needs and interests will attract more members than if it seeks only to serve its internal groups and to convert the community to its beliefs.

Members of the Trinity Church of the Nazarene, Lompoc, California, congregation report that the key to its quite phenomenal growth was Pastor Tom Wilson's success in turning its attention to serve human needs within the local community. The congregation adopted as its mission the statement, "We will find a need and fill it, find a hurt and heal it."

In an interview with Pastor Wilson, we learned his philosophy, "If a congregation sets out to find hurts and heal them, it will never have to plead for money or search for new people. People and money will come to you."

This responsive approach to ministry and marketing the church certainly seems to have worked at the Trinity Nazarene Church in Lompoc. In reflecting upon Pastor Wilson's tenure of 6 years, one member told us, "Every day the driveway of our church was lined with ambulances, police cars, and even an occasional fire truck. The emergency care providers of the community knew where they could find help to assist anyone in need. People who passed by wondered what was happening inside. Every hospital, social worker, and policeman thought first of Tom when they needed a pastor. We didn't have to advertise. People just came because this church had a reputation for caring for hurting people."

As in the case of Pastor Wilson's later tenure at the First Church of the Nazarene in Salem, Oregon, we see that when these congregations became genuinely responsive to the needs of targeted publics, they experienced phenomenal growth. Growth and ministry continue at both of these churches, even though Pastor Wilson is now in Tempe, Arizona, achieving similar results with the same ministry-marketing strategy.

**Activist publics.** Religious organizations are increasingly petitioned by consumer groups, environmental groups, minority organizations, and other public interest groups for certain concessions or support. In congregations, activist publics often arise from within the membership. We know of several congregations recently in which dissatisfied members have joined in petition campaigns to remove the pastor or the ruling board, thus becoming an activist public. Likewise, on a larger scale, within ecclesiastical bodies, members from across the nation are joining together as activist publics to protest or change denominational edicts.

Religious organizations would be foolish to attack or ignore demands of activist publics. Responsive organizations can do 2 things. First, they can train their leaders and administrators to include social criteria in their decision making in order to strike a better balance between the needs of the members, community populations, and the organization itself. Second, they can assign a staff person to stay in touch with these groups and to communicate more effectively the organization's goals, activities, and intentions.

**General publics.** An effective organization must be concerned with the general public's attitude toward its activities and policies. The general public does not act in an organized way toward the organization, as activist groups do. But the members of the general public form images of the organization, which affect their patronage and legislative support. Every congregation should monitor how it is seen by the general public, and should take concrete steps to improve its public image where it is weak. Managing the organization's image will be discussed later in this chapter.

**Media publics.** Media publics include media companies that carry news, features, and editorial opinion—specifically, newspapers, magazines, and other journals. Religious organizations are acutely sensitive to the role played by the press in affecting their capacity to achieve their marketing objectives. Congregations normally would like more and better press coverage than they get. Getting more and better coverage calls for understanding what the press is really interested in.

The person responsible for press coverage at the national level of a denomination will make it a point to know most of the editors in the major media and will systematically cultivate mutually beneficial relations with them. The same is true for pastors and rabbis at the local level. They will make it a point to know the religious editors and the managing editors of the local newspapers. They will offer interesting news items, informational material, and quick access to religious information. In return, the media editors are likely to give the congregation more and better coverage.

**Competitive publics.** In carrying out its task of producing and delivering services to a target market, a congregation will typically face competition. Many congregations deny the importance or the existence of competition. Some think that competition is evil. Some feel that it is more characteristic of business firms. Thus congregations do not prefer to think of other congregations as competitors, for fear of treating each other as winners and losers. They would rather think of all congregations as providing needed services.

Nonetheless, a congregation or other type of religious organization must be sensitive to the competitive environment in which it operates. The competitive environment does not consist only of similar organizations or services. Perhaps the major competition facing congregations today is such things as professional sports, leisure activities, and competing philosophies of life.

A local congregation may experience itself in competition with another congregation nearby. If so, that congregation, in order to provide effective services, must decide how it will position itself as unique from the other congregation. For example, if a small congregation is living in the long shadow of a megachurch, it must market itself in some way as "the alternative church."

A religious organization can face up to 4 major types of competitors in trying to serve its target market.

1. *Desire competitors:* other immediate needs that the publics might want to satisfy.
2. *Generic competitors:* other basic ways in which the publics can satisfy a particular need.
3. *Service form competitors:* other service forms that can satisfy the public's particular needs.
4. *Enterprise competitors:* other enterprises offering the same service form that can satisfy the public's particular need.

Exhibit 4-8 illustrates these 4 types of competitors in relation to the selection of a congregation. Consider a young woman working to clarify her world view. She faces several competing desires (desire competitors): organized religion, humanism, New Age philosophy, and so on. Suppose, because of her upbringing, she is inclined toward organized religion. She then considers the best way to pursue this interest (generic competitors): Christianity, Judaism, or an Eastern Religion. She decides in favor of Christianity. She then considers what type of Christian religion (service form competitors): Baptist, Methodist, Catholic, Lutheran, and so on. She favors the Roman Catholic Church. This leads her to consider a specific church to attend (enterprise competitors): St. John's, St. Mary's, St. Paul's, and so on. Thus St. Mary's Catholic Church faces different levels of competition in attempting to meet the needs of this young woman.

These levels are not meant to simulate the decision to join a church, but rather to make the point that churches and synagogues hoping to influence such a decision will face various forms of competition, which they must meet in different ways.

## TYPES OF COMPETITORS FACING A CONGREGATION

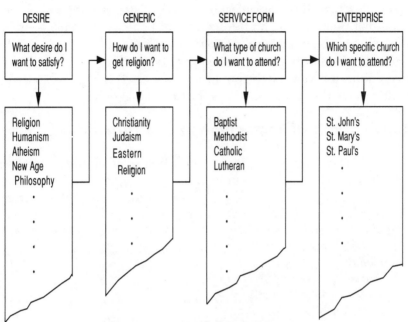

**Exhibit 4-8**

## *The Relationship Between a Public and a Market*

Having demonstrated that every organization is surrounded by a multitude of publics, we can now pose this question: What is the relationship between a public and a market? The term *market* has a different origin than does the term *public*, and yet has several affinities with it.

From the point of view of an organization, a market is *a potential arena for the exchange of resources.* For an organization to operate, it must acquire resources through trading other resources. In each case, it must offer something to the market if it is to receive in return the resources it seeks.

We can now see the affinities between a market and a public. A

> *A market is a distinct group of people and/or organizations that have resources they want to exchange, or might conceivably be willing to exchange, for distinct benefits.*

*public* is any group that has an actual or potential interest or impact on an organization. If the organization wishes to attract certain resources from that public through offering a set of benefits in exchange, then the organization is taking a *marketing viewpoint* toward that public. Once the organization starts thinking in terms of trading values with that public, it is viewing the public as a market. It is engaged in trying to determine the best marketing approach to that public.

## The Concepts of Segmentation and Targeting

In order to target a public, one must first segment the population into distinct, identifiable groups.

> Segmentation: *identifying groups (segments) in the population who have different wants and needs.*
>
> Targeting: *choosing the segments who will become the organization's focus for 1 or more of its programs or ministries. That specific segment becomes the target the organization will aim to reach with its message and activities, and from whom it will seek a mutual exchange of value.*

Recall that both Willow Creek Community Church and Saddleback Valley Community Church conducted marketing research in their communities to discover the various groups (segments) and their interests and needs. From a review of the various groups, Willow Creek decided to target "Unchurched Harry," and Saddleback decided to target "Saddleback Sam."

The Guthrie Church of the Nazarene did its own segmentation research and decided to focus on the needs and interests of the uneducated, distressed families in the community.

Targeting involves learning the unique needs and interests of the target group, developing specific resources to meet their unique needs and interests, and promoting the resources in such a way that the information will connect with the persons the organization wishes to attract and serve. Targeting is a wise move whenever the organization does not have enough resources to reach and minister to the unique needs and interests of every public represented in the internal and external communities, or when it is felt that concentrating on a particular segment might produce results beyond the ordinary.

Many local congregations never experience anything beyond the ordinary, or perhaps fail altogether, because they feel they must try to be all things to all people. Thus they fail to seize the extraordinary opportunities God puts before them. The truth is there isn't a congregation in the world that has sufficient resources to minister to the unique needs of each of the many publics represented in its community. It is by targeting some of the specific publics that the dynamics are put in place to capture the attention, support, and/or response of other publics.

Remember 2 things about segmenting and targeting. First, targeting a ministry to one group does not mean all other groups will be cut off or denied that ministry. "Unchurched Harry" is the *target* of Willow Creek's Sunday service, Christianity 101, and its evangelism efforts. However, this does not cut off or exclude the thousands of women and children who attend the same Sunday service, and for whom many special ministries are offered. Second, targeting may cause growth or ministry to expand among 1 segment of the population. If the congregation's resources are too meager to be all things to all groups, and to do it well, it makes sense that the congregation should target 1 (or 2) groups that, by focusing its resources, it might serve with excellence.

So long as Guthrie Church of the Nazarene tried to reach all segments of the population alike, they failed to reach any. But when the congregation of 13 members decided to target the uneducated, distressed families in the community they found themselves able to minister to this group with excellence. These 13 persons were able to prepare these persons to function more adequately in society. As a by-product, attendance at Sunday worship and Sunday school grew from 13 to 190 in less than 2 years.

The process of segmentation and targeting will be discussed in greater detail in chapter 6, including how some congregations use state-of-the-art techniques to efficiently and effectively reach chosen population segments.

## The Concept of Exchange

The concept of exchange helps us to understand how a religious organization can fulfill its mission by interacting with various targeted publics. Two key dimensions underlie the concept of exchange. The first is that each party believes the other party can offer something of genuine value and benefit—so that both parties feel mutually benefited and satisfied in the transaction. The second important dimension in exchange is that both parties are free in deciding to participate in the exchange. *Without value and free choice, there can be no exchange.* There may be extortion, manipulation, acquiescence, or accommodation, but not exchange. Whenever a congregation or other religious organization fails to subscribe to the concept of exchange, it will sooner or later fail to attract the attention and/or support of its publics, whether external or internal.

Exchange within the church or synagogue is carried on at 2 levels. One is the "something of value" a person is willing to give to the congregation in exchange for its meaning and services to the person's life. The second level of exchange is between the individual and God.

All religious organizations have reason to be leery of working toward exchanges that are merely transactional in nature: "You give us a dollar, and we'll give you a box of soap"; "You give us your tithes, and we'll give you a good sermon and Sunday school." The business of the church is a transformed person, and exchanges that are *transformational,* rather than merely *transactional,* are healthy for the religious organization and the individual alike.

### Conditions Underlying Exchange

Exchange assumes four conditions:

*1. There are at least 2 parties.* In the simplest exchange situation, there are 2 parties. If one party is more actively seeking an exchange than the other, the first party becomes the *marketer* and the second party the customer or *consumer.* A secular marketer is someone seeking a resource from someone else and willing to offer something of value in exchange. The religious "marketer" (evangelist, missionary, pastor, rabbi) is also seeking to effect exchanges between the individual and God, and within the individual alone.

*2. Each party can offer something that the other perceives to be of value.* If one of the parties has nothing that is valued by the other party, exchange will not take place. Each party must consider what it has to offer that may be perceived as benefits by the other party. "Something of value" may be various "products" or a "response."

Products offered in an exchange can consist of:

**goods:** Sunday school materials, worship bulletins
**services:** counseling, a visit, Sunday school classes
**persons:** rabbi, pastor, counselor
**places:** spiritual retreat center, synagogue, holy sites
**organizations:** congregation, Scouts, women's club
**activities:** stop smoking, sports program, sing in a choir
**ideas:** self-denial, commitment to a belief, hope in the future.

Responses to products may consist of:

**money**
**another product:** exchanging a skill, helping to install plumbing in a new synagogue
**a social behavior:** the performance of some desirable activity or non-performance of some undesirable activity
**acceptance or adoption** of an idea, value, or view of the world.

3. *Each party must be capable of communication and delivery.* For exchange to take place, the parties must be capable of communicating with each other. They must be able to describe what is being offered and when, where, and how it will be exchanged. Each party must state or imply certain expectations or guarantees about the expected performance of the exchanged objects. In addition to communicating, each party must be capable of finding means to deliver the things of value to the other party.

4. *Each is free to accept or reject the offer.* Exchange assumes that both parties are engaging in voluntary behavior. There is no coercion. For this reason, every transaction is normally assumed to leave both parties better off. Presumably each ends up with more value than it started with, since they entered the exchange freely.

Exchange is best understood as a process rather than an event. Two parties can be said to be engaged in exchange if they are anywhere in the process of moving toward an exchange. The exchange process, when successful, is marked by an event called a transaction, or an outcome, called a relationship or a transformation.

Transactions are the basic unit of exchange. A transaction takes place at a time and place and with specified amounts and conditions. Thus when a minister agrees to accept a new church position, a transaction takes place. Every organization engages in countless transactions with other parties—clients, employees, suppliers, distributors. Transactions themselves are a subset of a larger number of events called interactions, which make up the exchange process. Transactions are interactions that involve the formal trading of values. If either party is actively trying to create or influence the nature and terms of an exchange, that is marketing.[16]

An exchange process will result in a transaction whenever the target recipient perceives that the benefits of the transaction exceed the "costs" or sacrifices the exchange entails—and that the ratio of benefits to costs is better than what can be hoped to be achieved by "spending" the costs in any other conceivable way. For example, the absent member will begin attending weekly worship services when he or she perceives that the personal benefit of participating in the worship services exceeds the benefits of whatever it is he or she is in the habit of doing at that hour. The "costs" which the absent member has to spend in this instance are time plus whatever he or she would be doing at that hour.

## Types of Exchanges

It is possible to categorize exchanges as resulting from 2 kinds of exchange processes.

1. *Unilateral exchange processes*, where only one party seeks to influence the outcome of the exchange process. For example, the congregation of Salem First Church of the Nazarene carried out a unilateral exchange process when it decided to give up its traditional Easter worship in its sanctuary to make it possible for unchurched persons to "come back" to church in a more neutral, less threatening setting.

2. *Bilateral exchange processes*, where both sides seek to influence the outcome of an exchange process. For example, the founders of Willow Creek Church entered into a bilateral exchange

process when they first asked unchurched persons what there was about attending church services that made them most uncomfortable and kept them away—and then designed a style of Sunday service that intentionally stays clear of those things.

Exchanges also vary in whether they are *two-party* or *multiple-party,* and whether they lead to transactions that are of *continuing* or *fixed* duration. Multiple-party exchanges in a religious organization can occur in a number of contexts. The additional party may be:

a. *allied with the recipient of the services*—for example, other family members, other members of the neighborhood, or other members of a buying group;

b. *allied with the religious organization*—for example, an advertising agency or consulting firm;

c. *independent of* either primary party but necessary to *facilitate* the transaction—for example, a state education official regulating a church elementary school; or

d. *independent* of either party but seeking to influence the existence or content of an exchange—for example, a Chamber of Commerce seeking to convince a synagogue to open a day-care center in the business district.

These additional parties are unique in the exchange process in that they do not bear any of the direct costs in the transaction but are involved because they expect to reap benefits, depending on the nature of the outcome.

"Continuing transactions" are those in which one or more parties must perform some continuing behavior as their part of the exchange agreement. Baptism as a requirement for membership in a church is a noncontinuing exchange in that the transaction is carried out only once and occurs at a fixed point in time. However, most exchanges sought by churches and synagogues are continuing transactions (usually designed to support the journey toward a transformed person) that require the party to change *permanently* some behavior or set of behaviors. Examples include tithing; requiring members to stop using alcohol, tobacco, or drugs; worshiping on a specific day of the week; observance of holy days; specific methods of birth control; and sending children to church school.

Implicit in continuing transactions—and therefore crucial to religious marketing—is the fact that marketing does not stop, and *should not stop,* with the parties' agreement to the transaction or when the exchange is first performed under the terms of the transaction. The church's mission is accomplished as new behaviors become habits and persons are transformed thereby. Just as marketing helped to bring the person to new behavior, so also marketing is needed to inform, sustain, and strengthen the person's resolve to stay with the behavior until it becomes fixed in his or her actions and attitudes.

## Analyzing Exchange Flows

Whenever two social units are engaged in exchange, it is useful to develop a diagram or map showing what is actually or potentially being exchanged between the two parties. An exchange between a synagogue and its members could be represented in Exhibit 4-9.

**THE EXCHANGE BETWEEN A SYNAGOGUE AND ITS MEMBERS**

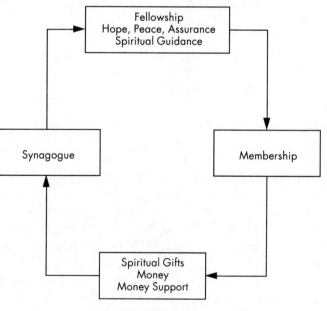

**Exhibit 4-9**

To give a sense of how an exchange framework can be used in the development of a marketing strategy, suppose a rabbi of a synagogue seeks to persuade a couple who have recently joined the congregation to send their seven-year-old son to the synagogue's elementary day school, instead of sending him to public school. We could represent this situation in the following abstract way.

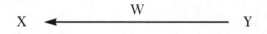

$$X \xleftarrow{\quad W \quad} Y$$

This says that X wants W from Y. In the concrete case, this is expanded to read:

$$\text{Synagogue's School} \xleftarrow{\quad W \quad} \text{Parents}$$

Wants:

1. Parents' acceptance of the importance of religious-based education.
2. Child's enrollment in school.
3. Tuition.

Thus the school wants the parents to enroll their child in the synagogue's school, support the ideals of religious-based education, and pay the required tuition.

The parents in turn hope to satisfy certain wants by the school's education. We could diagram these as follows:

$$\text{Synagogue's School} \xrightarrow{\quad W \quad} \text{Parents}$$

Wants:

1. Training in parents' values and religious beliefs.

2. Education in academic subjects exceeding that of public schools.
3. Healthy, safe environment.
4. Socialization with other "quality" children.

It would be helpful for the rabbi (teachers and principal) to know the relative importance parents attach to each of these wants.

Many religious organizations adopt a selling or product orientation that assumes everyone will recognize the obvious and inherent value of their product. This is an *inside-out* perspective. In contrast, a marketing orientation, as we saw in chapter 2, always takes an *outside-in* perspective by looking at the congregation's programs and ministries from the perspective of the other party (the consumer). We may think that the value of religious education is real, significant, and obvious, but if parents do not perceive its value *as they define value*, or if this value does not equal or exceed the value of what they must offer in response, then exchange will not take place.

> These diagrams illustrate an important aspect of exchange: Value is in the eye of the beholder. It doesn't matter how much value we see in the product we are offering. What matters is the perception of the party whom we wish to engage in exchange.

## Elaborating the Exchange Process

We have examined the exchange process as if it involved only two parties. But an exchange process may involve multiple parties. We can illustrate a multiple party exchange process by introducing the child into our example. In Exhibit 4-10 we see three sets of wants and/or values being considered in the exchange process.

*The child* wants to feel loved and cared for by the parents, including parental concern for doing what is good for the child in the long-run. *The school* is looking for children who have the capacity and desire to learn, who will be well-behaved, and who can be used as examples of the type of children enrolled in the day school. The synagogue values this type of student in order to encourage other parents to enroll their children in its school. *The parents* want a happy, well-adjusted child with the values and beliefs they prize, as well as an academic training that prepares the child for further education.

## THREE-PARTY EXCHANGE MAP
## SHOWING WANT VECTORS

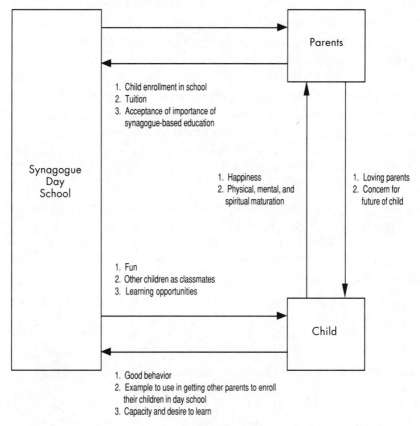

1. Training in values and religious beliefs supported by parents
2. Quality academic education
3. Healthy, safe environment
4. Socialization with other "quality" children

**Parents**

1. Child enrollment in school
2. Tuition
3. Acceptance of importance of synagogue-based education

**Synagogue Day School**

1. Happiness
2. Physical, mental, and spiritual maturation

1. Loving parents
2. Concern for future of child

1. Fun
2. Other children as classmates
3. Learning opportunities

**Child**

1. Good behavior
2. Example to use in getting other parents to enroll their children in day school
3. Capacity and desire to learn

**Exhibit 4-10**

Not included in the diagram, but still pertinent parties to the 3-way exchange, would be, on the school's side, accrediting associations and other agencies that could affect the parents' perception of the value of the school's program. On the parents' side would be other institutions, such as financial institutions, that might affect the parents' financial ability to enroll their child in the day school. Clearly the synagogue, as marketer, must take these various needs and weightings of value into consideration when formulating strategies to attract students to its school.

When marketers are anxious to consummate a transaction, they may be tempted to exaggerate the actual product benefits. Thus the rabbi may be tempted to overstate the competence of the teachers or understate the total costs to the parents, financial and otherwise. By doing so, he may succeed in getting the parents to enroll their child, but the parents and/or child will become dissatisfied because of the difference between their *expectations* and the school's *performance*. As unhappy participants in this exchange, they can be expected to complain a great deal, talk negatively about the school to other parents or playmates, or leave the school and synagogue. In the case of the day school, these dissatisfactions could carry over into other exchanges between the synagogue and the family.

The best transactions are those in which it is realized that both (or all) parties are not simply seeking a single transaction but a continuing expected behavior on the part of the other party, and where parties behave in such a way as to ensure the other will receive the expected values from the exchange.

*Good marketing will not serve to compensate for an inferior ministry or program.* A church or synagogue cannot market a value its product does not have. Marketing can never be a substitute for the diligent effort required to build an effective ministry. Members and outside targeted publics are too sophisticated to be taken in for very long. If an inferior program or ministry is marketed, the results will always be worse than before. Effective marketing must begin with a product of sufficient value (as perceived by the targeted public, not by the organization) to convince the consumers that the benefits to their lives will outweigh the costs.

## The Cost of an Exchange

In the consumers' perspective of an organization's programs, they are being asked to incur cost or make sacrifices (that is, to give up something of value) in return for promised benefits. There are 4 types of "costs":

1. *Economic costs*—e.g., to give up money or goods as tithes or offerings, or simply to buy a product or service.
2. *Sacrifices of old ideas, values, or views of the world*—e.g., to give up believing that women are inferior, that abortion is evil (or not evil), that God is vindictive, that one can't be forgiven.
3. *Sacrifices of old patterns of behavior*—e.g., to start a daily devotional or attend church services regularly.
4. *Sacrifices of time and energy*—e.g., to perform a voluntary service or give blood to a church blood drive.

In return for these types of sacrifices, consumers of ecclesial services receive benefits of three basic kinds: *goods and services, social,* and *psychological.* The combination of these kinds of sacrifices and benefits yield the matrix outlined in Exhibit 4-11.

We have presented this discussion of exchange theory because it is central to a responsive congregation. To be responsive requires analyzing the other party's needs and interests and determining how far the organization can go toward satisfying them. A congregation that is oblivious or indifferent to the needs of the other party cannot, by definition, be responsive.

Father John J. Wall, pastor of Old St. Patrick's Catholic Church in Chicago's downtown area, practices a market orientation with tremendous success. In a day when most churches have left the downtown area, and when the membership in those that remain tends to dwindle, Old St. Patrick's is flourishing. By targeting the downtown office workers as a weekday congregation, Father Wall has been able to install a weekday mass with more than 3,000 persons attending. He is also keenly aware of his competition and the need to effect meaningful exchanges of mutual value. Following is a report of "The Largest Block Party in the World."[17] It deals with virtually every marketing concept discussed so far.

## COST/BENEFIT MATRIX FOR RELIGIOUS ORGANIZATIONAL EXCHANGES

| COSTS | A GOOD | A SERVICE | BENEFITS SOCIAL | PSYCHOLOGICAL |
|---|---|---|---|---|
| Give up economic assets | Buy a tape of sermons | Church School education | Donate to building fund | Church tithes and offerings |
| Give up old ideas, values, opinions | Receive free clothing donated by church members | Premarital counseling, marriage counseling | Prison ministry by laypersons | God can be trusted, sins can be forgiven |
| Give up old behaviors, undertake or learn new behaviors | Stay drug free and receive a "how to" video tape | Participate in stop smoking program, home budget counseling | Go to divorce recovery group once a week | Start daily devotion, attend church services |
| Give up time or energy | Come to revival meetings and get a free Bible | Attend a free religious concert | Volunteer for Vacation Bible School | Give blood in church blood drive |

**Exhibit 4-11**

On a warm summer Sunday, as the sun streams in through the brilliant stained-glass windows of Old St. Patrick's Church and the worshipers wait expectantly for the 9:45 A.M. mass to begin, Father John J. Wall, dressed in white and green vestments, steps from the sanctuary into the center aisle.

"What a great day!" he says, smiling. "Welcome to Old St. Patrick's. If you're a visitor, we hope you enjoy Chicago. The Blues Festival seems to be the place to be this weekend.

"We have kind of a tradition here at St. Pat's. If you're parishioners, please stand up and introduce yourselves to the visitors."

And so they do. One enthusiastic older woman, apparently surrounded by familiar faces, even crosses a side aisle to shake hands with some flabbergasted newcomers clustered in a pew in the back of the nave.

The brief welcoming ritual over, the mass begins. The church is crowded with young adults, some of their parents, a sprinkling of toddlers, and two vocal babies.

It is a far cry from the first Sunday mass Father Wall celebrated at Old St. Patrick's, shortly after Labor Day in 1983, when he took over as pastor. He preached to a mere 25 people. There were no readers and no music.

"I spent a lot of time just wandering around," he remembers. "I mean, trying to meet people in the neighborhood. I would say 'Hi. I'm Jack Wall. I'm new here; tell me what to do.' "

In the spring of 1984, Wall noticed some blue-and-white-striped tents on Madison and Monroe Streets. He walked over to see what was going on and ended up "crashing" the opening festivities for the first residents moving into the new Presidential Towers. The complex of four 49-story buildings containing rental apartments and other amenities is geared for the affluent young people who want to walk to their offices in the Loop, and it could not have been a better omen for Old St. Patrick's.

Quite a few residents of Presidential Towers and other nearby developments in Dearborn Park, Printers Row, and University Village are among its 800 registered parishioners and about 10,000 associates who attend mass and participate in the lecture series and other activities. According to Wall, one-third of the parishioners come from downtown and the Near North and Near Southwest Sides, another third comes from outlying areas of the city, and the last third from the suburbs.

"About 60 percent of the congregation is young adults in their 20s and 30s, and 40 percent are their parents," Wall says. "I did not expect that. It's a family church, but it's the adult family as opposed to the family with children in grammar school." Consequently, there are very few funerals but plenty of weddings—200 a year—though the majority of the younger members are single.

The 11:00 A.M. mass on the first Sunday of each month is geared to young adults, who flock to the church on those Sundays and partake of a complimentary breakfast in the social hall afterward.

But there are enough young married couples with new babies and toddlers who live or work in the neighborhood and its environs to warrant a school, and this fall St. Patrick's opened the first new Catholic school in the archdiocese since 1967. Preschool and kindergarten classes are being held in a space in the Presidential Towers complex.

Under Wall's leadership, Old St. Patrick's major fund raiser is the annual World's Largest Block Party, held on a Friday and Saturday night in midsummer on the streets around the church. It began in 1984, when someone donated the use of a band, and on the spur of the moment Wall said, "Why don't we throw the world's largest block party?"

His early encounters with block parties came during his first assignment as a priest at St. Ita's parish in Edgewater-Uptown, where, he says, "Social life in the summer was sitting on your front porch, and block parties provided such a sense of neighborhood."

Another important part of Old St. Patrick's mission is service to the community. As Wall puts it, "We're not a congregational church looking inward to ourselves; we're a church that's reaching out toward others."

Under the umbrella of a Community Outreach Group (COG), several hundred members and associates are involved in 3 programs: a tutoring program for children at St. Malachy School, helping out 4 evenings a week at the Franciscan House of Joseph and Mary, a shelter for the homeless, and a sports program for teenagers from Pilsen, held at the Old St. Patrick's gym on Saturday afternoons. An adult literacy program at Providence of God Church in Pilsen is in the planning stages.

In addition to service and hospitality, Wall also wants to offer a good worship experience. He hired a permanent music director, Mary Prete, to organize a choir and a musical repertoire.

"Most of the music that we know is passive in context," says Prete, who is president of Alverno Religious Articles & Books and a professional musician. "It's been a challenge to find outward, active kinds of text and music. You would probably not hear 'Holy God, We Praise Thy Name' at St. Patrick's, but you will hear 'Amazing Grace.' "

And homilies, which have traditionally been neglected in Catholic churches, are emphasized.

"We are trying to listen deeply to the everyday experiences in people's lives because we think that's where God is present," Wall says. "Scripture says God is present in all the decisions and moments of your life. We use the Scriptures as a blueprint to look over one way God may be speaking to us a paradigm of how God is working in life today. The only way into God is through your own human experience."

Perhaps the parishioners are the best judges of the sermons. "They're great," says John Bredemann, a vice-president and account media director at J. Walter Thompson Advertising Agency who has been a member of Old St. Patrick's for five years. "The key for me is getting a different perspective. The sermons are food for thought. You try and figure out how to fit the message into your everyday life."

## The Concept of Image

One consequence of the exchanges between a church or synagogue and its targeted audiences is that the audiences develop an image of the congregation. Every congregation has an image. *Your* congregation has an image. Do you know what it is?

The most important point about the image of a religious organization is "To market a positive image, you need a product worth marketing. Without that, you are doomed to failure. Image makers' efforts and resources would be better spent on needed improvements in the product."[18] To put it simply, *you cannot market what you have not got*.

Responsive religious institutions have a strong interest in how their publics view their structures, ministries, and services. It is the institution's image, not necessarily its reality, that people initially respond to. Publics holding a negative image of the congregation will avoid or disparage everything it does, while those holding a positive image will be drawn to it. The congregation has a vital interest in learning about its image and in seeking to create a more positive image in the minds of members and non-members alike.

A congregation does not acquire a favorable image simply through public relations work. Its image is a function of its *deeds* and its *communications*. Good deeds without good words, or good words without good deeds, will not work. A strong favorable image is achieved when the congregation creates real satisfaction for its members and other users of its ministries and services, and lets others know about this.

Leaders of religious organizations want to know the following things about image:

1. What is an image?
2. How can it be measured?
3. What determines the image?
4. How can an image be changed?
5. What is the relationship between the person's image of a program or ministry and his or her behavior toward the church or synagogue?

## Definition of Image

The term *image* came into popular use in the 1950s. It is currently used in a variety of contexts: organization image, corporate image, national image, brand image, public image, self-image, and so on. Its wide use has tended to blur its meaning.

Our definition of image is:

Image is the sum of the feelings, beliefs, attitudes, impressions, thoughts, perceptions, ideas, recollections, conclusions, and mindsets that a person or group has of another person, organization, or object.[19]

This definition enables us to distinguish an image from similar sounding concepts, such as *impressions*, *attitudes*, and *stereotypes*.

An image is more than a simple impression. The impression that the Roman Catholic Church takes a strong stand against abortion would be only one element in a large image that might be held about the Roman Catholic Church. An image is a whole set of impressions about an object.

On the other hand, people's images of an object do not necessarily reveal their attitudes toward that object. Two persons may hold the same image of the Catholic Church and yet have different attitudes toward it. An attitude is a disposition toward an object that includes cognitive, affective, and behavioral components.

How does an image differ from a stereotype? A stereotype suggests a widely held image that is highly distorted and simplistic, and that carries a favorable or unfavorable attitude toward the object. An image, however, is a more personal perception of an object that can vary among groups. Actually, a specific religious organization will have several images, depending on the particular group.

## Image Measurement: Discovering the Organization's Image

We will describe a 2-step approach to measuring a congregation's image.[20] The first consists in measuring how familiar and favorable the congregation's image is. The second consists in measuring the organization's image along major relevant dimensions. These approaches are suggestive only.

*Familiarity-favorability measurement.* The first step is to establish how familiar each public is with the congregation and how favorable they feel toward it. To establish the degree of familiarity, respondents are asked to check one of the following:

| Never heard of | Heard of | Know a little bit | Know a fair amount | Know very well |
|---|---|---|---|---|
| | | | | |

The results indicate the public's level of awareness of the congregation. If most of the respondents check the first 2 or 3 categories, the congregation has a serious awareness problem.

If most of the respondents indicate they know the congregation "a fair amount" or "very well," they are then asked to describe how favorable they feel toward it by checking one of the following:

## FAMILIARITY-FAVORABILITY ANALYSIS

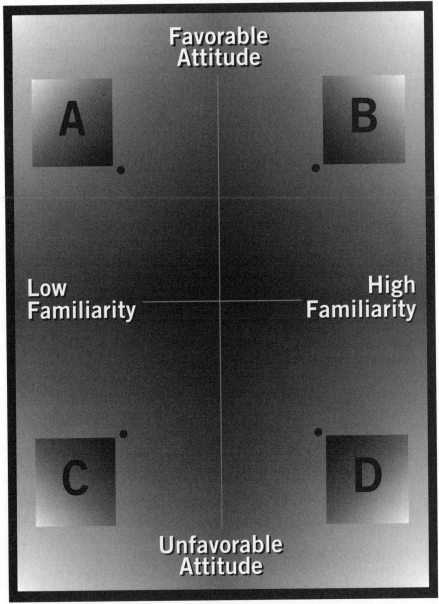

**Exhibit 4-12**

| Very unfavorable | Somewhat unfavorable | Indifferent | Somewhat favorable | Very favorable |
|---|---|---|---|---|
| | | | | |

To illustrate these scales, suppose the residents of an area are asked to rate four local congregations: A, B, C, and D. Their responses are averaged and the results displayed in Exhibit 4-12.

The exhibit depicts Congregation A as having the strongest image; most people know it and like it. Congregation B is viewed favorably, but too few know about it. Congregation C is negatively viewed by the people who know it; fortunately not too many people know about it. Congregation D is in the weakest position; it is seen as an undesirable congregation, and everyone knows it.

Clearly, each congregation faces a different task. Congregation A must work at maintaining its good reputation and high community awareness. Congregation B must bring itself to the attention of more people, since those who know it find it to be a good church. Congregation C needs to find out why people dislike the church and take steps to mend its ways, while keeping a low profile. Congregation D would be well advised to lower its profile (avoid news), mend its ways, and when it is a better church, it can start seeking public attention again.

**Semantic differential.** Each congregation needs to go further to research the *content* of its image. One of the most popular tools for this is the semantic differential.[21] It involves the following steps.

*1. Developing a set of relevant dimensions.* The researcher first asks people to identify the dimensions they would use in thinking about the object. People could be asked what things they think of when they consider a church. If someone suggests "quality of preaching," this would be turned into a bipolar adjective scale, with "inferior preaching" at one end and "superior preaching" at the other. This could be rendered as a 5- or 7-point scale. A set of additional relevant dimensions for a church is shown in Exhibit 4-13.

## Exhibit 4-13
### IMAGES OF THREE CHURCHES (SEMANTIC DIFFERENTIAL)

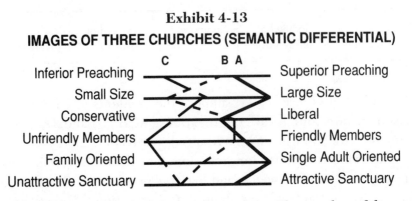

2. *Reducing the set of relevant dimensions.* The number of dimensions should be kept small to avoid respondent fatigue in having to rate several congregations on a number of scales. Osgood and his coworkers feel that there are essentially 3 types of scales.

* Evaluation scales (good-bad qualities)
* Potency scales (strong-weak qualities)
* Activity scales (active-passive qualities)

Using these scales as a guide, the researcher can remove redundant scales that fail to add much information.

3. *Administering the instrument to a sample of respondents.* The respondents are asked to rate 1 organization at a time. The bipolar adjectives should be arranged so as not to load all of the poor adjectives on one side.

4. *Averaging the results.* Exhibit 4-13 shows the results of averaging the respondents' impressions of congregations A, B, and C. Each congregation's image is represented by a line that summarizes how the average respondent sees that institution. Thus Congregation A is seen as large, liberal, friendly, singles-oriented with superior preaching. Congregation C, on the other hand, is seen as a moderate-sized, conservative, unfriendly group with inferior preaching. Congregation B is seen as small, liberal, friendly, with good preaching.

5. *Checking on the image variance.* Since each image profile is the result of averaging the respondents' answers, it does not reveal how variable the image is among different respondents. If there were 100 respondents, did they all see Congregation B, for example, exactly as

shown, or was there considerable variation? If the responses were very similar, the image is highly *specific*. If the responses were greatly varied, the image is highly *diffused*.

An institution may or may not want a very specific image. Some religious organizations prefer a diffused image so that different groups can project their needs onto it. The organization will want to analyze whether a variable image is really the result of different subgroups rating the organization, with each subgroup having a highly specific image.

The semantic differential is a flexible image-measuring tool that can provide the following useful information:

1. *The congregation can discover how a particular public views the organization and its major competitors.* It can learn its image strengths and weaknesses, along with those of the competitors, and take remedial steps toward creating a more desirable image.

2. *The congregation can discover how different publics and market segments view it.* One can imagine that the image profiles in Exhibit 4-13 represent the images of one congregation held by 3 different publics. The congregation would then consider taking steps to improve its image among those publics who view it most unfavorably.

3. *The congregation can monitor changes in its image over time.* By repeating the image study periodically, the congregation can detect any significant image slippage or improvement. Image slippage signals that the organization is doing something wrong. Image improvement, on the other hand, verifies that the organization is performing better as a result of some steps it has taken.

### Image Causation

What determines the image a person holds of an object? A theory of image determinants will help the organization understand the factors that have shaped its present image and help in planning to change the image. Two opposite theories of image formation prevail. One holds that image is largely *object-determined*—that is, persons are simply perceiving the object's reality. If an attractive synagogue is located next to a lake and is surrounded by beautiful trees, then it is going to strike people as a beautiful synagogue. A few individuals might describe it as ugly, but this would be dismissed as the peculiarity of certain individuals. The object-determined view of images assumes that: (1) people tend to have firsthand experience with objects; (2) people get reliable sensory data from the object; (3) people tend to process the sensory data in a similar way in spite of having different backgrounds and personalities. These assumptions imply that organizations cannot easily create false images of themselves.

The other theory holds that images are largely *person-determined*. Those holding this view argue that: (1) people have different degrees of contact with the object; (2) people placed in front of the object will selectively perceive different aspects of the object; (3) people have individual ways of processing sensory data, leading to selective distortion. This set of assumptions implies that people are likely to hold quite different images of the object. That is, there is a weak relation between the image and the actual object.

The truth lies somewhere in between. An image is influenced both by the object's objective characteristics and the perceiver's subjective characteristics. We might expect people to hold rather similar images of a given object mainly under the following conditions: when the object is simple rather than complex; when it is frequently and directly experienced; and when it is fairly stable in its real characteristics over time.

Conversely, people may hold quite different images of an object if it is complex, infrequently experienced, and changing through time. People have quite different images of a particular church or synagogue because it is complex, infrequently experienced in direct contact, and changes through time.

## Image Modification

The leaders of an organization are often surprised and disturbed by the measured image. Thus the leaders of a congregation might be upset that the pubic sees the congregation substantially different from their own perceptions. Their immediate reaction is to disbelieve the results by complaining that the number of persons interviewed is too small or unrepresentative. But if the results can be defended as reliable, the leaders must consider what they should be doing about this image problem.

The first step is to develop a picture of the *desired image that they would like to earn in the general public's mind—in contrast to the current image.*

The second step is to decide which image gaps they want to work on initially; for example, is it more desirable to improve the congregation's image of friendliness (through staff training, etc.) or to improve the condition of the facilities (through renovation)?

Each image dimension should be separately reviewed in terms of the following questions:

1. What contribution to the organization's overall favorable image would be made by closing the image gap in this dimension?
2. What strategy (combination of real changes and communication changes) would be used to close the particular image gap?
3. What would be the cost of closing that image gap?
4. How long would it take to close that image gap?

For example, the leaders might decide it would be more apparent, quicker, and less costly to improve the congregation's image of friendliness than to improve the buildings' physical facilities. An overall image modification plan would involve planning the sequence of steps through which the congregation would go to transform its current image into its desired image.

An organization seeking to change its image must have great patience. Images are "sticky" and last long after the reality of the organization has changed. Thus a congregation may be more family oriented and yet continue to be considered singles oriented in the public mind. Image persistence is explained by the fact that once people have formed a certain image of an object, they tend to be selective perceivers of further data. Their perceptions are oriented toward seeing what they expect to see. It will take highly disconfirming stimuli to raise doubts, and open them to new information. Thus an image enjoys a life of its own for a while, especially when people are not likely to have new firsthand experiences with the changed object.

## The Organization's Image and the Way Persons Respond

Organizations should be interested in image measurement and modification because there is a close relationship between the public's image of the organization and their behavior toward it. Organizations can obtain better public response by acquiring a better image.

However, the connection between image and behavior is not as close as many organizations believe. Images are only one component of attitudes. Two people may view a church as large and have opposite attitudes toward a large church. Furthermore, the connection between attitudes and behavior is also tenuous. A person might prefer a large church to a small one, and yet end up in the small one because it is closer to home, or their friends go there.

Nevertheless, one should not dismiss image measurement and planning simply because images are hard to change and their effects on behavior are unclear. Quite the contrary. Measuring an object's image is a very useful step in understanding what is happening to the object, what results its efforts are achieving, and in planning steps toward changing its image. Furthermore, though the connection between image and behavior is not always strong, it does exist. The connection should neither be overrated nor underrated. The organization should attempt to make an investment in developing the best image it can for the advantages this might bring.

## The Concept of Satisfaction

A responsive organization is one that makes every effort to sense, serve, and satisfy the needs and wants of its members and publics. Each organization must determine how responsive it wants to be, and develop the appropriate systems for measuring and improving its satisfaction-creating ability.

Since responsive organizations aim to create satisfaction, it is necessary to define the term *satisfaction*. Our definition is:

> *Satisfaction is a state felt by a person (or group) who has experienced a performance (or outcome) that has fulfilled his or her expectation.*

Thus satisfaction is a function of the relative levels of expectation and perceived performance. A person will experience 1 of 3 states of satisfaction: If the performance exceeds the person's expectations, the person is *highly satisfied*. If the performance matches the expectations, the person is *satisfied*. If the performance falls short of the expectations, the person is *dissatisfied*.

In the last case, the amount of dissatisfaction depends on the person's method of handling the gap between expectations and performance. Some members and participants try to *minimize* the felt dissonance by imagining better performance than there really is, or reasoning that they set their expectations too high. Other persons will exaggerate the perceived performance gap because of their disappointment.[22] They are more prone to reduce or end their contacts with the organization.

### Measuring Satisfaction

Member or participant satisfaction, in spite of its central importance, is difficult to measure. Religious organizations use various methods to make an inference about how much member or participant satisfaction they are creating. The major methods are described below.

**Performance-related methods.** Many congregations feel that the extent of member and participant satisfaction created by their activities is revealed by such objective measures as:

*Growth statistics*: the increase or decline of the number of persons attending or participating in their programs and ministries.

*Market share*: the number of members and of persons participating, as compared to the other congregations nearby;

*Repeat ratio*: the percentage of persons who attend more than once, and how long they keep returning;

*Active ratio*: The percentage of active members out of the total membership ("active" must be defined).

If these measures are rising, the leaders draw the conclusion that the organization is satisfying its members and participants. Thus if

Congregation X is crowded at the worship services and 100 percent of its members subscribe to support the budget, the leaders conclude that the members must be satisfied. If a Sunday school class attracts more teenage students each year, even though the number of teenagers in the congregation is declining, it implies that the teenagers in the congregation must be satisfied.

These indirect measures are important, but hardly sufficient. In situations of no competition, or of excess demand, these measures may be high and yet not reflect actual satisfaction, because persons have no alternatives. In other situations, attendance can remain strong for a while, even after satisfaction has started to decline, because dissatisfied members might continue to participate for a period of time out of habit, or inertia.

**Complaint and suggestion systems.** A responsive congregation will make it easy for its members and others to complain if they are disappointed with the service. Leaders will want complaints to surface, on the theory that members who are not given an opportunity to complain might reduce their level of participation and/or support for the organization, bad-mouth it, or abandon it completely. Not collecting complaints represents a loss of valuable information that the organization could have used to improve its services.

To facilitate the opportunity for persons to register complaints, the leaders can set up systems that make it easy for dissatisfied (or satisfied) persons to express their feelings. Several devices can be used in this connection. For example, a church or synagogue could place *suggestion boxes* in convenient areas. It could supply members and participants with a *comment card,* allowing responses to several of the congregation's services. These cards encourage the submission of complaints, compliments, suggestions, and requests for information.

An organization should try to identify the major categories of complaints. Thus a congregation might count the number of complaints about the timing of worship services, sermon topics, and youth ministry and focus its corrective actions on those categories showing a high frequency, high seriousness, and/or high remediability.

A good complaint management system will provide much valuable information for improving the organization's performance. At the same time, a complaint system tends to understate the amount of real dissatisfaction felt by members and by participants. The reasons are (1) Many people who are disappointed may choose not to complain, either being too angry or feeling that complaining would do no good. One study found that only 34 percent of a group of dissatisfied people said they would complain. (2) Some people overcomplain (the chronic complainers), and this introduces a bias into the data.

Some critics have argued that complaint systems do more harm than good. When given an opportunity—indeed, an incentive—to complain, people are more likely to feel dissatisfied. Instead of ignoring their disappointment, they are asked to spell it out. They are also led to expect redress. If the latter is not forthcoming, they will be more dissatisfied than ever. Even though this might happen, it is our view that the value of the information gathered by soliciting complaints far exceeds the cost of possibly overstimulating dissatisfaction.

**Consumer panels.** Some organizations set up a consumer panel to keep informed of member and participant satisfaction. The panel consists of a small group of members and participants who are periodically sampled about their feelings toward the organization or any of its services.

Some provision is usually made to rotate membership of the panel, in order to get fresh views from new people. The panel is typically a source of valuable information to the organization. At the same time, the information may not be completely reliable. The panel's representativeness can be called into question. People who do not like to be members of panels are not represented. Those who join the panel may be more loyal to the organization, and thus less likely to see its faults.

**Member and participant satisfaction surveys.** Many organizations supplement the preceding devices with direct periodic surveys of members and participants. They send questionnaires or make telephone calls to random samples of volunteer workers, members, and participants to find out how much they like or dislike a particular program or ministry. In this way, they avoid the possible biases of complaints systems, on the one hand, and consumer panels, on the other.

The level of satisfaction a group holds for a particular program or service can be measured in a number of ways, 3 of which will be described here.

*1. Directly Reported Satisfaction.* A church or synagogue can distribute a questionnaire to a representative sample of members, asking them to state their felt satisfaction with the organization as a whole, and with specific components. The questionnaire is distributed on a periodic basis either in person, by mail, or through a telephone survey.

The questionnaire might contain questions of the following form:

Indicate how satisfied you are with _____ on the following scale:

| 1 | 2 | 3 | 4 | 5 |
|---|---|---|---|---|
| Highly dissatisfied | Dissatisfied | Indifferent | Satisfied | Highly satisfied |

Here 5 intervals are used. When the results are in, a bar graph (histogram) can be prepared, showing the percentage of respondents who fall into each group.

If the histogram is highly skewed to the left, the congregation is in deep trouble. If the histogram is bell-shaped, then it has the usual number of dissatisfied, indifferent, and satisfied members. If the histogram is highly skewed to the right, the congregation can be satisfied that it is a responsive organization, meeting its goal of delivering high satisfaction to the majority of its members and participants.

The survey should be repeated at regular intervals to spot any significant changes in the distribution. Furthermore, the respondents should check scales for other components of the organization, such as its community service activities, youth programs, choir, and the like. It would help to know how the various components of satisfaction relate to overall satisfaction.

*2. Derived Dissatisfaction.* The second method of satisfaction measurement is based on the premise that a person's satisfaction is influenced by his or her expectations and perception of the object. The respondent is asked 2 questions about each component of the organization, for example:

The quality of the youth program:

a. How much quality is there now?

| minimum | 1 | 2 | 3 | 4 | 5 | 6 | 7 | maximum |

b. Considering costs, how much quality should there be?

| minimum | 1 | 2 | 3 | 4 | 5 | 6 | 7 | maximum |

Suppose the respondent circles 2 for part a and 5 for part b. A "need deficiency" score can then be derived by subtracting the weight given to part a from that given to part b. In this instance the difference would be 5 minus 2, or 3. The greater the need deficiency score, the greater the respondent's degree of dissatisfaction (or the smaller his or her degree of satisfaction).

This method provides more useful information than the previous method. By averaging the scores of all the respondents to part a, the researcher learns the average perceived level of that attribute of the object. The dispersion around the average shows how much agreement there is among the members. If all members see the congregation's youth program at approximately 2 on a 7-point scale, the program is pretty bad. If members hold widely differing perceptions of the program's actual quality, this will require further analysis of why the perceptions differ so much and what individual or group factors might be related to the differing perceptions.

It is also useful to average the scores of all the respondents to part b. This will reveal the average member's view of how much quality is expected in the youth program. The measure of dispersion will show how much spread there is in member opinion regarding the desired level of quality.

By finding the need deficiency score for each program or ministry, the leaders will have a good understanding of current member and participant moods, and where to make the necessary changes. By repeating this survey at regular intervals, the leaders can detect new need deficiencies as they arise, and take timely steps to remedy them.

3. *Importance/Performance Ratings.* Another satisfaction measuring device is to ask members and participants to rate several programs and ministries provided by the congregation in terms of (1)

the importance of each service and (2) how well the organization performs each service. Exhibit 4-14 shows how church members rated 14 services. A service's importance was rated on a 4-point scale of "extremely important," "important," "slightly important," and "not important." The congregation's performance was rated on a 4-point scale of "excellent," "good," "fair," and "poor."

For example, the first service, "youth program," received a mean importance rating of 3.83 and a mean performance rating of 2.63, indicating that members felt it was highly important, although not being performed all that well.

The ratings of all 14 services are displayed in Exhibit 4-14. The figure is divided into 4 sections.

Quadrant A shows important services that are not being offered at the desired performance levels. The church should concentrate on improving these services.

Quadrant B shows important services that the church is performing well. Its job here is to maintain the high performance.

Quadrant C shows minor services that are being delivered in a mediocre way, but do not need any attention since they are not very important.

Quadrant D shows a minor service that is being performed in an excellent manner, a case of possible "overkill."

This rating of services according to their perceived importance and performance provides the church with guidelines as to where it should concentrate its efforts for increasing levels of satisfaction.

## Consumer Satisfaction and Other Goals

Many people believe that the marketing concept calls upon the organization to *maximize* the satisfaction of its members and participants. This, however, is not realistic. The marketing concept says the organization should strive to create a high level of satisfaction among its members and participants. The reasons for this are explained below.

First, consumer satisfaction can always be increased by incurring additional cost. Thus a congregation might hire more associate pastors, build better facilities, and institute more programs to increase the satisfaction of its members. But obviously a congregation faces a financial constraint in trying to maximize the satisfaction of a particular public.

## IMPORTANCE AND PERFORMANCE RATINGS
## FOR SEVERAL CHURCH SERVICES

| Service | Service Description | Mean importance rating (a) | Mean performance rating (b) |
|---|---|---|---|
| 1 | Youth Program | 3.83 | 2.63 |
| 2 | Premarital Counseling | 3.63 | 2.73 |
| 3 | At Home Visitation | 3.60 | 3.15 |
| 4 | Sermon Quality | 3.56 | 3.00 |
| 5 | Community Service | 3.41 | 3.05 |
| 6 | Evangelistic Outreach | 3.39 | 3.29 |
| 7 | Church School Quality | 3.38 | 3.03 |
| 8 | Sunday School Classes | 3.37 | 3.11 |
| 9 | Bible Camp | 3.29 | 2.24 |
| 10 | Vacation Bible School | 3.27 | 3.02 |
| 11 | Mid-week Prayer Meeting | 2.52 | 2.25 |
| 12 | Pastoral Counseling | 2.43 | 2.49 |
| 13 | Social Events | 2.37 | 2.35 |
| 14 | Infant and Toddler Care | 2.05 | 3.13 |

(a) Ratings obtained from a four-point scales of "extremely important," "important," "slightly important," and "not important."
(b) Ratings obtained from a four-point scale of "excellent," "good," "fair," and "poor." A "no basis for judgment" category was also provided.

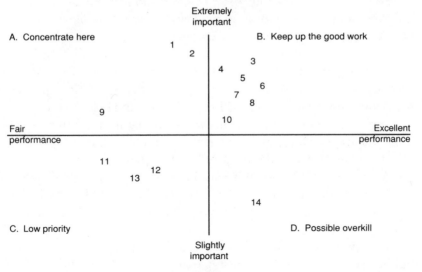

**Exhibit 4-14**

Second, the congregation has to satisfy many publics. Increasing the satisfaction of one public might reduce the satisfaction available to another public. The organization owes each public some specific level of satisfaction. Ultimately, the organization must operate on the philosophy that it is trying to satisfy the needs of different groups at levels that are acceptable to these groups within the constraint of its total resources. This is why the organization must systematically measure the levels of satisfaction expected by its different constituent publics and the current levels they are, in fact, receiving.

The organization hopes to derive a number of benefits as a result of creating high satisfaction in its publics. One benefit is that the members will participate with a better sense of purpose and pride. Another benefit is that the organization creates loyal publics. This reduces the costs of market turnover. Finally, the loyal publics say good things to others about the organization. This attracts new participants without requiring as much direct effort on the part of the organization. In chapter 10, we will discuss in greater detail various ways to create satisfied customers and consumers.

## Summary

Religious organizations exist to be responsive to the needs of their members and constituents, and responsive to the needs of society. A responsive congregation is one that makes every effort to sense, serve, and satisfy the needs and wants of its members and participants within the constraints of its budget. The concept of a responsive congregation rests on the concepts of mission, publics, segmentation and targeting, exchange, image, and satisfaction.

Every organization starts with a **mission** that answers these questions: What is our business? Who is the customer? What is of value to the customer? What will our business be? What should our business be? A mission is best when it is feasible, motivating, and distinctive.

Congregations interact with several **publics**. A public is a distinct group of people and/or organizations that has an actual or potential interest and/or impact on an organization. Publics can be classified as input publics (donors, suppliers, judicatory agencies), internal publics (trustees, board, ministry team, volunteers), intermediary publics (facilitators, publishers, agents, radio and TV media, marketing firms), consuming publics (members, other participants, recipients of services), and external publics (local publics, activist publics, general public, media publics, and competitive publics).

When an organization seeks some response from a public, this public is called a "market." A market is a distinct group of people and/or organizations which has resources it (or they) want to exchange, or might be willing to exchange, for distinct benefits.

No single organization can serve all the needs and interests of all the people surrounding it. A congregation that attempts to do so will likely dissipate its resources and accomplish little. Therefore it is important that the congregation **segment** the population into identifiable groups in order to decide those which it will **target** with its programs and ministries.

To carry out its mission with targeted publics, a religious organization needs resources. A congregation can attract resources through self-production, force, begging, or **exchange**. Marketing is based on exchange, and it assumes that there are at least two parties; each able to offer something of value to the other, each capable of communication and delivery, and each free to accept or reject the offer. Exchanges take place when both parties expect to be better off after a transaction is completed.

Responsive religious organizations are interested in their **image**, because it is their image to which people respond. An organization's image is the sum of the beliefs, ideas, and impressions that a person or group has of it. Images can be measured by scaling techniques. Organizations can work to modify undesirable aspects of their image through changing their practices and their communications.

The acid test of a congregation's responsiveness to its members, and society's physical and social needs, is the **satisfaction** it creates among the publics it serves. Religious organizations range from those that are unresponsive and casually responsive, to those that are highly responsive and fully responsive.

The more highly responsive religious organizations make use of complaint systems, surveys of satisfaction, surveys of needs and preferences, person-oriented personnel, and empowered members and participants. Responsive organizations create more satisfaction for their publics. Satisfaction is a state felt by a person or group that has experienced organizational performance that has matched their expectations.

This concludes Part One of our discussion. In this section we have focused on defining marketing and on setting it within the context of religious organizations. Marketing is an appropriate and important resource for religious organizations in today's environment, and application of the marketing concepts will serve to make any religious organization more responsive to the needs and interests of its members and participants. The members and participants, in return, will find greater satisfaction in their contacts with the organization.

In Part Two, we will discuss ways for analyzing ministry opportunities and targeting the opportunities best suited for a particular religious organization.

# PART TWO

# *How Religious Organizations Can Develop Marketing Plans*

## Introduction to Part Two

At this point we have arrived at an understanding of the role of marketing for religious organizations. More specifically, we have learned that marketing can help religious institutions structure their exchanges with key publics, both internal and external to the organization, to be mutually beneficial. Mutually beneficial exchanges are those that result in satisfaction of the organization's goals while addressing the relevant needs of those key publics. Marketing, therefore, provides the means by which religious organizations can become more responsive to their sometimes dramatically changing environments. The question at this point concerns how marketing can achieve these desirable ends.

The next 2 parts of this book are intended to follow a step-by-step process, showing how to develop marketing programs to achieve exchange-related organizational goals. Part Two details the development of marketing plans. Part Three shows how to put those plans into action.

Part Two consists of 3 chapters, which are the "front end" of developing marketing programs: researching ministry opportunities, segmenting the publics, and developing a marketing plan. Chapter 5, "Finding Out What People Need and Want: Marketing Research," suggests simple research methods by which we can discover the most attractive opportunities for ministry development. In the process of finding out what people need and want, we also become knowledgeable about the means by which we may capitalize on these opportunities—the "raw material" of marketing plans.

Chapter 6, "Ordering Your Priorities: Market Segmentation and Targeting," shows one important use of research findings: how we can divide a large amorphous "market" into manageable "segments" with similar characteristics, allowing us to develop responsive programs for each segment and, in turn, generate the response we are seeking from that segment. This chapter will give clues for understanding segment behavior, in order that one may plan how best to engage that segment in desired exchanges.

Finally, chapter 7 makes use of the segmentation and targeting outcomes to develop a strategic marketing plan that details what will be done to make these mutually beneficial exchanges with targeted segments a reality. Such a marketing plan starts with a well-defined mission for the organization, looks at the current situation to see what objectives should be pursued and what resources will be needed to achieve these mutually beneficial exchanges, specifies what target market the organization should pursue, and determines the marketing strategy, tactics, and budget best suited for achieving organizational goals with that target market.

Chapter 7 will also discuss ways to ensure the marketing plans are put into action. This is called "Marketing Control." Program evaluation is a key factor in marketing control. Evaluation will be discussed briefly in chapter 7, and at greater length in Appendix B.

# 5

# Finding Out What People Need and Want:

## Marketing Research

In the preceding chapters, we described the critical role that marketing research must play in understanding customers' needs, perceptions, behavior, and satisfaction. In the following chapters, we will see its usefulness in segmenting the market, planning marketing strategy, and developing program and promotional plans.

Marketing research covers a diverse number of activities. It can involve conducting one-time field research studies. It can comprise the analysis of data provided by internal record systems or by secondary sources of information. It can involve experiments or panel studies. What distinguishes marketing research from simple observation and "straight thinking" is that it is (1) planned and (2) tied to specific decision-making situations.

> *Marketing research is the planned acquisition and analysis of data measuring some aspect(s) of the organization, or its environment, for the purpose of improving its marketing decisions.*

Child Evangelism Fellowship (CEF) is an interdenominational organization operating in 85 countries. It has had fruitful ministries in its more than 50-year history, but found in the 1980s that two of its ministries—Good News Club, a children's Bible class meeting during the school year; and 5-Day Club, a Bible class for children meeting during the summer—had membership declines between 12 percent and 58 percent. The decline was particularly precipitous in Chile. CEF administration turned to marketing research to help determine the cause of the decline and to suggest marketing strategies to turn the organization around. Administrators conducted in-depth interviews with 30 pastors, 10 in each of the 3 major social classes. They discovered that 40 percent of the responses to questions about their needs concerned desired services that CEF did not then provide.

Major changes were made in the Good News and 5-Day Clubs programs and in the teacher training classes used to prepare adults to teach the Bible to the children enrolled in the clubs. Formerly, a teacher was required to study in the CEF teacher training classes yearly without ever graduating. Based on research findings, the training classes are now taught in 4 levels with graduation upon completion of each level.

Distribution of the club services was changed from central locations to the local churches, resulting in greater numbers of teachers willing to participate and more "ownership" by the local church. Instead of having one price for the club services for the entire country, a differential price structure was instituted, allowing each local CEF area in Chile to decide how much it would charge for the services it provided. This allowed for pricing structures in keeping with economic situations in different parts of the country.

Finally, promotion began to be done through personal contacts, public speaking, posters, direct mail, exhibitions in conferences, and Christian newspaper advertising where research indicated best media placement for reaching the target audience. Results? The two basic ministries grew by 2,500 percent in 6 years. Total income increased by 349 percent during that same period.

The role of marketing research in this case was put into perspective by the Chilean National Director of CEF:

Why does an evangelical organization need marketing research? Our organization, like many others, is up against a lot of competition. We are competing for the precious time of children and housewives, whom we train to teach the Bible to children in the Good News Clubs. We need to study the segments of women and children so we can better help them and attract their attention. Regular marketing research needs to take place to review our services and determine whether to change them.[1]

## Marketing Research in Religious Organizations[2]

Religious organizations conduct much less marketing research than they can or ought to. This is a consequence of their limited budgets, their relative newness to a marketing orientation, and their limited research expertise. Increasing the amount of marketing research, therefore, calls for both education and motivation, showing administrators what marketing research can do and how to do it properly, as well as encouraging them to do it more often.

Five myths keep religious organizations from engaging in more marketing research:

The "big decision" myth
The "survey myopia" myth
The "big bucks" myth
The "sophisticated researcher" myth
The "most-research-is-not-read" myth

### The "Big Decision" Myth

Religious leaders may consider doing marketing research only for decisions where large financial investments are at stake. Certainly in such cases research makes sense, but if we view research from a cost/benefit perspective we can better determine if research could prove useful, whatever the stakes. Marketing research costs commonly consist of 2 types—the expense incurred from doing the research itself and the costs incurred from delaying a decision until the results are available. The benefits in the cost/benefit analysis consist of improved decision making based on the research results. The value of the improvement, in turn, is a function of the stakes involved and how certain the leaders are about the rightness of the contemplated decision.

The cost/benefit ratio may sometimes come out against doing research, even when the stakes are high. Take the case of a pastor who was considering adding a day-care center to the church plant, and investing in a series of advertisements to promote this new service. She called in a research professional to design a study of neighborhood consumer interest in day care to determine the likely acceptance of such a service. In extended conversations with the pastor, the researcher determined that unless the survey found virtually no interest in day care, the congregation should go ahead with the decision to add the daycare. Given that such a study could cost several thousand dollars, and that in all likelihood the day care would be started, the benefits of the research would not justify the cost. The pastor was highly uncertain about the size of the market, but she was certain that it was adequate and that the decision to add the day-care center was best. The researcher convinced the manager that the money that would have been spent on research could more productively be used to ensure that the new day care got the promotional support needed to have the best chance of succeeding. It is not hard to think of other parallels to this example when a congregation has reached a concensus decision.

Conversely, research can often be justified even when the stakes are low. This is the case whenever the research is minimal, takes little time, and will help clarify which decisions to make.

Decisions involving advertising of the congregation often embody these conditions. A congregation, for example, may be investing a relatively small amount of money for advertising, but have two or three candidate ads that could be run with the funds. A modest research program may consist of exposing a small but representative group of the target audience members to the ads, revealing the superior ad, or at a minimum, revealing the problem with the ads and helping to narrow the choice. A pleasant by-product of such research is to "hear the voice of the market," suggesting new ads or alternative means of reaching your audience with meaningful messages.

Research may also be called for when the stakes seem modest at first, but upon reflection turn out to be high. When one considers the potential effects of making a wrong decision on such things as the congregation's image in the community, its ability to raise funds and attract volunteers, and its ability to attract new members, the costs may indeed be high. Such is often the case when a congregation tries to mimic what was proven successful by a sister congregation in a different geographic area with different target audiences, assuming what worked there will be equally successful here. What sometimes results is a marketing gaffe, of regrettable results and long-term consequences, which could have been avoided with a little research.

One may concede the argument to this point, but counter that the costs of such research seem high and that the alternative "quick and dirty" study is rarely quick but always dirty and therefore worse than no research at all. The only good research, one might argue, is a carefully conducted sample survey. This leads us to the next major myth.

## The "Survey Myopia" Myth

Any reliable information that improves our ability to make better marketing decisions can be considered marketing research. If one takes this view, many alternatives to conducting surveys come to mind. Consider the communications department of a denomination interested in selling a cassette tape and printed material to congregations or Sunday schools experiencing racial or ethnic disharmony among their members. The tapes are intended to help the listeners better understand their prejudices and find the solution for the disharmony among their people. The head of the communications department doesn't know whether there is a market for the tapes, how many to produce, or if the tapes can accomplish their intended task. The manager could conduct a survey to reduce this uncertainty. However, to make the research 95 percent certain of correctly predicting the percentage of congregations who would purchase the tapes, the manager must use a sample of at least 900 people.

Assuming the questionnaire and sampling plan are already designed, and ignoring analysis and report preparation costs, the interviewing alone could cost between $5,000 and $10,000. (The amount would depend on the length and type of interviews.) Clearly, this is more than many denominational departments could afford and, in fact, may be more than the entire sales potential of the tapes. More important, will the research yield valid data in any case? One should ask whether it is reasonable to expect respondents to be candid about their ethnic prejudices and willingness to listen to material that addresses "someone else's" problem!

How else, then, might we address the research objectives at lower cost? The decision in this case was to produce 40 copies of the tapes and material and call pastors and Sunday school superintendents to find 40 congregations who expressed an interest in testing the material in their churches. The sensitive issue of a pastor admitting to these types of problems in his or her church was avoided by having a third party (i.e., a student in a college marketing research class) conduct the interviews and place the material in the churches and schools. After the pastors and superintendents had time to use the material, follow-up telephone interviews were placed to determine satisfaction with the material. The interviews with the users were open-ended questions using a loosely structured interview guide intended to obtain some basic feel for their enthusiasm for the material. As it turns out, the response was lukewarm at best, and the communications department manager decided to scrap the project. The total cost of test packets, phone calls, and report was less than $200. Elaborate probability sampling designs were simply not necessary to satisfy the research objectives.

Another low-cost approach would be to commission focus group interviews of 5 to 9 members of the target audience at a time.[3] Although strictly speaking, the results cannot be projected to the larger market because the groups are not randomly selected, these results can cut the cost of interviewing by 35–50 percent. Interviewers can sometimes develop a deeper understanding of the issues in the relaxed, chatty format of the focus group. Also, the groups can alert leaders to problems with the new program. Focus groups have been found to be a cost-effective approach for other types of religious marketing research occasions as well. Consider the following use of focus groups by the Baptist Church.

In 1977, the Baptist General Convention of Texas prepared an extensive sales campaign to increase membership in its church. As a test, 4 commercials were shown to separate groups consisting of active Christians, inactive Christians, and non-Christians. All 3 segments gave their highest rating to testimonials in which the speakers indicated how important their faith in Christ had been in overcoming their own problems. In one, the speaker said that he had been a revolutionary, but his life had been changed by another revolutionary. He closed with the statement: "My name is Eldridge Cleaver. I'm living proof."

This "living proof" campaign was later widely used throughout the United States. Focus groups were also used to help set criteria for acceptable spokespersons.[4]

## The "Big Bucks" Myth

We have already seen that there are often low-cost alternatives to the kinds of field surveys most religious marketers normally consider. To be knowledgeable users of marketing research, persons must know how and when to do traditional survey research, and how and when to use a wide range of alternative low-cost research techniques. We shall consider these low-cost research techniques in later sections, since religious organizations typically have seriously restricted budgets (probably not news to our readers).

## The "Sophisticated Researcher" Myth

Just as marketing research does not always involve complex sampling and elaborate designs, neither is it always essential to have a high level of sophistication in sampling techniques, statistics, and computer analysis. Simple approaches can be highly effective. For example, both Bill Hybels (Willow Creek Community Church) and Rick Warren (Saddleback Valley Community Church) used door-to-door surveys to gather information to guide them in planning the philosophy and style of their churches. They then tabulated the responses to discover the major reasons persons did not attend church, and they designed programs to avoid these hindrances.

Religious leaders anticipating undertaking more formal research programs should acquaint themselves with at least the rudimentary principles of random sampling, questionnaire design, and graphic presentation of results (see Appendix A for sources of information on these and other marketing topics).

Even when the situation calls for high levels of sophistication—for example, when planning elaborate experiments or careful field study projects—low-cost assistance on an ad hoc basis is generally available. Instructors at local colleges are one resource. An alternative that is particularly appropriate to religious organizations is the voluntary help of local professional researchers. Generally a large congregation will have members who are, or who know, researchers.

## The "Most-Research-Is-Not-Read" Myth

Persons who would rather not bother doing research, or who subconsciously fear the results, may be especially interested in this last myth. Poor research certainly is undertaken, but when it is, it is usually a testimonial to poor planning. In our experience, few pieces of well-planned research are rejected as unhelpful, although they may be ignored on other, often political, grounds.

How can one ensure that precious resources will not be wasted on research of little effect? The responsibility rests with both the person requesting the research and the researcher conducting it. Research will be most valuable when:

1. It is undertaken after the religious leader had made clear to the researcher the decision alternatives and what additional information will add to better decision making.
2. The relationship between the results and the decision is clearly understood.
3. The results are communicated well.

In order to help them understand the unique characteristics of their California audience, the leadership team at Saddleback Community Church reads and discusses social theorists, psychographs in life-style sections of newspapers, and geodemographic sources, such as *American Demographics.* An example of how they use their findings to plan their ministries can be found in another of Rick Warren's comments: "One of the trends we have discovered in our research is that of the fragmentation of the American family. So we have designed questionnaires to survey the community, and we use the results in our program planning, and as material for preaching. Since many persons are experiencing the loss of intimate family ties, the church says, 'We want to be your family.' "

## Doing Marketing Research

Once a religious organization has overcome the myths discussed above, it is then free to develop a plan for conducting the necessary research for improving its ministry effectiveness. Three important components for a research process are (1) a budget for carrying out the research, (2) a statement of the objectives of doing the research, and (3) the specification of how the research will be carried out (methodology).

Since most religious organizations will perform research on an ad hoc basis (the alternative being research carried out by research professionals on a regular basis), the cost of each research project may be calculated and the money found to pay for the costs. Rarely will a church or synagogue include in its annual budget an amount earmarked for marketing research, so the funds must either be allocated from an existing account or raised from members for the purpose of the research study.

As was indicated in the "big bucks" myth, it should not be assumed that "marketing research" and "expensive" go hand-in-hand. It is important, however, that all the costs of the research are anticipated, so appropriate funding will be available. Again, one inexpensive (sometimes free) source of help is the marketing teacher at the local college, whose marketing research class may take on the organization's research problem as a class project.

In order to have a budget, the organization must first develop a plan. The research plan begins with a *statement of the objectives* for the research—what exactly do we need to know in order to make the best decision? An example of such a statement is shown below.

---

**Problem:** Attendance at the planned program for our teenage church members is consistently poor.

**Research Objective:** Discover the reasons for poor attendance and what, if anything, can be done to improve attendance.

**Research Questions:**
1. What has been the pattern of attendance for planned programs? Do the same few people come to each one? Do

---

different youth attend each program (but only come to a few before dropping out)?

2. What is common to those attending, and those not attending (age, gender, social class, home location, personality, etc.)?
3. Why do those attending come?
4. Why do some teenagers stop attending?
5. Why have some never attended any programs at all?
6. Have the youth been informed of the programs before they were conducted? Was the advertising/communication prepared and delivered in a manner that would interest young people?
7. What programs do non-attenders say they would attend if offered?
8. How satisfied have attenders been with the offered programs?
9. What roles do parents and peers play in encouraging or discouraging attendance?

A statement of the research objectives should clearly indicate the questions for which answers are necessary to help the decision makers solve the problem.

While it may appear that developing such a statement is simple and easily done, such is rarely the case. More often, the statement of research purpose and objectives is the product of much soul searching and extensive discussion among the interested parties and decision makers. Far too often research explores the *symptoms* of a problem, rather than the *core* problem. Someone who has experience in defining marketing problems carefully (college marketing research professor, volunteer retired marketing person, consultant, etc.) could help guide the discussion of the problem and research objectives.

The importance of developing a careful statement of the research purpose can hardly be overemphasized. Expensive, elaborate, scientifically conducted research that does not explore the *real* problem, or that fails to address the *important* research questions, will *not* result in better decision making. A simple, inexpensive, but carefully conducted study that explores issues of direct relevance to the decision maker would be of far greater use in solving the actual problem. The researcher is advised to spend all the time necessary and to involve all relevant parties in the development of the statement of research purpose—before beginning to conduct any research.

The following sections will consider the problem of conducting effective research. Then a number of major pitfalls will be identified, which the researcher may well expect to encounter in carrying out a specific research design.

## Research Process

Exhibit 5-1 describes the 5 basic steps in good marketing research. We will illustrate these steps in connection with the following situation.

Camp Star (name disguised) is an overnight summer camp operated by the Jewish Federation of a major U.S. city. The camp has experienced an enrollment decline over the past few years, resulting in operating at about 70 percent of capacity. The camp director is not sure whether the decline is due to a general decline in overnight camping in the nation as a whole (a shrinkage in market size) or is specific to Camp Star (a shrinkage of market share). Not knowing the causes, the camp director is not sure about what marketing actions, if any, can halt the enrollment decline. He recognizes the need to do some marketing research, although his budget will not permit a large-scale study. He decides to hire Social Marketing Consultants, a small marketing research firm that was recommended to him. Arthur Sterngold, proprietor of the firm, agreed to design and implement a low-cost study that would yield useful findings and recommendations.

## THE MARKETING RESEARCH PROCESS

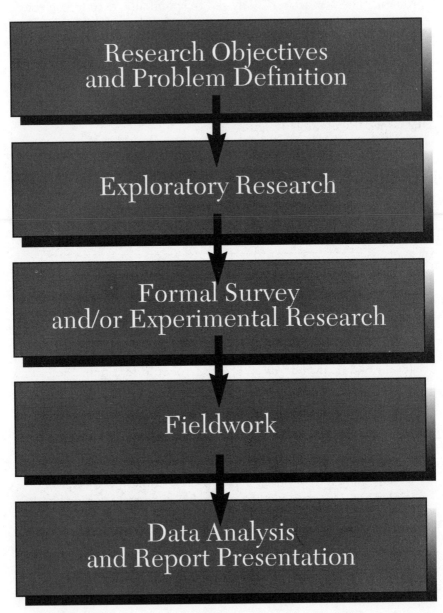

Research Objectives
and Problem Definition

Exploratory Research

Formal Survey
and/or Experimental Research

Fieldwork

Data Analysis
and Report Presentation

**Exhibit 5-1**

## Research Objectives and Problem Definition

The first step in research is to define carefully the research objectives. The objective may be to learn about a market, or to find a practical idea for increasing the demand for a product or service, or to measure the impact of a marketing tool. The research objectives make it easier to arrive at a useful definition of the problem. If the problem is stated vaguely, if the wrong problem is defined, or if the uses of the research are not made clear, then the research results may be useless or even misleading.

The marketing researcher working on the Camp Star case defined the overall research objective as that of discovering the main factors affecting parents' decisions to send their children to an overnight summer camp and, on the basis of these factors, recommending specific marketing actions available to Camp Star to increase its enrollment. To accomplish this objective, the researchers identified the following questions that required answers.

1. What is the decision-making process people go through in selecting an overnight camp?
2. What are people's images of overnight camps in general, and of Camp Star in particular?
3. What are the alternative activities people consider in making summer plans?
4. What are people's motives for selecting overnight camps?
5. What do people look for in an overnight camp?
6. What are the important consumer characteristics and divisions among groups of consumers (market segmentation)?
7. What is the role and effectiveness of different promotional material?

## Exploratory Research

This step calls for carrying out preliminary research to learn more about the market before any formal research survey is undertaken. The major procedures at this stage include collecting secondary data, doing observational research, and carrying out informal interviewing with individuals and groups.

**Secondary data research.** In seeking information, a researcher should initially gather and review secondary data if any exists. *Secondary data* are relevant data that already exist somewhere, having been collected for other purposes. Secondary data are normally quicker and less expensive to obtain and will give the researcher a start on the problem. Afterward, the researcher can gather *primary data*—namely, original data to meet the problem at hand. In looking for secondary data the Camp Star researchers can consult the following major sources of secondary data.[5]

1. *Internal records.* The researchers should check Camp Star files for past figures on enrollment, dropouts, complaints, competitive advertising, and other data that might be relevant.

2. *Government.* The federal government publishes more marketing data than any other source in the country. Many organizations depend on data found in the *Census of Population, Census of Housing, Census of Business, Census of Manufacturers, Census of Agriculture, Census of Minerals,* and *Census of Governments,* as well as on special research reports issued at all levels of government. The Camp Star researchers can use local census data to determine what is happening to the number of children aged 8-11 who are normal prospects for overnight camps.

3. *Trade, professional, and business associations.* Camp Star is a member of the American Camp Association, which provides information on camp enrollment and capacity by state, year, and type of camp. The researchers can ascertain whether Camp Star's enrollment decline is in line with a normal decline in its area, or whether it is exceptional.

4. *Competitors and other private organizations.* The researchers could see whether any useful secondary data can be obtained directly from other camps in the area.

5. *Marketing firms.* Marketing research firms, advertising agencies, and media firms may possess some useful past studies of the overnight camp market.

6. *Universities, research organizations, and foundations.* These organizations may have conducted studies of the camping industry.

7. *Published sources.* Researchers should examine published material in libraries on the subject of camping. Among the marketing journals, marketers like to consult *Journal of Marketing, Journal*

of *Marketing Research,* and *Journal of Consumer Research.* Useful general business magazines include *Business Week, Fortune, Forbes, Harvard Business Review,* and *Sales & Marketing Management.* Newspapers such as the *Wall Street Journal* and *The New York Times* are very useful. Use of a computerized indexing service of articles, such as InfoTrac or ABI/Inform (see Appendix A) can help locate related articles.

These secondary data are likely to provide useful ideas and findings. The researchers must be careful in making inferences, however, because the secondary data were collected for a variety of purposes and under a variety of conditions that might limit their usefulness. Marketing researchers should check these data for relevance, impartiality, validity, and reliability. The researchers are also likely to find that the secondary data leave many questions unanswered, for which they will have to collect primary data, either through observation or interviewing.

**Observation research.** A major means for collecting primary data is to carry out personal observations in various situations. The researchers could visit the camp during the season and observe the campers' reactions to the food, facilities, and various activities. Off-season, the researchers could observe how the camp staff handles telephone inquiries and personal visits of prospects. The researchers could also examine the camp's brochures and mailings for possible deficiencies. The purpose of the observational method is to discover factors that affect enrollment, the importance of which can be measured later.

**Qualitative interviewing.** In addition to gathering data through observation, the researchers need to conduct some interviewing during the exploratory stage of a marketing research project. The purpose of the interviewing is to gain further insight into the factors playing a role in the marketing problem being investigated. In the exploratory stage, the interviewing should be qualitatively rather than quantitatively oriented. Qualitative interviewing is largely open ended. People are asked questions requiring extended (not yes or no) answers as a means of stimulating them to share their thoughts and feelings regarding overnight camps or other relevant topics. The distinct uses of qualitative research are to:

1. probe deeply into consumers' underlying needs, perceptions, preferences, and satisfaction;
2. gain greater familiarity and understanding of marketing problems whose causes are not known;
3. develop ideas that can be further investigated through quantitative research.

On the other hand, quantitative research seeks to generate statistically reliable estimates of particular market or consumer characteristics. Quantitative research entails sampling a much larger number of people than qualitative research, and it assumes one knows in advance what specific questions to ask.

Qualitative research is not only a desirable first step, but it is sometimes the only step permitted by the budget of many religious organizations. For the Camp Star project, the researchers decided to interview new prospects for the camp as well as people associated with Camp Star in the past. The new prospects included parents and their children. The Camp Star group included past campers, counselors, and parents of returnees and non-returnees. In addition, the researchers interviewed staff members about their attitudes toward the camp. Two methods were used: individual interviewing and group interviewing.

*Individual interviewing* consists of interviewing one person at a time either in person, via the telephone, or by mail. The Camp Star researchers conducted about 50 individual interviews, half in person and half over the phone.

*Focus group interviewing* consists of inviting from 5 to 10 persons to meet with a trained interviewer to discuss a product, service, organization, or other marketing entity. The interviewer needs good qualifications, such as objectivity, knowledge of the subject matter and industry to be discussed, and some understanding of group dynamics and consumer behavior.

The participants are sometimes paid a small sum for attending. The meeting is typically held in pleasant surroundings (a home, for example), and refreshments are served to increase the informality. The group interviewer starts with a broad question, such as "How would you like to see your children spend their summer vacation?" Questions would then move to the subject of summer camps, then to overnight camps, and then to Camp Star versus other camps. The interviewer encourages free and easy discussion among the participants, hoping that the group dynamic will bring out real feelings and thoughts. At the same time, the interviewer "focuses" the discussion, and hence the name *focus group* interviewing. The comments are recorded through note taking, tape or video recording, and are subsequently studied to understand the consumers' decision process. The Camp Star researchers conducted two focus group discussions, one with the parents and another with the children, and learned a great deal from this form of interviewing. Focus group interviewing is becoming one of the major marketing research tools for gaining insight into consumer thoughts and feelings.[6]

## Formal Research

After defining the problem and doing exploratory research, the researchers may wish to carry out more formal research to measure magnitudes or test hypotheses.

Suppose the Camp Star researchers found that some of the past campers reported dissatisfaction with their camping experience at Camp Star. The researchers, however, were not sure how extensive the dissatisfaction was and the relative importance of different factors. In addition, they learned that some camp prospects had little or no knowledge of Camp Star and, among those who did, several had a negative image of this camp. The researchers, however, were not sure of how extensive this was. The camp director agreed that it would be desirable to quantify these factors.

At this point, the marketing researcher can design a formal survey or a marketing experiment. Each is described below.

### SURVEY RESEARCH

Many managers take an overly simplistic view of survey work. They think that it consists of writing a few obvious questions and finding an adequate number of people in the target market to answer them. The fact is that amateur research is liable to many errors that can waste an unconscionable amount of the organization's funds. Designing a reliable survey is the job of an experienced marketing researcher. Here we will describe the main things that users of marketing research should know about developing the research instrument, the sampling plan, and the fieldwork.

**Research instrument.** The questionnaire is the main survey research instrument. The construction of good questionnaires calls for considerable skill. Every questionnaire should be pre-tested on a pilot sample of persons before being used on a large scale. An experienced marketing researcher can usually spot several errors in a casually prepared questionnaire (see Exhibit 5-2).

### Exhibit 5-2

### A "Questionable" Questionnaire

*Suppose the following questionnaire was prepared by a summer camp director for interviewing parents of prospective campers. How do you feel about each question?*

1. What is your income to the nearest hundred dollars?

   > People don't necessarily know their income to the nearest hundred dollars nor do they want to reveal their income that closely, furthermore, a questionnaire should never open with such a personal question.

2. Are you a strong or weak supporter of overnight summer camping for your children?

   > What do "strong" and "weak" mean?

3. Do your children behave themselves well in a summer camp?

   > "Behave" is a relative term. Besides, will people want to answer this? Furthermore, is "yes" and "no" the best way to allow a response to the question? Why is the question being asked in the first place?

4. How many camps mailed literature to you last April? This April?

   > Who can remember this?

5. What are the most salient and determinant attributes in your evaluation of summer camps?

   > What is "salience" and "determinant attributes"? Don't use big words on me.

6. Do you think it is right to deprive your child of the opportunity to grow into a mature person through the experience of summer camping?

   > Loaded question. How can one answer "yes," given the bias?

A common type of error occurs in the types of questions asked: the inclusion of questions that cannot be answered, or will not be answered, or need not be answered, and the omission of other questions that should be answered. Each question should be checked to determine whether it is necessary in terms of the research objectives. There is a difference between asking for "interesting" information and "essential" information. Questions should be dropped that are interesting but not essential because they lengthen the time required, anger the respondent, and cause unnecessary work in analyzing the data.

The form of questions can make a substantial difference to the response. An *open-end question* is one in which the respondent is free to answer in his or her own words. For example, "What is your opinion of Camp Star?"

A *closed-end question* is one in which the possible answers are supplied. A close-end question can take several forms.

*Dichotomous question:* Have you heard of Camp Star? yes ( ), no ( ).

*Multiple-choice question:* Camp Star is run by (a) the YMCA, (b) the Jewish Federation, (c) the Black Panthers, (d) some other group.

*Itemized-response question:* Camp Star is (a) a very large camp, (b) a large camp, (c) neither large nor small, (d) a small camp, (e) a very small camp.

*Likert scale question:* Camp Star plans to turn itself into a music camp. How do you feel about this? (a) strongly approve, (b) approve, (c) undecided, (d) disapprove, (e) strongly disapprove.

The choice of words also calls for considerable care. The researcher should strive for simple, direct, unambiguous, and unbiased wording. Other "dos" and "don'ts" arise in connection with the *sequencing of questions* in the questionnaire. The lead questions should create interest, if possible. Open questions are usually better here. Difficult questions or personal questions should be introduced toward the end of the interview, in order not to create an emotional reaction that may affect subsequent answers or cause the respondent to break off the interview. The questions should be asked in as logical an order as possible to avoid confusing the respondent. Classificatory data on the respondent are usually asked for last, because they tend to be less interesting and are on the personal side.

**Sampling Plan.** The other element of research is the sampling plan. The sampling plan calls for 5 decisions.

*1. Sampling unit.* This answers the question: Who is to be surveyed? The proper sampling unit is not always obvious from the nature of the information sought. In the Camp Star survey of camping decision behavior, should the sampling unit be the father, mother, child, or all 3? Who is the usual instigator, influencer, decider, user, and/or purchaser?

*2. Sampling frame.* This answers the question "From what list do we draw the sample?" A sampling frame is nothing more than a listing of sampling units that can be used to select a sample. A phone book, for example, could be considered a sampling frame for a survey of local voter opinions on some issue. Care must be taken, however, to choose an unbiased sampling frame. If the phone book were used to sample opinions of voting-age citizens, there might be an under representation of lower social classes without phones, or upper social classes with unlisted numbers. In the Camp Star situation, a sampling frame consisting of a list of families who had enrolled children in the camp might be biased in omitting the opinions of those who had chosen not to send their children to the camp because of some real or imagined problem with the camp, or those who had not heard of the camp. If the director is to make marketing plans intended to stimulate demand for the camp's services, obviously these two groups', as well as users', opinions need to be surveyed. Perhaps a membership list of Jewish congregations in the area serviced by the camp would be a good sampling frame. A "perfect" sampling frame consisting of every member of the target population and only those members might not be available. Researchers must make those trade-offs necessary to acquire a sampling frame with few and non-critical biases.

*3. Sample size.* This answers the question: How many people should be surveyed? Large samples obviously give more reliable results than do small samples. However, it is not necessary to sample the entire target market or even a substantial part of it to achieve satisfactory precision. Often samples amounting to less than a fraction of 1 percent of a population can provide good reliability, given a credible sampling procedure.[7]

4. *Sampling procedure.* This answers the question: How should the respondents be chosen? To draw statistically valid and reliable inferences about the target market, a random sample of the population should be drawn. Random sampling allows the calculation of confidence limits for sampling error. However, random sampling is almost always more costly than nonrandom sampling. Some marketing researchers feel that the extra expenditure for probability sampling could be put to better use. Specifically, more of the money of a fixed research budget could be spent in designing better questionnaires and hiring better interviewers to reduce response and nonsampling errors, which can be just as fatal as sampling errors. This is a real issue, one that the marketing researcher and decision makers must carefully weigh. A standard marketing research text can help in making decisions regarding sampling procedure.

5. *Means of contact.* This answers the question: How should the subjects be contacted? The choices are telephone, mail, or personal interview. *Telephone interviewing* stands out as the best method for gathering information quickly. It also permits the interviewer to clarify questions if they are not understood. The two main drawbacks of telephone interviewing are that only people with telephones can be interviewed, and the interview must be kept short and not too personal.

The *mailed questionnaire* may be the best way to reach persons who will not give personal interviews or who might be biased by the interviewers. On the other hand, mailed questionnaires require simple and clearly worded questions, and the return rate is usually low and/or slow.

*Personal interviewing* is the most versatile of the three methods. The personal interviewer can ask more questions and can supplement the interview with personal observations. However, personal interviewing is the most expensive method and requires more technical and administrative planning and supervision.

## EXPERIMENTAL RESEARCH

We have talked about formal research in its most common form, that of designing a survey. An increasing number of marketing researchers are eager to go beyond measuring the perceptions, preferences, and intentions of a target market to measuring actual cause-and-effect relationships. For example, the Camp Star researchers might like to know the answers to such research questions as:

Would an expensive, four-color Camp Star brochure sent to prospective campers produce at least twice as many inquiries as the normal one-color plain brochure?
Would Camp Star attract more parent interest if it emphasized the educational or the recreational aspects of summer camping?
What impact would a 20 percent increase in tuition costs have on next summer's enrollments?

Each of these questions could be answered by the survey method by asking people to state their reactions. However, they may not give their true opinions or carry them out. Experimental research is more rigorous. Situations are created where the actual behavior of the target market can be observed and its causes identified. In applying the experimental method to the first question, the Camp Star director would need to design an expensive four-color brochure as well as a traditional one. The researcher would select a subsample—say, 100 families—from the mailing list. Half of these families would receive the expensive brochure, and half would receive the traditional one. As inquiries came in, the director would check whether the family received either the first or second brochure. The inquiry rate would be calculated for the 2 groups of families to see whether the more expensive brochure stimulated at least twice as many inquiries to cover its higher cost. If it did, and the camp director could think of no other factor that could explain the difference in the inquiry rates, he or she would want to mail only the expensive brochure to the rest of the families on the mailing list.

The experimental method[8] is increasingly recognized in marketing circles as the most rigorous and conclusive, if the proper controls can be exercised and the cost afforded. The method requires selecting matched groups of subjects, giving them different treatments, controlling extraneous variables from making a difference, and checking on whether observed differences are statistically significant. To the extent that the design and execution of the experiment eliminates alternative hypotheses that might explain the same results, the research and decision makers have confidence in the conclusions. One early example of experimentation is found in Scripture.

> Then Daniel asked the guard whom the palace master had appointed over Daniel, Hananiah, Mishael, and Azariah: "Please test your servants for ten days. Let us be given vegetables to eat and water to drink. You can then compare our appearance with the appearance of the young men who eat the royal rations, and deal with your servants according to what you observe. So he agreed to this proposal and tested them for ten days. At the end of ten days it was observed that they appeared better and fatter than all the young men who had been eating the royal rations. So the guard continued to withdraw their royal rations and the wine they were to drink, and gave them vegetables.
> (Dan. 1:11-16)

## Fieldwork

The fieldwork phase of survey or experimental research follows after the research design has been finished and pretested. Some organizations use volunteer interviewers. Other organizations will hire professional interviewers. Marketing research firms work hard to select and train interviewers who can be trusted, who are personable, and who are able to do their work in a reasonably short time. The fieldwork phase could be the most expensive, and the most liable to error. Three major problems must be dealt with in this phase.

1. *Not present.* When randomly selected respondents are not reached on the first call, the interviewer must either call them back later or substitute another respondent; otherwise, nonresponse bias may be introduced.

2. *Refusal to cooperate.* After reaching the subjects, the interviewer must interest them in cooperating; otherwise, nonresponse bias may be introduced.

*3. Respondent interview bias* can also be a problem at this stage of the research.

## Data Analysis and Report Presentation

The final step in the marketing research process is to develop meaningful information and findings to present to the decision maker. The researcher will tabulate the data and develop 1-way and 2-way frequency distributions. Averages and measures of dispersion will be computed for the major variables. The researcher might attempt to apply some advanced statistical techniques and decision models in the hope of discovering additional findings.

The researcher's purpose is not to overwhelm management with numbers and fancy statistical procedures. The researcher's purpose is to present major findings that will help the manager make better marketing decisions.

## Summary

Most religious organizations carry out much less marketing research than they should. This is because they have accepted certain myths. They assume that marketing research should be used only for major decisions, that it involves big surveys, that it takes a long time, that it is always expensive, that it requires sophisticated researchers, and that, when it is finished, it is usually not read or used. But research using a diversity of techniques, many at low cost, can be extremely valuable to a wide range of decisions.

Having a well-defined statement of objectives for the research provides a good framework for decisions about budgets and for the designing of specific research projects.

The research process consists of 5 steps: developing the research objectives and problem definition, exploratory research, formal survey and/or experimental research, fieldwork, data analysis, and report presentation.

# 6

# Ordering Your Priorities:

## Market Segmentation, Targeting, and Positioning

This is the generation of the baby boomer—those persons born between 1946 and 1964. In almost every way, the baby boomer generation is drastically different from any American generation alive today.[1] The baby boomer generation is a watershed; things will not soon return to former ways or values.

The baby boomer is the first American who has little or no loyalty to a church or denomination. He or she is the first American who feels little or no loyalty to the religion of his or her parents.

When baby boomers turn to the church, they shop for the services they want, much like they shop for items at the supermarket.[2] It is not unusual today to find a baby boomer family attending Sunday school at one church, because the school has excellent classes for the children, and then going down the street to attend worship services in another church, because it has an outstanding music program and/or preacher.

The baby boomer is anti-organization and anti-institution. The baby boomer favors decentralization of government and power. Perhaps above all, the baby boomer wants, indeed demands, goods and services styled for his or her needs and interests. A generic approach will never do.

---

### Young Adults Lean to "Megachurches"

Associated Press, The Bismarck Tribune, January 4, 1991

Small "mom and pop" grocery stores have the charm of first-name familiarity, and you can get credit if needed, but despite the personal touches, most people patronize supermarkets.

The contrast, says church planner Lyle E. Schaller, is a key pointer to the effectiveness of today's Christian congregations, and a hallmark to their future.

---

165

"The emergence of the 'megachurch' is the most important development of modern Christian history," he said.

"In today's world, big churches are more attractive to younger adults," he added. "People nowadays want a church that offers a broad range of choices in teaching, scheduling and programming."

"Adults born in the '50s and '60s don't carry the institutional loyalty of older generations," he said. "People today expect to make choices about things—about a new TV, an automobile, what they eat, their housing."

He said the same approach applies increasingly in choosing a church, which is done mainly on the basis of large, varied, well-run programs, with little regard for denomination.

"It's a part of the consumer orientation," he said. "Parents and grandparents stayed with their denomination, but people from age 40 down to 25 don't have that denominational loyalty. They shop around."

He said the widespread fading of particular denominational distinctions among people, surpassing official ecumenical relationships, also characterizes the mood of worshipers.

The leaders of a religious organization, knowing that marketing strategy should be tailored to consumer perceptions, needs, and wants, might see the task as almost overwhelming. Three factors contribute to the complexity of tailoring a ministry package to meet the unique culture, needs, and interests of a target group.

The first factor is *conceptualizing* the life-style and decision-making characteristics of individuals within a target group. Persons involved in a particular exchange may differ from each other in dozens of ways. For some, deciding their response might be a trivial decision. However, for others the decision might be highly complex, requiring cognitively rich evaluations. Among the latter, some could be inexperienced, some experienced.

Persons differ in their knowledge of religious alternatives—in the choice criteria they use, in where they go for information, in how much information they want to collect, in how malleable their present views are, and so on. The combinations seem almost endless, especially when one adds the possibility that the persons being targeted may also differ in gender, age, geographical location, level of spiritual commitment, and so on.

The second factor is *quantifying* the number of people in each group and the number of different groups within the populace. This is the task of defining the different segments that may be available to religious opportunities. Because of the newness of the field, few secondary data exist for the religious marketer.

Third, the final factor is *strategizing* which groups to reach and how to reach them. The fact that a marketer can identify different groups does not mean that they should (1) be treated separately or (2) be treated at all.

How, then, does one deal effectively and efficiently with the issues surrounding conceptualization, quantification, and strategizing? First we need to define 3 key concepts that will help: *market segmentation, targeting,* and *positioning* (see definitions below).

The alternative to a specifically designed, well-positioned, *target marketing* approach is to use a "scatter shot" *mass marketing* approach where a single appeal is made to an undifferentiated mass market. The scatter shot approach pays no attention to differences in consumer needs, preferences, or behaviors. It is primarily concerned with meeting the organization's own needs, or clinging to its pet programs.

At least 4 benefits of target marketing can be identified. First, religious organizations which have cultivated a market orientation are in a better position to spot emerging opportunities. Because they look at things through a different lens, they can more readily notice segments whose needs are not being fully met by current ministries offered by themselves or their competition.

*Market segmentation is the process of classifying the population into groups with different needs, characteristics, or behaviors that will affect their reaction to a religious program or ministry offered to them.*

*Target marketing is the process of selecting one or more of these segments to focus on and developing ministries and marketing plans to meet the unique needs and interests of each chosen segment.*

*Positioning is the art of developing and communicating meaningful differences between one's offer and those of other organizations serving the same target market.*

Second, market-oriented leaders can make finer adjustments in the way they package their ministries to match the unique interests of the market. They can interview members of the target market and get a good picture of their specific needs and desires and track how these change over time.

The Willow Creek ministry team, lay and clergy, is methodical and tough in evaluating every aspect of the church's ministry. Immediately following the Sunday services, a group of staff and participants gather to evaluate every aspect of the Sunday experience—for that Sunday—to see how it might have been done more effectively. Likewise, the leaders are in constant search to predict and plan for changes in the needs and interests of their target markets.

Third, religious marketers can make finer adjustments to their offer to match the desire of the target market. They regularly interview members of the target market to get a clear picture of their specific needs and desires and track how these change over time.

Fourth, organizations that approach ministry through a market orientation are ready to make adjustments to the elements of their marketing plans, for example, using different ministries to target young families versus older families.

### Understanding Behavioral Differences

Segments exist because certain factors cause people to behave differently from one another. Consider, for example, the differences between people based on their level of "involvement" in a decision to join a particular church.

Consumer behavior theorists make a distinction between *low-involvement* and *high-involvement* exchanges. The higher the level of involvement, the more a person will exercise deliberation and care in making a decision. As defined by Engel, Blackwell, and Miniard, with respect to products and services, *involvement* is the degree of perceived relevance and personal importance accompanying the product choice within a specific situation.[3]

High personal involvement has been found to occur under one or more of the following conditions. (1) The behavior required of the consumer will reflect his or her self-image. (2) The economic and personal costs of behaving "incorrectly" are perceived as high. (3) The personal or social risks of a "wrong" decision are perceived as high. (4) Outside (non-marketer) reference group pressures to act in a particular way are strong, and the target consumer's motivation to comply is strong. (5) The behavior assumes importance by offering significant ability to provide satisfaction.[4]

A high number—perhaps the majority—of exchanges with which religious marketers are involved carry high involvement and, therefore, are highly cognitive. They include decisions about changing health habits, taking a stand on abortion or other emotionally charged issues, giving a significant donation of time or money, joining a church, changing religious beliefs, choosing a new pastor, women's ordination, and so forth.

In addition to their involvement level, persons may vary according to the needs they are seeking to satisfy through religious affiliation. Abraham Maslow developed a schema for viewing human needs in an ascending order, with survival being the basic need and self-actualization being the highest order need (see Exhibit 6-1).

**Exhibit 6-1**

Each level of need can potentially lead people to seek a different benefit from religious affiliation and involvement.

Just as persons experience a hierarchy of physio-social needs, they may also experience a hierarchy—or cycle—of religious/spiritual needs. These needs are shown in Exhibit 6-2.

**HIERARCHY OF NEEDS RELATING TO CHURCH INVOLVEMENT**

**Spiritual Motivators**
Love of God
Joy of salvation
Inner peace
Deeper Spiritual Life,
Service

**Religious Motivators**
Deliverance from sin
Guilt
Desire for religious stimulation or ecstasy
Sense of alienation from God
Search for truth

**Social Motivators**
Family pressures to belong to church
Personal problems
Finding an acceptable mate
Need for social interaction

**Material Motivators (Physiological/Safety)**
Tithe paying advantages
Meeting potential customers and business associates

Source: Adapted from Dan Day, *A Guide to Marketing Adventism*, (Boise: Pacific Press, 1990).

**Exhibit 6-2**

We will now describe the major concepts and tools for segmenting, targeting, and positioning in religious markets, which take into account the factors which cause behavioral differences among people.

## The General Approach to Segmenting a Market

Exhibit 6-3A shows a market consisting of 6 consumers before it is segmented. The maximum number of segments that a market might contain would be the total number of consumers making up that market—that is to say that each person might be a separate market, if each were uniquely different from all the others.

## DIFFERENT APPROACHES TO
## SEGMENTATION OF A MARKET

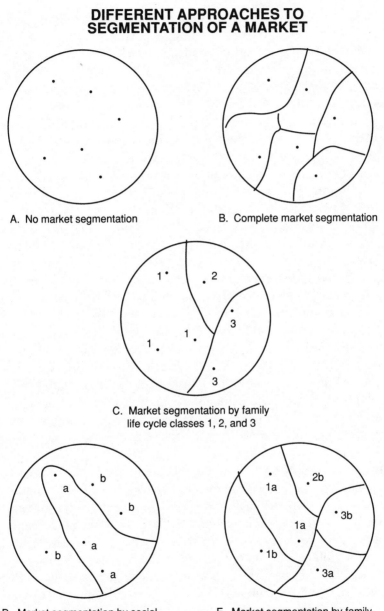

A. No market segmentation

B. Complete market segmentation

C. Market segmentation by family
life cycle classes 1, 2, and 3

D. Market segmentation by social
classes a and b

E. Market segmentation by family
life cycle-social class

**Exhibit 6-3**

Therefore, for a religious organization, each person holding an interest in one or more of the organization's ministries is potentially a separate market, because of his or her unique needs and desires. Ideally, an organization might study each individual, in order to tailor the best offering to that person's needs. Where there are only a few persons, this may be feasible. A therapist, for example, tailors a different treatment to each patient, depending on what each patient needs. This ultimate degree of market segmentation is illustrated in Exhibit 6-3B.

Most religious organizations will not find it worthwhile to "customize" their services or programs to satisfy each individual's specific requirements. Instead, the religious organization identifies broad classes of persons who differ in their ministry program requirements, responses to marketing programs, or both. The congregation may discover, for example, that *family life-cycle groups* (i.e., unmarried, newly married, "full nest", "empty nest,", etc.) differ in their program requirements and marketing responses. In Exhibit 6-3C, a number (1, 2, or 3) is used to identify each consumer's family life-cycle class. Lines are drawn around stakeholders in the same family life-cycle class.

Segmentation by family life-cycle class results in 3 segments, the most numerous one being life-cycle class 1 in the illustration. On the other hand, the congregation may find pronounced differences in response behavior between people from different *social classes*. In Exhibit 6-3D the same individuals are shown, except a letter (a or b) is used to indicate the individual's social class. In this exhibit, segmentation of the market by social class results in 2 segments, each having 3 members.

It may turn out that family life cycle and social class both count heavily in differentiating the persons' behavior toward the program or ministry. The planners may find it desirable to partition the market according to those joint characteristics. In terms of the illustration, the market can be broken into the following 6 segments: 1a, 1b, 2a, 2b, 3a, and 3b. Exhibit 6-3E shows that segment 1a contains 2 stakeholders (e.g., middle-class bachelors). Segment 2a contains no persons fitting into this segment (e.g., upper-class newly marrieds), making this a null segment, and each of the other segments contains 1 person.

In general, as the market is segmented on the basis of a larger set of joint characteristics (e.g., adding education level to social class and life cycle), the planners achieve finer precision, but at the price of multiplying the number of segments and reducing the population in each segment. If the religious organization segmented the market using all conceivable characteristics, the market would again look like Exhibit 6-3B, where each person would be a separate segment.

Experience has suggested that, for congregations, the total impact rises faster than total costs as one begins to segment markets beyond a simple mass-marketing approach. Indeed, those who are responsible for planning the congregation's ministries are almost always better off looking for ways to segment. Only if that approach is infeasible should an undifferentiated strategy be adopted.

## Criteria for Segmentation

There are many ways in which a given market can be divided for purposes of marketing strategy. In determining which way to proceed, the planners should first consider why segmentation is to be carried out. Planners may wish to consider segmenting a market to help make the following strategic decisions.[5] (1) *Quantity decisions: How much* of the congregation's financial, human, and mental resources are to be devoted to each segment (if any)? (2) *Quality decision: How* should each segment be approached in terms of specific offerings, communications, place of offerings, costs, and the like? (3) *Timing decisions: When* should specific marketing efforts be directed at particular segments?

Given the seemingly infinite array of segmentation possibilities, planners need to decide which is best. In theory, the choice is relatively straightforward. A segmentation base is optimal if it yields segments possessing the following characteristics.

1. *Mutual exclusivity.* Each segment should be conceptually separable from all other segments. Breaking donors into present givers and past givers, for example, would be confusing, because a contributor could be both a past and a present giver.
2. *Exhaustiveness.* Every potential target member should be included in some segment. Thus if there is to be segmentation according to household status, one should have categories to cover relationships like unmarried couples and religious communes, where the notion of "head of household" really does not apply.

3. *Measurability.* This is the degree to which the segment sizes and profiles of the resulting segments can be readily measured. Certain segments are hard to measure, such as the segment of "white, upper-income, teenage, female drug addicts," since this segment is engaged in secretive behavior.

4. *Accessibility.* This is the degree to which the resulting segments can be effectively reached and served. Thus it would be difficult for a ministry designed specifically for white female drug addicts to develop efficient media to locate and communicate with persons comprising this segment.

5. *Substantiality.* This is the degree to which the resulting segments are large enough to be worth pursuing. The pastoral counseling center may decide that white affluent female drug addicts are too few in number to be worth the development of a special treatment and marketing program.

6. *Differential responsiveness.* This is the degree to which each segment responds differently to different offerings and marketing programs. If several segments respond exactly alike to several ministries, although it may be *conceptually* useful to develop separate segments, it would not be useful in terms of ministry effectiveness.

### Alternative Segmentation Variables

Here we will describe the most frequently used variables in attempting to identify different market segments (see Exhibit 6-4).

**Geographical Segmentation.** In geographical segmentation, the market is divided into different geographical entities, such as nations, states, regions, countries, cities, or neighborhoods, based on the notion that consumer needs or responses vary geographically.

Saddleback Community Church, for example, has started 20 "sister" congregations, each planning its own program to fit the particular needs and interests of its congregations and community. This is in contrast to structuring the churches so that they would all be carrying out identical programs. A local church may select specific census tracts or zip codes in which to operate within a geographic area.

The organization either decides to operate in one, or a few parts of the country as a specialist in meeting the needs of the populace, or to operate broadly but pay attention to variations in the population's needs and preferences within the various geographical areas.

**Exhibit 6-4**

| MAJOR SEGMENTATION VARIABLES | |
|---|---|
| Variable | Typical Breakdowns |
| **GEOGRAPHIC** | |
| Region | Pacific, Mountain, West North Central, West South Central, East North Central, East south Central, South Atlantic, Middle Atlantic, New England. |
| County size | A, B, C, D |
| City or MSA size | Under 5,000; 5,000-20,000; 20,000-50,000; 50,000-100,000; 100,000-250,000; 250,000-500,000; 500,000-1,000,000; 1,000,000-4,000,000; 4,000,000 or over |
| Density | Urban, suburban, rural |
| Climate | Northern, southern |
| **DEMOGRAPHIC** | |
| Age | Under 6, 6-11, 12-19, 20-34, 35-49, 50-64, 65+ |
| Gender | Male, female |
| Family size | 1-2, 3-4, 5+ |
| Family life cycle | Young, single; young, married, no children; young, married, youngest child under 6; young, married, youngest child 6 or over; older, married, with children; older, married, no children under 18; older, single; other |
| Income | Under $2,500; $2,500-$5,000; $5,000-$7,500; $7,500-$10,000; $10,000-$15,000; $15,000-$20,000; $20,000-$30,000; $30,000-$50,000; $50,000 and over |
| Occupation | Professional and technical; managers, officials, and proprietors; clerical, sales; craftsmen, foremen; operatives, farmers; retired; students; housewives; unemployed |
| Education | Grade school or less; some high school; high school graduate; some college; college graduate |

| Religion | Catholic, Protestant, Jewish, other |
| Race | White, Black, Oriental |
| Nationality | American, British; French, German, Scandinavian, Italian, Latin American, Middle Eastern, Japanese |
| **PSYCHOGRAPHIC** | |
| Social Class | Lower lowers, upper lowers, lower middles, upper middles, lower uppers, upper uppers |
| Lifestyle | Straights, swingers, longhairs |
| Personality | Compulsive, gregarious, authoritarian, ambitious |
| **BEHAVIORAL** | |
| Use occasion | Regular occasion, special occasion |
| Benefits sought | Inspiration, fraternity, comfort |
| Member status | Nonmember, ex-member, potential member, new member, regular member |
| Attendance rate | Light attender, medium attender, heavy attender |
| Loyalty status | None, medium, strong, absolute |
| Readiness stage | Unaware, aware, informed, interested, desirous, intending to commit |
| Attitude toward program | Enthusiastic, positive, indifferent, negative, hostile |

**Demographic Segmentation.** In demographic segmentation, the market is divided into different groups on the basis of demographic variables, such as age, gender, family size, family life-cycle, income, occupation, education, religion, race, and nationality. Demographic variables have long been the most popular bases for distinguishing target groups. One reason is that an individual's or a group's wants and preferences are often highly associated with demographic variables. Another is that demographic variables are easier to measure than other types of variables. Even when the target market is described in non-demographic terms (say, a personality type), the link back to demographic characteristics is necessary, in order to know the size of the target market and how to reach it efficiently.

Here we will illustrate how certain demographic variables have been applied creatively to market segmentation.

*Age.* Persons' wants and capacities change with age. Congregations have developed different programs for children, youths, singles, married adults, and senior citizens. The congregations try to "customize" the religious and social experiences to the interests of these different age groups. Some congregations go further to subsegment the senior citizens into those between 55 and 70 ("the young old") and 70 and up ("the old old"). Others distinguish between the psychological and physical differences among older individuals: the "go-goes," the "go-slows," and the "no-goes."

*Gender.* Gender segmentation appears in many nonprofit sectors, such as male and female colleges, service and social clubs, prisons, and military services. Within a single sex, further segmentation can be applied. The Christian education department of a congregation segments the female adult learners into "at homes" and "working outside the homes." The "at homes" are subdivided into "homemakers" and "displaced homemakers." Homemakers are attracted to courses for spirituality of children, self-enrichment, and improved homemaking skills, while displaced homemakers are more interested in fellowship, spirituality for women, and career preparation.

The "working outside the home" segment breaks into 2 subsegments, "married working," and "single working." Each segment has a different set of motivations and fellowship/learning interests. Furthermore, each segment faces certain problems not common to the other. By addressing the specific problems and interests of each segment, the Christian education department is in a better position to attract more women to its programs.

*Family life-cycle.* The family life-cycle concept is based on the notion that over one's lifetime, there are critical transition points when major changes in consumer and other behavior take place. These transition points are generally defined in terms of objective variables such as marital status, work force status, and the presence and age of children. Eight stages are typically specified as the modal family life-cycle pattern:

1. *Young single* (under 40, not married, no children at home)
2. *Newly married* (young, married, no children)

3. *Full nest I* (young married, youngest child less than 6)
4. *Full nest II* (young, married, youngest child 6 to 13)
5. *Full nest III* (older married, dependent children 14 or older)
6. *Empty nest I* (older married, no children at home, head working)
7. *Empty nest II* (older married, no children at home, head retired)
8. *Solitary survivor* (older single, working or retired)

It should be noted that while the family life-cycle concept can prove a useful segmentation variable, it is not exhaustive in that it omits important groups of households. For example, older never marrieds and divorced or single parents with spouses absent are not included.[6] For some religious social service marketing programs, such households may be very important.

*Income.* Income segmentation is another long-standing practice in the nonprofit sector. Religious organizations, including congregations, segment the membership into income levels for fundraising purposes. In addition, the amount of income and how it is earned—wage earner, self-employed, new money, old money, etc.—suggests unique interests and needs that the religious organization may want to focus on in ministries and program offerings to each group. By doing so, the church or synagogue is able to assist persons within each segment to connect stewardship with spirituality and responsibility.

The market researcher may want to distinguish between the amount of income and the components of income.

Miller, for example, found that donation behavior in various zip codes in Oklahoma is more closely associated with the source of income than the amount of income.[7] He found that the number of households in a zip code area receiving interest or dividend income was a better predictor of total donations than was total adjusted gross income. Clearly, the market researcher must carefully define the measures used for each variable.

**Psychographic Segmentation.** Marketers also segment markets on the basis of variables that suggest more about the psychological orientation of the particular group.

*Social class.* Social classes are relatively homogeneous and enduring divisions in society that are hierarchically ordered and whose members share similar values, interests, and behavior. Social scientists have distinguished 6 social classes: (1) upper uppers (less than 1 percent); (2) lower uppers (about 2 percent); (3) upper middles (12 percent); (4) lower middles (30 percent); (5) upper lowers (35 percent); and (6) lower lowers (20 percent), using objective variables such as income, occupation, education, and type of residence. Denominational preference seem to vary closely with variations in social class.[8]

*Life-styles.* Life-style segmentation is based on the notion that "we do what we do because it fits into the kind of life we are living or want to live." There are several different approaches to identifying life-style groups in the population. Most, however, are based on measures of consumers' *activities, interests,* and *opinions* (AIOs). Life-style measures developed from these data can be general or more specific as in the case of one's leisure life-style. The VALS (Values and Life Styles) approach to categorizing U.S. population life-styles has received wide publicity.[9] Here the population is divided into 4 major categories and 9 life-style groups. While at any point in time a household can be categorized in one life-style group, over time the household would be expected to move upward within each major category. For example, the most basic category—Need-Driven —has two groups, Survivors and Sustainers. Survivors are the most disadvantaged in American society. Sustainers are at the edge of poverty, but are better off than survivors. Just as Maslow's Hierarchy of Needs (p. 169) suggests, when people move up the need's hierarchy as the lower level needs are fulfilled, so do people move between life-style groups (e.g., from being Survivors to becoming Sustainers).

The objective of religious marketers in using a life-style segmentation scheme such as VALS is to relate specific life-style patterns to religious behavioral patterns. In this way the marketer can use membership in a life-style category to predict how a person will react to a specific marketing program or religious product. Therefore, if someone is classified as a Survivor, we expect certain religious products will be more appealing to him or her than to someone who leads the life-style of an Experiential (another of the VALS groups).

**Behavioral Segmentation**. In behavioral segmentation, people are divided into groups on the basis of their knowledge, attitude, use, or response to a religious organization. Such behavior might be manifested in several ways of interest to religious leaders.

*Benefits.* A powerful form of segmentation is the classification of people according to the different benefits they seek from exchanges with the religious organization. Some simple marketing research can identify what the various internal and external markets are seeking. It is possible to then profile the benefit-seeking groups with respect to their demographic, behavioral, and psychographic characteristics. Each segment will also have attitudes toward various religious organizations as well as other benefit-delivering agencies (i.e., government agencies, community groups, self-help groups, etc.). Religious organizations will necessarily need to determine which benefit group it will seek to satisfy.

*Loyalty Status and Decision Process.* A market can be segmented by the loyalty patterns and behavioral processes used by people in choosing a church or synagogue. To illustrate, consider the hypothetical example of 4 families searching for a new church after moving to a moderate-sized Southern city from their home in the Northeast. Different levels of loyalty patterns and complexity of decision processes will be used by these archetypal people as they select a new church.

---

Joyce Evans, 23, illustrates a pattern of highly complex decision making. Joyce attended the ecumenical campus church at the private college from which she recently graduated. While in her senior year, she had a spiritual awakening, brought on by a search for a meaning to life and talks with the church's associate pastor for campus ministries. She is eager to find a church in the Southern city with people who share her enthusiasm for her newfound faith. Her dad grew up a Northern Baptist, but went to church only at Easter and Christmas, and her mother belonged to a Pentecostal congregation, but Joyce never felt comfortable with the people at either of her parents' churches. At her new job, she talks to people about where they go to church, what the people are like, the size of the church, whether there are other young singles, and if the church is reasonably close to her apartment complex. Engaging some of the young women in conversation in the laundry room of her apartment complex, she learns of several more churches that have a large number of active young people who share her religious fervor.

She begins to attend a variety of churches—some Catholic, some mainline Protestant, some Evangelical—on her own and with new friends from work and from her apartment complex, and with a few women she met at the health club. She also reads the churches' material and is asked to dinner by several church members after weekend services. She notes that some churches are more family oriented, while others seem to have a special ministry for singles. Some large churches actually seem more warm and friendly than some smaller churches. Some people seem to have the same sort of deep spiritual feelings she first felt in college, and seem to live their faith, while others seem to be uncomfortable when she starts asking about their beliefs. Joyce, after 3 months, finally chooses a moderate-sized, interdenominational, independent church with many young couples and singles who are active in Bible study and social events with the church. She drives by 7 other churches every Sunday to get to her new church family.

\* \* \*

The Kingmans, Frank and Theresa, both 32, and their children, Jason, 6, and Casey, 5, are an example of a family undergoing simplified decision making. Frank has accepted a transfer and promotion to a job in the Southern city and is eager to fit in with the other executives where he works. Theresa ran a catering business in the Northeastern city they moved from and wants to open another catering business, but not until they get settled.

Both Frank and Theresa are concerned that Jason and Casey be brought up with a strong moral foundation and traditional values. They each grew up in different Protestant faiths and attended the churches of their parents, but are now seeking to enroll their children in a church school and start attending the same church together as a family. Frank asks his fellow executives what church they attend, whether it has a church school attached to it, and how good the school is. He is pleased to see that there are 2 Episcopal executives, since Theresa is Episcopal, and that the Lutheran school is highly regarded. They attend a few other Protestant churches near them to see what they are like, but finally settle on the Episcopal church and Lutheran school suggested by Frank's fellow workers. The Kingmans' decision making could be characterized as simpler than that of Joyce Evans, but not as routine as is the case for the Bells.

\* \* \*

Kevin and Edith Bell, whose children are married with homes of their own, have decided to move to the South after Kevin took early retirement at his plant. They have been lifelong Southern Baptists and are looking for a Southern Baptist church in their new city. They don't have to look very far—the phone book's yellow pages list 18 Southern Baptist churches within 10 miles of their home. They decide to visit 4 that are conveniently located and about the size of their previous church. After several weeks, their choice is narrowed to 2. They decide on one after receiving several phone calls from church members and a visit by the pastor (who seems very young, but who is an excellent preacher).

\* \* \*

Before Tanya and Stanley Goldman and their son, Robert, 15, packed for their move to the South, they asked the rabbi at their synagogue whether he was aware of a temple in the Southern city near them. Their rabbi knew the rabbi at a temple near their new home and said he was sure they would like it there. The Goldmans are glad not to have to worry about finding a synagogue and plan to transfer their membership there once they get settled in their new home. The Goldmans could be considered largely uninvolved decision makers.

As these 4 examples suggest, the religious organization needs to understand whether target segments are undergoing complex, simple, or routine evaluations or are simply uninvolved. The congregation's approach to each family would be very different simply because of the way they went about making decisions.

Several points about people's decision styles need to be made.

1. The fact that a potential member adopts a particular style for a particular exchange does not mean that the member would use the same process for other decisions. Thus the Goldmans might be highly complex decision makers with regard to some decisions at the synagogue because they feel strongly about the issue. At the same time,

Joyce Evans might be uninvolved in some issues at her church because she doesn't feel that it would make much difference which way the church decided.

2. The fact that a consumer adopts a decision style on one occasion doesn't necessarily mean that he or she will adopt it the next time for the same decision. Three kinds of circumstances could alter the decision style. First, the consumer could simply acquire more experience, and a highly complex decision could become simplified and then routinized. If the Kingmans move again they may choose a church the same way the Bells did. Second, the consumer could change in his or her perceptions, needs, and wants. If Jason were to die from leukemia, Frank and Theresa Kingman may question their faith and stop going to church. Third, circumstances surrounding the next decision occasion could change. Some churches have lost members when questions are raised about the church founder's authenticity, when the church takes a stand on an explosive issue counter to that of the individual believer, or when church leaders are found to have embezzled church funds.

3. Although the consumers in a market at a given time will undoubtedly represent all 4 decision styles, the majority may be characterized as one type or another. This may be the case when a crucial subject is at issue and everyone must choose for the first time (for example, when a new church is being formed by members of one congregation and everyone chooses between the old and new churches). Or it may just be that, although the decision is not new or unique, the behavior in question is one that is almost always routine (for example, perhaps contributing to the annual Christmas offering) or always highly complex (for example, choosing a new faith).

4. Although a certain type of exchange may most frequently involve a particular decision style for most consumers, virtually everyone in the market may be predicted to change before the next time they decide. Again, this may be due to the passage of time and the maturing of a market over its life cycle. Thus when consumers were first asked many years ago to consider relatively narrow anti-smoking ordinances, the decision for many was highly complex. Today, as society seems to have generally accepted such restrictions on individual freedom, voting on similar ordinances will be more simplified.

Behavioral segmentation could prove very useful to religious leaders who are seeking to identify and understand how and why certain congregations are selected by people in different market segments to satisfy some of their needs. However, great care must be taken when interpreting this behavior and drawing implications from it.

**Geodemographic Segmentation.** One of the promising new tools for segmentation is geodemographic segmentation, which combines many preceding variables in a superior way and permits much finer targeting of groups in the populace. Religious marketers have typically turned to inexpensive, easily obtainable objective measures, such as the census demographic data, to segment populations and tried to infer what needs might exist among the local population so that specific ministries can be designed to meet those needs. This approach has met with limited success. For example, consider the following demographic data for census tract 1051 in Oklahoma City, Oklahoma.

### DEMOGRAPHIC DATA
Oklahoma City Census Tract 1051

| | |
|---|---|
| Population | 2387 |
| White | 59% |
| Black | 36% |
| Other | 5% |
| Median Age | 46 years |
| Ave. Yrs. School | 13 years |
| Ave. Family Size | 2.97 people |
| Median Income | $31,390 |
| Housing Owned | 54% |
| % White Collar | 57% |
| % Blue Collar | 26% |

Census Tract 1051 appears to be fairly "middle America" in its demographic profile. What ministry would you direct toward this census tract? Now consider the following description of the 2 dominant types of people located in census tract 1051.

|  | *Affluent Singles* | *Low Income Single Retirees* |
|---|---|---|
| Demographic Description | Apartment and Condominium, High Rent, Above Average Income, Well-Educated, Professionally Employed, Mobile, Singles, Few Children, Urban Areas | Old, Few Children, Low Income, Below Average Education, One-Person Households, Retirees |
| Product Preferences | High Quality Clothing, Bottled Water, Movies, Cordials and Liqueurs, Burglar Alarm, Car Rentals | Cigars, Relatively Low Weekly Grocery Expenditures, Fast Food Restaurants |
| Selected Demographics<br>Median Age<br>Median Income<br>Median Yrs. School<br>% Professional<br>% Moved Last 5 years | 40.1<br>Top 1/3<br>14<br>36.4<br>63 | 54.8<br>Bottom 1/3<br>12<br>20.7<br>50 |

What ministry(s) would you now use in this census tract? Chances are that you have changed your mind based on the new information. This "new information" (which is, by the way, actual data) is called *geodemography*. Geodemography represents a major step forward for religious marketers who are seeking to address conceptualization, quantification, and strategizing segmentation issues in order to target their ministries.

Since 1980, several firms (see Exhibit 6-5) have used census and other databases to segment the population of the United States into 40 or more socioeconomic or life-styles segments. These companies now have the ability to classify anyone with a street address into one of the more than 40 segments. This process, called *geodemographic profiling*, is based on the concept that people who live in close proximity to each other share many key socioeconomic traits. Since census data are available at the Block Group/Enumeration District level (approx.340 households per BG/ ED), these companies can use a person's street address to attach a "geocode" to that individual, signifying the socioeconomic segment that best describes what the census data reveal about people living in the BG/ED of that street address. Although these systems differ in some minor details, they are basically similar in their approach. A description of one of these systems will help clarify the advantages of these systems over ordinary demographic data.

## GEODEMOGRAPHIC PROFILING SERVICES

| Company | CACI | Donnelley Marketing Information Services | Claritas | National Decision Systems[2] |
|---|---|---|---|---|
| **Service Name** | ACORN | CLUSTERPLUS | PRIZM | VISION |
| **Number of Segments** | 44 | 47 | 40 | 48 |
| **Example of Segment Name** | Old Money | Established Wealthy | Blue Blood Estates | Suburban Gentry |
| **Report Cost Per Unit of Geography**[1] | $169 | $55 | $150 | $95 |

[1] Prices as of July 1990. Prices may vary by composition or number of units of geography ordered (e.g. quantity discounts may apply).

[2] Acquired by Equifax and now known as Equifax Marketing Decision Systems.

## Exhibit 6-5

ClusterPlus is a geodemographic segmentation tool developed by Donnelley Marketing Information Services. Donnelley analyzed more than 75 million households in America, comparing 1,600 variables for each address. Through multivariate analysis, Donnelley created 47 basic types of life-styles (called clusters) for Americans. The clusters describe life-styles ranging from the very privileged (Cluster 1—highest income, highly educated, professionally employed, lives in prime real estate areas, sends children to private schools, drinks imported wines, and buys expensive clothes) to the very disadvantaged (Cluster 47—consisting primarily of urban blacks with very low incomes, low education, unskilled, high rate of unemployment, high incidence of female householders with children, and buys malt liquor, menthol cigarettes, and insecticides.) See Exhibit 6-6 for a listing of the 47 clusters comprising the ClusterPlus system.

# AN OVERVIEW OF THE
# CLUSTERPLUS CLASSIFICATION SCHEME

| Code | Cluster Description | 1988 Adult Population | % Pop. | 1988 Hhlds | %Hhlds. | Median Household Income |
|---|---|---|---|---|---|---|
| S 01 | Established Wealthy | 2,669,555 | 1.5 | 1,178,161 | 1.3 | $66,432 |
| S 02 | Mobile Wealthy with Children | 2,096,122 | 1.2 | 950,170 | 1.1 | 57,459 |
| S 03 | Young Affluents with Children | 4,071,046 | 2.2 | 1,881,725 | 2.1 | 47,003 |
| S 04 | Surburban Families with Teens | 3,162,873 | 1.7 | 1,359,710 | 1.5 | 46,905 |
| S 05 | Established Affluents | 4,837,530 | 2.7 | 2,239,581 | 2.5 | 45,383 |
| S 06 | Highly Mobile Young Families | 5,610,429 | 3.1 | 2,699,400 | 3.0 | 35,016 |
| S 07 | Affluent Urban Singles | 5,232,446 | 2.9 | 2,907,383 | 3.3 | 29,715 |
| S 08 | Older Mobile Well Educated | 3,614,975 | 2.0 | 1,833,420 | 2.0 | 29,980 |
| S 09 | Non-urban Working Families | 7,581,228 | 4.2 | 3,606,516 | 4.0 | 32,879 |
| S 10 | Young Professionals | 2,590,603 | 1.4 | 1,375,287 | 1.5 | 26,950 |
| S 11 | Small-town Families | 5,299,664 | 2.9 | 2,370,570 | 2.6 | 34,716 |
| S 12 | Highly Mobile Working Couples | 6,936,753 | 3.8 | 3,471,871 | 3.8 | 29,920 |
| S 13 | Older Small-town Households | 3,755,937 | 2.1 | 1,822,708 | 2.0 | 31,622 |
| S 14 | Urban Retirees & Professionals | 2,209,997 | 1.2 | 1,235,366 | 1.4 | 28,851 |
| S 15 | Older Non-mobile Urban Hhlds. | 4,648,323 | 2.6 | 2,337,506 | 2.6 | 29,543 |
| S 16 | Urban Working Families | 5,676,709 | 3.1 | 2,563,990 | 2.8 | 34,946 |
| S 17 | Young Urban Educated Singles | 4,104,659 | 2.2 | 2,312,714 | 2.6 | 21,912 |
| S 18 | Working Couples with Children | 2,486,808 | 1.4 | 1,162,766 | 1.3 | 31,284 |
| S 19 | Young Ex-urban Families | 3,784,532 | 2.1 | 1,768,539 | 2.0 | 31,707 |
| S 20 | Group Quarters | 2,406,590 | 1.3 | 590,932 | 0.7 | 22,429 |
| S 21 | Rural Families with Children | 7,102,917 | 3.9 | 3,394,065 | 3.8 | 25,164 |
| S 22 | Older Below Avg. Inc. Homeowner | 2,909,102 | 1.6 | 1,518,549 | 1.7 | 21,130 |
| S 23 | Low-mobility Rural Families | 3,229,028 | 1.8 | 1,571,502 | 1.7 | 20,537 |
| S 24 | Young Urban Ethnics | 4,760,922 | 2.6 | 2,768,664 | 3.1 | 17,328 |
| S 25 | Young Apartment Dwellers | 4,643,898 | 2.6 | 2,494,365 | 2.8 | 20,411 |
| S 26 | Old Rural Retirees | 3,827,476 | 2.1 | 2,027,591 | 2.2 | 19,091 |
| S 27 | Avg. Income Families in SFDUs | 3,611,430 | 2.0 | 1,821,533 | 2.0 | 23,359 |
| S 28 | Mobile Less-educated Families | 6,708,536 | 3.7 | 3,268,938 | 3.6 | 20,493 |
| S 29 | Old Urban Ethnics | 3,997,341 | 2.2 | 2,012,400 | 2.2 | 23,072 |
| S 30 | Low-income farmers | 3,652,674 | 2.0 | 1,830,085 | 2.0 | 19,984 |
| S 31 | Older Low-income Couples | 3,288,279 | 1.8 | 1,744,069 | 1.9 | 16,915 |
| S 32 | Low-income Single Retirees | 2,306,871 | 1.3 | 1,279,658 | 1.4 | 16,193 |
| S 33 | Stable Blue-collar Workers | 3,387,919 | 1.9 | 1,701,848 | 1.9 | 22,360 |
| S 34 | Rural Blue-collar Workers | 2,409,218 | 1.3 | 1,208,755 | 1.3 | 19,031 |
| S 35 | Small-town Apartment Dwellers | 3,183,566 | 1.8 | 1,764,250 | 2.0 | 17,613 |
| S 36 | Middle-income Hispanics | 3,104,808 | 1.7 | 1,466,137 | 1.6 | 23,001 |
| S 37 | Avg.-inc. Blue-Collar Families | 2,827,787 | 1.6 | 1,439,077 | 1.6 | 22,570 |
| S 38 | Lowest-income Urban Retirees | 2,162,583 | 1.2 | 1,340,402 | 1.5 | 12,436 |
| S 39 | Low-income Blue-Collar Workers | 4,230,723 | 2.3 | 2,196,736 | 2.4 | 19,209 |
| S 40 | Lowest-inc. Retirees-Old Homes | 2,014,100 | 1.1 | 1,121,917 | 1.2 | 13,892 |
| S 41 | Rural Manufacturing Workers | 3,927,628 | 2.2 | 1,911,165 | 2.1 | 17,969 |
| S 42 | Southern Low-income Workers | 5,310,678 | 2.9 | 2,579,258 | 2.9 | 17,357 |
| S 43 | Low-income Black Families | 4,989,471 | 2.7 | 2,337,592 | 2.6 | 16,919 |
| S 44 | Center-city Blacks | 2,984,503 | 1.6 | 1,633,368 | 1.8 | 12,182 |
| S 45 | Lowest-income Urban Blacks | 2,414,264 | 1.3 | 1,235,657 | 1.4 | 12,791 |
| S 46 | Lowest-income Hispanics | 3,697,240 | 2.0 | 1,804,429 | 2.0 | 14,126 |
| S 47 | Lowest-inc. Black Female Hd. HHs | 2,280,256 | 1.3 | 1,125,422 | 12.0 | 13,018 |
| | **TOTALS** | 181,649,997 | 100.0 | 90,328,747 | 100.0 | |

Source: Enhanced Cluster Description Guide 1988/89, and American Profile, 21 June 1989: Donnelley Marketing Information Services, a Dun & Bradstreet Company

**Exhibit 6-6**

Based on what various data banks, including census data, reveal about households, every United States household is assigned a cluster code, indicating that each household belongs to 1, and only 1, of the 47 clusters. A profile can be prepared of a specific area (i.e., a census tract, zip code, city, country, circle of set radius, polygon of specified boundaries [such as 4 city streets bounding a 4 square-mile area], block group, etc.) which will determine the number of households in that area that "belong" to each of the 47 clusters. Therefore, a high-rent district census tract may have representation of only 4 or 5 clusters, all of which are low numbered (i.e., high socioeconomic standing), while a county may have 25 or 30 clusters spread out among the 47 clusters because a greater variety of life-styles would be represented in the larger geographic area.

An analysis of a given area using ClusterPlus information (or another geodemographic service) provides greatly enriched information for program planners than demographics alone can provide. This is because Clusters capture more information about life-styles than does a large set of demographic statistical averages. For example, consider how much more useful it is to know that a given zip code has large concentrations of either Young Influentials (PRIZM cluster 7) or Blue-Collar Nursery (PRIZM cluster 16), than to know the age, income, or other demographic data for that area. Both of these clusters are similar along some demographics, but very different in terms of their values, behaviors, preferences, and lifestyles (see Exhibit 6-7). Obviously, different ministries may be needed to appeal to these two groups; yet demographics alone would not reveal that such dramatic life-style differences might exist between the people in that zip code who had similar demographic profiles.

So one purpose for using a geodemographic system would be to gain more insight into the types of people living in an area where a congregation might be planning to do some types of outreach ministry. The Oklahoma City census tract example illustrates this application. However, it would be even more useful if we could enhance the life-style description of these people by learning whether they were very similar, or different, from those people who had responded favorably to types of ministries similar to ours in the past. In this way we can identify whether an area is "fertile ground," whether it contains many people similar to those who have joined the congregation, or whether it represents "rocky soil" with few people similar to new members.

## Exhibit 6-7

## A COMPARISON OF TWO PRIZM CLUSTERS*

| | *Young Influentials* | *Blue-Collar Nursery* |
|---|---|---|
| Cluster Code 2Q# | ZQ7 | ZQ16 |
| % of U.S. Hlhds. | 2.9% | 2.2% |
| Primary Age Range | 18-34 | 25-44 |
| Median Hlhd. Income | $30,398 | $30,007 |
| Median Home Value | $106,332 | $67,281 |
| Predominant Political Ideology | Moderate | Conservative |
| Life-style | | |
| *High Usage* | Travel by Cruise Ship Environmentalist Organizations | Campers Unions |
| *Low Usage* | Bowling Balls Nonfilter Cigarettes Compact Pickup Trucks | Electric Fry Pans Watch Tennis Foreign Tour Packages |
| Food | | |
| *High Usage* | Yogurt Whole-wheat Bread | Canned Stews Pretzels |
| *Low Usage* | Whole Milk White Bread | Canned Orange Juice Whole-wheat Bread |
| Television | | |
| *High Usage* | "At the Movies" "60 Minutes" | "Night Court" "Highway to Heaven" |
| *Low Usage* | "Knots Landing" "Wheel of Fortune" | "Miami Vice" Sunday Morning Interview Programs |
| Cars | | |
| *High Usage* | VW Cabiolets Acuras | Ford EXPs Chevrolet Chevettes |
| *Low Usage* | Pontiac Bonnevilles Chevrolet Monte Carlos | Jaguars BMWs |
| Magazines/Newspapers | | |
| *High Usage* | *Rudder* *Barron's* | *Lakeland Boating* *Industry Week* |
| *Low Usage* | *The Star* *True Story* | *Forum* *Atlantic Monthly* |

*Adapted from *The Clustering of America*, by Michael J. Weiss (New York: Harper & Row, 1988), 288-89, 316-17. Copyright © 1988 by Michael J. Weiss. Used by permission.

How do we know what types of people have joined the church or synagogue? In the same way that geodemographic firms can profile an area to determine the concentration of the population by clusters, they can take a list of new members with their street addresses and, based on what their constantly updated databases tell them about people living at that address, determine a profile of new members along the same 40+ clusters. Therefore, The United Methodist Church could profile its membership (or just newly joined members) in northern Indiana to determine the types of people who have been attracted to The United Methodist Church. They could then examine areas where they were considering locating a new church to determine if there were many unchurched people who were similar to those who have joined the church in northern Indiana (i.e., from the same life-style clusters). This list profiling could be done successfully for any list with several thousand names, and therefore could be done at an entire denominational level, for all members, for new adult members, for new adult members in a geographic area, and so on.

---

### The Seventh-day Adventist Church Uses Geodemographic Analysis to Target New Members

A Protestant denomination with a worldwide membership of over 6 million, the Seventh-day Adventist Church set an objective in 1985 to increase its United States membership by 100 percent by 1990. To achieve this objective, they sought a means by which they could identify those segments of society offering the greatest potential for gaining new members. More specifically, they sought answers to the following questions:

What population groups have been shown to be most responsive to our message in the past?
Where are these people located, and how many are in specific geographic areas (i.e., a zip code, county metro area, etc.)?
What types of programs will appeal to these people, satisfy their needs, and get them into an escalating commitment process that will result ultimately in becoming a church member?

To answer these questions they elected to use Donelley Marketing Information System's ClusterPlus geodemographic program. The church's first objective was to determine the segments of society where they have had their greatest success in the past. It was decided that although it would be useful to profile the church's total U.S. membership (approximately 300,000 households), the best profile of where the church was gaining new members would be derived from a profile of the 53,000 households that contained one or more adults who had joined the church during 1982–85. This group presents a more valid representation of people who have responded favorably to the church's appeals. A list of these new members was compiled, including their street addresses, and it was submitted to Donnelley. The resulting profile appears in Exhibit 6-8. The bar graphs illustrate the church's success in drawing members from each of the 47 clusters. This penetration index was computed for each cluster by dividing the percentage of new members for that cluster by the percentage of U.S. households for that cluster and multiplying the result by 100. An index of 100 means average performance.[10]

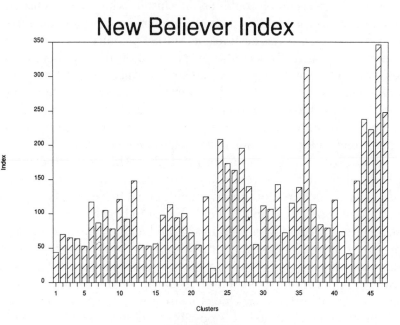

**Exhibit 6-8**

**Exhibit 6-9**

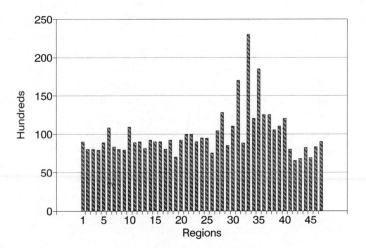

## Opportunity Index
### Illinois Region

From this, the church could see the clusters where success has been greatest. However, in the analysis of a given region, just identifying high penetration clusters was insufficient. Market potential of any region is a function of consumer acceptance (penetration rate) and population size. An "opportunity index" was created by calculating the proportion of households belonging to each cluster for an area and multiplying this proportion by the penetration index for that cluster. These weighted indices were summed for the clusters present in the area to give the opportunity index for the unit of geography being profiled.

In addition to the "opportunity index" that indicated overall potential for differing regions, clusters were studied to ascertain what kinds of church programs might appeal to the respective clusters. Illinois provided an excellent chance to perform such an analysis. Units of analysis varied from several block groups within Chicago to groupings of several rural Illinois counties. A graph of the opportunity index for Illinois appears in Exhibit 6-9. (100 represents average opportunity, index numbers above 100 offer better opportunity, below 100 offer less.) Once the areas with the greatest opportunity have been identified, it is possible to determine what segments contributed to the high index for the area.

**Exhibit 6-10**

# Piatt Co.

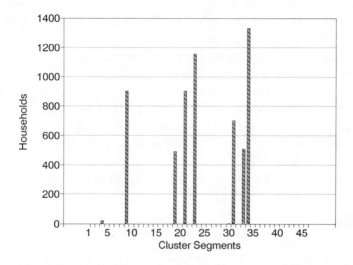

To illustrate, 2 regions—Piatt County and a portion of West Chicago—are represented. From the opportunity index (Exhibit 6-9), one can see that West Chicago (region 33) scores the highest on the opportunity index, while Piatt County (region 42) scores the lowest. A full profile of these areas (Exhibits 6-10 and 6-11) reveals that West Chicago is populated by clusters in which the church has had above-average success (high penetration indices), while the converse holds for those clusters found in Piatt County (note difference in vertical axis units). Geodemographic analysis, therefore, makes it possible to estimate the overall potential by targeting specific segments within any given region under study.

After the market has been segmented and targeted areas are selected based on the opportunity index, it is necessary to develop a positioning strategy for church programs directed at gaining new members. A detailed description of the people in each cluster has been developed by Donnelley (including information such as product preferences, leisure activities, media habits, demographics, etc.), which can be used to develop positioning strategies for the targeted segment. (See Exhibit 6-7 for an example of the type of information these geodemographic firms can make available for each of the geodemographic segments.)

For example, the Seventh-day Adventist Church has a variety of programs that can be used to generate interest among population clusters. Parenting seminars may be most appropriate for cluster 28 with its high incidence of children, while Bible study classes may be best for cluster 25 (young apartment dwellers with below-average income and high school education). Stress management seminars are best targeted at cluster 10 (young, dual-income professionals). Such program positioning for targeted clusters has generated encouraging results around Chicago and in other metro areas across the United States. Future research should help match program with clusters for further outreach. Additionally, new "products" must be designed to appeal to those clusters with low penetration rates where current programs have not been successful.

**Exhibit 6-11**

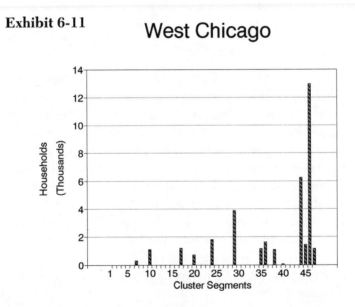

## West Chicago

While generally not advisable for smaller congregations (under 1,000 members), it may be possible to profile a single large congregation for subsequent local area targeting purposes. Contact Church Information and Development Services (see Appendix A) for more information on profiling a single congregation. CIDS also has the ability to produce color-keyed maps of a congregation's local community to identify high concentrations of groups of particular interest to that congregation (e.g., young single parents, Hispanic families, middle-income empty nesters, etc.).

While geodemographic marketing is a major advance for religious organizations, much remains to be done. The congregation needs to identify attitudes for each cluster that are related to the adoption of religious "products." The more directly applicable the cluster descriptions are to religious organizations, the more effective segmentation, targeting, and positioning strategies will be. Additionally, work is needed to discover appropriate outreach strategies for each of the 40 or more different clusters.

Geodemography may prove to be a useful segmentation approach for persons considering any of the following objectives.[11]

1. Planting new congregations is considered by church growth experts to be the best way to reach unchurched populations. Many denominations use a very capital-intensive model for planting new congregations. Making a poor decision can cost up to $100,000 or more. They use the best demographic data available to pick the location for the new church. However, data on the life-style characteristics of the targeted population would dramatically increase the probable success of the venture.
2. If a church wants to relocate, decisions can again be guided by having in-depth information on the population living in the area.
3. Churches that are located in transitional neighborhoods can use this data to understand the factors that motivate the new residents of a different ethnic background to attend religious services. This could revive a church that does not want to relocate, but instead begin new ministries with the new population.
4. Evangelism is a high priority for many denominations. Having data on the life-styles of the unchurched would be very valuable. Life-style characteristics would help suggest modifications in the church's image and services, as well as help to target the appeal.
5. Fund-raising campaigns may be enhanced by knowing the types of people living in an area in addition to demographic data on the number of people by income category.

6. Stratified sampling designs for image research or other types of marketing research could be better planned if life-style segments could be identified in an area. Follow-up research after the introduction of a new church program could help determine whether the church had been more successful with some segments than others in improving the church's image.

7. Geodemographic data firms can provide the media characteristics of the various segments, mailing lists, and phone numbers for people in selected segments for a specified geographic area for churches interested in cost-effectively reaching households in targeted segments.

## THREE ALTERNATIVE MARKET SELECTION STRATEGIES

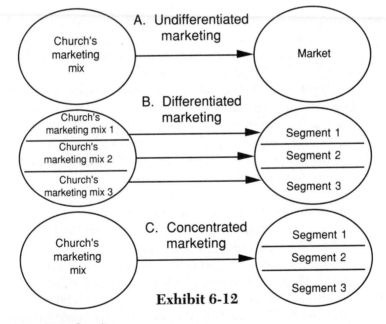

Exhibit 6-12

## *Target Marketing*

Market segmentation reveals the market segment opportunities facing the organization. At this point, the planners must decide between three broad market selection strategies. (1) *Undifferentiated marketing:* The organization can decide to go after the whole market with 1 offer and marketing mix, trying to attract as many new members as possible (this is another name for mass marketing). (2) *Differentiated marketing:* The organization can decide to go after several market segments, developing an effective offer and marketing mix for each. (3) *Concentrated marketing:* The organization can decide to go after 1 market segment and develop the ideal offer and marketing mix. Here we will describe the logic and merits of each of these strategies. (See Exhibit 6-12.)

## Undifferentiated Marketing

In undifferentiated marketing, the congregation chooses to ignore the different market segments making up the market.[12] It treats the market as an aggregate, focusing on what is common in the needs of consumers rather than on what is different. It tries to design an offer and a marketing program that appeal to the broadest number of people. It would be exemplified by a church that has only 1 weekend service for everyone, or a bishop who travels his or her area preaching the same sermon to all groups.

Undifferentiated marketing is typically defended on the grounds of cost economies. It is the marketing counterpart to standardization and mass production in manufacturing.[13] Program costs, research costs, media costs, and training costs are all kept low through promoting only 1 church ministry. The lower cost, however, is accompanied by reduced consumer satisfaction through failure of the congregation to meet individually varying needs.

## Differentiated Marketing

Under differentiated marketing, a congregation decides to operate in 2 or more segments of the market but designs separate ministries and/or marketing programs for each. By offering ministry and marketing variations, it hopes to attain a higher number of exchanges and a deeper position within each market segment. It hopes that a deep position in several segments will strengthen the consumers' overall identification of the congregation with the ministry. Furthermore, it hopes for greater loyalty because the ministry's offerings have been bent to the customers' desires rather than the other way around.

The net effect of differentiated marketing is to create more exchanges for the congregation than undifferentiated marketing. However, it also tends to create higher costs of doing business. The leaders and workers have to spend more in ministry development, marketing research, communication materials, advertising, and training. Since differentiated marketing leads to more exchanges and higher costs, nothing can be said in advance about the optimality of this strategy. Some organizations push differentiated marketing too far in that they run more segmented programs than are economically feasible; some should be pruned. The majority of religious organizations, however, probably err in not pushing differentiated marketing far enough, in the light of the varying needs of their consumers.

## Concentrated Marketing

Concentrated marketing occurs when an organization decides to divide the market into meaningful segments and devote its major marketing effort to 1 segment. Instead of spreading itself thin in many parts of the market, it concentrates on serving a particular market segment well. Through concentrated marketing the organization usually achieves a strong following and standing in a particular market segment. It enjoys greater knowledge of the market segment's needs and behavior, and it also achieves operating economies through specialization in program development, distribution, and promotion. Churches that concentrate on reaching single adults or young families or homosexuals are examples of concentrated targeting. Concentrated marketing does involve higher than normal risk in that the market may suddenly decline or disappear. In this case, the congregation is faced with relocation, a change of focus, or a broadening of targeted groups.

---

Saddleback Valley Community Church is an example of a congregation that from its beginning utilized concentrated marketing. Part of the genius of Pastor Rick Warren is displayed in the fact that he not only *named* the target segment (Saddleback Sam), but he also helps the members and ministers to *see* the segment by providing a pictorial description of Saddleback Sam (see Exhibit 6-13).[14]

---

## Choosing Among Market Selection Strategies

The actual choice among these 3 marketing strategies depends on specific factors facing the organization. If a congregation has *limited resources,* it will probably choose concentrated marketing because it does not have enough resources to relate to the whole market and/or to tailor special services for each segment. If the market is fairly *homogeneous* in its needs and desires, the congregation will probably choose undifferentiated marketing because little would be gained by differentiated offerings. If an organization aspires to be a leader in several segments of the market, it will choose differentiated marketing. If *competitors* have already established dominance in all but a few segments of the market, the organization might try to concentrate its marketing in 1 of the remaining segments. Many churches and synagogues start out with a strategy of undifferentiated or concentrated marketing and, if they are successful, evolve into a strategy of differentiated marketing.

If the congregation elects to use a concentrated or differentiated marketing strategy, it must evaluate carefully the best segment(s) to serve. The best way to do this is to follow the marketing planning approach that will be outlined in chapter 7. Each segment should be rated on its intrinsic market attractiveness in relation to the congregation's particular strengths. The congregation should focus on market segments where it is capable of satisfying that segment's needs.

## Positioning the Religious Organization

Having selected its target market, the religious organization will now need to develop a strategy to create a competitive position vis-à-vis other religious organizations serving the same market. The *position* of an organization is "the relationship of the institution and its products to competing institutions and their products—as perceived by constituents (a person or group)."[15]

*Positioning* is "the process of adjusting persons' perceptions of an institution and its products to achieve a specific position in relation to competitors."[16]

## "SADDLEBACK SAM" - OUR TARGET

### The likely Mr. Orange County

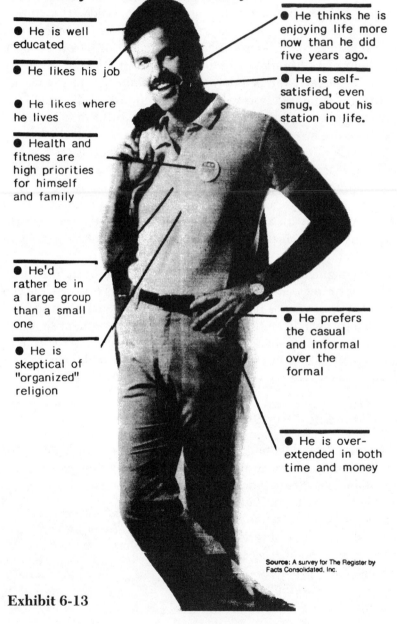

● He is well educated

● He likes his job

● He likes where he lives

● Health and fitness are high priorities for himself and family

● He'd rather be in a large group than a small one

● He is skeptical of "organized" religion

● He thinks he is enjoying life more now than he did five years ago.

● He is self-satisfied, even smug, about his station in life.

● He prefers the casual and informal over the formal

● He is over-extended in both time and money

Source: A survey for The Register by Facts Consolidated, Inc.

**Exhibit 6-13**

*Positioning* describes the efforts of an organization to locate or relocate itself in the *minds* of the persons it is trying to attract or serve. Positioning is attempting to find a niche, a "hole" in the mind of the consumer in which the organization might be lodged.

Perhaps an illustration from the car rental industry will shed light on how an organization can position itself to find a "niche" in the market, a "hole in the mind" of the potential customer.[17]

---

Hertz was the first car rental agency, and as such became a powerful competitor for any company entering the field. For years Avis tried to go head-to-head with Hertz, with the result that Hertz only became more popular. (It is very difficult to unseat the first entrant to any enterprise.) Finally Avis decided to stop trying to get Hertz's place in the mind of the consumer, and to position itself as the number 2 company. Avis began its "We're number two, we try harder" campaign. In short order Avis succeeded in finding a new hole in the mind of the customer, "They are smaller, therefore they will give me more personal attention, and better value—because they do have to try harder." Avis's business soared; the company had found its niche in the market. Even if Avis were to far outgrow Hertz, they would be wise to continue to project their "We're number two, we try harder" image. After all, everyone knows that "big boys" don't have to try harder.

---

There is little that is of greater importance to a church or synagogue than knowing what position it occupies in the minds of the persons it is attempting to attract to its services and ministries. Temple Beth Schul, discussed below, offers much insight into the position a rabbi (or pastor) might occupy in persons' minds, and possible attempts to *reposition* the rabbi. The story also reveals the position of a synagogue, and the effects of this upon its programs.

---

Temple Beth Schul (the name is fictional to protect confidentiality), an established synagogue in a major metropolitan area, began to lose members. A dynamic high profile "competitor" began to dominate the "local market." Temple Beth Schul clearly needed information and a marketing plan.

To identify the major issues, the synagogue organized a series of focus groups involving current members, former members, and nonmembers from the Jewish community at large. Following this, it developed a questionnaire for phase 2 of the research process: a phone survey targeting the same 3 population groups.

The key issues, it turned out, ran the gamut from the purely practical to the purely emotional. They ranged from the amount and quality of the religious education offered by the institution to whether the respondents liked the rabbi.

On most of the key issues, Temple Beth Schul received high ratings from its current members. However, it seriously lagged behind its chief "competitor" on these same issues, in the estimation of nonmembers.

Was this because Temple Beth Schul had somehow acquired a "bad" reputation in the community? Not at all. Much of the synagogue's problem stemmed from the Jewish community's overall lack of information about the synagogue's programs and practices, even though these same people were much more familiar with the programs and practices offered by its competition.

One major issue was the importance of available educational programs and activities for children. Although Temple Beth Schul offered many excellent programs and activities for children, few respondents outside the congregation were aware of them. The result: a higher number of "don't knows" and generally lower ratings on this key issue for Temple Beth Schul.

The same lack of knowledge was also partially responsible for the comparatively low ratings given to Temple Beth Schul's rabbi by nonmembers. In the focus groups and phone survey, the rabbi was named as the most important aspect of any synagogue and was considered by many as the one factor that could persuade them to change from one synagogue to another.

While the rabbi at the main competitor had a high recognition factor and received high ratings from the general Jewish population, the rabbi at Temple Beth Schul, while receiving high ratings from members of his own congregation, was not nearly as well-known by nonmembers.

During the focus groups involving Temple Beth Schul members, it was also noted that the synagogue's rabbi was much more effective at relating to people on a one-to-one basis than at services. Another logical conclusion was that even nonmembers who said they were familiar with the rabbi may not have seen him at his "best."

To help Temple Beth Schul solve its recognition and familiarity problems, some fairly simple "repackaging" and "repositioning" strategies were proposed.

First, it was suggested that the synagogue initiate a campaign of targeted communications emphasizing its many family- and youth-oriented programs and activities to nonmembers with children.

It was also recommended that Temple Beth Schul organize and encourage its members to participate in a "bring a friend" program of small, informal gatherings hosted by the rabbi. These gatherings would also present the rabbi in his best environment and allow him to establish a personal rapport with prospective members.

But repackaging and repositioning could solve only 1 part of the temple's problems. In at least 1 basic and very sensitive area, it became clear that the synagogue would need to undergo some "reformulation" as well.

Because reformed synagogues attract members from all types of Jewish upbringing (reformed, conservative, and orthodox), it is crucial for these institutions to be aware of and sensitive to the practices and traditions that are most prevalent in the communities they serve.

In the community served by Temple Beth Schul, most people had come from orthodox or conservative backgrounds and had been brought up with their more formal traditions. Although a significant portion of the general Jewish population identified itself as reformed, most of those who were familiar with Temple Beth Schul perceived it as too reformed for them. On the other hand, they perceived the synagogue's leading competitor, also a reformed temple, as being much more successful at blending reformed liberalism with tradition.

If Temple Beth Schul hoped to survive in the community, it would have to reformulate its atmosphere and practices to attract the more tradition-oriented prospects. At the same time, reformulation had to be subtle enough to avoid sacrificing the open, relaxed atmosphere that was so important to its less tradition-oriented current congregation.

To accomplish these goals, it was recommended that the temple make a concerted communications effort, emphasizing its long history in the community and, indirectly, its high regard for and adherence to basic traditional standards and customs.

At the same time, more traditional elements, such as wearing traditional garb, could be introduced as options for congregants, with emphasis on how the synagogue's openness and acceptance of a wide range of customs and traditions make it possible for Jewish people of all backgrounds to worship and socialize together.[18]

The Temple Beth Schul story is one of repositioning an existing institution. Positioning, however, is also an important concern for a new institution, which as of yet occupies no position in persons' minds.

When Rick Warren decided to start a new church in the Saddleback Valley of southern California, no less than 7 of the largest churches, served by some of the most popular preachers and Bible teachers in the United States, were located within driving distance of the location he had chosen. The list of pastors included Chuck Swindoll, Robert Schuller, John MacArthur, Jack Hayford, and John Wimber.

Rick reasoned that if he was to establish a strong congregation, surrounded by these great churches, he would need to position his church as being different, an alternative to the great churches in the valley. He further reasoned that the people attending these great churches were there because they wanted the style of service and preaching being offered. Therefore, he would organize a church whose style could be clearly seen as different. Thus came a church for Saddleback Sam, the unchurched baby boomer who was turned off by religious ceremony and structure.

By doing this, Rick succeeded in *positioning* Saddleback Valley Community Church as the place for persons who were searching for spiritual values, but who felt organized religion had nothing to offer them in their search. He succeeded in positioning Saddleback Church as the place where spiritual values are taken very seriously, and where religion is unorganized and informal.

It would have done little good to the 7 people who started Saddle-back Valley Community Church in the Warrens' condo to have presented the church as another Crystal Cathedral or Vineyard. Those niches were already "owned" in the mind of the potential "customer." So they went looking for a place in the mind of their potential customer, Saddleback Sam, which was not yet taken—and they found it by positioning themselves as a church for those who don't like church.

Positioning is akin to *image*, but different from *attitude*. One person may fully understand that Saddleback Church is very different from the other large churches surrounding it (position), and at the same time believe it to be a "cheap grace" church where everything goes (attitude). Another person may see Saddleback Church as being very different from the other large churches in the area, and believe it is the best place to go in order to discover and strengthen one's spiritual values within an informal, relaxed atmosphere (attitude).

What we learn from the examples is that a responsive church will actively take steps to develop its image and position because this determines the target publics it will attract. Responsive churches will think through the position they wish to occupy in the minds of their target publics.

The final step in market segmentation and target marketing is the development of a "marketing mix" that will support and reinforce its chosen position. (See Exhibit 6-14.) If the Saddleback Church wants to attract Saddleback Sam, it must develop programs that meet Saddleback Sam's needs, develop promotional methods and means of informing Sam of those programs, be fully cognizant of the "costs" (economic, social, psychic) Sam incurs in moving toward membership in the church, and develop "delivery systems" by which Sam might be able to "consume" the church's programs and become an active part of the congregation. This describes the "four Ps" of the marketing mix—*product, promotion, price,* and *place*—which an organization puts together in order to attain its chosen position in the minds of those it is trying to reach. In other words, the chosen competitive position dictates the elements of the marketing mix that will be emphasized. These 4 elements will be more fully discussed in chapters 8 and 9.

**MARKETING
MIX**

**PRODUCT**
Ministries
Programs
Services
Goods

**PLACE**
Locations
Atmospherics

**TARGET
MARKET**

**PRICE**
Psychological costs
Social costs
Time
Money

**PROMOTION**
Advertising
Publicity
Telemarketing
Direct Marketing

**Exhibit 6-14**

## Summary

Churches and synagogues are by nature a refuge for persons seeking a haven where they can commune with God and with fellow sojourners. Consequently, with few exceptions, they are open to anyone and everyone. However, this is not the same as saying that congregations should approach everyone with the same message or ministry. The most successful congregations have effectively identified groups in the population with homogeneous needs (segmentation) and determined which of these groups they can best serve (targeting) with their various ministries. Peter Wagner's fifth "vital sign" of a healthy congregation is that it draws its membership primarily (though not exclusively) from a homogeneous group.[19]

The problems facing religious leaders, then, are several. First, bases for segmenting the market must be determined. Then, profiles of resulting segments must be identified and their attractiveness assessed. Concern with strategic issues then turns to questions of how to target and develop appropriate marketing programs for some or all of the identified segments.

Markets are segmented to help leaders make decisions about the quality, quantity, and timing of marketing efforts. A scheme for segmenting markets for these purposes is ideal if the segments are mutually exclusive, exhaustive, measurable, accessible, substantial, and, finally, if the segments differ from one another in responsiveness to marketing approaches.

Once markets have been segmented, the leaders must decide whether to pursue them with an undifferentiated, differentiated, or concentrated strategy. Choices among these alternatives depend on market conditions and the congregation's own goals and resources. In particular, the congregation should seek to position itself and focus on the segments that have an intrinsic attractiveness and that correspond to the congregation's strengths.

# 7

## Capitalizing on Opportunities:

### Strategic Marketing Planning

The first step toward becoming a market-oriented congregation is to make a commitment that all of the ministries and programs will be planned from the perspective of the persons the program is intended to serve, "outside-in thinking" as opposed to "inside-out thinking." For many religious organizations, this requires a change of attitude, perhaps even of heart, regarding the way ministry is to be decided and carried out.

The idea of changing the ministry planning orientation of a religious organization is not to be taken lightly. It is no simple matter. For many staff and volunteer workers in a congregation, the very idea that the ministry programs and services should be planned from the "outside-in" will be received as anathema. Changing the way people have thought about planning ministry is, if you will, "where the rubber meets the road." Once this commitment is made, however, the entire organization will begin to experience subtle and obvious changes in the attitudes and activities of ministry planning.

The next step is to review all existing programs to determine the extent to which each one measures up to the commitment. It perhaps goes without saying that all future ministries will also be created from this perspective.

Delivering satisfaction to those who benefit from a ministry program rarely occurs serendipitously. It is more often the expected consequence of planned actions than a fortuitous by-product of unplanned good intentions. Recent research has shown that planning is most likely to take place when a congregation perceives its environment to be complex and dynamic—conditions that face an increasing number of churches and synagogues today.[1]

## Life Cycles of Religious Organizations

An adaptive organization, through making timely and appropriate changes, increases its chances for survival. This does not mean, however, that it will enjoy continuous stability or growth. Organizations, including congregations, tend to pass through life cycle stages. Adaptability may help to prolong these phases or produce new life cycles. Exhibit 7-1 shows the 4 stages in the life cycle of a typical organization.

**Exhibit 7-1**

# Typical Life Cycle Curve

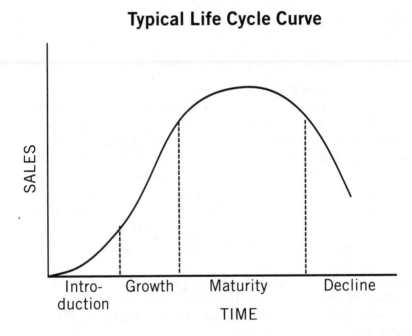

The organization is founded at some point and grows slowly (introduction stage). This is followed by a more rapid growth if the organization is successful (growth stage). The growth eventually slows down and the organization enters maturity (maturity stage). This is followed by a period of decline as long as the organization fails to find a new mission (decline stage). This life cycle model has been used not only to describe organizations, but also the history of product categories, product forms, and brands.

Dr. John Shope, a church planning consultant, refined this model and described the "theoretical life cycle of a church" as falling into 8 stages:

Stage 1—The church is organized.

Stage 2—The nucleus of the church organization survives and grows slowly.

Stage 3—The growth rate increases due to the confidence of potential members being translated into church participation and membership.

Stage 4—The membership plateau. Membership in the church stabilizes and contentment and routine become obvious in the membership and church programs.

Stage 5—Initial decline; membership of the church declines and little is done to reverse the trend.

Stage 6—Rapid decline; membership decline accelerates and members find logical excuses to join other churches.

Stage 7—Nothing but a small nucleus of members remains, the church is a financial burden to those who stay.

Stage 8—Dissolution; the congregation disbands and the church dissolves.[2]

Shope's church life cycle has much validity. For example, it describes accurately the history of Second Presbyterian Church of Evanston, Illinois.[3]

The Second Presbyterian Church of Evanston is a magnificent edifice built in 1926 in the then-affluent southeast Evanston at a time when south Evanston was synonymous with wealth and gracious living. After a slow start, membership started to grow rapidly and the eventually 1,300 adult voices gave life to the sanctuary. Eventually the character of south Evanston began to change. The monied Evanston social classes were dying or leaving for southern climes, to be replaced by less affluent, younger people who either were not interested in joining a Presbyterian church or were likely to move a bit farther north where two other Presbyterian churches were closer. In the mid-1960s, the church's Reverend David H. Pottie was attacked by minority groups as anti-Semitic and bigoted, and sidewalk demonstrations by human rights groups took place. Pottie resigned in 1967, and the church dropped almost 500 members in the next year. Shortages of funds led to the cutting of youth programs, and, as a result, young families never came for a second visit. Finally in 1977, the church was down to a membership of 200, with regular Sunday attendance of only 60 to 80 persons in a sanctuary built for 1,300. The church finally closed its doors in 1978, a victim of a changing neighborhood and social environment.

With little effort, it is simple to trace the life cycle of Second Presbyterian Church through the 8 life-cycle stages identified by Shope. It should not be difficult for each reader to locate his or her own congregation in the life cycle stages.

When viewing these institutional life cycles, one must recognize some exceptions. In fact, some institutions enjoy a second life cycle as a result of the coming of a new leader or other key development. Consider the following case.[4]

Tom and Margie Williams always slept in on Sunday mornings—until seven years ago when they joined Broad Street Presbyterian Church downtown. "We heard John Buchanan preach once, and that was that," says Tom Williams, a chest surgeon. As do many who worship in the old, Romanesque structure, the Williamses bypass other churches on the way to 11 A.M. services. Like its surrounding neighborhood, the church has reversed a decline, largely because of Buchanan's 10 years of outstanding preaching and quick responses to parishioners' concerns. Among signs of progress:

* Membership has grown by 200 to 1,400 at a time when many Presbyterian churches have lost congregants.
* The annual budget has risen from $280,000 to about $500,000.
* A $1 million building addition was just completed.
* Education programs enroll 250, the most since the 1950s.

The life cycle of congregations enjoying a second life cycle might be depicted as seen in Exhibit 7-2.

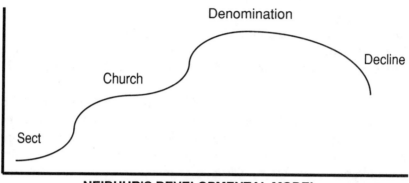

**NEIBUHR'S DEVELOPMENTAL MODEL**
**Exhibit 7-2**

The life of a church or synagogue often is like a roller coaster. This "oscillating life cycle " suggests that a church or synagogue need not necessarily enter into decline, and ultimately, dissolution. Rather, the congregation can seek to renew itself. By continually adapting to its environment, the church may operate indefinitely through stages 1-4, and avoid stages 5-8.

There is nothing inevitable about maturity leading into decline. One of the major contributions of marketing analysis is to identify new opportunities for a religious organization to return to a period of healthy growth or extended maturity.

The growth stage of the organization's life cycle is particularly important to understand. Carman and Langeard have observed that the growth stage of a service organization tends to consist of 5 sub-stages, shown in Exhibit 7-3.[5]

**SUBSTAGES OF THE GROWTH STAGE**

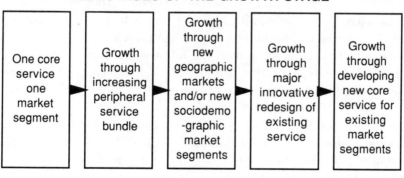

**Exhibit 7-3**

The organization starts by successfully introducing a new service to a single market segment. Thus a congregation starts by attracting a certain type of member to its core service—namely, its worship services. Its strategy for growth is to attract as many more similar members as possible.

Over time, the congregation adds peripheral services that will appeal to current and potential members, such as religious schooling, pastoral counseling, and spiritual direction. At some point the congregation may decide to launch a second congregation in another geographic area to serve a similar type of member; or to start attracting new sociodemographic groups, such as black or Hispanic members.

Later, the congregation may undertake to redesign its physical plant and services to bring them more into line with the new groups it is serving.

Finally, the congregation may start some new core ministry ventures, such as operating nursing homes or day-care centers. The model does not say that all churches or institutions go through this particular sequence of growth stages, but it describes a growth pattern that some congregations have exhibited.

What has been said here about the life cycle of congregations can also be said about the life cycle of denominations or ecclesial bodies. Since 1900 many church bodies have passed from the American religious scene. Today many others barely cling to survival.

In his book *The Social Sources of Denominationalism,* H. Richard Niebuhr defines the life cycle of denominations as passing through 4 stages of development: sect, church, denomination, and decline.[6]

*Sect.* The sect is a small, exclusive, separatist group that its members must *join.* One cannot be born into a sect, in that the sect attaches primary importance to the religious experience of its members prior to their joining with the fellowship. As such, a sect can survive only one generation. In that time it must gain sufficient size and strength to survive the transition into becoming a church. If it fails this test, the sect will die.

*Church.* The sociological character of sectarianism, Niebuhr asserts, is almost always modified in the course of time. This modification is given an added impetus by the children of the first-generation members of the sect. Change in structures is accompanied by change in doctrine and ethics. Furthermore, wealth frequently increases among the members of the sect, as they give themselves to the discipline of asceticism in work and expenditure, which is always placed upon its members by the sect. With the increase in financial standing comes an involvement in the economic and social life of community and nation. Compromise begins, and the ethics of the sect approach the churchly type of morals. *So the sect becomes a church.*

*Denomination.* As a church grows, Niebhur asserts, the varying degrees of commitment of the people regarding ethics, structures, and morals make compromise an ever-increasing necessity. It is in the failure of the churches to transcend the social conditions that fashion them into caste-organizations, to sublimate their original loyalties to standards and institutions only remotely relevant, if not contrary to the original ideals of the founding group, and to make the self-preservation of the organization of primary importance, that the denomination is born.

The denomination is even more concerned with being accepted by the environment and in its self-preservation than in the church. Accordingly, Niebuhr contends, the denominations seek to represent the ethics of classes and nations, rather than a common and Christian morality. The boundary between denomination and society becomes ever more diffuse. Denominations, Niebuhr claims, are the emblems of the victory over the church, of the secularization of Christianity, of the church's sanction of that divisiveness which the church's gospel condemns.

So Niebuhr defines the life cycle of denominations as that of maturing from sect, to church, to denomination, to decline. It is the decline of denominations that gives rise to the sects, as both necessary and desirable.

The life cycle theories described here hold in common the implication that the failure to adapt to a changing environment can spell the end of the organization's existence.

## Strategic Planning and Marketing Planning

Religious organizations have increasingly turned to formal planning methods as the way to adapt to rapid environmental change. Large and growing churches tend to be more formal planners.[7] It is not clear, however, whether formal planning is the cause or the consequence of being a large church. Nevertheless, a planning approach has caused some churches or denominations to become large.

The authors hold 3 principles of utmost importance to the success of planning in congregations: (1) **Keep it simple.** Einstein is credited with saying that "a theory should be kept as simple as possible—but no simpler." The simpler the planning process, the easier it is for members to participate in it, and the less resistance it will encounter. (2) **Keep it natural.** The planning processes used in any congregation should take into consideration the culture, work experiences, and abilities of the people. What feels natural to one congregation may not feel natural to another. (3) **People tend to support what they have helped to create.** Any person, or group, whose support is needed to carry out the plan should be involved in making the plan. Where this is not possible, they should be kept fully informed throughout the planning process, and invited to comment on it.

---

For example, during the 1970s, the Presbyterian Church introduced a PPB (Program Planning & Budgeting) process, encouraging local congregations to adopt the method. The materials were heavily oriented toward the use of paper and pencil materials and methods. The materials were sent to the Dakota Presbytery (all Native American churches, whose culture, abilities, and experiences were not oriented to paper and pencil procedures). The program lasted about as long as it took the congregations to carry the forms to the waste basket.

---

In mid 1991, the authors spent a day with the staff of the megachurch Fullerton First Evangelical Free Church, Fullerton, California. Chuck Swindoll is the pastor. In the course of the day he said, "We never had a plan. We just love people and do what we can to serve them. We just keep expanding our ministries to meet the needs of those God sends our way." The authors doubt that this statement tells the whole story regarding ministry planning at Fullerton Evangelical Free Church. It does, perhaps, indicate that for Chuck Swindoll, and his capable staff, planning is done naturally, as a matter of course.

Most religious organizations pay more attention to *budgeting* than they do to planning. For many religious organizations, budgeting comes so naturally that when they are building the budget they think they are planning. Planning is not the same as budgeting or forecasting, although both would find a place in a good plan.

Planning, from a marketing perspective, can be thought of as 2 processes: (1) **Strategic planning** is the process of developing and maintaining a *strategic fit* between the organization's goals and resources, and its changing marketing opportunities. It seeks to answer these questions: What kind of church are we? What kind of church do we want to be? (Mission and goals). (2) **Marketing planning** is the process of selecting *target markets* (groups to be focused upon), choosing a *strategic position,* and developing an effective *marketing mix* to reach and serve the target groups and achieve organizational goals. It seeks to answer these questions: What ministries do we want to offer? How do we implement these ministries? (Strategy and tactics).

Admittedly, drawing a distinction between strategic and marketing planning is more for illustration than for operational purposes. For our purposes, we will use a marketing plan to show how strategic planning and marketing planning can be used by a religious organization to help identify and accomplish its goals. We will describe the objectives of a marketing plan and the steps in developing one.

## *Objectives of the Marketing Plan*[8]

Cohen specifies 7 marketing plan objectives for any marketing plan.

**1. Act as a road map.** A marketing plan should act as a road map, telling the organization how to get from the point of launching the planned ministry to reaching its objectives. Like a road map, the plan must describe the environment in which the religious organization will find itself along the way. A marketing plan will embrace 4 environs that have influence upon the ministry plan. They are:

A. *The organization itself.* The congregation becomes a very important and influential environment for any of its plans and ministries. The congregation may act as a resource, providing needed resources for the plan, or it may act as a constraint, failing to provide the needed resources.

As consultants to congregations, the authors often discover that the staffs and ruling boards of all types of churches fail to consider the membership as an environment. They fail to "bring the members along." They make plans without the members' involvement, input, or understanding—then they blame the members for the failure of the programs.

A cardinal rule in planning is "people tend to support what they have helped to create." If the staff or ruling board rely upon the congregation for financial support, final approval, and so on, it only makes sense that the planning process should involve the congregation. We are not talking about "rubber-stamp" involvement, but about having input and influence on the plan as it is developed.

What has been said about the membership as an environment can also be said about any group or agency within the organization, whose responsibilities or activities are relevant to the plan. For example, doesn't it make sense for a congregation building committee to involve young parents in deciding the location, space requirements, toys, and furnishings of a new or remodeled nursery? Yet, in our experience, very few building committees satisfy this test. Then they complain when, "after we spent all this money to remodel the nursery" the young parents refuse to put their children there.

*B. The competitors:* The congregation, in general, has its competitors. However, each new ministry will likely have its *specific* competitors. The marketing plan must identify the general and the specific competitors and decide how to neutralize, or control, the effects of the competition.

*C. Neutral environs:* The environment in which a planned ministry will be launched is composed, in part, of a number of "neutral" entities with which the congregation must contend (i.e., ecclesiastical judicatories, local, state and federal governments, media, and special interest groups). Any one of these "neutral" entities may become a very important resource or constraint on a particular plan or ministry.

For example, if the congregation is planning to launch a day-care center for children of working parents in the surrounding downtown area, the state may suddenly become an important environmental factor by way of imposing several code restrictions. In this case the state environment becomes a constraint. On the other hand, several financial institutions, or the chamber of commerce, may provide ample finances for remodeling building space and equipment, thus becoming a resource.

D. *Situational environs.* The situational environment—which includes politics, laws and regulations, economic and business conditions, technology, demand, social and cultural factors, and demographics—will have an impact on the planned ministries.

At any point in time a number of these environs may be acting as resources to the plan, while others are acting as constraints. The planning of any significant ministry should include a review of all the environs. This will go a long way to strengthening the plan and avoiding many unpleasant surprises along the way.

The problem in dealing with all of these environs is how to do it well, while at the same time keeping it simple and natural. If effort is not made to do this, the average volunteer planning group will become bogged down, overwhelmed, angry, and the like.

**2. Assist in administrative control and monitoring of implementation of strategy.** A marketing plan assists in administrative control and allows better decisions to be made, and to be made much more quickly than would otherwise be the case.

**3. Inform new participants in the plan of their role and function.** All individuals involved in carrying out the plan should be familiar with the plan in its entirety. Individuals need to know what they are responsible for, what actions they will be required to take, and how their part is necessary for the success of the ministry. Everyone, especially volunteers, wants to know the ultimate goal for the ministry and exactly how their efforts will help accomplish it.

**4. To obtain resources for implementation.** The implementation of any marketing strategy requires a congregation to allocate the resources necessary for its accomplishment. No plan is complete until the resource decisions are clearly decided and agreed upon.

Resources are not automatically made available. Therefore, those who have the authority to provide the resources—whether financial groups, volunteer workers, denominational hierarchy, or the congregation—must be convinced that this is the best use of the resources. A marketing plan is the "sales" vehicle to assist in persuading the resource providers that the plan will help them meet their *personal goals* in supplying the resources, as well as helping the organization accomplish an important ministry.

**5. To stimulate thinking and make better use of resources.** Strategy in marketing depends on building on one's strengths and making one's weaknesses irrelevant. As one develops a marketing plan, thinking is stimulated. The plan is changed and modified. As a result, the strategy and tactics necessary to achieve the marketing objectives and goals of the marketing plan are continually improved as the plan develops.

**6. Assignment of responsibilities, tasks, and timing.** Any marketing plan is only as good as those who implement it. Therefore, it is absolutely crucial that the responsibilities of everyone be indicated and that tasks be thoroughly understood by all individuals who have roles to play in implementation. Further, these actions must be scheduled—so that the overall plan is executed in a coordinated fashion.

There is an old adage that "if *everyone* is responsible for accomplishing a task, then *no one* is responsible." The marketing plan assures that every task is assigned to someone who is responsible, and the scheduling is coordinated to maximize the effectiveness of what is done.

**7. Awareness of opportunities and threats.** The preparation of a marketing plan requires investigation into the environs in such a fashion that opportunities and threats are precisely identified. The more one plans (instead of shooting from the hip), the more one understands the nature of these opportunities and threats, and what can be done about them.

In no case should opportunities or threats be ignored. Rather, the marketing plan should have enough flexibility in it to allow modifications along the way—to take advantage of the opportunities and to avoid or overcome unanticipated threats.[9]

### Exhibit 7-4

### MARKETING PLAN FORMAT

A.  Mission Statement (Who are we? Who do we want to be?)
    Purpose of your church (what it is we are trying to accomplish?)
    Objectives of the church consistent with the purpose
B.  Situation Analysis (Where are we now?)
    1.  Internal Environment

Describe your past experiences relative to the financial, human, and capital resources, and strengths and weaknesses of your internal publics (administration, board, staff, volunteers). Take a "spiritual gifts inventory" to determine what your members can contribute to achieving the church's objectives.

2. Input Environment

Describe the aspects of the donor, supplier and judicatory publics which could impact on your objectives. Also, your expectations for intermediary publics such as financial, marketing or other facilitator publics to help achieve your objectives. Ask such questions as:

—How does the availability or nonavailability of funds affect the situation?

—How will judicatory action or anything else in current or future state, federal, or local government actions likely affect this plan?

—Does current media publicity favor or disfavor church activities?

3. External Environment

Describe the cultural, societal, economic, and demographic trends existing on a national and local scale which could positvely or negatively impact the ability to achieve your objectives. These environmental trends or events are categorized as opportunities or threats.

C. Target Market (Where do we want to go?)

Describe your target group using detailed information on demographics, geographics, life style and life cycle, needs, psychographics, or whatever is the most appropriate basis for segmentation. Why are you interested in this group rather than some other segment?

D. Marketing Strategy (How are we going to get there?)

1. Goals

What are the quantifiable goals for the church's programs? How will they be measured? What constitutes "success"?

2. Marketing Mix

—What program services will be offered to satisfy target market needs? (Product)

—How and where will the target market make use of the service? (Distribution)

—What will be said to the target market and how will they hear it? (Promotion)

—What must the target market give up to use the services offered? (Price)

E. Marketing Tactics (What and when?)

Give a detailed breakdown of how each aspect of the strategy will be put into operation, who will be responsible for the tactical implementation of each task, and when it must be accomplished.

F. Marketing Budget (How much and where?)
Who will be involved in the program? How much time will each person involved have to devote in order to make the program successful? How much money will each task take, when must the money be available, and what is the allocation priority?

G. Marketing Control (How did we do?)
What are the results of the program's implementation? How do they compare to our stated objectives? What corrections are necessary to improve performance?

## Steps to Developing a Marketing Plan

We will now examine the basic components of a marketing plan (see Exhibit 7-4), using the following hypothetical example.

---

The Hope United Methodist Church of Valparaiso, Indiana, has a membership of 400 on the church books, with a typical attendance of fewer than 300 at worship services on Sunday (less in Sunday school). Brice Merrill, 31, has only recently been appointed to the head pastor position at Hope. He was pleased to find that his personal desire to reach out to the unchurched in Valparaiso was shared by the Sunday school superintendent and other church leaders. There was also a deep concern for reviving the church's current inactive members. While some members were content with the status quo, there seemed to be a sizable number of relatively young couples, many with children, who were eager to reach out to the community and build a more "vibrant, spirit-filled congregation." To that end, Brice met with the church leaders to put together a marketing plan that would help the church accomplish its objectives.

---

### Mission Statement

Responsive religious organizations seek to clarify two questions: *responsive to whom and to what?* These questions help the religious organization to define its mission the *guiding principle* to what it does.

Suppose that after much soul searching and prayerful discussion, the planning group of the Hope United Methodist Church settles on the following mission statement.

## HOPE UNITED METHODIST CHURCH[10]

WE EXIST TO PRAISE GOD.
through celebrating new life in Jesus.
through responding to His presence in our lives.
through allowing His Holy Spirit to lead us.
Praise is our way of expressing our deep love for God. In worship we submit to His lordship in our lives and reflect His majesty, glory, and power.
PREPARE OURSELVES FOR SERVICE.
through the study and application of Scripture.
through developing our talents and spiritual gifts.
through becoming mature in Jesus Christ.
Preparation and growth are vital. It is not merely an option. However, growth is not an end in itself. Therefore, we seek to grow and become mature so that we can be prepared for service to our Lord, Jesus Christ.
PROVIDE LOVE AND CARE FOR ONE ANOTHER.
through sharing each other's needs, burdens, and joys.
through serving each other in a sacrificial way.
through learning how to love and be loved.
God, in His grace, has given us to each other.
An integral part of our life as His body is caring for and supporting each other.
PROCLAIM CHRIST TO THE WORLD . . .
through the penetration of our society.
through reproducing ourselves by evangelism and discipleship.
through applying ourselves and our resources in reaching out to our community, our nation and our world.
We take seriously our Lord's command to go and make disciples. Mission is the bedrock of our reason for being.

## Situation Analysis

Following the mission statement, the planning group prepares a situation analysis consisting of examining the internal environment, the input environment, and the external environment.

**Internal Environment.** Exhibit 7-5 shows the background data for Hope Church's performance and resources. It would appear from the information in Exhibit 7-5 that the church has had a decline in both membership and attendance over the past 3 years, although the percentage of members attending services is holding at around 70 percent, well above the national average of 42 percent. This leads to the next major section of internal analysis—listing the church's strengths and weaknesses.

## BACKGROUND DATA FOR HOPE CHURCH

|  | *1989* | *1990* | *1991* |
|---|---|---|---|
| Membership | 450 | 430 | 400 |
| Average Worship Attendance | 325 | 300 | 280 |
| Attendance as % of membership | 72% | 70% | 70% |
| Annual Capacity[1] | 26,000 | 26,000 | 26,000 |
| Main Worship Attendance[2] | 16,900 | 15,600 | 14,560 |
| Worshipers as % of Capacity | 65% | 60% | 56% |
| Income[3] | 75,000 | 75,000 | 79,000 |
| Expense[4] | 74,000 | 74,000 | 75,000 |
| Net operating surplus or (deficit) | 1,000 | 1,000 | 4,000 |

[1]Church sanctuary capacity is 500, multiplied by 52 Sundays
[2]Congregation per week x 52 weeks
[3]From member tithes, offerings, donations
[4]From operations

**Exhibit 7-5**

*Resources and Constraints.* Following the background study on the congregation's performance, planners should undertake an analysis of the church's resources and capabilities. An organization should pursue goals, opportunities, and strategies that are suggested by, or congruent with, its strengths/resources, and avoid those where its resources are insufficient.

We understand that God's people have always been called upon to accomplish tasks quite beyond their normal ability. This is part of the meaning of being "faith-full," and living by faith. However, there is a big difference between faith and stupidity. An example follows.

The authors worked with a congregation of 75 members whose pastor led them into a half million dollar debt to establish a Christian day school, saying God had instructed them to teach their children the laws of God, and to protect them from the evils of public education. The members mortgaged personal property, borrowed against pensions, and tried other means of raising money. In addition, the congregation mortgaged its own parsonage and sold junk bonds to relatives and friends. The school failed, the denomination had to assume the debt, the pastor left the scene, and the congregation was left with the pain and sorrow.

A "resource" is whatever the organization has of value in accomplishing its plans. Resources may be money, good will, people, skill, or common sense. A "constraint" is whatever the organization does not have enough of to accomplish its plans. Exhibit 7-6 shows a form that the congregation can use to develop an analysis of its resources (strengths) and constraints (weaknesses). The major resource areas are people, money, facilities, systems, and image. The analysis is to indicate whether the church's position with respect to each constitutes a strength (high, medium, low), is neutral, or constitutes a weakness (low, medium, high).

Suppose the checks reflect Hope Church's evaluation of its resources. The church believes that (1) it has an adequate number of spiritually gifted members who are highly enthusiastic, loyal, and service-minded.[11] (2) As for money, the church is somewhat short of funds, and almost all funds are committed. Therefore, the church does not have the flexibility to take on many new projects. (3) The church's facilities are adequate, but not flexible for multipurpose uses. Also, the church location is somewhat inconvenient. (4) The church's management system for planning and information is reasonably good, but it is weak in feedback (control) systems. (5) Finally, the church's image with the general public is neutral, as it is with the targeted group. (Ratings for image would be filled in after the congregation had selected its target group, discussed in chap. 6.)

## STRENGTHS/WEAKNESS ANALYSIS

| Resource | Strength | | | | Weakness | | |
| --- | --- | --- | --- | --- | --- | --- | --- |
| **People** | H | M | L | N | L | M | H |
| 1. Adequate number? | | ✓ | | | | | |
| 2. Spiritual gifts? | | ✓ | | | | | |
| 3. Enthusiastic? | ✓ | | | | | | |
| 4. Loyal? | ✓ | | | | | | |
| 5. Service-minded? | ✓ | | | | | | |
| **Money** | | | | | | | |
| 1. Adequate? | | | | | ✓ | | |
| 2. Flexible? | | | | | | ✓ | |
| **Facilities** | | | | | | | |
| 1. Adequate? | | | | ✓ | | | |
| 2. Flexible? | | | | | | | ✓ |
| 3. Location quality? | | | | | ✓ | | |
| **Systems** | | | | | | | |
| 1. Information system quality? | | | | ✓ | | | |
| 2. Planning system quality? | | | | ✓ | | | |
| 3. Control system quality? | | | | | ✓ | | |
| **Image** | | | | | | | |
| 1. General reputation? | | | | ✓ | | | |
| 2. Among target group? | | | | ✓ | | | |

Notes: H=high; M=medium; L=low; N=neutral

**Exhibit 7-6**

**Input Environment.** The relevant input publics should be evaluated to determine the possible impact they will have on achieving the church's objectives; for example, the community, judicatories, neighbors, and so on.

**External Environment.** The major components of the external environment should be analyzed to determine their impact on the church's ability to achieve its objectives. The procedure is (1) listing the major factors and subfactors making up the environment component, (2) describing the major trends in each factor, (3) converting the implications of these trends into specific opportunities and threats, and (4) assessing the threats—by their probability of occurrence and potential severity—and assessing the opportunities by their potential attractiveness and probability of success.

*Threat Analysis.* Every organization needs to identify the major threats it faces.

> *An environmental threat is a challenge posed by an unfavorable trend or specific disturbance in the environment which, in the absence of purposeful marketing action, would lead to the stagnation, decline, or demise of a religious organization or one of its ministry programs.*

Suppose the congregation's planning committee identified the following 4 threats:

1. A small local factory is in financial difficulty and has announced that it may close. If this happens, the congregation might lose the membership of 4 to 6 families.
2. The congregation's cost of operation—heating, lighting, salaries, and so on—might rise 15 percent next year.
3. A major financially contributing member has retired and is talking of moving to Arizona. This might cause the congregation to lose $10,000 a year in contributions.
4. A local radio station might stop broadcasting the church's main worship hour on Sunday.

The threats must be weighed to determine their potential severity and probability of occurrence. Suppose the results are those shown in Exhibit 7-7. For those threats that are most severe and highly probable, contingency plans should be made (upper left cell). Threats that are quite severe but of lower probability should be monitored (upper right cell). Those that are neither very severe nor probable can be ignored (bottom cells). By identifying and classifying threats, the organization knows which environmental developments t o plan for, monitor, or ignore.

**Exhibit 7-7**

Probability of occurrence

| | High | Low |
|---|---|---|
| **High** | 1, 2 | 3 |
| **Low** | | 4 |

*Potential severity* (vertical axis label)

A. Threat Matrix

*Opportunity Analysis.* While threat analysis is important, opportunity analysis is much more important. Managing threats and problem solving is maintenance oriented—it will not develop a quality organization or facilitate growth and expansion. But by managing its opportunities successfully, the congregation will grow and strengthen its ministries. Here we are concerned with marketing opportunities.

> A marketing opportunity is an attractive arena of relevant marketing action in which a congregation can apply its strengths to satisfy significant needs of a target group.

Suppose the planning committee perceived the following opportunities, which are located in the four cells of Exhibit 7-8, according to their probability of success (measured by the ability of the church to develop the opportunity) and potential attractiveness (measured by the likelihood of achievement of church objectives.)

**Exhibit 7-8**

Probability of success

| | High | Low |
|---|---|---|
| **High** | 1 | 3 |
| **Low** | 4 | 2 |

*Potential attractiveness* (vertical axis label)

B. Opportunity Matrix

1. The church could develop programs to satisfy the needs of unchurched young families. (Through geodemographic analysis [see chap. 6], the planning committee learned that young families constituted the largest number of households in Valparaiso).
2. The church could start an ecumenical men's prayer breakfast during the week at the church.
3. The church could open a day school for grades 1-9.
4. The church could start a branch Sunday school at the large local nursing home.

Starting some outreach programs to meet the needs of unchurched young families seems to be the best opportunity for the church, since it fits nicely with the church's objectives, its "market" conditions, and the ability of the church to capitalize on their current strengths of enthusiasm, service-mindedness, and related spiritual gifts. The idea of a church school fits church objectives well, but lack of funds, an insufficient "critical mass" of children in each grade, and strong competition from other private schools locally gives it little chance of success. A branch Sunday school at the local nursing home could prove successful, but seems lower in attractiveness than other outreach programs. The men's prayer breakfast is a pet project of a few parishioners, but the church's relatively inconvenient location and inflexible facilities make it relatively unattractive and its success uncertain.

In considering opportunities, congregations should generally avoid those for which necessary resources are weak or inadequate. But a weakness is not fatal to a project if the congregation can see a way to acquire the needed resources. Therefore, what is an opportunity for one church may not be a possibility for another, and what is a mediocre idea at one point in time may become an attractive possibility at another time.

## Target Market

The first step in preparing a marketing strategy is to understand the target market(s) thoroughly. Selection of a target market(s) follows a segmentation of the entire market, where different segments are identified and evaluated for attractiveness (see chap. 6).

In the case of Hope Church, suppose the segmentation approach was to use geodemography to identify the households in the various life-style segments. The choice was then made to target a specific segment—young families—because it represented an attractive opportunity with a good chance of success. Although some demographic and product preference information is available for this segment, the church may want to conduct a market research study to discover the specific needs, concerns, values, and behaviors of this group in order to plan an outreach ministry.

## Marketing Strategy

For each targeted market, the organization must develop a marketing strategy for succeeding in that segment. Marketing strategy represents the organization's responsive strategy to that segment. Marketing strategy consists of specifying marketing goals and formulating a *marketing mix* that will be used to reach the targeted segment.

**Goals.** Specific goals need to be set for each targeted group. In the case of the young families target market, the goals may read as:

* To provide at least 1 program ministry that will prove successful in helping young mothers cope with the stresses of caring for small children, in the next 12 months. For example, a "mother's day out" program, or a day-care program for children of working mothers.
* To provide a training program of at least 12 sessions for parents of hyper-active children, to be followed by an ongoing support group for the parents.
* To provide nursery services during Sunday school and worship hours, and on Wednesday evening, to allow young parents to participate in Sunday and Wednesday evening services without concern for the care of their children.

**Marketing Mix.** The next step in marketing strategy is to develop a marketing mix. We define marketing mix as follows.

Although many variables make up the marketing mix, they can be classified into a few major groups. McCarthy formulated a popular classification called the "four Ps: *product, price, place,* and *promotion*.[12] These variables can be translated for religious marketing as follows:

> *Marketing mix is the particular blend of controllable marketing variables that the religious organization uses to achieve its objectives in the target segment.*

Product—The program(s) and ministries that the religious organization offers a target segment.

Price—The sacrifices or commitments that the target group must make to use or adopt the organization's program(s).

Place—The means or location by which the program is delivered to the target segment.

Promotion—The means used to communicate the attributes of the organization's program(s) to the targeted segment.

In the case of Hope Church, it might have a marketing mix consisting of several programs, with different "prices," delivered through a variety of means and communicated with different messages using several media. For example, young families are found to move frequently. The marketing mix for this target group might, therefore, include the following elements:

Product—A "New Home Welcome" program where new families are identified and given welcome baskets with information, gifts, and offers of help in getting the new family settled.

Price—Targeted families may be asked to give up time to come to a welcome dinner for recently arrived residents.

Place—The congregation might rent a hall instead of using the church facility for the welcome dinner.

Promotion—A printed invitation, followed by a personal phone invitation to the welcome dinner.

When delivering the welcome basket, informal marketing research might be done, consisting of a few questions to determine the needs and interests of the young family, including their entertainment interests. If certain entertainment activities frequently surface during these welcome visits/interviews, some specific ministries might be developed to satisfy those needs. Some programs might be directed at the couples, others at the entire family. By asking a few questions and making simple observations, this informal marketing research could prove valuable in suggesting other specific outreach programs to this targeted segment.

The objective of developing the marketing mix is to put together the most *effective* and *efficient* means possible to achieve the marketing goals. This means developing an action program or set of tactics and establishing a marketing budget.

## Marketing Tactics

The marketing strategy needs to be turned into a specific set of actions for accomplishing the marketing goals. Each strategic element should be elaborated into appropriate actions. For example, the strategic element "Reach newly arrived young families" could lead to the actions of obtaining the names and characteristics of new young families moving into the community, preparation of the welcome baskets, delivery of the welcome baskets by church couples, and so on.

## Marketing Budget

The goals, strategies, and planned actions allow the planners to build a budget. A schedule should be prepared such as in Exhibit 7-9 where each task is listed, along with its cost and time of occurrence.[13]

## Marketing Control

Plans are useful only if they are implemented and monitored. The purpose of a marketing control system is to maximize the probability that the organization will achieve the short-term and long-term objectives of the organization's ministries. It accomplishes this purpose by measuring the ongoing results of a plan against the plan's goals, indicating where corrective action should be taken before it is too late.

## Exhibit 7-9
# MARKETING BUDGET AND PLAN SCHEDULE

**WEEK**

| Task | 1 | 2 | 3 | 4 | 5 | 6-8 | TOTAL |
|------|---|---|---|---|---|-----|-------|
| Program Development | $25 | | | | | | $ 25 |
| Material | | $100 | $100 | $100 | $100 | $100 | 700 |
| Printing | | | 75 | 75 | 75 | | 225 |
| Promotion | | | | | 80 | 80 | 320 |
| COST TOTALS | $25 | $100 | $175 | $175 | $255 | $180 | $1270 |

An example of controls for an action plan of Hope Church is shown in Exhibit 7-10. Also see Appendix B for a more thorough discussion of how to evaluate the success of your programs.

## Exhibit 7-10
# MARKETING ACTION PLAN CONTROL SHEET

| Time | Responsibility | Goal | Results | Deviance from Goal |
|------|----------------|------|---------|--------------------|

1. Call Apartment Complexes and Housing Authority for names of new residents. Determine which are young families, ethnic composition.

| | | | | |
|------|----------------|------|---------|--------------------|
| Every | J. Smith | 6/3 | | |
| Wednesday | | 6/10 | | |
| | | 6/17 | | |
| | | 6/24 | | |

2. Fill Welcome Baskets with materials.

| | | | | |
|------|----------------|------|---------|--------------------|
| Every | R. Jones | 6/6 | | |
| Saturday | H. Brown | 6/13 | | |
| | | 6/20 | | |
| | | 6/27 | | |

3. Have baskets delivered by young couples of similar ethnic background. Dinner invitation made.

| | | | | |
|------|----------------|------|---------|--------------------|
| Every Tuesday | A. Couple | 6/2 | 50% acceptance | 60% accceptance |
| or Thursday | B. Couple | 6/12 | of dinner | for June |
| | C. Couple | 6/16 | invitation | |
| | D. Couple | 6/18 | | |
| | | 6/25 | | |

Again, planning is necessary to the success of any major effort. However, it need not be overwhelming in complexity. Neither does planning have to be boring. Keep it natural; keep it simple. Remember: a plan should be kept as simple as possible, but no simpler.[14]

## *Summary*

Numerous societal events have created a dynamic environment, challenging the existence of many denominations and local congregations. While organizational life cycles do exist, individual churches need not always face decline. Success stories abound of congregations that have successfully met challenges to their existence by adapting to the changed environment. Becoming a responsive religious organization that can adapt to environmental conditions requires careful planning and skilled leadership.

Marketing planning can help leaders of religious organizations by acting as a road map, assisting in administrative control and monitoring of strategy implementation, informing participants in the plan of their role and function, obtaining resources for implementation, stimulating thinking, assigning responsibilities, and making planners aware of opportunities and threats.

A marketing plan consists of a mission statement; situation analysis covering internal, input, and external environments; description of target markets; a marketing strategy to reach the target market, consisting of goals and a marketing mix; marketing tactics to implement the strategy; a marketing budget to carry out the strategy; and marketing controls to provide feedback on the strategy's effectiveness and to identify where programs are failing to achieve the marketing goals.

# How to Put Marketing Plans into Action for Religious Organizations

## Introduction to Part Three

Thus far we have explored marketing's role in religious organizations, marketing's importance to contemporary religious institutions, and we have discussed the essential concepts necessary to incorporate such a marketing orientation by religious organizations (Part One). Following that, we discussed how religious organizations can actually "do" marketing by first researching opportunities, then segmenting and targeting religious markets, positioning their ministries to those targeted markets, and developing marketing plans that incorporate the research findings and decisions (Part Two).

We now continue that discussion of "doing" marketing by focusing on the "marketing mix"—the mix of product (ministries or programs), price (what target audiences must give up in terms of time, money, and psychological or social costs), place (the location or means of delivering the ministry), and promotion (the message and media by which we communicate the product's benefits). These 4 tools are the means of implementing the position we desire in the minds of the targeted segment. These tools are discussed in chapter 8 (product, place, price) and chapter 9 (promotion—i.e., advertising and public relations).

"Doing marketing," however, involves more than simply implementing a marketing mix. Religious institutions are also very much concerned with "internal marketing"—delivering satisfaction to current members and managing exchanges with volunteer workers (chap. 10). "Doing" also includes obtaining resources to fund our ministries, which is discussed in chapter 11 ("Fund Raising"). It is prudent for religious leaders to evaluate the effectiveness and efficiencies of their marketing programs, so we have included in

Appendix B a discussion of program evaluation. From these cases we have evidence of the very real value a marketing orientation brings to the search for solutions to these organizations' problems. However, as we stress in our final chapter (chap. 12), we are not of the opinion that marketing is the source of answers to all the problems of contemporary religious organizations. Those answers must come from the Source, which has been a very present help in times of trouble throughout all generations.

# 8

# Designing Your Program Offerings

## Product, Place, Price Decisions

In previous chapters, we examined several tasks of religious marketers: using research to obtain and use information about "market opportunities," segmenting and targeting groups whom the organization most wishes to engage in exchange, developing a positioning strategy, and developing a planning process and document (marketing plan) that specifies the who, what, where, when, why, and how of achieving our marketing objectives. One key component of a marketing plan is your marketing mix: developing a *product*, setting its *price*, determining the *place* where it will be available, and how it will be *promoted*. These are the 4 "Ps" of marketing: product, price, place, promotion.

This chapter will focus on the first 3 "Ps" of the marketing mix: product, price, and place. The following chapter will address the last "P," the promotional component.

---

A special word to the reader:

When presenting new ideas to an audience, the burden is on the writer to translate the ideas into the reader's vocabulary and to show how they apply to his or her institution. This is not a simple task in writing a text on marketing for leaders of religious organizations. The religious world does not have corollaries for many of the marketing terms that are familiar to other institutions, such as *customer, consumer, product, price,* and so on. Having noted this, we now alert the reader to the fact that in this chapter we will use marketing terms borrowed from secular marketing vocabulary, without any attempt to cast them in "religious" terms. We do this for the sake of simplicity in reading, and because we assume that by now you have progressed in your understanding of marketing concepts to the point where more "secular" marketing terms will cause no problem, and may even add to the learning.

---

## The Nature of Products

Chapter 4 suggests that products can consist of goods, services, persons, places, organizations, activities, or ideas. Exhibit 4-11 displays congregations that are engaged in offering different products or benefit bundles whose consumption incurs different types of costs. In the definition below, as well as in Exhibit 4-11, it is important to note that products are to be viewed from the perspective of the *consumer* rather than the *producer.* The religious organization must determine what type of product will have value in the eyes of the product's consumers, if it is to successfully engage them in exchange.

> A product is anything that can be offered to a market to satisfy a need. Other names for a product would be a value package or benefit bundle. For a religious organization, these products are sometimes called ministries, programs, services, or offerings.

A producer's sense of a product's value is determined not by its intrinsic characteristics, but rather by what *results* it can produce (see Exhibit 8-1). Sometimes a pastor or rabbi will see a ministry as important because he or she has a personal desire to offer it, even though this same opinion is not shared by the congregation nor by the target consumers. Exhibit 8-1, however, suggests that the value a pastor or rabbi places on a product should be based on its abilities to provide true need satisfaction for the consumer and to satisfy other mission related objectives, not because it is someone's "pet" project.

Research that produces results such as in Exhibit 4-14 for the consumers will help to determine which ministries are perceived as most important and satisfying.

### Levels of Products

In developing a product for an external or internal market, the organization must distinguish between 2 conceptual levels of a product, the *core* and the *tangible* levels (see Exhibit 8-2).

**The Core Product.** At the most fundamental level stands the core product, which answers the questions: What is the consumer

**Exhibit 8-1**

## VALUES OF PRODUCTS TO PRODUCERS AND CONSUMERS

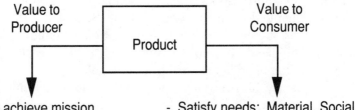

Value to Producer | Product | Value to Consumer

- Help achieve mission
- Satisfy customer needs
- Generate revenue or attract other resources
- Move consumers to next stage of commitment process

- Satisfy needs: Material, Social, Religious, Spiritual
- Improve quality of life: Physical, Cultural, Social, Spiritual

**Exhibit 8-2**

## LEVELS OF PRODUCT

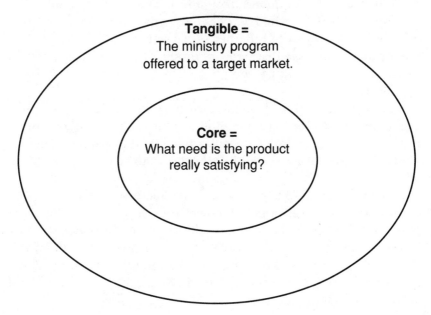

**Tangible =**
The ministry program offered to a target market.

**Core =**
What need is the product really satisfying?

really seeking? What need is the product really satisfying? People don't *need* products for the sake of products; they *want* products which satisfy needs. For example, people don't need youth programs, but they need to expose their children to entertainment and educational experiences that will enhance their children's spiritual lives. People don't need Vacation Bible School, but they need to have a means of concerted religious education for children and adolescents. The classic example given, which illustrates this point, is that people don't need drill bits; they need holes!

Consequently, all present or potential ministries should be subjected to this test: Does this program do the most effective and efficient job of satisfying the core need that the consumer is seeking to satisfy?

**Tangible Products.** The core product is always made available to the consumer in some tangible form. The *core benefit* of spiritual inspiration can be provided through the *tangible products* of a sermon, a Sunday school lesson, a midweek prayer service, religious literature, and the like.

As mentioned in chapter 1, for religious organizations, some core products are considered unalterable or non-negotiable. Adopting a marketing orientation *does not* require a congregation to alter the core product (e.g., a statement of beliefs, a part of the organization's mission, its theology, etc.). Rather, a marketing orientation requires the organization to see that the core product can take many tangible forms, and not to confuse the unalterable core with the alterable tangible product.

Failure to make this distinction causes religious leaders to stubbornly insist on offering a tangible product to the market, which has outlived its usefulness, because they feel they would be failing God or compromising the faith if they were to change the tangible product.

Religious leaders can find various tangible means of offering the core product without doing violence to faith or creed. This is an important distinction, because it spells the difference between mistakenly concentrating on improving the characteristics of the product (making better drill bits) rather than finding ways of satisfying enduring needs (making holes). Our loyalties, after all, are to God and his laws, not to programs.

In addition to satisfying the core benefit, the tangible product must also satisfy several other criteria of importance to the religious organization.

## Objectives for Products

The introduction or continuation of any ministry, program, or activity should be based on that ministry's potential for accomplishing some basic objectives growing out of a marketing plan. These objectives are related to balancing the product portfolio from 3 perspectives: the organization's mission, the decision processes of target consumers, and concern for resource attraction.

**Missional Objectives.** The first step in developing a strategic marketing plan is to establish the organization's mission. The intent here is not to discuss how a mission might be developed, but rather to indicate how a church's products should relate to that mission.[1] In the previous chapter, the mission statement of the hypothetical Hope United Methodist Church contained 4 major components: praise, prepare, provide, and proclaim. If the church is to fulfill such a mission, it needs a balanced *product portfolio*, which would include products for each of these 4 missional objectives—products relating to the worship experience, products intended to edify members and enhance their talents, products that permit the church to foster loving fellowship among all its constituents, and outreach products that use the church's resources to meet the spiritual, physical, and social needs of the world around the church.

> A product portfolio is the set of all product lines that a religious organization makes available to consumers, internal and external to the organization.
> A product line is a group of products, within a product portfolio, that are closely related in the organization's objectives, target audience, or function.

Developing a balanced product portfolio requires having products related to each missional area, specifically designed for each targeted consumer group.

**Exhibit 8-3**

# PRODUCT OBJECTIVES CONSISTENT
# WITH MISSION OF CHURCH

**Targeted Public of Mission Component**

|  | Internal | External |
|---|---|---|
| Faith (Vertical Relationships)<br><br>**Core Product of Mission** | Exaltation and Discipleship | Evangelism |
| Fraternity (Horizontal Relationships) | Koinonia | Social Action |

In general, we could say that all products in the portfolio would have core benefits consisting of either faith or fraternity. That is, the core benefit of any ministry would consist of enhancing a person's vertical (faith in God) or horizontal (fraternity with others) relationships. These core benefits would be directed at publics either internal or external to the congregation. Exhibit 8-3 shows the 4 product objectives that would result from a combination of targeted publics of a congregation's mission, and the core products aimed at achieving the mission.

A religious organization's identity is, to a large degree, dependent on how it defines and carries out its mission. It is important, therefore, that the organization plans product portfolios to enhance the organization's identity along the relevant 4 dimensions. Of course, not every religious organization may have a mission statement that stresses all 4 cells of Exhibit 8-3.

An example will help to illustrate these concepts. Exhibit 8-4 lists the major products (ministries) offered by Willow Creek Community Church. (Willow Creek has over 90 ministries or programs, only the major ones are listed here.) For each major component of their mission, a product line is listed, consisting of products targeted at different age groups. The entire set of product lines comprises the product portfolio.

Every religious organization should establish a mission that reflects its answers to the question of why the organization exists.

## WILLOW CREEK COMMUNITY CHURCH—PRODUCT PORTFOLIO

| Missional Objectives: Ministries by Age Group: | Exaltation Product Line: | Koinonia Product Line: | Evangelism Product Line: | Social Action Product Line: |
|---|---|---|---|---|
| All Ages | Saturday night service; Sunday 9am, 11am service; Seeds Tapes of weekend services | Saturday night service; Sunday 9am, 11am service; Seeds Tapes of weekend services | Wednesday night service; Verbal witnessing by laymembers | Heartbeat—hospital visitation; Food Pantry—emergency food and clothing for families in need; Hearthstone—homebound visitation |
| Children | Promiseland—Nursing care and creative playtime for Toddler during adult service | Promiseland—birth thru 6th grade Bible classes, other activities | | Rainbows—children suffering from parental loss |
| Youth | Camp Paradise—250 acre camp in Michigan | Sonlight Express—jr. high Saturday am social activities, spiritual study; Son City—high school, Thursday evenings social activities and spiritual study; Camp Paradise—250 acre camp in Michigan | Son Village—high school Bible study classes | Premarital Counseling; Alateen—children in alcoholic families |
| Single Adults and Couples | PrimeTime Community Core Events—Bible teaching, singing, worship; 4 Weeks in Focus Bible study small groups; Odyssey (singles mid 40s+) social and spiritual events; Grasp—single parent families; Women's Ministries | PrimeTime Community Nights (age 18-30); All-Community Nights (ages 30-mid 40s); Odyssey (singles mid 40s+) social and spiritual events; Grasp—single parent families; Voyagers—(couples in mid 40s+) social and spiritual events | Outreach Events (ages 18-30); All-Focus Events (ages 30-mid 40s); Small Groups | CHILD—pregnant single women; Rebuilders—marriage breakdowns; Good Sense—budget counseling; HEAL—sexual addiction counseling; Heritage—nursing home visitation; Exodus—families of people in prison |

Failure to carefully plan a product portfolio that is consistent with the missional objectives will result in an identity that is vague and confusing to internal and external publics alike.

**Influencing Behavior in Faith and Practice.** A portfolio of products should also have as its objective the leading of persons along toward increasing maturity in their faith. Individual ministries should be planned with regard to how they contribute to a commitment of persons to enter a process by which they will become aware of the church or synagogue, develop interest in its offerings, go through a period of exposure to its offerings, and experience spiritual and social growth. Products should be targeted to meet the needs of people at each stage of this process, and to move them to the next stage. For example, at Willow Creek the Sunday morning service is intended to appeal to the general public with a sermon, drama, and music, while the Wednesday night service is intended to prepare those who have moved from curiosity to a more serious interest in membership through a study of the Bible and church doctrines.

**Securing Financial and Volunteer Resources.** Some products of a church or synagogue have the objective of attracting volunteers, funds, or donated resources. Annual fund drives, sales of goods, stewardship programs, and the like are products designed with the objective of attracting resources necessary for the congregation's continued operation. Just as a product portfolio must be balanced to achieve missional objectives, and to fulfill consumer needs at various stages of a commitment/assimilation process, so also churches and synagogues must have a balance of products that generate and absorb resources.

Failure to design attractive products that generate revenues can result in the perception that a church or synagogue is constantly begging for money. Such a perception may well inhibit the consumption of other products by people who are afraid to come near the place for fear of being asked to contribute funds for its operations.

## Developing New Products

A religious organization that wishes to develop new products to achieve a balanced portfolio must establish a process that will lead to successful new product launches. *The ability to slough off old products and to successfully launch new products can hardly be overemphasized.* The church or synagogue that fails this test can hardly hope to satisfy the needs and interests of its target markets.

> In 1975 the Bethel African Methodist Episcopal Church, located in a low-income area of Baltimore, was stagnant. Only half of its 600 members attended Sunday services. That was before John Bryant, 32, arrived with dreams of what a city church could do. Pastor Bryant envisioned a church that would reach out to the "whole person" and the surrounding community. Among the church programs started were sign language instruction for about 50 deaf parishioners; a prison missionary project for adults and youth; an outreach center that provides job counseling, clothing, food, and vouchers for emergency payment of rent and utility bills; an energy cooperative that sells fuel oil at reduced prices; and a 2,000-member food cooperative. The Senior Citizens Eating Together program serves free meals to members and non-members alike.
>
> Yet the religious message was not forgotten. In addition to 3 Sunday services, Bethel sponsors Sunday school classes for all ages and daily Bible classes and discussion groups. Bryant's spirit has spread to his congregants, one of whom recently gave money to start a ministry for cancer patients and their families—a program that several other churches have copied. By 1984 membership had climbed to 6,000 with a paid staff of 31 and dozens of volunteers. As one church member noted, "We're not just adding people to the church rolls. Reverend Bryant has shaken our consciousness and awakened us as Christians."[2]

While the marketing plan will specify to whom the product will be marketed, how it will be offered, and what the offering's objectives will be, the organization must first be capable of generating new product ideas, and then be able to screen the ideas so that the best ones can be incorporated into the marketing plan. These steps of idea generation and screening are described in the following sections.

## Generating New Ideas

Religious organizations differ in their need for new product ideas. Some are quite busy carrying out their current activities and do not need new things to do. Others need one or two big new ideas to balance their product portfolio. Still others need several new ideas simply to keep up with the changing local environment. Shifting demographic compositions of the population surrounding an urban congregation, for example, may require substantial changes in its portfolio.

The idea generation stage is most relevant to congregations that need one or more ideas to maintain or expand their ministries. It may be argued that the more ideas a congregation generates—and the more diverse they are—the greater chance it will have of finding *successful* ideas. Ideas can occur spontaneously from the following "natural" sources:

* Personal inspiration of one or more members.
* Serendipitous stimuli from the environment—for example, learning of a new idea from another congregation or in discussion with religious workers from other parts of the country or the world.
* Requests for new offerings or modification of existing offerings from persons in a target market or key public.
* Suggestions from a participant in one of the organization's program offerings.

Ideas that arise spontaneously should not be ignored. They indicate areas where "something is trying to be born." However, spontaneous ideas are not the only approach a congregation should rely on for new ideas—for at least 2 reasons. First, they rely on a chance combination of an idea's appearing *and* someone's alertness in recognizing it.

These casual approaches have a second problem. As noted by Crompton: "There is a great deal of evidence which suggests that many efforts to produce new programs which meet client needs are incestuous. That is, there is a tendency to reach for prior experiences, prior approaches, or moderate distortions of old answers, as opposed to really searching for new ideas. We become victimized by habit."[3]

Therefore, the organization should create a climate in which spontaneous ideas are welcomed, and at the same time employ a systematic methodology for generating ideas. A systematic process requires 4 steps. (1) A *commitment* must be made to routinely and formally search for new ideas. (2) *Responsibility* for this task must be specifically assigned to someone or some group. (3) A *procedure* must be put in place for *systematically* seeking new ideas. (4) The procedure must contain a *creative* component if truly new ideas are sought.

## PROCEDURES FOR GATHERING NEW IDEAS

Establishing the idea generation *procedure* involves the entire organization in listing all possible sources for new ideas, and then developing a strategy for generating or collecting ideas routinely from each source. Major sources and procedures for mining them are listed below.

1. Similar organizations
   (a) A jointly funded clearing house could be established to share new ideas among congregations in the same denomination or a group of independent congregations.
   (b) Scheduled, routine visits or telephone conversations with similar organizations on specific dates; for example, the first Tuesday of every February and July.
2. Journals, newspapers, magazines
   (a) Probable written sources of ideas should be identified, subscriptions acquired, and someone (or several people) assigned to peruse these sources routinely.
   (b) A clipping service might be subscribed to.
   (c) A librarian might be hired and assigned these tasks.
   (d) A computer-based information retrieval system could be subscribed to.
3. Conferences, lectures
   (a) People should be routinely assigned to attend important gatherings to collect ideas and useful literature.
4. Members
   The organization should solicit members for their ideas rather than waiting until they spontaneously offer them. Many religious organizations obtain most of their best new ideas by soliciting or actively listening to members and other stakeholders, whether internal or external.
5. Evaluation of Market Data
   Idea suggestions may surface when market data is evaluated (e.g.,

how to best serve the needs of newly arrived young families for Hope Church in Valparaiso).

Three features should characterize the idea-generation system. First, specific dates should be set for carrying out each information-gathering technique. Second, a formal reporting and assessment mechanism should be developed to assure that each idea comes before the appropriate group for consideration. Finally, the system should be *unblocked*. A few vocal persons should not be able to kill ideas as "too outrageous" or "not really appropriate for us right now." This stage is intended to generate, not evaluate, ideas.

One technique for improving the emergence of new ideas is to assign responsibility to someone who might be called a *ministry idea manager*. A ministry idea manager would perform 5 major functions:

1. *Idea finding.* The ministry idea manager would conduct an organized and continuous search for new ideas by reading journals and newsletters, attending conferences, and talking to consultants.
2. *Idea stimulating.* The ministry idea manager would use creativity-generating techniques to stimulate others to create new and useful ideas.
3. *Idea collecting.* The ministry idea manager would serve as a receiving station for the good ideas spotted by others. Everyone would know that good ideas should be sent to this person.
4. *Idea evaluating.* The ministry idea manager would do a preliminary analysis and evaluation of the ideas and identify the really good ones.
5. *Idea disseminating.* The ministry idea manager would know to whom each worthwhile idea should be sent. The ministry idea manager would act as an idea champion of the better ideas.

This important responsibility should be assigned to someone who has some power and stature in the congregation.

Generating ideas involves both spontaneous and systematic techniques for routinely scanning or prodding various systems for ideas.

This will yield a high proportion of ideas. If an organization seeks "breakthrough-quality" ideas, it can utilize a number of proven techniques. Some techniques can be used by individuals; others are best done in groups where persons can spark ideas off each other.[4]

**Brainstorming.** This is probably the best-known technique for forcing creativity. Brainstorming involves putting 5 to 9 people, preferably of diverse backgrounds, together and giving them a very broad problem mandate. They are then told (1) to come up with as many solutions as possible; (2) no solution is too wild to suggest; (3) no one is to evaluate—most particularly, criticize—any idea at this stage; and (4) it is possible to build upon another's idea. The objective is to place the participants in a non-threatening environment where they can let their imaginations soar as they use one another's input to suggest new and increasingly creative solutions.

**Attribute listing.** Here, the major attributes of the idea, product, or service are listed and each attribute is scrutinized to see if it can be adapted, modified, magnified, substituted, rearranged, reversed, or combined. The traditional approach to borrowing a book from a synagogue library, for example, involves (1) going to the library, (2) looking up the book in the card catalogue, (3) going to the shelf to obtain the book, (4) taking it to the library table or office, (5) filling out the record of borrowing details, (6) taking the book home, and (7) bringing it back to the library when the borrower is finished with it. The idea-generating process would involve trying to think of new ways to accomplish each of the 7 steps to produce greater product use. Step 1, for example, could be done by using a telephone or the mail, by using a computer terminal, by bringing the "library" to the borrower's home in a mobile van, or by having volunteers bring the book to the member's home. Then one would proceed to step 2, imagining innovative ways to look up and retrieve the book, including voice-activated computer systems and the use of automatic conveyor belts, or even robots.[5]

**Forced relationships.** Here, several objects or elements are listed, and each is considered in relation to the other. Thus, a product portfolio for children might include a Saturday afternoon story telling hour and picnic, a children's worship service, and a Sunday School "pre-confirmation series" dealing with the sacraments of the church. An analysis of possible relationships might suggest stories to be told to children to indirectly teach them what the sacraments are, and how they fit into worship. Perhaps the stories might be of children in other cultures i.e., American Indian, and sacraments and worship in that culture.

**Problem analysis.** Here consumers are asked about problems they encounter in making a particular exchange. *Each problem can be the source of new ideas.* Library patrons, for example, could express frustration at sometimes having to wait a long time to check out a book. The librarian might think of installing some form of diversion—for example, a computer game, an interesting exhibit, or closed-circuit television—to engage and occupy patrons while they are waiting.

William J. J. Gordon suggests that it is sometimes useful to propose as broad a problem as possible, such as, "How can the library match people and ideas?" and only later in the session should one narrow it to specific issues, such as, "How can our synagogue library use its limited budget to have the most study and reference materials available for the most users?"[6] Imaginative leaders should be able to use this same process to stimulate creative thinking among members of a church or synagogue for generating new product ideas in any ministry area.

## Idea Screening

As ideas accumulate, an effort must be made to identify the most promising and to eliminate those that do not warrant further attention. There is some chance that screening might result in an excellent idea's being prematurely dropped (a drop-error). What might be worse, however, is accepting a bad idea for further development (a go-error) as a result of poor screening. Each idea that is developed consumes substantial paid or volunteer time and money. The purpose of screening is, therefore, to eliminate all but the most promising ideas.

Several steps are necessary to ensure effective idea screening:

1. *A screening committee should be established to evaluate new ideas.* The committee should include representatives of each key program area and ministry department. Selection of those to serve on the committee should assure that the committee will represent experience and expertise on the proposed new ministries and programs.

*2. Regular meetings should be scheduled to evaluate new ideas.*

*3. Criteria should be developed against which the ideas are to be evaluated.* The criteria would be consistently applied over many evaluation sessions. Each religious organization will want to establish criteria most appropriate for their circumstances. Weights for the criteria should be developed prior to *each* evaluation session. These weights should be set by the ministry leaders and ruling board, since they will directly affect where the organization wishes to go in the future.

*4. Prior to the evaluation meeting, committee members should prepare briefs on each idea, as a basis for group discussion.* The briefs should present data that is relevant to each of the major criteria.

*5. The group should meet and discuss each idea.* Afterward, they should rate each idea, either individually or collectively, on each criterion. (A form should be devised for this purpose.)

It is not enough to generate and screen product ideas. It is also important to understand the process by which people will adopt the new product, so that an implementation plan can be devised with maximum likelihood of success.

## *The Innovation Adoption Process*

Rogers and Shoemaker have identified 4 steps that individuals typically go through in adopting some new pattern of behavior.[7]

1. *Knowledge.* First, the targeted consumer must (a) become aware of the program or new life pattern, and (b) learn enough about it to deduce whether it has relevance for his or her needs, wants, and life-style.
2. *Persuasion.* Next, the target consumer must move from simple awareness and vague interest to being motivated to take action. This is primarily a matter of attitude change. However, it is also possible that a *behavioral response* could be achieved through offering incentives, with relatively little *attitude change.*
3. *Decision.* At some point, the target consumer thinks through the probable consequences of the proposed behavior change and makes a decision to adopt or reject it.

4. *Confirmation.* After the initial decision, it is hoped that the target consumer will continue the behavior. This can be a major problem for social change agents. For example, over 70 percent of those who have stopped smoking resume the habit within a year.

The value of the Rogers-Shoemaker adoption model is threefold. First, it points to the *sequence* of tasks necessary to move a given target group to adopt a product. Thus early messages must create awareness and interest, subsequent messages persuade, and later messages secure and reinforce decisions.

Second, the Rogers-Shoemaker adoption model provides a monitoring device to identify reasons for a slow rate of acceptance. For example, research on how persons quit smoking shows that many smokers are blocked at the decision stage. For these persons, attempts to persuade them to stop smoking are no longer necessary, and effort should focus on inducing a decision.

### Innovation Characteristics

The innovation's characteristics will affect the rate of adoption. Five characteristics have an especially important influence on the adoption rate.

The first is the innovation's *relative advantage,* the degree to which it appears superior to previous ideas. The greater the perceived relative advantage (higher quality, lower cost, and so on), the more quickly the innovation will be adopted.

For example, a 5-evening Vacation Bible School, with transportation provided at a tuition of $10 per child, being offered in a neighborhood with a high percentage of single-parent households will be *adopted* (utilized) by more households than a school providing no transportation with a tuition of $5. Even though one costs less, which will certainly be appreciated by the working parent, the other may have more appeal because of the convenience of the parent's not having to rush the child off to church, after just returning from work.

The second characteristic is the innovation's *compatibility*—the degree to which it is consistent with the values and experiences of the individuals in the social system. Thus persuading women in

Third World nations to practice birth control when they believe that their number of children is "in God's hands" will take more time than persuading them to boil water before drinking it, because the latter has no religious significance.

The third characteristic is the innovation's *divisibility*—the degree to which it may be tried on a limited basis. The evidence of many studies indicates that divisibility helps to increase adoption. For example, a prospective member may more readily sign up to attend a 3-month Sunday school series on spiritual formation than to pledge life-long allegiance to God for all affairs of one's life.

---

When Rick Warren publicly launched Saddleback Valley Community Church, the congregation (15 people) hand-addressed and hand-stamped 15,000 letters to homes in the neighborhood. The letters announced that the church's first public service would be held on Easter Sunday, two weeks after the letters were mailed.

The letter also stated that Rick would be doing a trial run of the service, in the high school, on the Sunday prior to Easter. Sixty people came to the trial run, by accident, thinking it was the real service, and 5 of them committed their lives to Christ that day and joined the church.

---

By inviting people to attend the trial-run service, Rick Warren made it possible for persons to give the new church "a try" on a limited, one-shot basis. If they didn't like the trial run, they would never attend the church once it was started. Also, attending the practice session was much less threatening than attending the Easter service, where many more people might be present and the service would be "for real."

The fourth characteristic is the innovation's *complexity*, the degree to which it is relatively difficult to understand. More complex innovations take a longer time to diffuse, other things being equal.

The fifth characteristic is the innovation's *communicability*—the degree to which the results are observable or describable to others. Innovations whose advantages are more observable will diffuse more quickly throughout the social system. Thus new believers will adopt regular attendance habits faster than tithing 10 percent of their income, because the benefit of tithing can be understood or experienced only over a long time of faithful practice.

The planning team should research how any proposed innovation is perceived by the target market in terms of these 5 characteristics before developing the marketing plan. The committee can then proceed to make the innovation relatively more advantageous, more compatible, more divisible, less complex, and more communicable.[8]

## Pricing the Product

Another element of the marketing mix, which must be planned along with the product, is *price.* In chapter 4, we discussed the cost of an exchange (see Exhibit 4-11). Consumers balance the expected benefits of an exchange against the expected costs. Money payment might be only one of these costs or sacrifices.

---

Consider the case of a man who is deciding whether to begin attending Sunday worship services regularly. His wife has begun attending, and he is noticing a marked difference in her demeanor and conversation. Further, he has been reading some of the materials about the congregation and its many programs. He knows regular attendance will cost him a significant amount of money because he can work overtime several Sundays a year at the steel mill where he is employed. He would have to give this up. Further, he imagines that being faithful to worship means one contributes money regularly. He is aware of another "cost." On most Sunday mornings, when he is not working overtime, he plays golf with his buddies. Regular worship attendance would wipe out Sunday morning golf.

There is yet another "cost" with which he is struggling. His crew at the mill loves to tease, and nickname, anyone who attends religious services. This seems to him to be the greatest "cost." The family can get along well enough without his Sunday overtime, and he might possibly be able to pick up some Saturday overtime to compensate. He has long remembered his

own father regularly contributing to the old family church. But he
is not sure he could endure the taunts of his fellow mill workers.

For many persons considering joining a church or synagogue, the financial cost may not be the most important factor. A number of psychic costs may be of greater importance, including:

> *A perceived cost* is any negative outcome of a proposed exchange perceived by a target consumer.

* awkwardness at having to ask for a change in work schedule or for time off;
* fear that turning down overtime might hurt chances for promotion;
* embarrassment at having to explain to co-workers why you aren't working overtime (or lying to them);
* regret of breaking up the golfing foursome;
* concerns of being ostracized by co-workers and friends.

All of these perceived costs will run through one's mind. A church marketing portfolio that focuses primarily on promoting the responsibilities of bringing the family to worship and on the joy of worship will probably fail to motivate many persons whose situations parallel what is described above. Many persons know that it would be good to take the family to church. It is the vast array of perceived costs that keep them from taking the step.

Likewise, in many of the exchanges a religious organization seeks, managing the perceived costs is often much more important than managing the benefits. Furthermore, the nominal financial price tag on the exchange may be the least important perceived cost that concerns the individual. In many religious exchanges, there is no financial price tag at all.

### Cost Management

Cost management (deciding a "price" for the organization's offering) presents a delicate problem for the religious marketing program. An optimal cost management strategy, from the organization's standpoint, is one that maximizes the number of exchanges for a given cost to the target market. This is a delicate matter, for the religious organization is concerned about several cost factors.

First, the religious organization is providing some products with a cost that has been determined by God.

Second, the religious organization knows that to price certain religious products too cheaply will result in "cheap grace"—and grace cheaply gotten is too often cheaply held.

Third, the organization wants to reach as many persons as possible, but simply hawking the message to the lowest bidder does not necessarily reach the most people, and those who are thus reached do not tend to make for a quality organization.

Deciding how to address these concerns makes up the very fabric of managing the costs of religious experience.

How can a cost management strategy be developed? The religious organization must begin by researching consumer perceptions of these costs. Otherwise, those who are planning the congregation's marketing portfolio may miss subtle, but crucial, barriers affecting particular consumer segments. Consider the following examples:

* The National Cancer Institute realized only within the last 10 years that a perceived cost keeping many people from trying to quit smoking is the fear of failure.
* In the rural areas of many countries, women who want to practice contraception do not do so because all of the methods they know require that someone (or many people) become aware of their behavior.
* Some potential attenders of symphony concerts won't go because they believe they have to "dress up."
* Many elderly people do not attend theater in downtown areas because they believe they will be mugged or robbed.
* Many elderly people will not accept nursing home care because this involves admitting that they are old.
* Many alcoholics avoid treatment because they don't want to admit to themselves that they are alcoholics.
* Some males do not take medication for high blood pressure because they believe it will make them sterile.

* Many uneducated women do not use IUDs because they believe (1) an unexpected baby could be born with the IUD embedded in its body, or (2) the IUD will work its way through their bodies, causing all sorts of unimaginable problems.
* Some organizations won't hire consultants because to do so would be an admission that they lack some competence.
* Sanitary water systems are resisted in some Third World villages because they disrupt established social systems (for example, the twice-daily convening at the village well).
* Many potential theater, ballet, opera, and symphony attenders avoid going because they don't want to feel ignorant about what's being presented.

Costs may be incurred in several forms: (1) *Sacrifices of old ideas, values, or views of the world*—for example, to give up believing in reincarnation, that women are inferior, that abortion is evil (or not evil), that God is vindictive, that you can't be forgiven. (2) *Sacrifices of old patterns of behavior*—for example, to start a daily discipline of prayer and Scripture reading or to attend church services. (3) *Sacrifices of time and energy*—for example, to perform a voluntary service or give blood to a church blood drive.

Once these costs are understood, the marketer can consider the following questions:

1. Are there strategies that can be used to reduce the perceived costs, while still avoiding becoming a purveyor of cheap grace?
2. What will be the effects on a product of reducing or increasing a perceived cost to the consumer?
3. What is the probable response of consumers to given levels of perceived cost reduction?

In summary, consumer responses to offers are usually a reaction to a *bundle* of costs (and, of course, a bundle of benefits). The problem in managing *costs* rather than *a cost* is to figure out *which* of many costs to reduce and *how much* to reduce them—if, indeed, the organization can reduce the costs to the consumer. Often this is not possible for a religious organization, since many perceived costs are not financial or tangible, but rather are psychic and intangible. Yet observations and other research methods (chap. 5) can, over time, provide decision makers with answers to many of the cost-related questions discussed here.

## Distributing the Product: Place

Every organization must think through how it will make its products and services available and accessible to its target consumers. This is the *place*, or *distribution*, decision, and it is one of the key decisions in the marketing mix.

Religious organizations can be thought of as operating a religious service distribution system. Robert Buford and Fred Smith suggest that one way to view the local congregation is as a marketing organization, or as a distribution system. The congregation is the "manufacturer" or originator of its products. Its program departments and ministers comprise its "wholesale" or distribution operation, the workers (Sunday school teachers, ministers, visitors, etc.) function as the "retailers," who come face to face with the "consumers"—the members, potential members, and other users of the congregation's products.

---

### Large Churches as Retailers of Religious Products

Robert Buford of the Leadership Network, a resource group for large churches, uses a distribution model to contrast the nineteenth-century church with the large independent churches emerging at the end of the twentieth century. The early churches, he says, were like a corner grocery store, "serving a blue-collar or agricultural constituency that had little free time, and had one pastor for 200 or fewer people, because that was as many as the pastor could keep up with." As the country changed, the neighborhood church had to make way for what he calls parachurch organizations. Buford compares them to national chain stores, specializing in one part of church work:

the Billy Graham Crusade, focusing on evangelism; Alcoholics Anonymous; youth groups, like the Inter-Varsity Christian Fellowship. The successor to both the small church and the parachurch organization is the large church, which Buford describes as being like a shopping mall. It contains all the specialized ministries of parachurch groups under one roof. It is often suburban, and its members are looking for a sense of community in a place that is often far from where they grew up. These large churches grow, according to Fred Smith of the Leadership Network, because they have identified their business differently. They see themselves as "delivery systems rather than as accumulators of human capital." The aim is to "distribute" ministry in the community rather than merely to get people to come to church. One thing they deliver better than small churches, paradoxically, is intimacy. Large churches are honeycombed with small "retail departments"— sharing groups, discipleship groups—organized around a subject, like caring for small children or growing older.[9]

When planning the distribution system for their products, congregations should pay careful attention to the characteristics of their target consumers and their possible reactions to the products. Some of Willow Creek's church products (Exhibit 8-4) would necessarily be distributed in locations more appropriate to the product type (e.g., a food pantry located in a low-income housing area for disadvantaged residents). The product's characteristics and the target market will combine to suggest the best form for the product's distribution.

## Selection of Physical Facilities

Churches and synagogues must make decisions on the "look" of their facilities, because the facilities' appearance affects how persons see the congregation, its programs and priorities. Charles Sineath, pastor of the megachurch First United Methodist, Marietta, Georgia, said of the influence of the facility's exterior, "Every blade of grass is an evangelist. People see the lawns and gardens before they see the inside of the building."

Churches and synagogues must make decisions on the "look" of their facilities, because the appearance and "feel" of the facilities affect the attitudes persons develop about the congregations, its programs, and its priorities. Church leaders must become skilled in the use of atmospherics. *Atmospherics* describes the conscious designing of space to create or reinforce specific effects on members and other consumers; such as feeling of well-being, safety, intimacy, or awe.[10]

A congregation that is designing a sanctuary for the first time faces four major decisions:

1. *What should the building look like on the outside?* The building can look awe-inspiring, ordinary, or intimate. The decision will be influenced by the type of message the congregation wants to convey about religion in general.
2. *What should be the functional and flow characteristics of the building?*
3. *What should the building feel like on the inside?* Every building conveys a feeling, whether intended or unplanned. The planners have to consider whether the facilities should feel awesome and somber, or bright and modern, or warm and intimate. Each feeling will have a different effect on the parishioners and their overall satisfaction of the services they attend in the building.
4. *What materials would best support the desired feeling of the building?* The feeling of a building is conveyed by visual cues (color, brightness, size, shapes), aural cues (volume, pitch), olfactory cues (scent, freshness), and tactile cues (softness, smoothness, temperature). The planners of the building have to choose colors, fabrics, and furnishings that create or reinforce the desired feeling.

When Doug Anderson (now at First United Methodist Church, Auburn, Indiana) came to serve as pastor of the United Methodist church in Wakarusa, Indiana, he found the church in about the same condition as the name of the little town implies. Wakarusa is an Indian term meaning "knee deep in muck." The congregation was experiencing a period of long decline and much turmoil. He convinced the congregation that it could grow if it would position itself to reach the young couples who were moving into the area. After much discussion, the congregation decided to repair the outdoor sign; tidy up the outside areas; refurbish the entry, the women's restroom, and the nursery; and redecorate the little sanctuary. They did this assuming these were the building areas of greatest concern to the young couple with children. They then began to advertise the church as a place for little children and their parents, including a new community nursery school. In a few weeks, young couples, new to the community, began to attend. The church experienced a significant growth in attendance and membership.

What has been said of the United Methodist churches in Marietta, Georgia (chap. 3), and Wakarusa, Indiana, can be said about dozens of large and small congregations who, in the past few years, have made the important discovery that the design and condition of the facilities either helps or hinders the ministry of the congregation—the effect is perhaps never neutral. The location, condition, cleanliness, smell, colors, acoustics, and so on are marketing decisions, either intentionally or by default.

## Summary

A "product" is anything that can be offered to satisfy a need. Products have value to producers based on their ability to satisfy producer objectives, and to consumers based on their ability to satisfy needs. Products exist at 2 levels. First, there is the "core product," which seeks to answer these questions: What is the consumer really seeking? What need is the product really satisfying? Second, there is the "tangible product," which is the actual ministry or program the organization offers. Failure to distinguish between these 2 levels generally causes a congregation and/or its clergy to misplace loyalties to an outdated tangible product, instead of developing a new tangible product that could do a better job of offering the enduring and unalterable core product's benefits.

A product portfolio should be balanced from 3 perspectives: the mission of the organization, consumer behavior, and resource attraction ability. If a congregation's mission includes several key areas, then products should be offered to address each area. Likewise, products should be offered to satisfy consumer needs at each stage of the process by which consumers are assimilated into the church or synagogue. Also, some balance needs to be achieved between products that absorb or generate resources.

New product development involves the generation and screening of product ideas. Several procedures can be used to generate new product ideas. Once ideas have been generated, they must be screened to winnow the set to the most promising ideas. A formal screening procedure may be helpful in conducting this winnowing.

Religious leaders must not only be able to develop new products but must also understand how those products are adopted by consumers. Administrators need to understand the steps the consumer follows in adopting a new product and how the product's characteristics can influence the rate of adoption.

Exchanges involve giving up something of value in order to obtain something else of value. A perceived cost is any negative outcome of a proposed exchange. Thus, costs may be both economic and non-economic in their consequences. Marketers must understand the nature of these costs to be able to devise strategies that can reduce the perceived costs, know what the cost is to the marketer to reduce costs to the consumer, and know what response will be made by the consumer in response to a reduction in consumer costs.

A church or synagogue may find that different means can and should be used in distributing its products. Also, the clergy and lay officers should be aware of how the atmospherics of their facilities will influence perception and consumption of the products they are offering to target consumers.

Crucial to the success of a marketing plan is the development of the marketing mix—the product, price, place, and promotion components of the organization's offering. This chapter addressed the first 3 components of the mix. The following chapter will focus on the fourth component, promotion.

# 9

# Communicating with Key Publics:

## Advertising and Public Relations

It is important that the preceding chapter, dealing with developing quality programs and ministries, come before this chapter on promotion. Before it undertakes advertising, the church or synagogue must be certain that the product will satisfy the target group's needs and interests.

Nothing will kill a bad product faster than good promotion. *Advertising rule #1: Never advertise or claim what you do not have!* Being effective in making false claims about a product's ability to satisfy a target market's needs will only increase the target group's disappointment with the product and the organization. If a program or ministry can't *deliver* on the promises, don't make the promises.

"It is better that you should not vow than that you should vow and not fulfill it" (Eccles. 5:5) is a good motto for advertisers.

It is a wise principle, therefore, to *market test* a new program or ministry among targeted consumers to ensure that it can deliver value to both the organization and the target group(s). Only after the product has been market tested should a promotional campaign be designed for it. As regarding existing programs and ministries, methodical evaluation should be conducted to assure the program is still of value to the target group(s), and to discover fine-tuning adjustments that will cause the program to deliver even greater satisfaction.

Seven years ago, Second Baptist Church in Houston, Texas, was a small, but affluent, congregation when it called H. Edwin Young as its pastor. Today the congregation of 12,000, known as Fellowship of Excitement, pack the octagonal sanctuary, which is the size of a basketball arena, with a quarter acre of stained glass, a 400-voice choir, and seats for 6,000. The facilities are located on a 32-acre campus.

The secret to its phenomenal growth, according to its staff, is its attention to market research, understanding the demographics of its target groups, its attention to quality, and constant, rigorous evaluation of all its programs, ministries, and workers.

The Reverend Young and his group studied the needs and interests of the area target groups: singles and young families. They compiled a list of characteristics of their target audience:

* They are pragmatic and pressed for time;
* They care passionately about amenities and services;
* They want spotless nurseries for their children, convenient parking, dazzling entertainment;
* They want sermons that are relevant;
* They want services that are suited to their age, culture, and tastes for music, drama, etc.

A spot check of Young's desk found several journals, including *Pulpit Digest, American Demographics,* and *Success.* Young studies these journals to help him understand the environment, needs, and interests of his target publics.

The congregation's first priority is getting people to church, so that they may be introduced to "born-again Christianity." To attract people, the church uses billboards, daily TV broadcasts, and crowd-pleasing events such as an original musical on the writing of the constitution.[1]

Edwin Young and his congregation take marketing seriously in planning the church's ministries. Advertising and public relations are used to communicate their offerings and to establish goodwill in the congregation and the community.

This chapter will examine the role and uses of promotion by religious organizations. It is divided into two sections, dealing with advertising and public relations, respectively.

## Advertising

Not all churches are willing to spend much money on advertising. In contrast to Edwin Young's church, the Willow Creek Community Church in Barrington, Illinois, pays virtually no attention to formal advertising. Less than 1 percent of the budget is spent on advertising. The great difference between these 2 successful churches highlights this question: Should religious organizations advertise?

Whether religious organizations should do marketing is not the question. Religious organizations are *always* doing marketing by attempting to satisfy needs via exchanges with internal and external markets and publics. Religious leaders can, however, choose not to do extensive advertising. In fact, some religious leaders have been outspoken in their criticism of secular advertising, and they have decried its use by any part of their organization.[2] On the other hand, other religious leaders have used bold advertising methods to promote their "product." The following example illustrates the Episcopal Church's advertising approach, which was considered excellent strategy by some and controversial by others.

---

### Admen for Heaven[3]

George Martin's office—the office of Saints Martha and Mary Episcopal Church—is in the basement of a funeral home. Public-school gymnasiums, library auditoriums, and all the other public meeting spaces in Eagan, Minnesota, have been taken by other church-planting efforts. Thus every Sunday, in one of the funeral home's parlors, Martin erects a portable screen on which to hang a cross and a banner in order to help the brand-new 90-member congregation feel as if it has gone to church.

In addition to his job as vicar, Martin is also executive director of the Episcopal Ad Project, a high-quality, but low budget, effort to get the attention of the unchurched. Appropriately, in a recent ad the vicar of this funeral-home church appeared as one of a half-dozen pall bearers carrying a casket. The headline of the ad read, "Will it take six strong men to bring you back into the church?" The fine print explained that the church welcomes everyone, "no matter what condition you're in, but we'd really prefer to see you breathing."

Tom McElligott's office—the office of the ad agency that produces Martin's church ads—is in downtown Minneapolis, 18 miles from Martin's mortuary meeting space. The Fallon McElligott agency occupies the fifteenth and sixteenth floors of a blue steel-and-glass building. On its walls, ads for Bloomingdale's, the *Wall Street Journal,* and Lee jeans are mixed in with the more socially conscious *pro bono* work they have done for the Children's Defense Fund and the Episcopal Ad Project.

"We're trying to stop people with these ads," McElligott says of the Episcopal Church promotions. "We're trying to make them open up their mental boxes. This is the first step in opening the possibility of regular church attendance."

The laid-back McElligott, relaxed in a green gingham-checked shirt and khakis, says he particularly enjoys beginning the ad brainstorming process with a piece of classical religious art. McElligott takes Titian's portrayal of Daniel in the lion's den as an example. "People have closed their minds to that art. But by pulling it out of its original context and giving it a contemporary point of reference, we've made it meaningful again. Although," admits McElligott sheepishly, "I'm not sure I'd want to explain that to Titian."

What McElligott and Martin saw in Titian's painting was stress. Like the biblical Daniel, Christians have often been at odds with conventional values and have had to live with stress—and help each other cope. So Martin and McElligott put a headline above the painting: "Contrary to conventional wisdom, stress is not a twentieth-century phenomenon."

Likewise, the television ads by the Church of Latter-Day Saints have been praised by many, but not all, critics. Should religious organizations advertise their product, or does the use of advertising somehow diminish the very product it seeks to promote? William Lynch, a Jesuit expert on literacy images, suggests: "Nothing is more sacred than the intentions of life of man, and nothing is more offensive to the religious instinct than that this interior life should be twisted and maneuvered as though it were a vulgar, unimportant thing."[4]

It is our contention that it is not the *act* of promotion that "twists and maneuvers" religion. Rather the *way* in which a religious product is promoted determines whether the end result confers honor or ignominy on the advertiser and his or her product. Religious writers have commented that promotion does not, per se, go against scripture from the Bible[5] or the Talmud.[6]

In a sense, almost all religious organizations do some promotion, since a listing in the yellow pages or an outdoor sign with a sermon title on it constitutes promotion. Consider the following "promotion" at the bottom of the front page of the Friday, June 15, 1990, *New York Times:* "JEWISH WOMEN/GIRLS Remember to light

Shabbat candles 18 minutes before sunset. In NYC 8:09 PM. Information call 718-774-2060."

Martin Marty makes this point: "Who is kidding whom? Religious advertising goes on all the time. A religious group that offers no presentation of itself in a competitive, complex society will go undiscovered—or if it is already known, it will wane and disappear. The question is not 'Will churches advertise?' but 'How?' "[7]

Most clergy seem to agree that religious advertising is appropriate and necessary. In fact, a survey of 1,000 clergy and 1,250 members of the general population revealed that, if anything, clergy are more favorably disposed toward religious advertising than is the general populace.[8]

## Advertising Methods

The religious marketer has a large number of methods available for carrying a message to a target audience. There are 5 main methods.[9]

**1. Paid Advertising** is any paid form of nonpersonal presentation and promotion of an offer by an identified sponsor through a formal communications medium.

Paid advertising permits total control over encoded message content and over the nature of the medium, plus substantial control of the scheduling of the message (and therefore its specific environment). On the other hand, paid advertising permits no control over message decoding by the audience and little (or, at best, lagged) feedback on the received message.

**2. Unpaid (public service) advertising** is any form of advertising in which space or time for the placement of the advertisement is free.

Marketer control is similar to that with paid advertising, except that there is very little control over the scheduling of the message. Many public service radio or television advertisements appear after midnight or on Sunday mornings, when the audience is small and the media have unsold spots.

**3. Sales promotion** is short-term incentives to encourage the purchase or sale of a product or service, or the performance of a behavior. Marketer control is substantial, although the "message," or the "meaning" attached to the specific promotion by the receiver is not controllable.

**4. Publicity** is nonpersonal stimulation of demand for an offering by securing the reporting of commercially significant news about the offer in a published medium or on radio, television, or the stage that is not paid for by the sponsor. Here, the marketer's control over message encoding and the medium varies, depending on whether journalists will use and revise the message. Some feedback is possible from journalists or from selected target audiences.

**5. Personal selling** is oral presentation of information about an offering in a conversation with one or more prospective target audience members for the purpose of securing a desired exchange.

In personal selling, the organization has less control over encoding—that is, what the salesperson actually says. The salesperson, however, has excellent opportunities to secure feedback on how the message is being received. According to this definition, sometimes a religious organization's leader or members will function as a salesperson when engaged in conversation with a prospective new member.

There are five major steps in developing an advertising program. They are detailed in Exhibit 9-1 and described below.

**Exhibit 9-1**

## MAJOR DECISIONS IN ADVERTISING MANAGEMENT

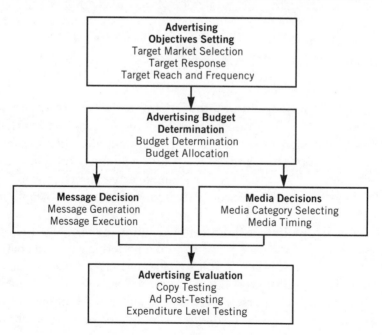

## Deciding on the Advertising Objectives

Before an advertising program and budget can be developed, advertising objectives must be set. These objectives must flow from prior decision making on the target market, market positioning, and marketing mix. The marketing strategy defines advertising's job in the total marketing mix.

Developing advertising objectives calls for defining the target market, target response, and target reach and frequency.

### Target Market Selection

A marketing communicator must start with a clear target audience in mind. The audience may be potential new members, current members, or key publics. The audience may consist of individuals or groups. The target audience has a crucial influence on the communicator's decisions on *what* to say, *how* to say it, *when* to say it, *where* to say it, and *who* should say it.

Consider this in terms of Hope United Methodist Church, described in chapter 7. Suppose the church seeks to reach the unchurched young families with children located in Valparaiso, Indiana, based on the planning committee's assessment of market opportunity and the congregation's strengths and mission. Young couples with children, therefore, constitute 1 target market for the church.

### Target Response

Once the target audience has been identified, the marketing communicator must define the target response that is sought. In this particular example, the Hope Church ultimately wants the targeted families to become a part of the Hope Church family. Any member of the target audience may be in 1 of 6 *consumer readiness states* with respect to the church or its members. These states—*awareness, knowledge, liking, preference, conviction,* and *action*—are described in the following paragraphs.[10]

**1. Awareness.** The first thing to establish is how aware the target audience is of the product (program, ministry, church, etc.). The audience may be completely unaware of the product, know only its name or 1 or 2 things about it. If most of the target audience is unaware, the communicator's task is to build awareness, perhaps just name recognition. This calls for simple messages repeating the name. Even then, building awareness takes time.

The Hope United Methodist Church may be unknown to most of the young families, particularly those families who have just moved to Valparaiso. Some inexpensive marketing research can help determine their level of awareness. Hope may set as its objective making 70 percent of the young families aware of the Hope Church's name within one year.

**2. Knowledge.** The target audience may be aware of the product but may not know much about it. In this case the communicator's goal is to transmit some key information. Thus Hope Church may want its audience to know that it is a young, friendly church, with programs (products) that address the needs of young families. Following its advertising campaign, Hope Church can sample the target audience to measure whether they have little, some, or much knowledge of Hope Church, and to assess the content of their knowledge.

**3. Liking.** If the target audience members know the product, the next question is How do they feel about it? We can imagine a scale covering a range of responses such as *dislike very much, dislike somewhat, indifferent, like somewhat,* and *like very much.* If the audience has an unfavorable view of Hope Church, the communicator has to find out why, and then develop a communications program to build up favorable feelings. If the unfavorable view is rooted in real inadequacies of the church (e.g., promoted as friendly, but when an interested prospect called the office she was treated rudely), then a communications campaign would not do the job and might make matters worse. The church would have to first improve and become the kind of congregation it claims to be, and then communicate this reality-based image.

**4. Preference.** The target audience may like the product, but may not prefer it over others. It may be one of several acceptable products available to the target audience. In this case the communicator's job is to build consumer preference. The communicator will have to tout its quality, value, performance, and other attributes. In the case of the Hope Church, it faces not only other churches, but also other generic competitors (i.e., other ways of spending time besides attending church services). This will influence the choice of messages intended to build preference for Hope over the alternative products. The communicator can check on the success of the campaign by subsequently surveying the audience to see if its preference has grown stronger.

**5. Conviction.** A target audience may prefer a particular object, but may not develop a conviction about entering into an exchange with it. Thus some young families might prefer Hope to other churches, but never can get themselves out of bed in time on Sunday to make it to church. The communicator's job is to build the conviction that going to church is the right thing to do. This requires an understanding of the *benefits* and *perceived costs* from the *consumer's viewpoint.* Hope Church must figure out how to generate conviction among its target audience that attending worship and Sunday school is the best thing they can do on a Sunday morning.

**6. Action.** Some target audience members may have conviction, but may not act. They may be waiting for additional information, may plan to act later, and so on. In this situation, a communicator must lead the consumer to take the final step, which is called "closing the exchange." Among the action-producing devices are offering an incentive (e.g., the welcome dinner), offering an opportunity to try the object on a limited basis (e.g., Willow Creek's Wednesday evening worship service), and other means of inducing an urgency to act.

This model assumes that persons pass through a hierarchy of states-of-readiness on the way to making a response decision to an offer. The communicator's task is to identify the stage that most of the target audience is in, and develop a communication message or campaign that will move them to the next stage.

It would be efficient if one message could move the audience through all stages, but this rarely happens. Most communicators seek a cost-effective communication approach to move the target audience one stage at a time. The critical thing is to know where the main audience is and what the next feasible stage is.

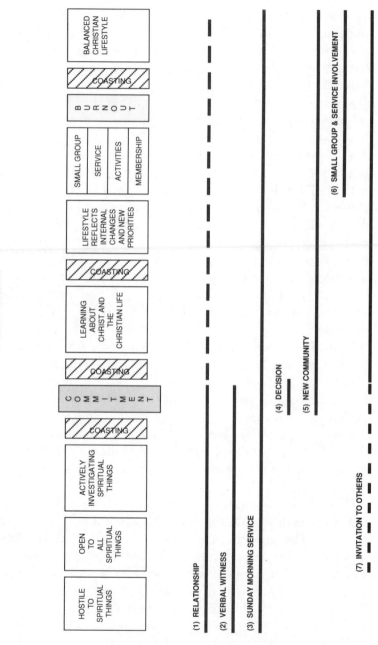

**STAGES OF SPIRITUAL GROWTH and the 7 STEP PHILOSOPHY OF MINISTRY OF WILLOW CREEK**

HOSTILE TO SPIRITUAL THINGS

OPEN TO ALL SPIRITUAL THINGS

ACTIVELY INVESTIGATING SPIRITUAL THINGS

COASTING

COMMITMENT

COASTING

LEARNING ABOUT CHRIST AND THE CHRISTIAN LIFE

COASTING

LIFESTYLE REFLECTS INTERNAL CHANGES AND NEW PRIORITIES

SMALL GROUP
SERVICE
ACTIVITIES
MEMBERSHIP

BURNOUT

COASTING

BALANCED CHRISTIAN LIFESTYLE

(1) RELATIONSHIP

(2) VERBAL WITNESS

(3) SUNDAY MORNING SERVICE

(4) DECISION

(5) NEW COMMUNITY

(6) SMALL GROUP & SERVICE INVOLVEMENT

(7) INVITATION TO OTHERS

**Exhibit 9-2**

Willow Creek Community Church has developed a 7-step philosophy called "Stages of Spiritual Growth," which is their way of describing the stages persons pass through in their spiritual development (see Exhibit 9-2). The model identifies seven stages, from being "Hostile to Spiritual Things" to adopting a "Balanced Christian Lifestyle." The leaders of the congregation use this model to track the growth of their parishioners and to inform the types of messages and experiences the person(s) should be receiving at each growth stage. Not only does this model suggest that different products are needed to meet the person's needs at different stages, but such a hierarchical model also assists in the planning of specific objectives for communications and advertising.

Saddleback Valley Community Church has also developed its unique model for understanding the hierarchy of states of readiness they see their parishioners passing through in their spiritual development. The religious organization's leaders have developed their ministry plan to move persons through the hierarchy of stages, and to inform their internal and external communications and advertising.

A careful study of the stages of growth models developed by the 2 churches makes it easy to understand that various advertising objectives can be developed for each stage—on the basis of whether their aim is to inform, persuade, or remind.[11]

The *inform* category includes such advertising objectives as telling the market about a new product, pointing out the benefits of a different religious behavior, informing the market of a "cost" change, explaining how the benefits of a ministry can be obtained, describing various available programs, correcting false impressions, reducing fears, and building an image. See Exhibits 9-3A and 9-3B for examples of *informative* church advertising.

The *persuade* category includes such advertising objectives as building preference for a synagogue's offering, encouraging switching to the advertiser's institution, trying to change the person's perception of the importance of different behavior attributes, persuading the member to act now, and persuading the unchurched person to receive a "sales call" (visit by clergy or layperson). See Exhibit 9-4A and 9-4B for examples of *persuasive* religious organization advertising.

**Exhibit 9-3A**
**INFORMATIVE ADVERTISING**

# The Episcopal Church welcomes you. Regardless of race, creed, color or the number of times you've been born.

Whether you've been born once or born again, the Episcopal Church invites you to come and join us in the fellowship and worship of Jesus Christ.
**The Episcopal Church**

**Exhibit 9-3B**
**INFORMATIVE ADVERTISING**

# Contrary to conventional wisdom, stress is not a 20th century phenomenon.

The Episcopal Church can't promise an end to stress. But we can promise to help you live better with stress through the love, support and fellowship of Jesus Christ. Come join us this Sunday.
**The Episcopal Church**

**Exhibit 9-4A**
**INFORMATIVE ADVERTISING**

# 2000 years later, Christianity's biggest competition is still the Lions.

Before you sit down for an afternoon with the Lions, Bears, Dolphins, Rams, Cowboys or Vikings, come spend an hour with some very nice Christians in the love, worship and fellowship of Jesus Christ.
**The Lutheran Church**

**Exhibit 9-4B**
**INFORMATIVE ADVERTISING**

# For fast, fast, fast relief take two tablets.

In the Episcopal Church, we believe that some of the oldest ideas are still the best.
Like the regular worship of God. Come join us as we celebrate this Sunday.
**The Episcopal Church**

The *remind* category includes such advertising objectives as reminding persons that the religious organization will be there when they need it in the future, putting the person in touch with earlier religious inclinations, and keeping the organization in their minds during "off-seasons." (Off-seasons for some is any time other than religious holidays!) See Exhibit 9-5 for examples of *reminder* religious organization advertising.

### Exhibit 9-5A
### REMINDER ADVERTISING

# Will it take six strong men to bring you back into the church?

The Lutheran Church welcomes you no matter what condition you're in, but we'd really prefer to see you breathing. Come join us in the love, worship and fellowship of Jesus Christ this Sunday.
**The Lutheran Church**

**Exhibit 9-5B**
**REMINDER ADVERTISING**

# Remember this tune from your childhood?

It's "Jesus loves me, this I know," and he still does, you know.
Come, bring your family, and begin getting acquainted with Him again this Sunday.
**The Lutheran Church**

*Target Reach and Frequency*

The third decision that must be made is determining the optimal *target reach and frequency* of the advertising. Funds for advertising are rarely so abundant that everyone in the target audience can be reached, and reached with sufficient frequency. Religious marketers must decide what percentage of the audience to reach with what exposure frequency per period.

Hope Church, for example, might decide to use direct mail, and decide on 500 advertising exposures. This leaves a wide choice available concerning target reach and frequency. Hope could send 1 letter to 500 different families, or it could send 2 different letters a week apart to 250 families, and so on. The issue is how much exposure is needed to create the desired response, given the market's (the target group) state of readiness. One exposure could be enough to move the targeted families from being unaware to being aware. It would not be enough to move families from awareness to preference.

## Determining the Advertising Budget

Suppose Hope Church wants to send 2 letters to each of 250 families. The gross number of exposures would be 500. Suppose that the average mailing piece will cost $.50 to design and mail. Then Hope Church will need a rough advertising budget of $250 to accomplish its objectives.

In addition to estimating the total amount of the required advertising budget, a determination must be made regarding how the budget should be allocated over different market segments, geographical areas, and time periods. In practice, advertising budgets are allocated to segments of demand according to their respective populations or response levels or in accordance with some other indicator of market potential (e.g., the presence of young families). It is common to spend twice as much advertising money in segment B as in segment A if segment B has twice the level of some indicator of market potential (e.g., young families without a church home). How does one know whether 1 segment has twice as much potential for a positive response as another segment?

In some cases, this judgment comes from experience—trial and error estimates of what works best with specific groups. Therefore, doing a bulk mailing to every home in census tract A vs. census tract B makes sense if it is believed there are more young families in census tract A, and if there is reason to believe young families will respond favorably to the promotion of the "product" designed with young families in mind. Geodemographics helps greatly in making such assumptions (see chap. 6).

## Developing the Message

Once the religious marketer has determined the objectives for the advertising program and established an advertising budget, the next step is to develop specific messages. Message generation involves developing a number of alternative messages (appeals, themes, motifs, ideas) from which the best one can be chosen.

In principle, the message that is desired to be communicated about the ministry (product, program, service) should be decided when the ministry was developed. If, as described in chapters 7 and 8, a specific ministry has been developed for a specific targeted group with a specific objective in mind which permits our mission to be achieved, there should already be a basic theme or appeal in mind for the ministry. Even so, there are a variety of messages which could be developed around this basic theme.

### Generating the Message

Messages can be generated in a number of ways. One approach is to talk with members of the target market and other influential parties to determine how they see the ministry or service, talk about it, and express their desires about it. A second approach is to hold a brainstorming meeting with laypeople in the church to generate several ideas. A third method is to use some formal deductive framework to tease out possible advertising messages. We will discuss one such framework—the rational, emotional, moral framework.

This framework identifies 3 types of messages that can be generated: rational, emotional, and moral.

**Rational messages** aim at passing on information, serving the audience's self-interest, or both. They attempt to show that the product will yield the expected benefits. Examples would be messages discussing a product's value or performance. In the case of the Hope Church, these might involve telling targeted young parents about how children will enjoy learning about the Bible via the children's Sunday school classes, which focus on famous Bible characters.

**Emotional messages** are designed to stir up some negative or positive emotion that will motivate the desired behavior. Communicators have worked with fear, guilt, and shame appeals, especially in connection with getting people to start doing things they should do (e.g., attend church, hold a church office) or stop doing things they shouldn't do (e.g., smoke, overimbibe, abuse drugs, or overeat). Advertisers have found that fear appeals work up to a point, but if there is too much fear the audience will ignore the message. Communicators have also used positive emotional appeals such as love, humor, pride, and joy. Evidence has not, however, established that a humorous message, for example, is necessarily more effective than a straight version of the same message. An emotional appeal for the Hope Church targeting young families might be showing a young family at worship with a message suggesting that family cohesiveness is enhanced by the bond of a common faith.

**Moral messages** are directed to the audience's sense of what is right and proper. They are often used in messages exhorting people to support such social causes as a cleaner environment, better race relations, equal rights for women, and aiding the disadvantaged. A moral appeal for the Hope Church might focus on the need for parents to instill a strong sense of values based on biblical principles in their children to better ensure their future happiness and contribution to society.

## Executing the Message

Once the basic message has been generated it must find a style of execution. That is, a *style, tone, wording, order,* and *format* must be found to make the message effective.

Any message can be put across in different *execution styles*. Suppose a denomination is planning to launch a national campaign to get people to read their Bibles and wants to develop a 30-second television commercial to motivate people to start reading their Bibles and having family worship. Here are some major advertising execution styles they can consider:

1. *Slice of life.* A wife suggests to her husband that they might end the day right if they could contemplate some Bible passages together. He agrees, and the next frame shows them talking together on the couch with the TV off and an open Bible in front of them.
2. *Life-style.* A 30-year-old man pops out of bed when his alarm rings at 6:00 A.M., races to the bathroom, races to the closet, races through breakfast, then slows down to take a few moments to read his Bible, then drives to work with a peaceful look on his face.
3. *Fantasy.* Parents read Bible stories to their children with the children imagine being in the lions' den or sitting on the lap of Jesus.
4. *Mood.* A jogger runs in a residential neighborhood on a beautiful spring day, noticing the beauty of nature. We hear Bible verses he is reciting to himself, which he read that morning from the book of Psalms, about God's handiwork. This ad creates a mood of beauty and harmony of humans with God's creation.
5. *Musical.* Ad depicts a family singing hymns around the family piano with great joy and gusto.
6. *Personality symbol.* A well-known sports hero is shown reading his Bible with a smile on his face.
7. *Technical expertise.* A seminary professor or librarian discusses the variety of study Bibles currently available.
8. *Testimonial evidence.* The ad shows a variety of family members from different ethnic backgrounds telling how beneficial studying the Bible has been for them.

The communicator must also choose a *tone* for the message. The message could be deadly serious, chatty, humorous, and so on. The tone must be appropriate to the target audience and target response desired.

*Words* that are memorable and attention-getting must be found. This is nowhere more apparent than in the development of head-lines and slogans to lead the reader into the message. There are 6 basic types of headlines: news, questions, narrative, command, 1-2-3 ways, and how-what-why.

The Hope Church, seeking to attract young families to their "Wel-come to Your New Home" dinner, might develop headlines using each of these styles.

> *News:* "The Hope Church has been welcoming new neighbors to Valparaiso for years. Just listen to these glowing reports. . . . "
>
> *Questions:* "Why are these young families taking time from busy schedules to share a meal with strangers?"
>
> *Narrative:* "The Campbell family didn't know a soul when they moved to Valparaiso, but that quickly changed when they attended a fellowship dinner last Wednesday night."
>
> *Command:* "You've always said you wanted to get to know your new community. Well, do it now and get a free meal in the bargain."
>
> *1-2-3 ways:* "We have scheduled our fellowship dinners during different times to make it easy to get to know you."
>
> *How-what-why:* "Getting to know your new community can begin tomorrow if you accept our invitation to meet your neighbors over dinner at the Hope Church."

Once the headline and the themes are determined, the communi-cator must consider the ordering of the ideas. There are 3 issues: con-clusion drawing, 1- or 2-sided arguments, and order of presentation.

The first is the question of *conclusion drawing*, the extent to which the ad should draw a definite conclusion for the audience, such as telling them to "give their fair share." Experimental research seems to indicate that explicit conclusion drawing is more persuasive than leaving it to the audience to draw their own conclusions. There are exceptions, however, such as when the communicator is seen as untrustworthy or the audience is highly intelligent and annoyed at the attempt to influence them.

The second is the question of the *1- or 2-sided argument*—that is, whether the message will be more effective if 1 side or both sides of the argument are presented. Two-sided arguments are of 2 types. First, there is the approach that admits that the offering has some defects. The classic example of this approach is the series of ads for the Volkswagen Beetle that admitted it was homely and that it didn't change its looks every model year, but that otherwise it was a marvelously sensible purchase. In the religious sector, there are many situations in which the target audience will know there is a negative side to a requested behavior:

* Potential tithers *know* they are committing scarce financial resources on a regular basis to the church.
* Attendees to a midweek prayer service *know* they are giving up leisure time and the comforts of home to attend.
* Potential blood donors to the church blood drive *know* the needle will hurt and that they might feel faint.
* People who are asked to hold a church office *know* they will have to devote time to carrying out those duties and may have to ask (beg, cajole, implore) others to carry out some responsibilities.
* Prospective new members *know* that giving up drinking or dancing to become new members will be a difficult change to make in their behavior.
* People *know* that being asked to observe the Sabbath means a major change in the way they spend their time on weekends.

The other kind of 2-sided argument recognizes the fact that there are other alternatives. The burger and cola "wars" are message campaigns that fully recognize that there are tough competitors "out there." In the religious sector, there are many parallel situations:

* Going to Sunday school means not being able to sleep in after being out late Saturday night.
* Paying tithes may mean not giving to the American Cancer Society or a university's alumni fund.
* Going to a church officers' meeting means not going bowling.
* Your child's choosing not to have sex before marriage means enduring the taunts of his or her peers.

* Not using artificial means of birth control means possibly having the economic pressures of a large family.

One-sided presentations are common in both the profit and religious sectors. They are often synonymous with what many would call a hard-sell approach. Yet social science research suggests that 1-sided approaches may be relatively more effective in 3 situations: (1) when the audience is less educated; (2) when the audience already favors the message's central proposition; and (3) when the audience is not likely to be exposed later to counterpropaganda. Two-sided messages are said to be more effective when the opposite is true.

There is another, perhaps more compelling, factor that should influence whether 2-sided messages are used. It is the degree of the audience's involvement in the behavior that the marketer is attempting to influence. In general, we would argue the following: the higher the audience's involvement in the behavior, the more frequently the religious marketer should use 2-sided messages.

There are several reasons for this. In high-involvement situations, target audience members are more likely to

* be very concerned about the costs of the behavior (see chaps. 4 and 8);
* be opposed to the action advocated, if it means change;
* be aware of very attractive alternatives.

In high-involvement situations, the target audience will engage in extensive internal cognitive activity, which will include considering costs and alternatives. They will engage in an extensive external search that will make available to them the "other side" of the argument. The religious communicator should seize the initiative and deal with the other side of the issue rather than leave it to the individual. A useful concept in this regard is what is called *inoculation theory*. If a communicator knows that a target audience member will *later* be exposed to counterpropaganda (the other side), a more favorable outcome will be achieved if the religious communicator deals with the counterarguments in advance, in effect "inoculating" the target audience against the later influence attempts.

Finally, it must be reemphasized that in situations in which a 2-sided strategy would be appropriate, the religious communicator must go to great lengths to understand what *the target audience* perceives to be the key costs of the behavior and what *they* consider to be the reasonable alternative. Only with a solid research base can an effective 2-sided strategy be developed.

A third issue for the communicator in cases where several ideas are to be conveyed is the best *order of presentation.* Social scientists have found that, other things being equal, people tend to remember the items in a message stream presented first (the primacy effect) and last (the recency effect). There are arguments for putting one's strongest statements in either position. Where one is using a 2-sided message, the case is more complex. However, the following approach appears reasonable.

1. If the audience is likely to attend to the message under most circumstances (that is, not filter it out), it is probably best to place the message about the "other side" in the middle of the message where it is more likely to be forgotten and the arguments for one's own position in the first and last position.
2. If the audience is opposed to the message and likely to screen it out, then beginning with the other side of the issue or with the other alternative may disarm the audience into "hearing' the marketer's message. Thus a religious marketer might say, "A night at home with the family watching TV by a warm fire would be great this winter. But the Hope Church has some good reasons for you to consider other pleasures."

*Format elements* can make a difference in an ad's impact, as well as in its cost. If the message is to be carried in a print ad, the communicator must develop the elements of headline, copy, illustration, and color. Advertisers are adept at using such attention-getting devices as *novelty, contrast, arresting pictures,* and *movement.* Large ads, for example, gain more attention, and so do 4-color ads, and this must be weighed against their higher costs. If the message is to be carried over the radio, the communicator must carefully choose words, voice qualities (speech rate, rhythm, pitch, articulation), and vocalizations (pauses, sighs, yawns). If the message is to be carried out on TV or given in person, then all of these elements, plus body language (non-verbal clues) must be planned. Presenters need to pay attention to their facial expressions, gestures, dress, posture, and hairstyle.

As we have already noted, individuals have a substantial background of experiences, categorization schemes, prejudices, association, needs, wants, and fears that can markedly affect what they "see" or "hear" in the message.

This potential for distortion can work to the communicator's advantage. Messages can be relatively economical in what they say by using association that they know people will bring to a symbol, a word, or an example. For example, readers need to see only 1 of these symbols depicted in an ad to know that a restaurant is *not* a fast-food outlet: a tablecloth, flowers on the table, silverware, a waiter taking an order, candles or subdued lighting, upholstered chairs, wine glasses, or china. Someone with glasses is supposed to be smarter than someone without them. Colors have symbolism: White is pure; gold is rich; blue is soothing; pastels are "modern"; and so on.

This is a major advantage to communicators. The problem, of course, is to choose the right symbols and to be assured that your audience sees them as you do. While the religious marketer should carefully plan the choice of association, one advantage of personal communication is that a sensitive communicator can secure feedback on how the message is actually preceived and fine-tune it so that it is perceived as intended.

Even if a message is perceived in an appropriate fashion, this does not guarantee that it will be retained or, more important, recalled at the moment it is "needed" to influence a particular behavior. One technique to reduce this possibility is, of course, repetition. Research has suggested that up to 3 repetitions will improve the probability of retention under high-involvement conditions. Another technique is to link the new information to existing cognition. Individuals are more likely to recall things that they can assimilate well.

### Selecting the Media

Once the advertising budget and message have been set for a given market segment, region, and time period, the next task is to allocate this budget across media categories and vehicles. There are

2 basic steps in the media selection process: (1) choosing among major media categories and (2) timing.

## Choosing Among Major Media Categories

The first step calls for allocating the advertising budget to the major *media categories*. These categories must be examined for their capacity to deliver reach, frequency, and impact. Exhibit 9-6 presents profiles of the major advertising media. In order of their advertising volume, they are newspapers, television, direct mail, radio, magazines, and outdoor. Religious marketers choose among these major media categories by considering the following variables.

1. *Target audience media habits.* For example, radio and television are the most effective media for reaching teenagers.
2. *Product or service.* Media categories have different potentialities for demonstration, visualization, explanation, believability, and color.
3. *Message.* A message announcing an emergency blood drive tomorrow requires radio or newspapers. A message containing a great deal of technical data might require specialized magazines or direct mailings. Messages that would benefit from consumers adding their own inputs might be most effective on the radio.
4. *Cost.* Television is very expensive, and newspaper advertising is inexpensive. What counts, of course, is the cost per thousand relevant exposures, rather than the total cost. That is, if one media cost $80 and reaches 5,000 members of the target audience (cost per thousand = 1.6¢), and another costs $70 and reaches 3,500 (cost per thousand = 2.0¢), then the more expensive medium is the "better buy."

The organization's leaders must decide how to allocate its advertising budget to the major media categories.

**Newspapers.** Newspapers have been a traditional tool of religious advertisers, perhaps because of the relatively low cost, and because other religious marketers seem to use the media. Newspaper advertising has the following features of interest to religious advertisers:

*1. Flexibility.* Ad placement, change, or cancellation can be done at relatively short notice. Also, for a small charge newspapers allow the organization to select the page or section where the ad will run. The church or synagogue should make these decisions based on its target market; if the organization is trying to reach the unchurched, it should not run the ad in the religious section.

*2. Timeliness.* The speed with which ads can be placed and the frequency of ad exposure combine to make newspaper ads a good option. However, a newspaper's "short life" (1 day or 1 weekend) can be a disadvantage.

*3. Production simplicity.* This can be both an advantage to the novice who needs the newspaper's production department to aid in the development of the ad and a disadvantage to the advertiser needing a sharp reproduction of a graphic.

*4. Good coverage.* The broad distribution of many local newspapers means that generally a high percentage of large population segments will be exposed to the ad.

---

When the ministry team at Salem First Nazarene launched their new ministry programs for singles, divorced persons, and children of single-parent households, they initially had very little response. After 3 disappointing months they asked themselves 3 questions: Did we misread the community and its needs (poor situation analysis)? Did we plan poor programs (poor product planning)? Are we failing to get our message to the right people (poor targeting)? They decided they had indeed listened to the community and that their programs were responsive to the needs. They decided they must not be getting the message to the target audience.

At that time the congregation was utilizing 3 modes of communicating with the community: the religious TV channel, its own radio programs, and the religion section of the newspaper. The decision was made not to advertise over the TV channel, nor to announce the programs on their own radio programs, nor to continue advertising in the religion section of the newspaper. Rather, they would run advertisements in the newspaper's sports and entertainment sections. Almost immediately large numbers of persons who were singles by choice, divorced persons, and children of single-parent households began to participate in the programs.

**Television.** This medium can be very expensive for a small congregation. No other medium, however, has the ability to reach as many people as fast and with the high sensory appeal as does TV. Religious organizations contemplating television advertising must consider several factors: channels, costs of spot ads, number of times the ads will be run, and costs and types of creative approaches. We can all cite examples of local ads that were either very effective or bordering on the offensive and infantile.

Using spot ads on local stations or on cable can be a forceful means of getting the message to a target audience, but religious marketers should be aware of the requirements for effective television advertisements before making such an investment.[12]

The VCR may revolutionize the television set as a way to reach members in their homes. Denominations are issuing news, special programs, and messages through this medium.

**Radio.** Radio stations should be considered on the basis of the audience they reach. Some of the advantages of radio advertising are:

*1. Target marketing.* Radio programming has increasingly segmented the listening audience. For example, where a station may have previously been known as a "rock" station, now there is "hard rock" for teenagers, "progressive" rock for college students, "soft" rock for the over-30 crowd, and "classic" rock for those in their late 30s and early 40s. Advertisers can "rifle" their message to sub-segments of the population more effectively with radio than "shotgunning" with a more mass audience media, like newspapers.

*2. Flexibility.* Radio ads can be placed or changed on relatively short notice. This could be of value to take advantage of fast-changing market or environmental conditions, such as messages of hope or inspiration when a local disaster strikes, messages of joy for local good news, and so on.

*3. Urgency and Frequency.* The use of sound can help convey a better sense of urgency to a message. Also, radio messages can reach target audience members more frequently than can some other media.

*4. Cost.* Radio advertising can generate low cost per thousand people reached (CPM).

**Direct Mail.** A medium increasingly being used by nonprofit organizations is direct mail. Novelli has suggested that direct mail has 6 important advantages for nonprofit organizations:[13]

1. It tends to be very focused; it can achieve maximum impact on a specific target market.

2. It can be private and confidential, a major advantage for religious organizations, whose spiritual messages are often perceived as very personal matters.

3. Cost per contact and cost per response can often be very low, which is an important appeal to religious organizations with very low budgets.

4. Results are quite often clearly measurable, and this can help make marketing programs more accountable. The Hope Church can learn very specifically the effectiveness of a direct mail piece that offers free literature to those who send in a response card, or by counting the number of families who visit the church as a result of the direct mailing.

5. Small-scale tests of proposed strategies are very feasible with direct mail. In fact, direct mail is an ideal field-test vehicle. A number of marketing factors can be varied over several mailings and the results compared to baseline measures. In tests of other media, it is often difficult to link a specific surge in response to, say, a flight of radio advertisements. By contrast, if more literature requests come in from those who receive a mailing with a message about "how to achieve peace of mind" than from those who are offered literature on "what happens when you die," it is easy to conclude that a "peace of mind" message works best.

6. The effectiveness of direct mail can be assessed directly in terms of *behavior* (for example, requests and inquiries), whereas other media assessments usually require attitude and awareness indicators, which, as discussed earlier, are fraught with measurement problems.

There are several steps in establishing a strategically effective direct mail campaign.

1. *Determine the objectives of direct mail programs in advance.* Is the program to generate behavior, create awareness, change attitudes, or make contacts to be followed up through other media? In some cases, a phased strategy is appropriate, in which earlier mailers are used to develop awareness and later mailers to generate action.

2. *Determine the target audience.* Some groups are more responsive to direct mail than are others. Refer to one of the direct mail

books listed in Appendix A for examples of response rate differences by population groups.

*3. Develop mail lists.* Outside services can be the source of highly tailored prospect lists defined by schooling; occupation area; socio-economic status of the neighborhood; patronage of particular products, services, or outlets; and so on. Whenever time permits, new rented lists should be tested with small mailings to see if they are productive before a modest budget is committed to an unknown target list. The best lists, however, are always those containing the addresses of people with whom the organization already has some form of contact. Thus the best prospects are those who have responded to past mailings, who have made inquiries in some other fashion, or who have visited the church or synagogue on some occasion. The geodemographic firms listed in Exhibit 6-5 can provide mailing lists for selected geodemographic segments.

*4. Develop effective copy.* Investment in effective graphics and compelling messages is seldom wasted. Direct mail pieces are meeting more and more competition every day in the "mail box arena." The religious organization needs powerful messages and compelling visual images to stand out. Attention must be paid to envelope design (to get the message exposed), the cover letter (to get it read), and motivational themes (to get it acted on). Many mailings fail because they are not consciously designed to stimulate responses.

*5. Pretest each mailer.* This can be done inexpensively and, if sample target audience members are used, can both indicate probable successes and point up potential problems.

*6. Schedule mailings carefully.* Some mailings have predetermined timings (i.e., for particular events). In those cases, the mailings should arrive just as the evaluation stage of consumer decision making is taking place. Thus mailings for church events are best when sent 6 to 8 weeks before the event. They are seldom effective in the last week unless they are targeted to an impulse-based audience. When the timing of mailings is discretionary, the marketer should carefully test different patterns, for example, with mailings bunched together in *flights* (a grouping of mailings, released at one time) or spread out over time.

*7. Use responses as feedback.* The savvy direct mailer learns from each mailing what works or doesn't work in the mailing design itself.

If a systematic program of experimentation is used over the years, much can be learned about effective tactics for particular audiences. Mail responses can also tell something about the responder.

As Tom McCabe of International Marketing Group notes: "You know exactly who responds and why. . . . Every time someone responds to a mailing, you learn something about that person. Direct marketing is very efficient because eventually you will be able to know what kind of return to expect on every marketing dollar you spend."[14]

**Telemarketing.** Among the newest media tools used by religious organizations today is telemarketing—and it is producing much success. Telemarketing is employed to start new congregations and new Sunday school classes, to invite persons to attend existing programs, to announce a new program, and so on.

Under the leadership of the Reverend Bruce R. Ough, the Reverend Nancy Allen, and the Reverend Wesley Daniel, the United Methodist Church of Iowa has launched a series of highly creative and effective telemarketing campaigns in small and large congregations. Bruce Ough is the Program Council Director for the Iowa United Methodist Church. Nancy Allen and Wesley Daniel are Program Consultants. They call their telemarketing program "teleinviting," and they use the program for church planting and growth. One comprehensive example is that of the Christ Community Church (United Methodist) of Cedar Rapids.

The Reverend Ron Blix was a member of the Congregational Development Committee, which decided to launch a new congregation in the northeast part of Cedar Rapids. He was appointed the founding pastor and was given a parsonage, a budget, and a copy of *The Phone's for You!* by Norman W. Whan, on telemarketing for churches.[15] Over 130 volunteer callers made 53,000 calls in a 6-mile radius of the new church location. The volunteers made calls over a period of 4 evenings.

The volunteers received a 15-minute training session. They were given call sheets (script), work tracks (phone numbers) and cards to record names and addresses. They practiced making calls in pairs, using the provided script.

The Church Information and Development Services (see Appendix A) guided which programs and ministries were emphasized in the calls. The average call lasted 60 seconds.

Sixty percent of the people called were at home. Sixty-five percent already belonged to a church. The remaining 35 percent went on the prospect list. This effort yielded a mailing list of 4,300 names. Blix sees the purpose of teleinviting to be the development of a qualified mailing list.

Each person on the list would receive 5 items:

1. A greeting letter from Blix;
2. A letter from Blix describing his theology and approach to ministry;
3. A postcard describing the church;
4. A statement of 10 ways the church could meet needs;
5. An invitation to attend the first service.

A call-back campaign reached 95 percent of the persons on the mailing list, who were invited to attend the church's opening. The church spent $1,000 on newspaper, radio, and TV ads.

Over 440 people attended the first worship service, held in October 1989. Some attending had not been phoned, but were invited by friends who had received a call. The service took place in a movie complex that had 5 theaters (screens). One was used for worship, 1 as a nursery, and 3 for Sunday school. The large lobby housed 2 classes. New attendees kept coming over the next year at a rate of 2 or 3 new persons each Sunday, as a response to the call they had initially received. One family did not attend until 14 months after they had been called. By 1991, the average attendance settled at 223. An information stub at the bottom of the Sunday bulletin continues to yield new prospect names.

The new congregation recently used teleinviting to plant a daughter church after making 25,000 phone calls. The daughter church now has 60 members.

Here is another example of the use of telemarketing.

The Reverend Gene Koth of the Walnut Hill United Methodist Church, West of Des Moines, launched the new congregation by dialing 25,000 phone numbers, yielding 2,600 names. He invested $200 in ads in the suburban paper. To support the effort, 180 lay and clergy volunteers were recruited from other congregations in the Des Moines area. The volunteers received training in a 15-minute session. The group used the phones of a local insurance company, which loaned their facilities and equipment.

The first service was attended by 312 people. Attendance settled at 233 people in June 1991. The original 2,600 names were also called to invite them to the congregation's first Easter and Christmas services. Today the congregation has 600 active members and constituents—50 percent brought in by friends, 40 percent by phone calls, and 10 percent from newspaper ads. Each year 7,000 calls are made to new residents.

The ministries and services are directed toward baby boomers. Continual feedback is garnered from survey stubs on the Sunday bulletin. As a result of the feedback, the church uses little printed material. The worship service is simple; there are no congregational readings, and the sermons deal with practical concerns. Ministries are designed for specific small groups (singles, couples, etc.).

Norman W. Whan indicates that his organization has facilitated the planting of 7,000 churches in 90 denominations with a Sunday attendance of 700,000. They have trained over 25,000 pastors. Generally he expects that 20,000 calls will yield a list of 2,000 interested people. In a church startup, 200 will show up, while in an existing church starting something new (service, ministry), 100 will show up.[16]

Telemarketing carried on within a congregation has a beneficial effect on the volunteers. Most persons in the congregation never had the experience of recruiting a new member. Telemarketing offers them a sense of excitement in seeing how persons respond to their calls, and a sense of gratification in helping their congregation grow.

## Deciding on Media Timing

The other major decision in media selection is *timing*. Timing the advertising breaks down into a *macro* problem and a *micro* problem.

The macro problem is that of *seasonal timing*. During religious holidays, audience size and interest are higher than at any other time. Some churches and synagogues have concentrated their ads during religious holidays to remind people of the year-round benefits of attending church (see Exhibits 9-5A and 9-5B).

The micro problem is that of the *short-run timing* of advertising. How should advertising be spaced during a short period of, say, one week? Consider 3 possible patterns. The first is called *burst advertising* and consists of concentrating all the exposures in a very short period of time, such as all in 1 day. Presumably, this will attract maximum attention and interest, and, if recall is good, the effect will last for a while.

The second pattern is *continuous advertising*, in which the exposures appear evenly throughout the period. This may be most effective when the audience needs to be continuously reminded.

The third pattern is *intermittent advertising*, in which intermittent small bursts of advertising appear with no advertising in between. This pattern is able to create a little more attention than continuous advertising, but it has some of the reminder advantage of continuous advertising.

Timing decisions should take 3 factors into consideration. *Audience turnover* is the rate at which the target audience changes between 2 periods. The greater the turnover, the more continuous the advertising should be.

*Behavior frequency* is the number of times the target audience takes the action one is trying to influence (for example, some social behaviors such as smoking or giving blood). The more frequent the behavior, the more the advertising should be continuous.

The *forgetting rate* is the rate at which a given message will be forgotten or a given behavior change relinquished. Again, the faster the forgetting, the more continuous the advertising should be.

## Evaluating the Advertising

The final step in the effective use of advertising is *advertising evaluation*. The most important components are copy testing, ad post-testing, and expenditure-level testing.

### Copy Testing

Copy testing can occur before an ad is put into actual media (copy pre-testing) and after it has been printed or broadcast (copy post-testing). The purpose of *ad pre-testing* is to make improvements in the advertising copy to the fullest extent possible prior to its release. There are several methods of ad pre-testing.

*1. Comprehension testing.* A critical prerequisite for any advertisement is that it be comprehensible. This can be a major problem when dealing with less educated or even illiterate audiences. When words are used in the advertisement, one or more readability formulas can be applied to predict comprehension. These formulas measure the length of sentences and the number of polysyllabic words.

*2. Direct mailings.* Here a panel of target audience members examines alternative ads and fills out rating questionnaires. Sometimes a single question is raised, such as "Which of these ads do you think would influence you most to (request literature, attend worship services, etc.)?"

A more elaborate form consisting of several rating scales may be used, such as the one shown in Exhibit 9-6. Here the person evaluates the ad's attention strength, read-through strength, cognitive strength, affective strength, and behavioral strength, assigning a number of points (up to a maximum) in each case. The underlying theory is that an ad must score high on all of these properties if it is ultimately to stimulate action.

At the same time, direct rating methods are judgmental and less reliable than harder evidence of an ad's actual impact on target audience members. Direct rating scales help primarily to screen out poor ads, those that are deficient in attention-getting or comprehension-creating abilities, rather than to identify great ads.

*3. Focus-group interviews.* Since advertisements are often viewed in a group setting, pretests with groups can often indicate both how a message is perceived and how it might be passed along. The focus-group technique has the following advantages:

* its synergism can generate more reactions than a one-on-one session;
* it is more efficient in that it gathers data from 5 to 9 people at once;
* it can yield data relatively quickly.[17]

*4. Self-administered questionnaires.* This approach can be valuable in reaching hard-to-get-at target audiences. Since response rates can be a problem with this technique, follow-up calls are necessary to yield a representative sample.

**Exhibit 9-6**

### RATING SHEET FOR ADS

(Possible PTS)

Attention:
How well does the ad catch the reader's attention? _____(20)
Read-through strength:
How well does the ad lead the reader to read further? _____(20)
Cognitive strength:
How clear is the central message or benefit? _____(20)
Affective strength:
How effective is the particular appeal? _____(20)
Behavioral strength:
How well does the ad suggest follow- through action? _____(20)

|   |   |   |   |   |   |
|---|---|---|---|---|---|
| 0 | 20 | 40 | 60 | 80 | 100 |
| Poor ad | Mediocre ad | Average ad | Good ad | Great ad | |

_____TOTAL

## Ad Post-Testing Methods

There are 3 popular **ad post-testing methods** to assess whether the desired impact is achieved, or what the possible ad weaknesses are.

*1. Recall tests.* These involve finding persons who are regular users of the media vehicle and asking them to recall advertisers and ministries contained in the issue under study. They are asked to recall or play back everything they can remember. The administrator may or may not offer to aid them in their recall. Recall scores are prepared on the basis of their responses and are used to indicate the ad's power to be noted and remembered.

*2. Recognition tests.* Recognition tests call for sampling the readers of a given issue of the vehicle and asking them to point out what they recognize as having seen or read before.

*3. Direct response.* The preceding techniques measure *communication outcomes* of advertising. But favorable communication outcomes may not translate into *behavioral* outcomes! However, behavioral responses can be tracked by using a direct mail approach as follows:

a. Placing mail-back coupons with a code number or P.O. box in the advertisement that varies by message and medium. For example, if a church advertises a ministry requiring a phone call or mail response in the morning and evening local newspapers, it can direct respondents to ask for offer E (for evening paper ad) or offer M (for morning paper ad). In this way, the church can determine whether the morning or evening paper is generating a greater response. The same approach could be used for radio stations, handouts, posters, and so on.

b. Asking target audience members to mention or bring in an advertisement in order to receive special treatment (for example, reserved seats at a religious concert).

c. Setting up a phone number and asking individuals to call for further information (on which occasion they can be asked where they saw the ad, what they remember, etc.).

d. Staggering the placement of ads so that this week's attendance can be attributed to ad A, while next week's can be attributed to ad B. This is also an effective method for assessing alternative expenditure levels.

Religious organizations can learn a great deal about the effectiveness of alternative message and media strategies by designing experiments coupled with careful post-test measures.

## Expenditure Level Testing

Expenditure level testing involves arranging experiments in which advertising expenditure levels are varied over similar markets (e.g., target audiences or people in different geographic areas) to see the variation in response. A "high spending" test would consist of spending twice as much money in a similar territory as another to see how much more response (attendance at service, requests for literature, and so on) this produces. If the response is only slightly greater in the high spending area, it may be concluded, other things being equal, that the lower budget is adequate.

## Public Relations

To carry out its mission, the church or synagogue needs the active support of many diverse publics, and at least the tolerance of a number of others. In chapter 4, we noted 4 basic types of publics: *input publics* (donors, suppliers, judicatory), *internal publics* (trustees, ruling boards, ministers, volunteers, and staff), *intermediary publics* (publishers, facilitators, broadcast media, agents, marketing firms), and *consuming publics* (members, other participants, recipients of services), and *external publics* (local residents, activists, the general public, media, competitors).

These publics can be further divided into (1) those that directly, indirectly, or actively involved in carrying out the religious organization's mission (for example, donors, suppliers, internal and intermediary publics) and (2) those whose goodwill and tolerance are needed for the organization to exist and to carry out its mission as efficiently and effectively as possible. These 2 groups can be designated as the *active* and *passive* publics, respectively.

The local community, news media, bankers, local politicians, government officials, social action groups—all may take an active, or reactive, interest in the congregation's activities. Of course, the leaders can attempt to influence these publics in the course of carrying out their other duties.

But sooner or later, even a congregation recognizes the advantages of consolidating or coordinating these activities through a public relations "manager."

In using a public relations manager (usually a qualified volunteer parishioner), the church or synagogue can gain several advantages:

* better anticipation of potential problems;
* better handling of these problems;
* consistent public-oriented policies and strategies;
* more professional written and oral communications.

In some churches and synagogues, the public relations manager sits in on all meetings involving information and actions that might affect public perceptions of the congregation. The public relations manager not only puts out fires, but also counsels the leaders on actions that will avoid starting fires. In other congregations, public relations is charged only with getting out publications and handling news and special events. The public relations people are not involved in policy or strategy formulation, only in tactics.

Public relations is often confused with one of its subfunctions, such as press agentry, organizational publications, lobbying, fire-fighting, and so forth. It is, however, a more inclusive concept. The most frequently quoted definition of PR is the following.

Sometimes a short definition is given, which says that PR stands for *performance* (P) plus *recognition* (R). The organization not only must perform *good deeds* but must also follow them up with *good words.*

Public relations is not coextensive with marketing. Important differences are that (1) Public relations is primarily a communication tool, whereas marketing also includes needs assessment, product development, pricing, and distribution; (2) public relations seeks to influence attitudes, whereas marketing tries to influence specific behaviors, such as joining, giving, and so on; (3) public relations does not define the goals of the organization, whereas marketing is intimately involved in defining the organization's target group(s) and products.

> Public relations is the management function that evaluates the attitudes of important publics, identifies the policies and procedures of an individual or an organization with the public interest, and executes a program of action to earn understanding and acceptance by these publics.[18]

A checklist of activities for the public relations manager for a church or synagogue would include the following.[19]

1. The physical plant
   a. Does the appearance of the grounds, buildings, and parking lot tend to enhance the desired image?
   b. Is the building properly lighted at night (outside, inside, behind the stained-glass windows, etc.)?
   c. If the building is situated near a busy highway or major intersection, is this fact being taken advantage of? Is a display sign properly established, edited, and kept up to date with provocative messages? Is it lighted at night?
   d. Are church bells or carillons utilized to remind the community of the church's existence?

    e. Are signs posted on main roads leading to the facility, pointing the way?

2. Media and publicity work

    a. Have local professional religious editors and other media people been contacted to learn their needs and interests? Are "thank-you" notes sent when good news coverage is achieved?

    b. Are all members periodically reminded (perhaps via a sermon) that PR is everybody's business? Are they aware of channels and procedures for submitting news?

    c. Are ideas for major features (for religious monthlies or Sunday editions of the local papers) farmed out from time to time by the PR manager or the editor of the congregation's newsletter?

    d. Has a basic publicity brochure been prepared for distribution to new members and prospective members? This would summarize the congregation's purposes, services, staff, facilities, benefits, and so on.

    e. Are a series of bulletin boards kept up to date, attractive, and newsworthy? Is a clearly designated editor in charge, and do the members know this? Are the bulletin boards in high-traffic areas? Are they well lighted?

    f. Is the newsletter editor being supplied with a steady flow of items from the designated "reporters" and others? Is the layout reasonably professional? Is the newsletter being mailed at the cheapest postal rate? Is it being sent to absent members (away at college, in the armed services, shut-ins, etc.)? Is a copy sent to local church editors? Are copies exchanged with other local churches? (This can lead to a number of new ideas.)

    g. When interesting people drop by (like missionaries back from India), are arrangements made for possible radio or TV interviews?

    h. Is the church or synagogue part of a regional plan for the occasional broadcasting of services on radio or TV?

    i. Are special events dramatized for possible photo or TV coverage? For example, a routine ground-breaking ceremony might be enlivened by the use of a team of oxen pulling an ancient plow.

    j. Is an appropriate ad announcing services placed on the newspaper's church page each Saturday?

3. Miscellaneous
   a. Are the staff members (including janitors) trained to answer the phone effectively? Is the Yellow Pages phone listing attractive and up to date?
   b. Are ushers and other greeters trained with PR in mind?
   c. Have cooperative efforts with other local congregations been considered for fund raising (billboards, bumper stickers, signs in buses, radio and TV spots, etc.)?
   d. Does the PR committee have a list of members who are in key positions in local clubs and organizations and who can make announcements or appeals?
   e. Is there an annual critique of the overall PR effort, and is it coordinated with periodic surveys and audience analysis efforts?
   f. Do the members of the PR committee occasionally read books on journalism or PR work? Do they attempt to interview experts in the field, or even take PR courses at local colleges?

In short, the church or synagogue is an institution with a "product" to deliver and an image to maintain. There is nothing wrong with its effort to be well-organized and professional. Its adversaries are hardly amateurs. As St. Augustine phrased it about 1,600 years ago: "Truth must not go unarmed into the arena."

---

One good example of the church developing well-organized and professional PR materials is "Mission 90," prepared by the Evangelical Lutheran Church in America. Mission 90 comprised a 6-videotape series, in which Bishop Herbert W. Chilstrom hosted a discussion series entitled "What Does It Mean to Be a Christian?"[20] The videotapes were produced by the Commission of Communication funded by the Lutheran Brotherhood. The videotapes are entitled: *Grace; Faith and Sin; Word, Sacrament, and Worship; Life in Family and Community; Personal Stewardship;* and *Creation.*

---

Individual churches and synagogues minister under tight budget constraints. Most congregations simply cannot afford to hire professional PR firms. Their only chance for excellence lies in the voluntary, part-time help of PR professionals, who also happen to be churchpersons, or with laypersons who are willing to apply themselves to learning how to do effective PR. To the credit of Christian and Jewish professional PR and marketing persons, we have yet to meet such persons who are not willing to volunteer their skills to their places of worship.

## Do's and Don'ts for Religious Advertisers

Below are some actions that should be taken or avoided by religious marketers on limited budgets.

### Do's

1. Radio stations, newspapers, magazines, and other media specialists will frequently give free, valuable help on advertising strategy, especially for small or nonprofit organizations. Sometimes to sell their own medium, the staffs will help you create dynamic ads. Don't be shy about picking their brains about advertising strategy.

2. Ads placed during off-hours or in unusual print locations are charged cheaper rates. Sometimes you can still reach your market targets in these inexpensive, unorthodox media slots.

3. Most of the time your audience needs more than one exposure to remember your business. Repeat and repeat the same successful ads. You'll also save on production costs instead of having to reinvent the wheel.

4. See if media sellers will give last-minute discounts for unused time or space. Late fill-ins could result in discounts of up to 60 percent!

5. If appropriate, consider providing a convenient toll-free number in your ads to get immediate responses and feedback.

6. Try cheaper classified advertisements to see if their drawing power is comparable to more expensive display ads.

7. Consider bartering products or services donated by members in exchange for the production of ads (e.g., artwork and printing) or for media time or space.

8. Use piggyback advertising material in other mailings, such as in newsletters or special announcements, to save postage and other related costs.

9. Try cooperative advertising with denominational or regional church offices. Some judicatory offices, for example, are receptive to sharing advertising costs with local congregations.

10. Take advantage of any media discounts you're offered by paying cash in advance.

11. Try reducing the physical size of the print ad or the time of a broadcasting spot. A full-page ad or 60-second commercial, for example, is not always twice as effective as a half-page or 30-second ad. Sometimes frequency (number of times an ad appears) is more essential than the size or time of an ad.

12. Develop tight production controls to minimize the need to reject finished ads. Don't get carried away with the artistic endeavors in which production concerns outweigh your original advertising objectives.

13. Carefully aim your ads at the prospects or consumers who are most receptive to the ad's message.

14. See if you can sponsor a community or civic event. Sometimes the sponsor is mentioned somewhere in the community ad. Although your congregation's name is not prominently mentioned, the ad is repeated often, which gives favorable and frequent recognition.

15. You can't afford saturation advertising. Instead, work on carefully matching the particular medium—radio, newspaper, or whatever—with the market targets you want to go after. Poor target marketing causes advertising dollars to be wasted. Challenge the media reps to identify clearly their viewers, listeners, or readers.

16. Fully exploit the advantages of the various types of media; otherwise, you're needlessly paying for the higher costs or rates of certain media. Television ads, for example, give you the opportunity to demonstrate your offerings and allow visual impact. If your ads merely "talk" through the time slot, you might as well opt for the cheaper time slots of radio, billboard, or some other alternative.

17. Saturation and blitz advertising is very costly; therefore, carefully coordinate all forms of communication to develop a consistent, systematic, and effective image. With judicious integration of public relations, one-on-one communications, telemarketing, and advertising, you'll develop a total, powerful synergistic impact on the marketplace—and you will better maximize your precious ad dollars.

18. Experiment with an editorial-style format. "There is no need for advertisements to look like advertisements," says David Ogilvy.

"If you make them look like editorial pages, you will attract 50 percent more readers." You could provide informative suggestions, written in editorial style, which positions you as an expert in the reader's mind. This strategy could overcome advertising clutter and give better readership for your small budget.

19. Develop copy that appeals to your market while still being different from the big-budget marketers. You can't match them dollar for dollar. Experiment with unusual approaches, such as color, music, slogans, humor, or in media selection to attract the viewers' attention and interest.

20. Consider the use of such alternative media as the Yellow Pages, billboards, leaflets, community bulletin boards, church signs, booths at fairs, and other methods that are consistent with the target audience media habits, the image you wish to portray, the particular religious product being advertised, the message you're sending, and the advertising budget.

21. Keep close tabs on how well certain ads and different types of media are doing. You cannot afford to spend hard-earned dollars on advertising that is not getting the job done.

### Don'ts

Here are a few common mistakes made by advertisers on low budgets, such as religious organizations have.

1. *Trying to do too much with too few advertising dollars.* You cannot afford to be something to everyone. Too often you may try to say too much, hit many different media or have a huge, one-time flashy ad to get "your money's worth." It could be a costly blunder. You might need a better focus, a clear niche, or just one powerful message for dealing with competitive advertising clutter.

2. *Choosing a medium based on its low rate rather than on its cost per 1,000 readers, listeners, or viewers.* You should compare audience size, image, and the response results for other religious organizations that have advertised in various media. Don't just look at the ad rates of a medium.

3. *Not advertising frequently enough.* You may need to run an ad several times to increase the awareness and recall of your message.

*4. Making an advertisement bigger than it need be.* Don't sacrifice quality and repetition just for size. Sometimes attention is increased at a diminishing rate as the ad is made bigger.

*5. Expecting too much from creativity in copy and art.* A flashy and innovative ad will not overcome weaknesses in a religious organization's product.

*6. Imitating instead of analyzing.* A frugal religious marketer cannot financially compete with big-bucks religious organization marketers. Avoid me-tooism advertising.

*7. Not concentrating the advertising on the reader, listener, or viewer.* This reinforces our marketing vs. product or sales orientation.

*8. Failing to fully utilize the unique advantages of the medium, especially television.* For example, if you decide on TV, then demonstrate the virtues of your ministries. Avoid just talking through a TV script without product demonstrations. If you use billboards, avoid copy with a number of words or statements. Passersby will not have time to read them.

*9. Failing to capitalize on the inherent nature of the product, service, or organization.* Carefully match your market's preferences with the strengths of your offerings and congregation.

*10. Having no objective measure of the advertising effectiveness.* Carefully watch and evaluate your ads and the resulting campaigns to see if they're getting the job done.

*11. Believing advertising is more powerful than it really is. Discover what it takes for advertising to succeed.* Advertising cannot overcome a structural organization weakness, nor is it an automatic solution to all of your problems. For example, Dan Danford recounts the lament of a minister who could not find a volunteer to direct Bible school after placing an ad in the church newsletter 3 weeks in a row. Danford's observation was that volunteer recruitment is a one-on-one activity, not a job for the impersonal media.[21]

## Summary

An important part of marketing is promotion, providing that the church or synagogue has developed a good product. Most clergy support the idea of advertising the congregation's products. Good advertising necessitates a systematic process of decision making, including the analysis of market information and an understanding of the communication process.

Advertising—nonpersonal communications conducted through paid media under clear sponsorship—must be planned strategically. Objectives must be set, budgets determined, messages generated, media selected, and an evaluation system established.

Advertising objectives must fit with prior decisions about the target market. It must be clear what response is sought from·the target audience. Typically, the sought response is 1 of 6 consumer readiness states: awareness, knowledge, liking, preference, conviction, and action.

Budgets must be (1) set in total and (2) allocated among different market segments, geographical areas, and time periods. Budgets must also be allocated across media categories and to specific media vehicles. Choices here depend on the marketing objectives, the intended target audience, the planned message, and media costs.

Messages must be generated, executed, and evaluated. Decisions must also be made regarding media timing. Ads should be scheduled seasonally to parallel changes in audience interest. Within seasons, decisions must be made on short-run timing. The major options are to advertise continuously, intermittently, or in pre-planned bursts. These choices should be based on audience turnover, behavior frequency, and forgetting rates.

Evaluation schemes involve pre-testing and post-testing advertising and expenditure level testing. Pre-testing can incorporate comprehension studies, direct mailings, focus-group interviews, or self-administered questionnaires. Post-tests are usually based on recall, recognition, or some direct behavioral response, such as inquiries or attendance at meetings. Expenditure level testing consists of experiments in which expenditure levels are varied to see the variation in response.

Public relations is a well-established function in for-profit and nonprofit organizations. The recent introduction of marketing into nonprofit organizations has raised the question of marketing's relation to public relations. Public relations is primarily as a communications tool, whereas marketing involves needs assessment, product development, pricing, distribution, and advertising. Public relations seeks to influence attitudes, whereas marketing influences attitudes and behavior. Public relations does not help define the organization's target groups and products, as does marketing. Finally, a checklist for public relations can help in identifying many areas requiring the attention of a congregation's public relations manager. A checklist of advertising do's and don'ts is equally helpful.

# 10

# Energizing Members and Volunteers:

## Internal Marketing

The theme of this book is being responsive to your publics and serving people more effectively. Much discussion to this point has addressed how congregations and other religious organizations can use marketing principles to attract new members and meet the needs of external publics.

This chapter focuses on being responsive to those persons who make the church or synagogue possible by their attendance, financial contributions, and work. These are the *internal* publics—the members, active constituents, and the workers, both paid and volunteer. It is these internal groups that the leaders often find the most difficult to serve, especially in the areas of communications and public relations. A singular cause for this is that persons in a congregation often relate to the organization in more than one role. At one time a person may be a recipient of a ministry, and at another time be providing a ministry. Each role calls for different communications.

All marketing and all advertising depend on the *right message* getting to the *right people* at the *right time*. This can happen only when the leaders are clear regarding the targeted group, whether leader, worker, active member, or inactive member.

This chapter will first consider the problem of creating satisfied members and then the problems or recruiting, managing, and motivating volunteers.

### Creating Satisfied Members

The mid-1980s marked the beginning of a major revolution in American business. Books and articles began to document the decline of customer service in U.S. businesses and the subsequent attempts of some organizations to gain a competitive edge by delivering improved customer service.[1]

What does it mean for a congregation to have "satisfied" members? It may mean they are satisfied with the minister's abilities as a preacher, counselor, administrator, enabler, teacher, leader, nurturer, and so on. It may mean any of these things or all of them. But one thing it must mean: *The member wants to continue to remain an active participant in the life and ministry of the congregation.* When members become inactive, they are signaling that they are *not* satisfied "customers." The "product" is no longer ministering to their needs and interests.

Member satisfaction rarely occurs by chance, or as a natural consequence of a pastor or rabbi being a good administrator or problem solver. It would be a mistake to assume that you have more satisfied members because *you* are better. Members are satisfied because you have made *them* better—better at seeking God's presence in their lives, better at relating to their family, better at relating to other members, better at understanding God's plan for them.

Pastors and rabbis should see what they do as "value-adding" activities—adding something of value to the lives of members along some dimension that is significant *from the member's perspective* (outside-in thinking). This magnifies the need for a shared frame of reference to exist between pastor and parishioners, between rabbi and congregation. The pastor or rabbi must be able to perceive value in church membership *from the parishioner's viewpoint* so that member satisfaction can be truly delivered by building value into the very experience of being a member.

Exhibit 10-1 illustrates the fact that "value" from being a member of a certain congregation will often differ among the members. This table is not meant to be a definitive categorization, but rather it emphasizes that pastors and rabbis must be cognizant of how members vary in their perceptions of what constitutes value from belonging to a church or synagogue.

**VALUE DERIVED FROM MEMBERSHIP
IN A CONGREGATION**

**Orientation**

| | Process | People |
|---|---|---|
| **High** | A spiritual lift from the worship experience | Sense of belonging to a body of believers |
| **Low** | A sermon that causes me to think | Friendly place to be |

**Desired Involvement** (row label, left side)

**Exhibit 10-1**

## How to Deliver Member Satisfaction

There are many examples from the business world that teach powerful lessons about customer satisfaction and how it is achieved. Perhaps one such example will help you gain insight into satisfaction within your own organization.

In 1981, Scandinavian Airlines System (SAS), posted an $8 million loss. A new president, Jan Carlzon, was appointed and immediately embarked on a bold plan to turn SAS around. His revolutionary approach was to focus the entire organization around serving consumer needs! By "turning on" the whole company to the mission of service, he believed consumers would notice and respond to such a difference between SAS and other airlines. Carlzon's belief was that people within SAS, like most organizations, had become so tuned into executing the narrow set of tasks assigned to them that few were putting consumer satisfaction at the top of their list of priorities. Employees were motivated to perform their assigned tasks to a high degree of technical competence but were not seeing what they did from the perspective of how those activities would ultimately contribute to or detract from customer service. "Who," asked Carlzon, "is paying attention to the real needs of the customer?" He set about changing the focus of employees from a process of "producing" airline flights to one of delivering service. In his words, "Our business is not flying airplanes, it's serving the travel needs of our public. If we can do that better than the other companies, we'll get the business. If we can't, we won't get the business, and we don't deserve to."

With the help of key executives, Carlzon began to teach the "gospel of consumer orientation" energetically and persistently throughout SAS, to all 20,000 employees. He and his managers personally shouldered this task of evangelism by traveling from country to country, talking to employees and preaching about service, creativity, and finding a better way. A formal training program was established as well as an internal consulting group, which worked with managers throughout the company to find ways to overcome obstacles and move ahead on various projects. Carlzon also took an aggressive lead in finding ways to serve the consumer. One way was to focus on the business traveler rather than trying to be all things to all people and end up being nothing to everybody. This service for business travelers become SAS's best-known feature and was a big success. Another new program initiated was regular market research studies of consumers to determine their satisfaction levels and to correct little problems in customer service before they became big ones.

The result of these changes? Even with an investment of $30 million to institute the improvements needed to deliver better customer service, SAS went from an $8 million loss to a *gross profit of $71 million in a little over a year.* Reflecting on this amazing turnaround, Olle Stiwenus, director of internal SAS management consultants, said, "Jan Carlzon really masterminded the turnabout maneuver. He had a great deal of help from many talented people, but he himself *supplied the vision* to get it going and the energy to see it through."

Albrecht and Zemke, in their book *Service America*, conclude the SAS story with these comments: "Carlzon . . . possessed . . . two key traits that made him the right man for the times: a creative

> mind and the ability to communicate his expectations [and visions] clearly and dramatically. He managed to get the top management of SAS to rethink the company's destiny and to come up with possibilities that enabled them to see beyond this previous conception of the business."[2]

The SAS example suggests an important lesson for congregation leaders. The story points out the crucial difference between internal markets and external markets. The internal markets Jan Carlzon decided to target were SAS's executives and ground crews, flight crews, and sales and reservations personnel. The external markets Carlzon targeted were business travelers and travel agencies.

In addition, the story explicates a number of key concepts for member and volunteer worker satisfaction.[3]

1. *The need for visible, personal leadership in instilling a "customer service" mentality throughout the organization.* Just as Carlzon made a point of being personally involved in building a customer service mentality throughout his organization, a pastor or rabbi must do likewise. The clergy should make it clear through their own actions that a philosophy of interpersonal relations will prevail in all interactions the paid and volunteer workers have with the members and all other persons relating to the congregation.

2. *Communicating a vision for the congregation beyond members' previous conception of possibilities or destiny.* We have talked at several points about "mission" and "vision." Perhaps Jan Carlzon's greatest contribution to SAS's success was to get the people of SAS to "rethink the company's destiny and to come up with possibilities that enabled them to see beyond their previous conception of the business." Such visionary leadership by the clergy can also enable paid and volunteer workers and members alike to envision the congregation's ministry in ways they had not previously seen as possible or necessary.

3. *Understanding what constitutes satisfaction for the target public.* Carlzon decided to focus his company's efforts on satisfying the needs of a specific target market—business travelers—and made a point of knowing what is required to make those customers feel satisfied. Similarly, religious leaders must focus on understanding their

targeted "customers" and being in tune with the needs, attitudes, perceptions, values, and motivations of their members.

4. *Having a clear service strategy, instead of assuming that member satisfaction will occur.* When altering SAS's approach to customer service, Jan Carlzon did not simply talk about delivering service, he "walked his talk." To install the service strategy, he:

* established what was expected of employees by defining what constituted superior service;
* established a service strategy to deliver that service;
* trained employees to implement the strategy;
* measured the performance of employees in delivering service;
* rewarded superior service accomplishments of those employees.

Jan Carlzon did not assume that just because he announced the vision it would be put into action whenever a service encounter occurred. Beyond announcing his vision, he built a structure to make it happen—in measurable terms.

A pastor or rabbi must also develop a service strategy for himself or herself, and the entire congregation. One thing is almost certain: If the pastor or rabbi does not do this, it simply won't happen. It is not in the character of a congregation for such radical change to happen if the leader is not leading in it.

5. *Researching member attitudes.* SAS and other service-oriented companies are constantly researching and monitoring consumers' attitudes to better understand their wants and needs and the extent to which the organization is delivering satisfaction. Such research is no less important with the internal market of one's own members and participants.

> *Specifically, an effective service strategy is a nontrivial statement of intent that noticeably differentiates the church or synagogue from others, has value in the members' eyes, and is deliverable by the leaders and workers.*[4]

When measuring the attitudes of internal markets, 2 concepts are especially crucial: *satisfaction* and *importance.* By *satisfaction,* we mean the degree to which a member or other participant is satisfied that a program or ministry is meeting one or more of his or her important needs or interests.

By *importance,* we mean the degree to which a member or other participant feels a program or ministry is addressing an important need of at least 1 target group.

By definition, then, it is possible that a member might be satisfied with what a particular ministry is accomplishing, but that he or she may feel that it isn't addressing any important need. On the other hand, a member may feel that a particular ministry is very important and may be highly dissatisfied with its present results. (See, for example, Exhibit 4-14.)

A responsive congregation is one that researches the major needs and interests of individuals and groups within the organization and then works to provide program ministries, with which those persons or groups are fully convinced of their importance and are highly satisfied with their results. This is the muscle and fiber of internal marketing. Exhibit 10-2 provides process ideas for measuring satisfaction and importance.

Soliciting member attitudes not only yields the benefit of knowing the extent to which persons are experiencing satisfaction in their contacts with the church or synagogue, but it also involves members in identifying the programs that:

* have outlived their usefulness and should be sloughed off;
* are still important, but satisfaction is waning, indicating an overhaul is necessary;
* need to be started in order to meet a need not currently being addressed.

Making members a part of the process of building a responsive church or synagogue builds "ownership" of the organization's mission and vision. It also has the side benefit of generating new ideas and suggestions that can result in ministries of importance, delivering even greater satisfaction.

## Satisfaction & Importance/Performance Measurement & Marketing Research in Local Congregation

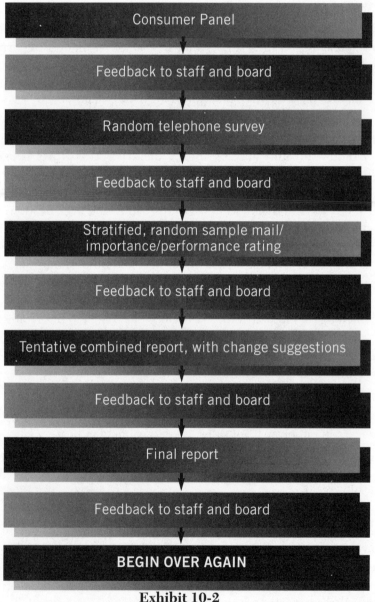

Consumer Panel

↓

Feedback to staff and board

↓

Random telephone survey

↓

Feedback to staff and board

↓

Stratified, random sample mail/ importance/performance rating

↓

Feedback to staff and board

↓

Tentative combined report, with change suggestions

↓

Feedback to staff and board

↓

Final report

↓

Feedback to staff and board

↓

**BEGIN OVER AGAIN**

**Exhibit 10-2**

It is important to remember that gathering member importance/ satisfaction information, and then not acting on it is worse—far worse—than not gathering the information at all. Importance/satisfaction studies generate high levels of expectation for changed behavior on the part of the congregation's leaders and its workers. A cardinal rule to follow is "if you don't want the answer, don't ask the question."

6. *Generating commitment throughout the organization.* Jan Carlzon made every effort to get his employees to rethink their responsibilities as centered around their customers. His approach was to constantly talk about how to deliver customer service, then he backed up his talk with structures to measure to what extent it was happening. Finally, he built reward systems to reinforce desired behavior.

For many churches and synagogues, asking the leaders and workers to think in terms of putting the needs and interests of members ahead of their own ideas about "what is right" is tantamount to asking them to change the color of their skin. Often no one has greater difficulty in making this change in attitude and behavior than the religious leader. A pastor or rabbi must get the ruling boards, the paid and volunteer workers, and the program committees to think in terms of their responsibilities in making satisfaction and importance happen. However, Rabbi Harold Schulweis demonstrates that it can be done.

Harold Schulweis describes his Valley Beth Shalom congregation as being "on the cutting edge of religion." Instead of hearing sermons at Saturday services, worshipers at the suburban Los Angeles synagogue are more apt to engage in lively discussions with the rabbi on the meaning of the Torah. In addition, to make the Jewish experience more than a once-a-week event, special programs are held in members' homes or in the temple, which has become a community center between Sabbaths. Some 27 trained laypersons assist Schulweis in his duties. "The laity has to be offered a coequality with the clergy," says Rabbi Schulweis, a nationally recognized leader in Judaism. In 14 years at Valley Beth Shalom, he has changed its country-club image to a model of innovation. Among his ideas is the wider use of the *havurah*, the

Hebrew word for "group of friends." Instead of confining the *havurah* to religious studies, Schulweis has promoted the concept of small groups as a way of counteracting isolation and providing a vehicle for "Jewishness" during the week. Now, members can join one of 61 *havurahs,* each of which includes about 10 families. Held in a synagogue member's home, the *havurah* acts as a monthly discussion or special-interest group, or as an extended family. Says Schulweis: "If there is a sickness, 9 times out of 10, by the time I get there, 9 families have already visited." In response to its success, Schulweis has helped many synagogues throughout the United States adapt *havurah* programs. Other activities supported by the $1.5 million annual budget include a counseling center staffed by 40 volunteers, which offers programs ranging from food distribution to childbirth classes, and a Gamblers' Anonymous group. "People come to the temple for everything, and we feel that's the way it should be," says congregation president Sylvia Bernstein. Membership has grown sixfold since 1970, to 5,000 drawn from a wide area. Says Diane Martin, who joined Valley Beth Shalom after visiting many other congregations: "Sometimes, I don't feel like driving so far, but I've tried different places, and I keep coming back."[5]

Successful large congregations are characterized by being "honeycombed" with groups of laypersons who provide for one another's needs. The pastor or rabbi should not, indeed cannot, take on a member service/nurturing program alone. The SAS example illustrates that successful service programs require the involvement and commitment of everyone throughout the organization. One or two workers who are not committed to serving the needs of the organization's constituents can undo the efforts of all the others—one bad apple can spoil the whole barrel.

7. *Making sure the basics are done well.* Excellent service organizations understand that no amount of extras, special touches, or "fancy packaging" can overcome failure to deliver the core benefits sought from their service by customers. Jan Carlzon understood that on-time flights and comfort in the air for business travelers would make or break SAS. Marriott understands that people are seeking comfort and convenience from a hotel room. McDonald's knows

quality, service, cleanliness, and value are the benchmarks of good fast-food. No amount of frequent traveler points or "win a million" games can make up for failure to deliver on the basics.

Satisfaction with being a member of a particular congregation will not occur unless that experience enriches the person's spiritual and social life. Changing the hours of worship to be more convenient, enlarging the parking lot, sending out a church newsletter, and so on will not overcome the limitations of an unfulfilling worship experience.

As the pastor of a church, one of the authors had occasion to work with a highly gifted music director/organist. For several months there was a good deal of amiable discussion, and some tension, as the pastor urged the music director to pay attention to what the congregation seemed to feel and say about various types of music. After a worship service in which a sense of praise and joy was manifest, the music director said, "I now understand what you want me to do. I thought my job was to teach these people music education. Now I see it is to lead them into worship, through music."

Successful organizations never lose sight of the basics; they know what they are there to do, and they are obsessive about making sure it's done right. Einstein's statement that "God is in the details" takes on a new meaning when seen in this light.

## Moments of Truth

Another of Jan Carlzon's legacies of value to pastors and rabbis is his concept of "Moments of Truth."[6] Carlzon said, "We have 50,000 moments of truth out there every day." He defined a moment of truth to be any episode in which the customer comes into contact with any aspect of the organization and gets an impression of the quality of its service.

A *moment of truth* for the church or synagogue may be defined as any episode in which a person comes into contact with any aspect of the congregation and gets an impression of the quality of the membership experience.

A moment of truth can be a phone call to the office to ask a question or obtain someone's address, the response a member gets when making a request for special prayer for a family member in a Sunday school class, the reaction of other members to a dish brought to the potluck dinner, looking in the pastor's eyes and shaking his or her hand at the end of a worship service, hearing (or not hearing) "Thank you for a job well done" when serving on a church committee, and so on. While the church or synagogue may not have as many moments of truth each day as SAS, it is safe to say they are no less important in their contribution to membership satisfaction, and they must be managed just as intentionally—toward creating participant satisfaction.

Positive moments of truth build member satisfaction and loyalty, while negative moments of truth can build a wall separating members from the church or synagogue to which they belong.

Moments of truth do not even have to involve human contact. A friend told one of the authors that she moved to a new town and sought out the local church on Wednesday night for mid-week prayer services. Upon arriving at the unlit church parking lot, she saw light coming from an upstairs window, where she expected to find the service being held. Trying several locked doors without success, she returned home without making contact with the worshipers. The following weekend she tried another local church of the same denomination and was made to feel most welcome. Needless to say, she made the second church her new church home.

Moments of truth can occur as people read your congregation's sign, see your ad in the paper, hear the worship service over the radio, or get approval for a group wanting to use a room without prior reservation. Moments of truth occur in "large, bold print," and in "fine print." But they occur, and persons' impressions of the church or synagogue are fixed thereby.

---

The authors have a friend living in Orange County, California, who decided, about a year ago, to seek out a new church home. This was happening at a crucial time in his life, when he was seeking comfort and support. Because he was favorably impressed with Wesleyan theology and the materials published by The Upper Room, related to spiritual formation, he decided to visit first a church of that tradition.

On his first, and only, visit to the church, he was asked to sign a guest register. This particular Sunday was toward the end of a calendar quarter. In a few days he received a quarterly financial statement from the church, with a note that he had given only one offering to the church that quarter. From then until now he continues to receive quarterly statements, with notes chiding him for not supporting the church. He has also received a letter from the pastor saying the congregation is behind in its mortgage payments and is unable to complete several necessary repairs. Since he had not been giving to the regular fund, would he please make a generous payment to the building fund?

If moments of truth are not managed successfully, the quality of the experience for the member or consumer regresses to mediocrity. This impression of mediocrity will then be transferred to other, unexperienced, aspects of the organization—"If the main worship service is this unfulfilling, I can imagine what the Sunday night service must be like." But this works both ways. A well-managed and positive moment of truth can provide a positive lens through which individuals view the organization, while negative moments of truth color a person's entire view of the organization. The scriptural adage is appropriate here: "It's the little foxes that spoil the vineyard."

One way to identify the various moments of truth occasions is to sketch out the "experience cycle" a member goes through when encountering the church in some way.[7] An experience cycle for the main worship service may appear as shown in Exhibit 10-3. Each point of the cycle represents a moment of truth that leaves an impression, and that should be successfully managed.

Similar experience cycles can be developed for other occasions where members and others come into contact with any aspect of the organization. Of course, it is not possible for the pastor or rabbi to be present at each moment of truth to manage its occurrence. Therefore, it is of utmost importance that all personnel (including members themselves) receive "customer service training" so that they see themselves as contributing to positive moments of truth for the entire organization. The paid staff, volunteer workers, ruling boards, program committees, and members must become the managers of their moments of truth—when encountering someone who will form an impression of the organization and its people.

## EXPERIENCE CYCLE FOR WORSHIP SERVICE

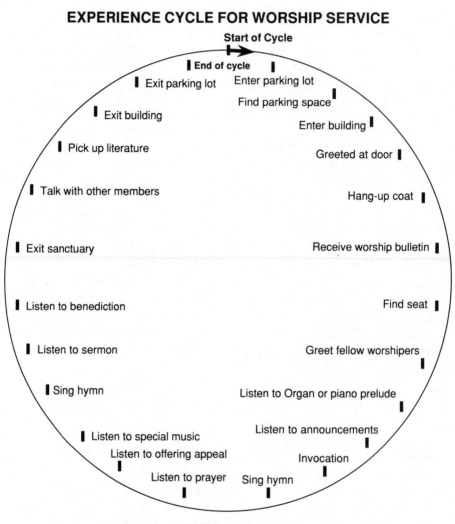

**Exhibit 10-3**

Likewise, because the moments of truth may sometimes not involve a person-to-person contact, the systems and "hardware" of each moment of truth must be devised in such a way as to leave a positive impression. For example, what does your organization's ad in the Yellow Pages suggest in the eyes of someone seeing it for the first time? What impression would someone have of your church or synagogue when driving by—what message does your lawn and sign communicate? What is the impression left by the moment of truth when someone hears the recorded message on the telephone answering machine at the office? In all moments of truth, we must be capable of seeing things through the eyes of the beholder.

It is important when considering how to manage the moments of truth to see them as specific occurrences, rather than as traits. That is, the trait of courtesy for greeters at the sanctuary entrance is not the same as a moment of truth for Mr. Doe when *he* enters for worship. If the greeters are generally courteous, but are having a bad day when Mr. Doe arrives, a failed moment of truth will occur.

Which of us is comforted with the thought that the airline on which we are traveling has an 88 percent on-time departure and arrival rate when *our* flight leaves hours late, causing us to miss an important event? Such occurrences are bound to happen. It is the way we recover from such events that determines whether our moment of truth is ultimately a failure or a success.

> A moment of truth is an episode, a specific event in time, in which someone will encounter the organization in some way—and form an impression based on that encounter.

## How to Recover from a Failed Moment of Truth

To err is human. To recover from your error is essential if you are to maintain good relations between paid and volunteer workers, the members, and external publics. A failed moment of truth can either leave a scar or, like a mended broken bone, result in an even stronger bond between the offender and the offended—if the proper recovery method is used.

The term *recovery* originated with Donald Porter of British Airways, based on that firm's efforts to understand customer expectations when they changed from a government-run entity to being privatized.

"Recovery" was the term we coined to describe a very frequently repeated concern: If something goes wrong, as it often does, will anybody make a special effort to set it right? Will someone go out of his or her way to make amends to the customer? Does anybody make an effort to offset the negative effects of [a mistake]? Does anyone even know where, when, or how to deliver a simple apology?[8]

A sequence of as many as 5 steps is involved in effective recovery from a failed moment of truth.[9] Whether all 5 are necessary in any particular instance depends on the severity of the failure. We will use as an example a failed moment of truth between an office worker, paid or volunteer, and a member of the congregation.

*1. Apology.* Recovery absolutely demands some acknowledgment of error *immediately following* a failed moment of truth involving a staff member and a congregation member. *Apology is more powerful when delivered in the first person, and as soon after the failure as possible.* An institutional "We're sorry" lacks the sincerity and authenticity of a person's acknowledging that a mistake has been made.

An apology should contain the following elements: a specific statement of the error to demonstrate that the worker knows what failure has been made, a confession that "I" am the one responsible, an expression of care for any inconvenience or embarrassment, a statement as to what will be done to correct the failure, and an inquiry as to whether this will be sufficient to resolve the matter.

Kenneth Blanchard has invented the creative "one-minute manager."[10] Blanchard teaches us that most apologies need not be long; one minute will do. They must, however, be sincere and genuine. Further, the worker committing the failure should make the apology. The offended person will resent any other person making the apology, even the pastor or rabbi.

If a very serious failure has been committed, the pastor or rabbi, as head of staff, will perhaps follow up with an apology and exploration of necessary corrective steps. But this need should be rare.

If the failure is a systems failure, for which no one person bears sole responsibility, the chairperson of the committee in whose responsibility area the failure has occurred should offer the apology. If the failure is a "total systems error," cutting across several departments, the pastor or rabbi, chairperson of the ruling board, or some other appropriate person should offer the apology.

*2. Urgent reinstatement.* The offended member must perceive that the worker is doing the best job possible to make things whole again without delay. If the member believes that the worker (and the church or synagogue) has his or her interest at heart, a great deal of progress has been made toward restoring goodwill between the offended and the offender.

3. *Empathy.* If a member has felt victimized by the actions of a worker or committee, he or she is likely to desire some demonstration of understanding of why they feel victimized *before* steps are taken to redress the grievance. Empathy is the expression of "I understand your hurt—I care about you—I can relate to your pain." In its highest form, the member feels heard, affirmed, and cared about.

*Empathy* is quite different from expressions of *sympathy*. Sympathy is the sharing of another's pain. Empathy is demonstrating compassion for the person in pain without personally taking on the pain—it's a shoulder to cry on, a source of strength. Sympathy is risky, because the helper enters the same condition as the one needing help or support. Sympathy is making someone weak feel better about his or her condition; empathy is being understanding and helping the person feel strong again.

An apology sends the message to the victim that it matters that there was a breakdown; empathy goes further to say that it matters that the person was hurt in the process. A service expert once said, "When service fails, first treat the person, then the problem."[11]

4. *Symbolic Atonement.* Rather than the proverbial pound of flesh, symbolic atonement is a gesture that says "We want to make it up to you." There are countless ways the worker can go beyond apologizing and empathizing with the mistreated member. Whether placing a phone call on behalf of the offended party, driving out of the way to deliver someone or something, or taking a person to lunch to establish broken connections, the symbolic atonement is communicating the worker's desire to make amends for a failed moment of truth.

The size of the recompense is not as significant as the symbolic impact of acknowledging that the injury has occurred. It is important that the worker demonstrates a sincere desire to atone for his or her role in the injury. Here, actions speak louder than words.

5. *Follow-up.* Depending on the severity of the failed moment of truth, it may be advisable to follow-up the symbolic atonement with inquiries to determine whether the relationship with the member

has been redeemed. This follow-up should perhaps be taken by the pastor or rabbi or some other official representative of the organization. Here, a perceived willingness of the organization to "go the extra mile" goes a lot further than earlier efforts to restore the relationship with the aggrieved party.

Research by the Technical Assistance Research Programs Institute of Washington, D. C., found that recovery methods, when done properly, help to build a loyal base of customers.[12] Customers who had complained and had their complaint handled to their satisfaction were even more "brand loyal" than customers who had never complained. However, the same research also showed that a poor or grudging recovery effort may be worse than no effort at all. Doubly dissatisfied customers or members will be less inclined to feel charitable toward an organization that has disappointed them than those who have suffered the first disappointment in silence.

## Establishing a Member Service Program

Five steps lead to the establishment of a service orientation in a religious organization.[13]

1. Evaluating the present level of service quality.
2. Clarifying the service strategy.
3. Educating the paid and volunteer workers.
4. Implementing new tactics at the front line.
5. Reinforcing the new orientation and making it permanent.

### Step 1: Evaluating the Present Level of Service Quality

The first step in becoming a service-oriented religious organization is to determine the satisfaction level of various served audiences. "Report cards" are needed, which cover the critical components of service delivery. For example:

Pastor to members in family counseling;
Rabbi to couples in pre-marital counseling;
Members to visitors at a worship service;
Members to needy persons in distributing food and clothing;

Staff to members in committees;
Nursery attendants to parents, regarding child's needs while
    under the nursery's care.

Marketing research methods, such as focus groups, user groups,
in-depth interviews, and surveys, can help the organization know
where it currently stands on delivering satisfaction. If experience
cycles have been diagrammed for all those occasions when persons
come into contact with someone in the organization (worship service, soup kitchen, prison ministry, teen counseling, etc.), it is fairly
simple to identify the particular moments of truth that are most
important to evaluate against the criteria of good performance. To
illustrate, if a report card is sought from visitors to the main worship
service, and one of the moments of truth to be assessed is the initial
greetings, we may include a series of questions such as the following.

When were you greeted? (check all that apply)

☐ Immediately upon entering the building
☐ Upon entering the sanctuary
☐ After being seated by those around me (us)
☐ I (we) were not greeted before service began
☐ Other, please describe:

How would you characterize the greeting(s) you received? (check
all that apply)

☐ Very friendly, made me (us) feel very welcome
☐ Somewhat friendly, I (we) felt welcome
☐ Neither friendly nor unfriendly
☐ I (we) did not feel welcome
☐ Too pushy, I (we) were embarrassed/prefer to be left alone
☐ Other, please describe:

The key for generating useful information on performance begins
with *knowing* what it is that the target group desires (outside-in
thinking), rather than *assuming* that we know (inside-out thinking).
When developing report cards on the pastoral staff, church members will often be reluctant to be perfectly candid. These reserva-

tions can usually be overcome if the clergy request their ratings anonymously. Efforts must be directed at obtaining unbiased, candid information.

## Step 2: Clarifying the Service Strategy

Developing a sound service strategy may require holding a retreat where the pastor or rabbi can engage staff and committee leaders in open discussion. There must be recognition that a problem exists ("We are not delivering 'customer' satisfaction as well as we should") and a willingness to be open-minded in considering solutions to the problem. Having report cards showing that a problem exists can provide the impetus for a serious discussion of what the shared vision of service strategy should be. The service strategy can be clarified by addressing the following questions.:

* How do our target groups see us at present?
* How well are we delivering on the precepts of our mission regarding service to our members and other participants?
* In what areas are we doing a good job of serving our target groups? What learnings can we transfer from these areas to those where we are not doing as well?
* How do we want to be known with respect to serving the needs of internal and external target groups?

Out of the retreat should come a strategy for delivering satisfaction to the organization's target groups. The following questions need to be asked of the strategy as it is being developed.[14]

* Can it differentiate our church from others? Does it reflect the fundamental values that bind our members together?
* Can people in and out of the church clearly see the benefits of associating with a congregation that serves people that way?
* Can we commit to it? Is it something that the clergy, staff, and members can believe in and work to support?
* Can we make it work?
* Can we communicate it to our target groups in ways they can understand?

* Can we dramatize its value to our members in concrete ways that will mobilize their efforts to make it happen?
* Can we make it real and experiential for our internal and external groups, rather than just an abstract slogan?

A final test of the service strategy is to relate it back to the report cards. Does the strategy zero in on those moments of truth and deliver true, meaningful satisfaction on those dimensions most important to the customer?

## Step 3: Educating the Paid and Volunteer Workers

As the SAS experience demonstrates, the leaders, workers, and committees must be trained to implement the service strategy. Since mass training on the scale of SAS is not practical for most congregations, the clergy and lay leaders must take the initiative to demonstrate by their own actions and decisions that they have made this service strategy a guiding principle. It is much easier to communicate the value of such a commitment if people witness the leaders' implementation of the strategy. Here a picture is worth a thousand words. Exhibit 10-4 suggests a pastor's influence on the members' service behavior.

### Exhibit 10-4

#### THE TRANSLATION OF SERVICE MESSAGES—
#### VISITOR RELATIONS MIRROR MEMBER RELATIONS

| Pastor to Member | Member to Visitor |
| --- | --- |
| What are your problems and how can I help you? | How can I be of assistance to you? |
| We want you to know what is happening in the church, so here is what is going on: | I am capable of helping you because I am in the know. |
| You are part of the corporate body; we all share in the victories of the church. | I take personal responsibility to see that you feel at home here. |
| We treat each other with respect. | I have respect for you as the individual you are. |
| We stand behind each other's decisions and support each other. | You count on me and my church to deliver on our promises. |

Source: Adapted from Robert L. Desatnick, *Managing to Keep the Customer* (San Francisco: Jossey-Bass, 1987), p. 20. Adapted by permission of Jossey-Bass, Inc., Publishers.

## Step 4: Implementing New Tactics at the Front Line

One of the best ways to get commitment is to let those facing the moments of truth define how the strategy should be implemented, rather than telling them how to do it. This does not mean they should be left alone to work it out for themselves, but each person should be fully involved in determining how the moments of truth can be carried out. People tend to support what they have helped to create. This approach generates a tremendous amount of creativity throughout the entire organization.

Many manufacturers have discovered the benefits of "quality circles," comprised of production workers who recommend and then implement ways of improving the quality of their own work. The same principle can deliver great results in the religious organization. The key is to focus persons' attention on ways to best handle the moments of truth they face, so that the end result is a satisfied member. By this means, the paid and volunteer workers are "lighting their own candles," so to speak.

## Step 5: Reinforcing the New Orientation and Making It Permanent

If a congregation is to become transformed into a true service organization, the clergy and lay leaders must find ways to reinforce desired behavior on the part of staff and members. Keeping an eye on the moments of truth these people face and providing immediate, positive reinforcement of well-handled moments is perhaps the best way to ensure continued positive behavior.[15] Virtually every person in the organization wants to know that the pastor or rabbi notices his or her efforts. Further, the program committees owe it to the paid and volunteer pastors to observe and compliment excellence in ministry. Finally, the ruling boards are co-equally responsible with the pastor or rabbi for the quality of ministry being offered at every level. All these people need to care enough about the congregation's ministries to know what is going on and to praise the workers who are doing well. Unless commitment to the service strategy and recognition of work well done are carried out at the top leadership level, it simply isn't going to happen.

On the other hand, leaders must also offer immediate and straight feedback to persons who are failing their moments of truth. Having been reminded of the congregation's service strategy, the person must be helped to plan his or her own strategy for correcting the behavior in future moments of truth.

It is sensitive and difficult for clergy to call paid and volunteer workers to accountability regarding the quality and results of their work. In a volunteer organization it is often very difficult to decide who works for whom. Does the pastor work for the members, or do the members, as workers, work for the pastor?

It would be wise, therefore, for lay personnel committees and ruling boards to assume this responsibility. They must recognize that they would be failing *their moments of truth* if they fail to do this. They shouldn't stick their heads in the sand when someone complains that the pastor or rabbi has criticized mediocre performance.

Supervising paid and volunteer workers isn't as difficult as most clergy make it. Peter Drucker is right when he claims that poor performance in religious organizations is perpetuated by the leaders' "temptation to do good"—to protect the mediocre worker. He is also right when he claims this style of personnel management will eventually bring the church or synagogue to regret and ruin.[16] But one should never ask of the staff and volunteer workers what one is unwilling to do oneself. There is no way around it; excellence in ministry and members' satisfaction begins with the pastor or rabbi. If it doesn't begin here, it doesn't begin.

Salaried and volunteer workers alike should know that a significant part of their performance evaluation will be based on their willingness and ability to successfully manage their moments of truth and deliver satisfaction in their contacts with members and other stakeholders.

Showing them the results of the report cards, rewarding excellence in service, and working with them to find innovative ways to deliver service satisfaction will pay dividends to church administrators seeking to lead their church into a new service orientation. Likewise, seeing church leaders who "walk their talk" and who are personally concerned with their own moments of truth provides a needed role model. Giving people the support systems and tools to deliver satisfaction is also critical. Asking them to "make bricks without straw" is a sure-fire way to dampen enthusiasm for the service strategy.

## Recruiting and Managing Volunteers

One common feature of virtually all churches and synagogues is their use of volunteers to provide a channel for committed people to contribute time to a cause or ministry they believe in, to become more involved with others who share a common spiritual bond, and, finally, to keep down expenses. Religious organizations are the largest volunteer organizations in the world.

The core concept of voluntarism is that individuals participate in spontaneous, private, and freely chosen activities that promote or advance some aspect of the common good, as it is perceived by the persons participating in it. Religious organizations hold a second, unique, core concept of voluntarism: the conviction that each and every one of God's people are called to use their time, talent, and tithe to further the work of God throughout the world. Each one is called to service.

Volunteers are the first to put their money where their heart is. In recent years, however, the number of volunteers has been declining. Churches and synagogues are having to give increased attention to the problem of attracting more volunteers, providing more volunteer satisfaction, and more effectively managing the entire volunteer enterprise.

The volunteer problem has been made more difficult because of several important trends in voluntarism.[17]

1. While people are still volunteering because they feel it's a good thing to do or because they have been taught to do so, new motivations are emerging, such as:
   a. The desire to change society
   b. The desire to obtain experiences that can eventually be useful on a "regular" paid job
   c. The desire to help a specific cause, such as improving the environment, electing a specific candidate, helping the elderly, removing discrimination, and so on
   d. The desire to improve one's life through meeting others

    e. The desire to engage in a volunteer career upon retirement

    f. The desire to get inside important institutions to see what they are doing and to make sure they are doing the right things.

2. A wider spectrum of people are volunteering. Rather than just the healthy, vigorous middle classes, we now find the "served" (for example, the elderly or the handicapped) and professionals also offering their services.

3. Volunteers are more demanding. They want more input into what they are doing and are no longer willing to only be drones in a larger enterprise.

4. Some groups are challenging the ultimate social desirability of voluntarism. While unions have traditionally worried that voluntarism was taking employment from those who could have been paid, the women's movement has recently challenged voluntarism as perpetuating the notion that what women do (that is, housework or volunteering) is not really valuable because it is unpaid.

The major consequence of these trends is that securing volunteers in the future will be harder than in the past.[18] The pool of those who come forward with little or no encouragement is shrinking. Those who might come forward are more hard-headed about their choices and are likely to be approached by more competitors vying for their volunteer commitment. For example, under the gifted leadership of Frances Hesselbein, the Girl Scouts of America has experienced a renaissance, and now utilizes over 60,000 volunteers.[19]

For churches and synagogues there is another factor affecting the shortage of volunteers quite apart from societal trends: *the size of the congregation.* Small congregations (fewer than 200 adult members) and large congregations (more than 600 members) tend to experience a perpetual shortage of volunteer workers—and for very different reasons. The small congregation simply does not have enough persons in its volunteer pool to draw upon. Consequently, in small congregations, a few faithful volunteers assume several responsibilities and keep them year after year. The large congregation finds itself short of volunteers because by the time the membership reaches 600, the members feel they can hire professional staff.

Medium-sized congregations tend to have a sufficient number of volunteers, or even an excess. They have a sufficient volunteer pool, but not a large enough financial base to cause members to think the work can be hired out.[20]

---

Cynthia Zacher lives with her husband, Clayton, and their 4 children on the family farm, 18 miles out of Elgin, North Dakota. A registered nurse, Cynthia has chosen to work, for less money, as a teacher's aide in the Elgin school system, because she feels her gifts and interests can best be expressed by working with children.

The family belongs to the Evangelical Lutheran Church in America in Elgin, a congregation of 538 baptized members. At the church, Cynthia is the organizing force behind all children and youth programming. Presently she serves as Sunday school superintendent, substitute teacher for all classes, teacher of a Sunday school class, and for the past few years has been the director of the daily Vacation Bible School. In addition, she serves on the church council and parish education committee.

Why does she carry so many responsibilities? "Because there just aren't enough people anymore who are willing to work with the kids." And Cynthia has a passion for the kids.

---

Cynthia Zacher is symbolic of uncounted thousands of deeply committed volunteer workers, hidden away in the churches and synagogues of America. Many carry 2 or more responsibilities because they have a passion for God's work, and there aren't enough volunteers to go around.

The need for effective strategic marketing aimed at volunteers is becoming ever more apparent. Religious leaders are confronted with 2 major concerns regarding volunteers: recruiting needed volunteers and managing them.

### Recruiting Volunteers

As with any marketing task, a crucial starting point for recruiting is understanding the target audience. Volunteer motivations are as diverse as consumer motivations. One classification of motivations is based on Abraham Maslow's hierarchy of needs (see chap. 6).

Maslow's understanding of changing motivational forces as one ascends or descends the scale of needs suggests important targeting and marketing considerations regarding volunteers. It would seem that a person would develop an interest in volunteering about the time he or she reached the third order of need. Having provided for one's own survival and safety, the individual may now aspire to the relationships and recognition voluntarism might provide.

Motivation for voluntarism might tend to remain high through the fourth order of need. Persons having reached the fifth order may be altruistic, in that they are no longer concerned about having enough for their own survival or security, they are less concerned about "belonging or status," and they care more about affecting systemic change.

The marketing task in recruiting volunteers is to (1) segment the membership into groups reflecting their own personal concerns, life situations, and motivations; (2) select the target groups or persons to be recruited; (3) prepare and present the recruitment plan to connect with their life situation and to appeal to their unique motivations and interests.

In this manner, it is possible to recruit volunteers from every position on the hierarchy of needs. The content and process of recruiting persons who are experiencing "survival" needs and motivations will, understandably, be different from the marketing approach taken with persons who have achieved self-actualization. This is true not only because they are at a different place economically and psychologically, but also because their spirituality is different—they are experiencing God differently and are asking different things of God.

Schindler-Rainman and Lippitt propose another strategy for targeting groups or persons for volunteer work.[21] They suggest that one might look upon a decision to volunteer as a response to forces pulling toward—and away from—volunteering. They propose that such forces be separated into (1) individual internal forces, (2) external interpersonal forces, and (3) situational forces.

There are still other approaches to identifying and attracting volunteers:

*1. Segmentation studies.* Here the interest is in isolating the demographic, motivational, and life-style characteristics that separate *current* volunteers from non-volunteers. The studies assume that the best prospects for future volunteers will resemble those who have volunteered in the past.

2. *Prospect studies.* Here the interest lies in recruiting volunteers from new segments. The focus is on learning more about clusters of congregation members who might have values or life-styles to which the congregation can appeal.

3. *Motivational studies.* Leaders of congregations have recognized the relatively superficial nature of using surveys to understand member motivation. Thus recent interest has developed in qualitative methodologies, such as focus groups and in-depth personal interviews as efficient, effective ways to reveal more fundamental reasons for volunteering and—just as important—for not volunteering.

4. *Positioning studies.* Leaders who feel they understand motivations typically progress to image studies as a basis for potentially changing their marketing strategies. They recognize that their success or failure as recruiters of particular segments of potential volunteers is tied closely to those segments' perceptions of the church and their perceptions of other organizations that might invite them to volunteer.

With information derived from such studies, the volunteer recruiter can decide whom to focus on, what to say, how to say it, and where to say it.

## Retention of Volunteers

Once recruited, volunteers must be retained. Retention has become a very important problem in recent years, as the demand on people's time and energy increases. Two techniques have proven particularly valuable. First, *former* volunteers should be studied to determine who they are and how they differ from volunteers who stayed on, why they ceased their volunteer work, and what steps could be taken to get them to re-volunteer.

Second, the church or synagogue should carry out routine formal assessments of *present* volunteers' satisfactions and dissatisfactions. Among the factors that frequently surface are the following.

1. Unreal expectations when volunteering. This is sometimes the recruit's own fault in that he or she has unrealistic fantasies about how rewarding it would be to teach a Sunday

school class, sing in the choir, work in the office. The recruit may also not realize how much time would be involved. But just as often the culprit is the recruiter, who, in his or her zeal to get volunteers, paints an excessively optimistic picture of the volunteer's time commitment, type of work, and probable influence.
2. Lack of appreciative feedback from leaders, paid staff, and co-workers.
3. Lack of appropriate training and supervision.
4. Feelings of second-class status vis-à-vis full-time staff.
5. Excessive demands on time.
6. Lack of a sense of personal accomplishment.

## Principles for Managing Volunteers

The use of volunteers is not an unmixed blessing. The mix of volunteers and full-time staff can be a volatile one, with problems arising on both sides.

On the side of the volunteer, many have the attitude that, since they are donating their services and are not being paid, (1) they don't really *work* for the church and so shouldn't be *told* what to do; rather, they should be *asked* whether they would be willing to do something; (2) they should have a great deal to say about the content and timetable for their assignments; and (3) they deserve continual appreciation for their generosity and commitment.

Further, some persons volunteer, not because they really want to, but because they have been coerced into volunteering by the pastor or peers, or because they wish to be perceived as loyal members doing their part. Just as bad, some volunteer only because they want a built-in group to visit with, a captive audience. Woe to the pastor or office staff when *they* become the captives. Worse yet, some volunteer simply because they want to "straighten things out down there at the church."

A major problem of managing volunteers is the matter of who works for whom.[22] Every pastor or rabbi with a volunteer corps has faced the issue at least once. The issue of who works for whom is unique to those organizations in which the members are the "owners," and the leaders are the "servants." This issue is especially acute in ecclesial bodies with congregational forms of government. The temptation of many pastors is to let volunteers do, or not do, as they wish. However, this is a trap for the organization and the worker alike. For the organization, it results in mediocre ministry, and it deprives the worker of the deep satisfaction that comes when one knows that one has done the job well.

One manager of a large volunteer force has developed what he calls his "rule of thirds." One-third of his volunteer force works avidly with very little direction and encouragement. One-third will work only with considerable motivation and are effective only under careful supervision. And one-third will not work at all under any circumstances and can't be relied upon.

On the side of the organization, there is considerable opportunity for friction to develop if the full-time staff look on the volunteers as second-class workers. Among the opinions professionals have been known to offer are:

* Volunteers are dilettantes. They are not there for the long haul and, therefore, don't have to live with the consequences of their impulsive or lethargic performance.
* Volunteers never really pay attention to their training and instructions, because they are only part-time, do shoddy work, and weaken the ministry.
* Volunteers often come from occupations in which they boss others and so cannot, or will not, take direction.

The potential for conflict between volunteers and full-time workers is considerable. The situation can be exacerbated if the pastor or rabbi does not take firm control of the situation. Again, it is a matter of *attitude*. If the pastor or rabbi is dominated by feelings of gratitude that individuals have so kindly volunteered, all is lost. Then he or she will be unwilling to "ruffle the feathers" of volunteers. This will only encourage the volunteers' tendencies toward undisciplined performance. At the same time, lay officers will be likely to squelch grumbling among the paid staff for fear that they will upset the volunteers and their friends in the congregation. This will only cause unrest and surreptitious insubordination among the paid staff, with the result that insubordination develops among *both* the full-time and the volunteer staff.

There is a solution, and it is a good one. The organization must develop the understanding that volunteer workers are expected to perform at the same level of excellence as the professional, full-time workers. And having set this standard, it must be enforced. Among other things, this means using the following volunteer standards and managerial practices:

1. Assessing the volunteer's skills and as nearly as possible matching these skills to the tasks to be performed;
2. Setting out job responsibilities clearly and in detail in advance;
3. Setting specific performance goals and benchmarks;
4. Clearly informing the volunteers of these goals and of the fact that they are expected to achieve them;
5. Nurturing and expecting excellence in performance of tasks by volunteers and paid staff alike.

This straightforward, professional style of volunteer management may seem risky to the inexperienced pastor or rabbi. But both volunteer and professional staff respond favorably to it. If they don't, they are the wrong choice.

Most volunteers like to be taken seriously and challenged. They appreciate the opportunity to be well-trained and well-supervised. Full-time staff appreciate the leader's firmness and the fact that they, too, can treat the volunteer seriously, giving orders as necessary and reprimands as required. Performance standards for both groups improve enormously, and the church's effectiveness, efficiency, and morale rise noticeably. Indeed, the church's volunteer positions can be highly coveted.

The authors are aware of one medium-sized city in the Midwest where the Chamber of Commerce runs a volunteer program for local non-profit organizations which requires volunteers to pay a stiff fee and have good references before they can do volunteer work. It is titled "The Leadership Program," confers status on those who are accepted, and has a long waiting list of applicants!

Perhaps what is most required is an elevated view of the worth and capabilities of today's volunteer. In almost any congregation there are persons who possess higher educational degrees than the clergy, and members who are more experienced in program planning and management, financial management, personnel supervision, and so on. Yet some clergy harbor low expectations of these volunteer workers, believing volunteers cannot perform "the important ministries," cannot be held accountable for excellence, or cannot be trusted to follow through on important tasks.

Leaders of religious organizations can overcome conflict and obstacles if they follow this brief set of operating principles to help in recruiting and managing volunteer leaders and workers:

1. There is little difference in deploying and managing paid and volunteer leaders and workers. If anything, the volunteer worker should be called to even higher levels of excellence in carrying out the tasks and ministries than the paid worker. Even if a paid worker does a poor job, he or she receives a periodic reward for the time given to the work—in the form of a paycheck. The essence of volunteer ministry, however, is that the worker receives no monetary reward. The only reward a volunteer receives is the satisfaction of knowing he or she performed the task to the best of his or her ability, and the recognition that may be given.

2. A congregation that is fully responsive to its volunteer workers' need for excellence and recognition will see it as the volunteers' right to have a competent supervisor, skilled in attracting good and reliable volunteers and in motivating and rewarding them.

A marketing approach means understanding the volunteers' needs and meeting them in a way that draws their support and best effort. The responsive volunteer manager is likely to sponsor social functions for volunteers, provide experiences designed for their spiritual renewal, confer awards for years of service, and arrange a number of other benefits that will recognize their contribution.

3. Volunteer leaders and workers have a right to know—and the recruitment process should make clear:

    a. What they are expected to accomplish, in terms of *results*, not activities;

    b. How these results fit into the overall mission of the church or synagogue and why these results are important to the life and work of the entire congregation and to God's work in this place;

c. What the position will cost them—how many hours will be required each week, what training will be necessary, what administrative meetings they will be expected to attend, etc.;

d. What their taking the position will "cost" the pastor or rabbi or the congregation—how much time is the pastor or rabbi, or some other leader willing to commit each week to working with the volunteers, what resources will be provided to do the job?

e. How they will be evaluated and in what form feedback will be given;

f. How they will be supported in their spiritual life journey.

When these items are built into the recruiting effort and the person to be recruited is carefully selected, fewer than 15 percent will decline to serve; once deployed, they will serve with excellence.

4. Volunteer leaders deserve the courtesy of personal recruitment by the pastor or rabbi or a respected lay leader. In recruiting topnotch volunteers and securing high commitment, nothing will take the place of a hand on the shoulder, face-to-face recruiting conversation.

5. Effective volunteer ministry requires double duty. Any worthwhile ministry requires hard work—and consumes spiritual and physical energy. The pastor or rabbi should see it as one of his or her major privileges to provide regular spiritual renewal experiences for "workers only"—a monthly meeting for spiritual renewal and fun, an annual retreat, private spiritual direction, and so on.

6. Match volunteer co-workers with care. Since they have different gifts, match them so that they complement one another, thus making one another's weaknesses irrelevant. Some volunteers *love* meetings; others hate meetings. Some are gifted in starting a program from scratch, but have no interest in administering a program once it is up and running. The following taxonomy of abilities will help match co-workers.

* *Idea Person*: highly creative at hatching new, innovative ideas, approaches, programs; not good at turning ideas into programs.

* *Planner*: not good at hatching new ideas or envisioning new programs, but very good at planning a program once the idea has arisen.

* *Trigger to Action*: highly creative at getting people started on an idea or program once it is ready for action.
* *Administrator*: not good at creating ideas or starting new programs, but gifted in keeping a program going, taking care of all the details after it is up and running.
* *Doer:* not good at ideas, planning, or triggering, but a faithful and effective worker, once the program is ready to go. Action oriented, wants to be where the "rubber meets the road."

Given these differences in people's abilities and interests, it makes sense to segment the volunteer pool into target groups according to interests and skills. If a "doer" is recruited to an "idea" or "administrator" role, the results will likely be disappointing. The person will either decline the request or, once on the job, will pick out one piece of the program where he or she can "work," to the total neglect of the details necessary to keep the program running.

7. After they have been on the job 90 days, invite each volunteer leader of a ministry area to rewrite his or her job description. By then, chances are they know more about their job and the ministry requirements than anyone else. Within 3 or 4 months as a leader, the person has insights and ideas for making the ministry area more effective. (If the volunteer doesn't, you know you recruited the wrong person.)

Ask the leader to put his or her ideas in writing. Discuss the ideas, being sure that the needs and interests of the target group(s) are addressed and that the ideas support the congregation's mission. Then, together, work the new ideas through with the ministry team or program committee. By this means, the leader and the entire ministry team will feel new commitment to their ministry area. People tend to support what they help to create.

## Summary

The theme of this book—building responsive religious organizations—is applied in this chapter to internal marketing issues. Part of internal marketing consists of being attentive to the needs of parishioners, training members to be attentive to one another's needs, and leading the congregation in developing ways for the church body to

serve the needs of the local community. This charge to service others' needs is given in the Bible and the Talmud, as well as having
practical relevance to church growth.

In the 1980s, commercial firms discovered the value of customer
service in retaining their current customers and attracting new ones.
Likewise for churches and synagogues, customer service is the right
thing to do from several perspectives. In the commercial field, Scandinavian Airline Systems (SAS) provides a valuable object lesson in
what it means for an entire organization to become service oriented.
The experience of SAS suggests several important lessons for leaders of religious organizations.

The SAS experience carries the lesson for religious organizations
to instill a "moment of truth" mentality throughout the entire organization, starting with the clergy and lay officers. A moment of truth
is any episode in which someone comes into contact with the church
or synagogue and develops an impression of the quality of the membership experience. This would be true for current members as well
as for those outside the membership who, through their contacts
with the church staff, clergy, or members, become aware of how the
organization treats its members and other participants. It is the outcome of these moments of truth that builds a firm foundation of
member loyalty and satisfaction, or a wall of separation between the
person and the organization.

By sketching out the various *experience cycles* in which members and
others encounter someone or something connected with their congregation, the myriad moments of truth can be identified and ways developed to make them success stories, instead of failed opportunities.

Failed moments of truth can, however, be recovered if the 5-step
*recovery plan* is followed. Establishing a service program to enhance
successful encounters with members and those outside the congregation can deliver long-term benefits to the church or synagogue.

Recruiting and managing volunteers is another internal marketing
task of importance to clergy and lay leaders. A number of societal
trends make securing volunteers increasingly difficult. Consequently, having a strategy for recruiting and managing volunteers is
becoming a prerequisite for success in many situations.

Pastors and rabbis need to use several practices when managing
volunteers: (1) assess the volunteers' skills and, as nearly as possible,

match these skills to the task to be performed; (2) set out job responsibilities clearly and in detail as a part of the recruiting conversation; (3) set specific performance goals and benchmarks; (4) clearly inform the volunteers of these goals and the fact that they are expected to achieve them; (5) expect excellence in performance of tasks by volunteers and paid staff.

# 11

# *Attracting Needed Resources:*

## *Fund Raising*

Few congregations have such an abundance of financial resources that the leaders can remain blissfully ignorant of fund-raising techniques. For-profit organizations get their funds primarily through issuing equities and debentures. Then they cover the cost of their "borrowed" funds by charging prices for their goods and services that exceed their costs and provide a return on investment for their shareholders. Congregations, however, must rely largely on donations, since the very act of doing their ministry results in "costs" rather than "revenues."[1] This is perhaps why there is no shortage of books on fund raising in religious organizations.[2]

This chapter will deal with the subject from a different perspective. The focus here will be on fund raising as a marketing task—consummating a mutually beneficial exchange between the congregation and its donors. Before discussing the marketing tools, concepts, and strategies for fund raising, we will review the ways in which local-congregation fund raising differs from that of other nonprofit organizations.

### *Fund Raising Is Difficult*

In 1988, churches and other religious organizations received 46.2 percent of the total gifts to nonprofit organizations. The next highest recipients, human service organizations, received 10 percent of the total.[3] A major characteristic of the people who gave more than 2 percent of their income to charity was that they attended religious services. Forty-two percent of people pledge a fixed dollar amount to their church or synagogue each week. Thirty percent of people pledge a proportion of their incomes to their church or synagogue. However, less than 10 percent pledge either a dollar amount or a proportion of their income to charities in general.[4]

349

Why then, with all this giving to the local congregation, do so many congregations find themselves in an almost constant shortfall of financial resources to achieve the objectives they would like to accomplish? One analyst of religious organization fund raising suggests the following reasons.[5]

1. *There is a proliferation of parachurch ministries.* Organizations abound that serve some specialized group or ministry. The ever-increasing number of parachurch organizations serve to siphon off money that otherwise might be channeled to a local congregation or other ecclesiastical agency.

2. *"Maxidollar" organizations.* Some high-profile ministries, many who use television as a primary means of transmitting their message, need tens of millions of dollars to finance their ministries. Many of these devote huge amounts of money to solicit contributions.

3. *Elementary and secondary religious schools.* The more than 32,000 elementary and secondary religious schools have tuition and donation needs that leave people with less money to donate to their church or synagogue. An increasing trend toward enrolling children in these schools, coupled with higher costs of education, will likely continue to reduce contributions to the congregation.

4. *The local church debt.* Many churches are saddled with very large building payments. Despite its other needs, the congregation must make its building payments first. Funding of these buildings means that fewer funds are available for ministry programs.

## The Heresies of Religious Fund Raising

In an effort to overcome these difficulties, some pastors, rabbis, and other fund raisers, have adopted tactics that could charitably be described as questionable. Are religious fund raisers subject to a different set of standards from other solicitors? Should they be? Church management writers have suggested potential heresies that should be avoided by *all* religious fundraisers.[6] Some of the heresies are:

**Don't lower God to your own standards.** Claiming God's blessings will be forthcoming to those who give to *your* cause is not only presumptuous, but it also lowers God to a supporting role in achieving your objectives. Opening a fund-raising letter with a scriptural text such as Luke 6:38, "Give, and it will be given to you," and then transitioning into a plea for money, which suggests a divine testimony as to the worthiness of a particular cause, is unsound exegesis.

**Don't use a prosperity gospel appeal.** People should give as an act of devotion to the will of God, not because they expect to profit from their largess. Giving to the church or synagogue should be first and foremost a response to God's goodness, rather than motivated by an assessment of the personal return on the investment.

**Don't play a "shell game" with the money.** Funds raised to support a specific ministry should be used for that purpose, no matter how pressing other expenses may be. Fund raisers for religious organizations should honor the wishes of the donor and the donor's expectations of the good that will be done with his or her donation. All religious organizations should be held accountable for the use of the funds solicited—as surely they will be. Luke 16:2, "Give an account of your management," suggests the clergy or lay leader should be concerned that he or she practice sound ethical procedures in all areas of fiscal management.

**Don't claim a false crisis.** Don't declare a financial exigency unless there is one, and then be transparently honest in presenting the facts about the crisis.

**Don't neglect proper business practices.** Fund raisers and finance committees should adhere "religiously" to proper financial and accounting standards, including full disclosure of finances (of course, honoring confidentiality of donors). Accounting sleight-of-hand which may be legal, but of questionable ethics, has no place in the church or synagogue.

**Don't raise funds to cover inefficient management.** Contributions should be used to advance the work of God through the congregation's ministries, not to subsidize poor management practices.

**Don't substitute slogans for Scripture.** The clergy and lay committees must be willing to submit every campaign to scriptural scrutiny. "Anyone soliciting funds for [religious purposes] must be fully persuaded that the ministry he or she represents not only is a response to human need or opportunity, but pre-eminently is a response to God's divine mandate."[7]

Given these admonitions, how can the officers of the congregation become more effective in obtaining resources necessary for achieving the congregation's goals? We will now examine how marketing practices may assist in soliciting funds.

## Motivational Attitudes in Fund Raising

Leaders who are responsible for meeting the budget typically adopt 1 of 3 attitudes regarding members' giving.

*1. Product orientation.* Here the prevailing attitude is "We have a good program; people ought to support us." Many congregations and judicatories operate on this concept. The leaders depend on the members to give the necessary funds and will use pleas and pressure if necessary to get it. Occasionally, the pastor or rabbi will approach a member or 2 for considerable contributions. A few loyal donors supply most of the funds. A rule of thumb in product-oriented congregations is that "20 percent of the members provide 80 percent of the funds."

This is also the main approach utilized by denominational hierarchies whose polity allows them to levy "apportionments" or "askings" on the local congregations.

*2. Sales orientation.* The prevailing attitude here is "There are a lot of members who should be giving more. We have to convince them to give." This type of thinking prompts the leaders to search for ways to convince the members they should support the budget, while paying little or no attention to the members' satisfaction level or sense of the importance of the programs they are being asked to support.

*3. Market orientation.* Here the prevailing attitude is "We must provide programs and ministries of importance and satisfaction to our members. To the extent that we do, we can count on them to support the necessary costs." This is the orientation toward ministries and budgets that, today, makes the most sense in a local congregation.

Use of the product orientation is perhaps the most damaging orientation used in congregations and by judicatories today. It bespeaks a mind-set that many members are finding increasingly unsatisfying. The mind-set is "We will tell you where your money will go—you give; we decide."

Under such circumstances, the faithful member gives—but also resents. As resentment grows, the members give less; in response to which the hierarchy applies threat and/or increases the per capita amount by legislation. Little by little members leave. Those who stay sink under the weight of important costs, which can hardly be cut or eliminated—i.e., clergy pensions and insurance.

However, it is not only the ecclesial supersystems that operate out of a product orientation. Many local congregations do also.

We will now discuss the topic of fund raising for religious organizations in 5 parts. Section 1 will analyze the major donor markets. Section 2 will examine how institutions organize their fund-raising effort internally. Section 3 will consider the important task of setting fund-raising objectives and strategies, while section 4 will take a look at the multiplicity of fund-raising tactics. Section 5 will consider how religious organizations can evaluate and improve their fund-raising effectiveness.

## Analyzing Donor Markets

A local congregation can tap into a variety of sources for financial support. The 5 major donor markets are the membership in toto, individuals, foundations, local businesses, and government. Following is a discussion of these donor markets as they relate to the congregation.

### The Membership and Individuals

Most congregations typically solicit funds primarily from 2 sources: the membership as a whole and individual members. Larger congregations tend, occasionally, to solicit funds from the other sources also. In fact, some (usually large) congregations are somewhat aggressive in finding resources for major programs, or programs of broad community appeal, from beyond the membership.

The exchanges of the congregation that involve its receiving economic benefit can be grouped into 2 broad categories: those in which goods or services are the something-of-value and those in which the something-of-value is a more intangible spiritual, social, or psychological benefit. Exhibit 11-1 lists some of the sources of funds exchanged for these benefits or goods and services for both individual and organizational donors.

**Exhibit 11-1**

## REVENUE SOURCES FOR CONGREGATIONS

| | GIVERS | |
| --- | --- | --- |
| | INDIVIDUALS | OGANIZATIONS |
| GOODS OR SERVICES | DINNERS<br>PUBLICATIONS<br>RENTAL PROPERTY<br>PLAYS OR CONCERTS<br>ARTS AND CRAFTS<br>EDUCATION | DENOMINATIONAL SUBSIDIES |
| INTANGIBLE SOCIAL OR PSYCHOLOGICAL BENEFITS | TITHE<br>PLEDGES/COMMITMENTS<br>OFFERINGS<br>MEMBERSHIP "DUES"<br>ANNUITIES<br>TRUSTS<br>LIFE INSURANCE BENEFITS | GRANTS<br>DONATIONS FOR SPECIFIC CAUSES |

(Row label spanning left margin: **Religious Organization "PRODUCTS"**)

**Goods and Services.** Congregations do raise funds by providing goods or services in exchange for money. Examples include a Jewish day school that charges tuition, a day-care center that charges a fee, a church that leases its parking lots to business concerns during the working hours, or a congregation that operates a retirement home and collects rentals and fees.[8]

However, when the congregation does enter into a serious venture, it should do so in the clear understanding that it has entered the marketplace and will face competition from for-profit and nonprofit organizations. All the prayers of all the staff won't compensate for poor planning or shoddy administration. Good stewardship of the congregation's resources dictates that the venture should be planned and operated in the light of sound planning and management principles.[9]

Understanding the target market's needs and interests and planning to satisfy them in some manner that affords the venture an advantage over its competition on some dimension of value to the target market group is the key to successfully attracting and keeping clients. Setting clear objectives, determining prices, and planning and delivering a quality product or service that capitalizes on the competitive advantage are all important steps in successfully exchanging a good or service for money.

Success in meeting the goods and services needs of clients has the added benefit of opening the door for the congregation to engage persons in exchanges of value regarding their spiritual, social, or psychological needs and interests, thus converting a transactional exchange into a transformational exchange.

**Spiritual, social, or psychological benefits.** Why do people give to religious organizations? What is the something-of-value received in return for their money if it isn't a good or a service? Is there such a thing as giving without getting? Altruism, as an answer to such questions, tends to mask the complex motives that underlie persons' giving or helping behaviors.

In giving, some people say they expect nothing back. But they almost certainly have some expectations or motives for giving. They may expect to feel good, to feel affluent and generous, to feel appreciated or admired, to feel special. While contributors to religious organizations may be motivated by these desires, there are some unique expectations present in religious contributive exchanges.

Several writers have examined the biblical motivational principles that may inspire a person to make a financial contribution to his or her church. By examining these motivations, one can begin to identify the intangible social or psychological "something-of-value" that should be built into an exchange with a contributor. Cunningham suggests that the following motivations may be present.[10]

* *Giving as a response to God's grace.* The person's ability to give is possible because God's grace frees the person to give as God has given to him or her.

* *Giving as a response to human need.* This principle is as old as the Pentateuch. In the New Testament, the good Samaritan best embodies this motivation.

* *Giving as an expression of thanksgiving to God.* Giving has been an integral part of the worship experience throughout antiquity. Thank offerings (see Lev. 7:12-13) were a formalized worship ritual intended to allow the giver to acknowledge his or her dependence upon God for blessings.

° *Giving as a way of symbolizing commitment of all of one's resources to the service of God and humanity.* All biblical giving practices are centered around this principle. God is portrayed as the owner of everything, having absolute claim upon God's people and all that they are and have. The believer's gifts, therefore, are symbolic commitments to serving God and humanity with all one's resources.

° *Giving as a concrete proof of love.* Scriptures admonish the believer to serve not just in word, but also in deed. Genuine love manifests itself in concrete action, of which giving is one act.

In addition to these uniquely religious aspects of an exchange involving gifts of money to a religious organization, donors may be motivated to satisfy other basic social/psychological needs.

---

In matters of fund raising, religious organizations are different in some significant ways from all other organizations. One of those differences is the way in which persons of faith view the whole matter of "giving to God." The people of God truly believe that they do not give *to* the religious organization. They believe that they give to God *through* the religious organization.

Religious organizations teach or utilize 3 major methods of fund raising: the tithe, the pledge, and the membership fee.

Our work as consultants with congregations and judicatories serves to convince us that congregations that have the tithe as the norm for giving to religious causes have far fewer financial problems to run pledge campaigns (anathema in most tithing congregations), or to methodically reduce ministries or staff to bring expenses into line with meager contributions.

We also observe that whenever a tithing church is experiencing financial difficulties, as many as 3 factors tend to be present.

First, the pastor has lost his or her integrity in the eyes of a substantial part of the congregation.

Second, the local leaders and/or the denomination's leaders are failing to practice sound marketing principles, such as measuring members' satisfaction with major programs, measuring members' feeling of "importance" regarding major programs or staff positions, practicing outside-in thinking, and making certain that the exchanges with members are transformational exchanges of value for both parties.

Third, the congregation is in serious, prolonged, and unresolved conflict.

We found it difficult to write about segmenting and targeting the congregation as a donor market. Especially difficult was wanting to use good marketing theory regarding what to ask of a donor; whether to make no specific request at all, to ask for less than the person should give (foot in the door), or to ask for more than the person would normally give (door in the face). It seems to us that the Scriptures and moral responsibility would suggest a different strategy; it isn't what's "low" or what's "high," but what's "right."

The fund raiser for a religious organization is left with the responsibility of discerning the right amount to ask for—without concern about which part of the anatomy may be bruised, whether foot or face. As a matter of consistency, the religious organization's fund raiser might ask for the tithe. Otherwise, when the church or synagogue or one of its most important ministries is in financial need, ask for what is needed, not what you think the person should give. Leave some room for God to speak to the donor. God is quite capable of directing one's giving, if one will but listen.

When the church operates on a pledge system, and the ministries are cut to fit the pledged amount, this is a "little faith, let's play it safe" approach. Do the leaders have the right to ask that the pledges be increased to fit the ministry? Yes, but only if they have done their homework, and through the process have discerned the will of God for ministry in that place. More likely than not, when pledges are reduced, forcing cutbacks in programs, it is because the donors do not see the programs as worthy of their support—they do not see the programs as important and/or satisfying.

Marketing and discernment can add a new dimension to any and all fund-raising efforts. Marketing is a powerful discipline. Every church and synagogue can benefit from its use. But marketing without discernment remains only a shadow of what it might be in the church and synagogue.

The main point is that the congregation must view the act of receiving money from an individual donor as an exchange—and the more clergy and lay leaders understand the motives for giving, the more capable they become of ensuring that the "something-of-value" will be received by the donor in exchange for the contribution.

For example, some congregations have a specific line on their tithe/offering envelopes for "Thanks Offerings," so that the donor can more specifically indicate the intended use of the offering.

---

Given the power of today's personal computer, it would be simple to print specific messages, relating to the use the offering was intended, on the member's quarterly statement of giving. This would assure the donor that the offering was noted and was directed to its intended purpose. These messages could be worded in such a way as to personalize the receipt of the gift, perhaps with some scriptural quotations and an accompanying statement that might help provide the "something-of-value" exchanged for the thanks offering.

Similar approaches could be developed to provide the benefits sought by donors with other motives for giving. The intent here is not manipulation, but simply to uphold the receiving organization's end of the exchange process; donors deserve to know their gifts are not only appreciated but also are understood regarding their motivations.[11]

---

The various motives for giving provide clues to marketing strategy for congregations. Harold Seymour has suggested that in many mass-donor markets, one-third of the people are *responsible* (they donate without being solicited), one-third are *responsive* (they donate when they are asked), and one-third *react to compulsion* (they donate because of pressure).[12] Each market can be investigated further to discover the specific motive segments that exist.

Too many congregations ask people to give to them as a poor and needy organization—rather than to support valuable ministries, through which the donor may find an exchange of value.[13] The former approach is tantamount to begging. The latter is far more effective. People respond to what they sense as the relevance, importance, and urgency of a giving opportunity. Seymour suggests that the case for giving must be bigger than the institution. And it must be presented in a way that catches the eye, warms the heart, and stirs the mind. People want to feel that they are worthwhile members of a worthwhile organization.

## Foundations

Many congregations do not realize that funding opportunities may exist from foundations. Of course, these foundations will not be interested in funding the operating expenses of a church or in evangelistic activities (unless the foundation has been established for that purpose), but opportunities do exist to receive grants for church programs, such as day-care center training facilities, classes for mentally retarded and emotionally disturbed children or adults, services for the aged, meals on wheels, family planning, alcohol and drug abuse, and many other social-service ministries.

Currently there are over 23,700 foundations in the United States, all set up to give money to worthwhile causes. They fall into the following groups:

* *Family foundations*, set up by wealthy individuals to support a limited number of activities of interest to the founders. Family foundations typically do not have permanent offices or full-time staff members. Decisions tend to be made by family members, counsel, or both.
* *General foundations*, set up to support a wide range of activities and usually run by a professional staff. General foundations range from extremely large organizations, such as the Ford Foundation and the Rockefeller Foundation, that support a wide range of causes and give most of their money to large, well-established organizations, to more specialized general foundations that give money to a particular cause, such as health (Johnson Foundation) or education (Carnegie Foundation).
* *Corporate foundations*, set up by corporations and allowed to give away up to 5 percent of the corporation's adjusted gross income.
* *Community trusts*, set up in cities or regions and made up of smaller foundations whose funds are pooled for greater impact.

With 23,700 foundations, it is important for the fund raiser to know how to locate the few that would be the most likely to support a given project or cause. Fortunately, many resources are available for researching foundations. The best single resource is known as the Foundation Center, a nonprofit organization with research centers in New York, Washington, D.C., and Chicago. The Foundation Center collects and distributes information on foundations. In addition, many libraries around the country carry important materials describing foundations and how to approach them. The most important materials are described below.

*The Foundation Grants Index* lists the grants that have been given in the past year by foundation, subject, state, and other groupings. The fund raiser, for example, could look up visual arts and find out all the grants made to support the visual arts and identify the most active foundations in this area of giving.

*The Foundation Directory* lists more than 2,500 foundations that either have assets of over $1 million or award grants of more than $500,000 annually. The directory describes the general characteristics of each foundation, such as type of foundation, types of grants, annual giving level, officers and directors, location, particular fields of interest, contact person, and so on. The directory also contains an index of fields of interest, listing the foundations that have a stated interest in each field and whether they gave money to this field in the past year.

*The Foundation News* is published 6 times a year by the Council on Foundations. *The Foundation News* describes new foundations, new funding programs, and changes in existing foundations.

*Fund Raising Management* is a periodical that publishes articles on fund-raising management.

## MATCHING WITH A FOUNDATION'S INTEREST AND SCALE OF OPERATION

The key concept in identifying foundations is that of *matching*. The religious organization should search for foundations matched to its *interest* and *scale of operation*. Too often a small nonprofit organization will send a proposal to a foundation because it would like to get the support of this well-known foundation. But that foundation accepts about 1 out of every 100 proposals and may be less inclined to fund a small project (in their scope) connected to a congregation than more regional or specialized foundations might be.

---

### Preparing a Grant Proposal

Writing successful grant proposals is becoming a fine art, with many guides currently available to help the grant-seeker.14 Each proposal should contain at least the following elements:

1. A cover letter describing the history of the proposal and who has been contacted, if anyone, in the foundation;
2. The proposal, describing the project, its uniqueness, and its importance;
3. The budget for the project;
4. The personnel working on the project, with their resumes.

The proposal itself should be compact, individualized, organized, and readable. In writing the proposal, the organization should be guided by knowledge of the "buying criteria" that the particular foundation uses to choose among the many proposals it receives. Like any other marketing communication, the proposal must be customer-centered. Many foundations describe their criteria in their annual reports or other memos, or their criteria can be learned by talking to knowledgeable individuals. Among the most common guiding criteria used by foundations are:

* the importance and quality of the project;
* the neediness and worthiness of the organization;
* the organization's ability to use the funds effectively and efficiently;
* the importance of satisfying the persons who are doing the proposing;
* the degree of benefit that the foundation will derive in supporting the proposal.

---

After identifying a few foundations that might have strong interest in its project, the congregation should try to estimate more accurately their level of interest before investing time in preparing a grant proposal. Most foundations are willing to respond to a letter of inquiry, telephone call, or personal visit and will indicate how interested they would be in the project. The foundation officer may be very encouraging or discouraging. If the former, the congregation can then expend the energy necessary to prepare a proposal for this foundation.

If the proposing organization knows the relative importance of the respective criteria, it can do a better job of selecting the features of the proposal to emphasize. If the particular foundation is likely to be influenced by who presents the proposal, for example, the congregation should send its highest ranking officials to the foundation. On the other hand, if the foundation attaches the most importance to the quality of the proposal, the congregation should put a lot of effort into fine-tuning the writing of the proposal.

Congregations that are interested in exploring foundation support for their program should not contact foundations only on the occasion of a specific proposal. Rather, the leaders should cultivate a handful of appropriate foundations in advance of specific proposals. This is called "building bridges" or "relationship marketing."

---

One major university sees the Ford Foundation as a "key customer account." The development officer arranges for one or more members of the university's board to see corresponding board members of the foundation each year. The university president visits the foundation's president each year for a luncheon or dinner. One or more members of the university's development staff cultivate relations with foundation staff members at their levels. When the university has a proposal, it knows exactly who should present it to the foundation and whom to see in the foundation. Furthermore, the foundation is more favorably disposed toward the university because of the long relationship and special understanding they enjoy. Finally, the university is able to do a better job of tracking the proposal as it is being reviewed by the foundation.

---

## Corporations and the Government

Marketing to corporations and government for the purpose of soliciting funds is sufficiently similar to warrant discussing them together. While businesses and the government are unlikely to be major funding sources for a congregation's program, they do represent a funding opportunity for certain programs sponsored by a church or synagogue. In fact, occasionally a business or the Chamber of Commerce will approach a congregation to launch a program that the business community feels is necessary to the welfare of its workers; for example, a day-care center in the business district. In such instances, the business community is prepared to offer substantial start-up funding.

For similar reasons, the right program can occasionally gain government (city, state, etc.) assistance. Both corporations and the government are likely to be interested in only nonsectarian programs. If the congregation can demonstrate that the funding will serve persons other than its members, these sources may be tapped.

Local corporations may have an interest in generating publicity and goodwill for themselves, even as they assist a project to benefit the community. Therefore, proposals to corporations should include a statement indicating the means by which the corporation will receive credit for its assistance. Congregation members employed in management positions for corporations can help the congregation fund raisers understand more of what the "something-of-value" is for companies contributing to local causes.

Congregations seeking government grants should obtain the catalogue of *Federal and Domestic Assistance*, published by the government, which lists thousands of funding sources. Here as well, nonsectarian causes have the greatest chance for consideration.

## Organizing for Fund Raising

Congregations must develop a strategic approach to fund raising. Three basic fund-raising approaches are used by congregations: the tithe, the pledge, and membership fees.

Small congregations tend to rely on one person who is chiefly responsible for fund raising—usually the pastor or rabbi. Medium-sized congregations tend to have a stewardship or finance committee. Large congregations tend to have a committee, plus a volunteer stewardship director or a paid minister of stewardship. Whatever the arrangement, the committee or stewardship person is responsible for identifying fund-raising opportunities and activating others—lay officers, staff, and volunteers—to assist. No matter what the structure, the pastor or rabbi will be heavily involved in fund-raising; it goes with the territory.

In the congregation, Knudsen suggests the use of task forces, each assigned responsibility for one source of funds.[15] Each task force would consist of 3 members who meet the following criteria:

* capable of maintaining the confidentiality of information, which can be very personal at times;
* must be known by—and know—many members of the congregation and have good relationships with the congregation and community leaders. This breadth of acquaintances will aid in enlisting the cooperation of key people when such circumstances arise;
* must be capable of organizing work and delegating work to volunteers.

Additionally, each task force should have high interest in its assigned source of funds, and some unique qualifications. These task forces would then focus on the following sources of funds:

> *Task force cardinal rule #1:* Never assign a task force more than 1 specific project. As soon as a task force is given 2 assignments, it becomes a committee.
>
> *Task force cardinal rule #2:* Task force members are hand-picked and recruited one-by-one. They are never nominated and elected by a nominating committee.

- stewardship enlistment and commitment;
- special gifts;
- memorials;
- gift annuities;
- wills and bequests;
- real estate and personal property;
- charitable remainder trust;
- grants;
- financial administration.

The task forces should be connected by a Financial Stewardship and Gifts Cabinet, composed of a representative from each task force and chaired by the pastor or a presiding officer elected by the task force members. If other sources of funds are to be explored (special events, thrift shops, etc.), a task force would be established for each source and represented on the cabinet.

## Fund-Raising Goals and Strategies

Congregations tend to establish a budget and set an annual goal for fund raising, even if this is merely the amount of increase of the current year's budget over the previous year's budget. Congregations use several different approaches to arrive at their fund-raising goal.

*1. Incremental approach.* The finance committee takes last year's contribution, increases it to cover inflation, and then modifies it up or down, depending on the expected economic climate. Thus a congregation may decide to raise about 15 percent more than it did in the previous year.

*2. Need approach.* The committee forecasts its financial needs and sets a goal based on its needs. Thus the leaders will estimate future program and building needs and costs, staff salaries, energy costs, and so on. Then it will subtract other sources of funds and set the portion that has to be covered by fund raising as its target.

*3. Opportunity approach.* The leaders and the committee make a fresh estimate of how much money they could raise from each donor group with different levels of fund-raising expenditure. They set the goal of maximizing the net surplus. The committee and leaders would be responsible for preparing this analysis by analyzing the potential of each donor group. If this goal is accepted, the group knows how much effort to allocate to each donor group.

Of the 3 approaches, the opportunity approach is the most sound. However, this is not to say that these are the only approaches, nor is it to say that the opportunity approach is the best approach for a specific congregation. There is an inherent flaw in all 3 approaches: each approach considers money and donors first, before considering the ministries, existing and possible, and what it would take by way of money for the ministries to reach their highest potential.

Also, we must recognize that there are congregations that never build a budget, but whose ministry is nonetheless secure and vital.

Over the years, the authors have discovered many congregations who do not operate on a budget and whose ministries are strong and growing. Interestingly, these congregations tend to have several things in common:

1. The pastor is of long tenure and is above reproach in his or her private and professional life. (This is, we are certain, a fundamental prerequisite.)
2. The norm for giving is the tithe, and offerings beyond the tithe. This is not a fancy ideal; the members live in covenant to tithe their income.
3. The leaders have committed themselves to the congregation to operate the church and its ministries within the amount of offerings received—and to spend all offerings received within 2 months of being received. The principle here seems to be that the money given will be (almost immediately) applied to ministry, and the ministry reach will not exceed the congregation's interests.
4. The leaders constantly keep before the congregation the results of its present ministries and other ministry opportunities, and the congregation knows at all times what it is getting for its money. Failures are openly announced and discussed.
5. The leaders make a monthly financial report to the congregation, listing the amount of contributions and how the money was spent that month. The report is made both verbally and in writing.
6. Many (not all) of these congregations do not receive public offerings. Rather an offering box is kept near the entrance, into which persons deposit their contributions.
7. A monthly meeting of the congregation is conducted in which the leaders make detailed reports of ministry and money, allowing much time for group discussion. Virtually all the people are in attendance.

Some time ago the authors interviewed a pastor whose congregation has followed these principles for several years. At the time of the interview, his central congregation had launched several other congregations, all following the same principles. The central congregation was the largest, with about 500 people. This ministry might be called a "mini-denomination."

A preferred strategy would see fund raising as 1 part of a larger picture, including:

1. An assessment of the present levels of *satisfaction* and *importance* of the present ministries and programs;
2. *Evaluation* of program and worker effectiveness;
3. *Searching* for new ministry opportunities, *segmenting* and *targeting* new ministry groups;
4. Creating *plans* to start new ministries and to continue existing ministries, each plan to include the *mission* and the expected *results* of the ministry;
5. Building *budgets* to support the proposed ministry plan;
6. The results of the ministry and budget plan will establish the *fund-raising goal* for the congregation.
7. As a part of arriving at the plan, the stewardship committee, or task forces working together, must do all the things listed above. It must also:
   a. analyze the potential of each donor group.
   b. develop its overall fund-raising strategy—including how it will present the ministry plans to each donor group, etc. Choices must be made concerning types of motivational appeal, how much effort will be devoted to seeking contributions from internal publics (members and denominational subsidies) and external publics (selling goods or services, seeking foundation grants, contributions from local corporations, etc.).

This approach takes time. It should become a way of doing things, an ongoing process, rather than a big push to get the budget approved—within the last 2 or 3 months of the current fiscal year. After such a long list of steps, it is perhaps appropriate to recall an earlier stated rule for planning: "Make the process *natural*. Keep it *simple*. If it isn't natural, the people *won't do it*. If it isn't simple, they *won't be able* to do it."[16]

## Fund-Raising Tactics

The fund-raising strategy sets the overall parameters for the fund-raising effort, which the committee or development officer must fill in with specific actions. The committee's job is to send messages to the potential donors through the most effective message channels and allow the donors to make their contributions through the most satisfying, and perhaps efficient, means. This view of the channel options is shown in Exhibit 11-2.

The various channel opportunities give rise to a set of specific, well-

**Exhibit 11-2**

**COMMUNICATION AND COLLECTION CHANNELS
FOR FUND RAISING**

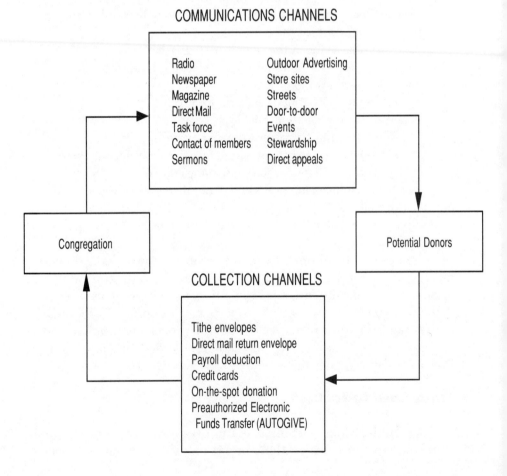

COMMUNICATIONS CHANNELS

| | |
|---|---|
| Radio | Outdoor Advertising |
| Newspaper | Store sites |
| Magazine | Streets |
| Direct Mail | Door-to-door |
| Task force | Events |
| Contact of members | Stewardship |
| Sermons | Direct appeals |

Congregation

Potential Donors

COLLECTION CHANNELS

Tithe envelopes
Direct mail return envelope
Payroll deduction
Credit cards
On-the-spot donation
Preauthorized Electronic
  Funds Transfer (AUTOGIVE)

known fund-raising tactics. Exhibit 11-3 lists the major tactics that are effective in 4 markets.

## Exhibit 11-3

## FUND-RAISING METHODS

### *Mass Anonymous Small Gift Market*

Charity cans in stores
Direct mail
Door-to-door solicitation
Street and sidewalk solicitation
TV and radio marathons
Thrift shops
Plate passing

Raffles
Rummage sales
Sporting events
Walkathons, readathons
  bikeathons, jogathons,
  swimathons
Yearbooks

### *Members and Their Friends Market*

Anniversary celebrations
Art shows
Auctions
Benefits (theater, movies, sports
  events)
Bingo games
Book sales
Cake sales

Dances
Dinners, suppers, lunches,
  breakfasts
Fairs
Fashion shows
Parties in unusual places
Phonathons (also called telethons)

### *Affluent Citizens Market*

Convocations
Dinners (invitational and/or
  testimonial)
Letters from high-status individuals

Parlor meetings
Telephone calls from high-status
  individuals

### *Wealthy Donors Market*

Bequests
Celebrity grooming
Committee visit to person's home,
  office
Memorials

Testimonial dinner for wealthy
  individuals
Wealthy person invited to another's
  home or club

*The mass anonymous small-gift market* consists of all persons who might be induced to contribute a small sum (say under $50) to a cause. The key idea is to use low-cost methods of fund raising, since the contributions from non-involved individuals are expected to be low. Such tactics include Campbell's soup label projects, annual church bazaar, and so on.

In recent years, direct mail has become an extremely important marketing tool to reach the mass anonymous small-gift market. There are 3 reasons for this. First, the cost of personal solicitation has increased dramatically. Second, the growing availability of highly specialized mailing lists permits careful targeting of the market. And third, the emergence of the small business and personal computers has permitted congregations to compile, use, and refine mailing lists at very low costs.

Direct mail fund raising might be considered by a congregation that conducts a ministry that serves a need or interest of the entire community and/or is highly visible, so that persons receiving the mailing would tend to see the ministry as responding to one of their personal needs or interests—such as a food distribution program for the poor, a summer sports program for children, or a ministry of giving job training and job placement to developmentally challenged adults.

Direct mail is relatively easy to get started. The first year's returns largely pay back the cost of the mailing lists and the system. This investment then begins to provide funds for ministry.

With computers, congregations can personalize correspondence and code into their data files who responds to what. With special mailing lists, they can tailor appeals to segments with known interests and life-styles. Each mailing allows the committee to acquire more experience and fine tune its approach.

*The members and their friends market* consists of congregation members and their friends who have a personal interest in supporting the congregation's ministry. This market can be tapped for donations in a number of ways—ranging from "second-time-around" sales, cake sales, and walkathons to dinners, mission fairs, and the like.

The unifying factor here is that something is being offered that members will support, and their friends will also support because of friendship connections. It goes without saying that these efforts need to be carefully planned and conducted; one doesn't want to lose a friendship over a congregation's appeal. Nonetheless, many members are willing to solicit funds from friends and acquaintances to support worthwhile ministries.

Each fund-raising method requires careful planning in order to maximize its potential. "Sweetheart dinners," for example, have to be planned and promoted far in advance of the day of their occurrence. Fund-raising consultants can be found who specialize in each method. These consultants can recommend the most effective and appropriate fund-raising methods to a congregation. Furthermore, they continue to invent new approaches each year.[17] No sooner had walkathons become popular than other organizations created readathons, bikeathons, and jogathons.

*The affluent citizens market* consists of persons whose income and interest in the congregation or its cause could lead them to give anywhere from $50 to several hundred dollars as a donation. This market can be approached by a congregation that is launching a ministry or service that will meet a community or specialized need. For example, a congregation launching a day-care center in the business district and is a highly felt need by business, and may even have received financial start-up from the chamber of commerce, might decide to market to affluent citizens.

A highly effective technique is to issue invitations to a special dinner featuring a popular personage as speaker (who will, of course, speak on a topic related to the ministry). The invitations can be issued in 2 different ways: the dinner may bear a set minimum price, perhaps $100 or the dinner may be free, with donations solicited after an inspiring program.

Another popular method of raising money from affluent donors consists of supporters sending letters or phoning their affluent friends to ask for donations.

*The wealthy donors market* consists of persons whose wealth and potential interest are such that they might be induced to contribute anywhere from $1,000 to several million dollars to a congregation or one of its ministries. This is perhaps the most neglected fund-raising strategy for congregations. Many congregations have at least 1 wealthy person in their own membership, who is being marketed by several other nonprofit organizations, but not by his or her own congregation.

A major concern of most wealthy persons is what will become of their wealth when they die and how a part of it may be used to perpetuate their memory or the memory of a loved one. For this reason, they are thinking about wills, trusts, and bequests of many kinds. Every congregation should have its own program for wills, trusts, and the like.

The congregation should not wait until someone inquires about wills to start such a program. Very often the person or family making the inquiry either needs to, or strongly feels the need to, make immediate arrangements. The time to set up the congregation's plan is when no one is asking. The plan will require legal assistance; don't do it without an attorney. Many ecclesial judicatories have departments to assist in this.

Many clergy and lay leaders need to think carefully about whom to market about including the church or synagogue in their wills, trust agreements, and the like. Virtually every congregation has a number of people who will leave an estate to others. Many faithful members would like to leave a gift to the congregation, but no one has ever asked or suggested it. While this type of marketing may not help today's fund raising, it will play a major role in sustaining the congregation's future ministries.

All of these fund-raising tactics can be organized under the umbrella concept of *campaign*.

> A campaign is an organized and time-sequenced set of activities and events for raising a given sum of money within a particular time period.

Congregations distinguish between an annual campaign and a capital campaign. The annual campaign is to raise a target amount of money each year, often called the general budget. The campaign plan spells out the mission of the church and its ministries, goals, events, and so on.

An annual campaign is not always the best step. At the end of 1990, reviewing the members' support of the church's programs and budgets and looking forward to a new year of ministry, Charles Sineath and the lay leaders of First United Methodist Church, Marietta, Georgia, decided that the strong and healthy state of the congregation did not warrant a campaign to underwrite the 1991 budget. Rather, they would use resources to thank the congregation for their faithful support over the years past. The decision was made to retain a professional public relations firm to prepare a 20-minute videotape, which would highlight the results of the congregation's ministry in the lives of real people. There were 3 false starts at the project, because the firm was much experienced in preparing media programs for churches to ask for money, but had never had a request to thank people for their support, with absolutely no appeal for future support. The crew finally developed an effective message of thanks for a job well done. The video was hand-carried to every home in the parish. The visitors left the tape, arranged a time to pick it up, and thanked the family for their support of the church. The result took everyone by surprise—total contributions to the church immediately increased by 15 percent—and did not decline.

Congregations conduct capital campaigns when they need to raise a large amount of money for major undertakings or expansions. These campaigns require the most careful planning. Following are some of the major considerations.

**A congregation should not run capital campaigns too often.** Many congregations space their capital campaigns at 3 to 5 years apart. This spacing is necessary if the capital campaigns are to retain their specialness in the minds of the donors. An exception to this is the case where a 2- or 3-phase campaign is launched, with the members knowing that the campaigns will follow one after the other.

**The planners have to make decisions about the capital campaign's goal and duration.** The goal should be achievable. There is nothing more embarrassing than failing to reach the goal. And the campaign should not last too long because it will eventually lose its momentum.

**The planners should try to add a matching-gift feature to the campaign,** where some wealthy donors or organizations promise to match the contributions of their employees, of the other members, and so on. Early in the planning, the committee has to find and cultivate challenge funds.

**The planners should prepare an attractive booklet showing the main items that the money will buy (called a wish list).** This will allow persons a choice of whether to give to the campaign in general or to "buy" a particular feature. This approach is often strengthened by allowing certain major items to be donated, such as memorials.

**Conventional wisdom has it that a capital campaign should not be started until much of its goal (35-50 percent) has already been reached.** That is, larger donors must be solicited for major grants before announcing the campaign kickoff. This will give the campaign significant momentum at the start, creating a sense of confidence and desire to see it succeed and erasing doubts that the project is not needed or that it will not soon achieve its goal.

This item, however, needs to be assessed in the light of the congregation's ethos. There are many congregations in which the "big gift" approach would offend the members as a "professional" approach—to be avoided by the church.

An issue in designing a campaign is to decide whether potential donors should be coached in how much to give or whether this should be left to their judgment. In fact, there are 3 possibilities:

1. Don't specify an amount.
2. Suggest a specific dollar amount on the low side.
3. Suggest a specific dollar amount on the high side.

The first approach is the most common. People differ in what they can give, and it is felt that this is best left to their individual judgments.

Suggesting a specific amount on the low side is seen as accomplishing 2 things. It helps prospects to know what is considered a proper minimum amount to give. And the "low-amount feature" allows people to get into the habit of giving (the "foot-in-the-door" theory).[18] While many people might have given more, research suggests that the technique can be quite effective.

Brockner and his colleagues found that in a campaign for a relatively obscure charity, the National Reye's Syndrome Foundation, concluding the sales presentation with the phrase "even a dollar will help" resulted in 20 times as much money being raised as when no amount was suggested.[19] Further, "even a dollar will help" was more effective than saying "even five dollars will help." The researchers found that the "five dollar" suggestion yielded more total dollars than the control condition (no request), but less than the "even a dollar" condition. Finally, the research found that the "even a dollar will help" technique applies to both telephone and face-to-face solicitation. Citing earlier research, they also claim that the technique has been shown to work for at least 3 different charities, Reye's Syndrome, the American Cancer Society, and the Heart Association.[20]

Suggesting a high amount to the person works on the theory of "door-in-the-face." It stretches people's idea of what they should give, and it is hoped that they will give this much, or something close to it. Thus the United Fund might suggest that citizens give 1 percent of their income, or a congregation might suggest that members give 10 percent of their income. Many people regard these amounts as too high and slam the door in the fund raiser's face, but end up giving more than they normally would.

## New Technological Fund-Raising Approaches

Modern technology has invaded every aspect of American life, including religion. One fund-raising tactic that could prove significant in generating a more constant, reliable source of funds is to provide a means of making systematic giving convenient and worry free for members. Electronic funds transfer is one contemporary way of achieving convenient systematic giving. A number of congregations have adopted the AUTOGIVE pre-authorized electronic fund transfer system (see Exhibit 11-4).

Bank credit cards are another means of making giving more convenient for parishioners. In Buffalo, New York, the Coronation of the Blessed Virgin Mary Church introduced the bank-card option, and total parish income increased by 300 percent in the first quarter.[21]

Modern technology allows, in some geographic areas, people to make fund transfers by using a personal computer or a touch tone phone. Congregations should not neglect opportunities for allowing members to make convenient, regular contributions using these technological tools. Strange as these methods may seem, they do fit our rules of "keep it simple" and "keep it natural." The use of the credit card is, for many, more natural than carrying cash.

## Exhibit 11-4

AUTOGIVE IS . . .

MAY

WE

* A banking process whereby donors may order their church commitment paid automatically by their bank.

SUGGEST . . . *

* A thoughtful action by responsible Christians who want to assure ministry and mission through regular, systematic giving.

. . . AUTOGIVE

* Convenient for donors . . . no checks to write or mail.

* Helpful in reducing administrative expense while assuring support even when you must be away, weather threatens or illness strikes.

* Easy to use. Merely complete the simple form and we'll do the rest.

a thoughtful tool of
Christian Philanthropy
for the 21st Century.

* Safely regulated by banking laws. You may terminate participation at any time.

* Now used by thousands and available to you in making your church commitment even more helpful.

## *Evaluating Fund-Raising Effectiveness*

As long as ministry requires money, congregations must make a continuous effort to improve the effectiveness of their stewardship and fund-raising efforts, through evaluating their most recent results, especially in the face of increasingly sophisticated competition and scarce funds.

Congregations use several methods to evaluate their overall fund-raising effectiveness. They are described below.

**Percentage of Goal Reached.** For congregations that set an annual goal, the first thing to look at is how close the congregation came to achieving the goal. Every congregation wants to achieve or to exceed its goal. This creates a temptation to set the goal low enough to be achieved. The clergy, however, tend to set a high goal to induce the parishioners to sacrifice in giving.

**Composition of Gifts.** The finance committee should examine the composition of the money raised, looking at trends in the 2 major components:

$$\text{Gifts} \;=\; \text{number of donors} \;\times\; \text{the average gift size}$$

**Number of Donors.** Each congregation hopes to increase the number of donors each year. The committee should pay attention to the current number of donors in relation to the potential number of donors. Many congregations have a disappointing "reach" or "penetration." Suppose 29 percent of congregation A's members have given each year. The question is not why congregation A has 29 percent penetration, but why 71 percent of its members do not give. The task force cabinet should interview a sample of nongivers and identify the reasons, and how often each is stated. They may hear, "We do not like the way the church is evolving"; "I disagree with policies of the synagogue"; "I couldn't care less"; "We were never asked"; and so on. Each of these reasons suggests a possible plan of action.

**Average Gift Size.** A major fund-raising objective is to increase the gift size in given donor segments. The task force cabinet should review the size distribution of gifts. It should estimate the potential number of gifts that might be obtained in each size class and compare it to the current number to determine the gift size classes that deserve targeted effort in the next period.

The marketing tactics of measuring "satisfaction" and "importance" members feel toward major programs and ministries, and working to increase feelings of satisfaction and importance, are primary strategies for increasing the number of donors and the average size of the contribution.

## *Summary*

Virtually all congregations need to raise funds in order to finance their operations and ministries. However, raising money for the most worthy of all causes is usually not easy. Moreover, the procedures used to raise money by religious organizations should be and are subject to a more stringent set of rules than govern fund raising by secular institutions. Marketing, as we describe it here, can be a useful tool for the fund raisers in congregations.

Religious organizations are gradually shifting from a product or a sales to a marketing orientation. A marketing orientation calls for carefully segmenting donor markets, measuring their giving potential, and assigning responsibility and resources to cultivate each market. Fund raisers for religious organizations need to assume that the act of giving is really an exchange process in which the giver gets something that the church or synagogue can offer in return for his or her contribution.

The first step in the fund-raising process is to study the characteristics of each of the 5 major donor markets: the congregation as a whole, individuals, foundations, corporations, and government. Each donor market has its own giving motives and giving criteria.

The second step is to organize the fund-raising operation in a way that it covers the different donor markets, matches potential donors with ministries, and selects the appropriate marketing tools.

The third step is to develop sound goals and strategies to guide the fund-raising effort. Goals are set on either an incremental basis, a need basis, or an opportunity basis.

The fourth step is to develop a mix of fund-raising approaches for the various donor groups. Different methods and materials are called for when approaching different groups, such as the mass anonymous small gift market, the members-and-their-friends market, the affluent citizens market, and the wealthy donors market.

The fifth step is to conduct regular evaluations of fund-raising results.

# 12

---

# Marketing Is
# Not Enough:

---

## Vision, Spirit, Integrity,
## and Discernment

Not by might, nor by power, but by my spirit, says the LORD of hosts" (Zech. 4:6).

Marketing is not enough for an effective ministry. It is, instead, an excellent management approach. It is a way of disciplined thinking and serves as a check list to be certain nothing important is overlooked or taken for granted in planning and carrying out ministry.

More important than marketing, or any management approach, are the spirit of the congregation and the spirituality of the leaders and workers. It is hoped that every religious organization is a spiritual entity. The Spirit that fuels and directs the religious organization is first and foremost the presence of God.

Most needed in the religious organization today is *vision*. This is not something new. It has always been the case. More than a few of the major denominations in America are presently much more maintenance-orientated than vision-driven. This is serious. The prophet Joel observed that "where there is no vision the people perish." For many years in the twentieth century the American church usually interpreted this to mean that where the church had no vision the unchurched perished. Since the 1960s, however, the church has had reason to interpret the prophecy to mean "where the church has no vision, the church will perish." How great is the need for vision-driven religious organizations in America today!

But vision, as presented in Scripture, cannot be planned; neither can it easily be transferred from one person or congregation to another. The vision we seek is God's vision—and God shares God's vision with whom God chooses. The vision cannot be wrested from God or purchased, though there is a price to be paid in placing oneself where one is able to hear the vision, when God chooses to announce it.

The price is not difficult to understand, though the preparation to discern God's vision may be costly, indeed. Scripture has a way of presenting vision within the context of suffering or sacrifice, a diligent seeking to understand "what now," along with a commitment and an ability to sustain prayer, silence, and solitude.

Spirit is the energy source of religious leadership and ministry. Most people know that the spirit that energizes a religious organization may be negative as well as positive, divisive as well as healing. The spirit that builds strong, viable religious organizations and ministries is the Spirit of God—always present, but not always welcomed, among the people of God.

The best marketing plan in the world cannot compensate for spiritual lethargy or confusion, so that none are able to listen in the silent closets of the heart where God awaits to communicate with us. Nor can a marketing plan counterbalance a lack of vision.

In the late 1980s, Leadership Network[1] retained a consulting firm, Shawchuck & Associates, to conduct research into what the pastors and laity of large Christian congregations felt were important aspects of the pastor's role. In a series of focus groups, and later a broad-scale questionnaire process, persons were asked to list the things a pastor must pay attention to in order to be effective in pastoring a large and growing church. High on the list of responses of laity and clergy alike was that the pastor must practice a disciplined life of prayer and other spiritual disciplines—the pastor must love God. Also high on the list was that the pastor must possess a vision, be able to articulate that vision, and be willing to advocate for it. The study indicated that clergy and laity alike did not see these items as mutually exclusive.

More recently, 1989–91, Shawchuck and Rath conducted a rather massive study for McCormick Theological Seminary, known as the Better Preparation for Ministry Project.[2] This study also utilized focus groups and survey questionnaires, which were sent to a large number of denominations and other church groups.

One of the purposes of the study was to identify the personal qualities and roles an effective pastor must fill in his or her ministry. Across the spectrum of groups surveyed, the item most often identified was the *pastor's personal integrity*. Integrity was followed by such items as a sense of call, wisdom, and personal spiritual renewal. These are items that a marketing program cannot provide.

What is coming clear in many studies and writings currently is that spirituality is the wetlands for vision and discernment. Persons who are most effective in their ministries understand this. No wonder, then, that Pastor Bill Hybels at Willow Creek Community Church wrote the book *Too Busy Not to Pray*,[3] and Martin Luther, during the Reformation, said, "I'm so busy that I have to pray an extra hour a day in order to get my work done."

*Discernment*, or discerning the will of God as a consensus-seeking, decision-making process, is based on the precondition that the people not only believe in prayer, but also that they actually pray. Discernment is not so much a thing the leaders and congregation do once in a while as it is a way of life. The necessity is that God's people should have discerning hearts, much more than they should know how to discern. The ability to discern the will of God for ministry is more a matter of who the discerners *are* than of what the discerners *do*.[4]

Spirituality, vision, discernment, the leaders' integrity—marketing cannot provide these. But marketing is not opposed to these; indeed, marketing can inform and support these essentials to effective ministry.

This book is finished. We send it abroad on its affairs. May this book and its topic serve you, your organization, and God's work through you.

We leave you, dear reader, between the hands of God, with this benediction:

> May the Lord answer you when you are in distress; may the name of the God of Jacob protect you. May God send you help from the sanctuary and grant you support from Zion. May God remember all your sacrifices and accept your offerings. May God give you the desire of your heart and make all your plans succeed.

We will shout for joy when you are victorious, and will lift up our banners in the name of our God. May the Lord grant you all your requests.

Now we know that the Lord saves his anointed; he answers them from his holy heaven with the saving power of his right hand. Some trust in chariots and some in horses, but we trust in the name of the Lord our God. They are brought to their knees and fall, but we rise up and stand firm.

O Lord save your people. Answer us when we call. Amen.
(Psalm 20, paraphrased)

# Appendix A

# *Marketing Resources for Religious Leaders*

W̲e list here marketing resources that are unlikely to be listed in church management literature. While you may be able to access and use all of these sources on your own, it is always wise to make use of the reference librarian at your local public or college library. He or she can help you save considerable time in locating sources of greatest practical use to you.

## *Computerized Data Bases*

One of the fastest ways of locating periodical literature addressing topics of interest to you is to use one of the following computer-based data retrieval services.

All of them allow search by author or by subject. The major difference between the Religion Index and the two business databases (InfoTrac and ABI/Inform) is the periodicals indexed. Therefore, searching the Religion Index using the key word *marketing,* you would locate articles such as August G. Lageman, "Marketing Pastoral Counseling," *The Journal of Pastoral Care* 38 (December 1984): 274-80.

Searching the business-related indexes, on the other hand, you would find thousands of articles on marketing, only a few of which would be of interest to a pastor. In these indexes a search strategy might be to use *religion* or *church* as the key search word with a subheading of *marketing.* This approach would locate articles such as Stephen McDaniel, "Marketing Communication Techniques in a Church Setting: Views on Appropriateness," *Journal of Professional Services' Marketing* (Summer 1986): 39-54. All 3 of these index search systems allow you to print out an abstract of the article so you can see whether it is worth the trouble for you to locate the article itself.

Below are listed some computerized data base systems you might contact.

* ABI/Inform. Louisville, Kentucky: Data Courier. Updated weekly, 1971–present. Available online and on CD-ROM. Indexes over 660 business and management periodicals worldwide.
* InfoTrac. Foster City, California: Information Access Company. Updated monthly, 1980–present. Available only on CD-ROM. Indexes over 800 business and general periodicals, including the *New York Times* and *Wall Street Journal.*
* Religion Index. Chicago, Illinois: American Theological Library Association. Updated monthly, 1949–present. Available online and on CD-ROM. Indexes 380 religious periodicals.

### The Religious Marketer's Bookshelf

Out of the thousands of marketing books that could prove useful to a religious marketer, those that would be of greatest value to the practicing pastor are:

* Jean Herold, *Marketing and Sales Management: An Information Sourcebook.* Phoenix: Oryx Press, 1988. This is an excellent, concise (167 pages) listing of the major sources of information of interest to marketers. Included are approximately 1,000 listings with most descriptions of abstracts, bibliographies, database directories, computer databases, dictionaries, guides to information sources, handbooks, indexes, proceedings, associations, and the like, organized around major marketing areas (general marketing, marketing research, advertising, consumer behavior, direct marketing, etc). If you can afford only one sourcebook on marketing, this is a good investment, since it will lead you to other works available in most large libraries.

One of the references under consumer based handbooks is given below to illustrate the form of the sourcebook's listings.

* George P. Moschis, *Consumer Socialization: A Life-Cycle Perspective*. Lexington, Mass.: Lexington Books, 1987 (353 pages). Understanding the nature of changes in consumer behavior is important for those interested in marketing. The nature of these changes, how and why they occur, is covered in this book. The topics include models of consumer socialization and family, peers, mass media, socioeconomic and racial influences, and the effects of age, life cycle, gender, and birth order.

## Marketing Research

It is hoped that the reader of this book is convinced by now of the wisdom of doing marketing research before making important church marketing decisions. Also, we hope you are convinced that such research can be done, in many cases, at a low cost. Many books are available to help clergy conduct research. Some are specifically written for those with very limited research budgets. Several books that can help clergy do valid, low-cost research are:

* Alan R. Andreasen. *Cheap But Good Marketing Research*. Homewood, Ill.: Dow Jones-Irwin, 1988. A very practical guide for doing marketing research, written by a well-known author of books for non-profit managers.
* George Edward Breen and Albert Breneman Blankenship. *Do-It-Yourself Marketing Research*. 3rd ed. New York: McGraw-Hill, 1989 (303 pages). A practical guide for the nonprofessional market researcher that explains how to conduct market studies necessary for making decisions in a small business, giving enough information so that the individual can decide when professional help is needed.
* Don Dillman. *Mail and Telephone Surveys: The Total Design Method*. New York: Wiley, 1978. A step-by-step method of conducting successful mail and telephone surveys. A bibliography provides additional sources of information.
* Alfred E. Goldman and Susan Schwartz McDonald. *The Group Depth Interview*. Englewood Cliffs, N.J.: Prentice-Hall, 1987 (197 pages in paperback). An excellent guide to

conducting focus groups, which could be of use to religious marketers who are attempting to better understand what motivates churchgoing behavior, testing new ministry ideas, pre-testing advertising, and so on. Every pastor considering using focus group research should read this book first.

* Stanley L. Payne. *The Art of Asking Questions.* Princeton, N.J.: Princeton University Press, 1979. Considered one of the best guides to writing questionnaires. Written for the nonprofessional surveyor.

* Seymour Sudman. *Applied Sampling.* San Francisco: Academic Press). A down-to-earth, practical look at sampling populations for survey research.

* Robert P. Vichas. *Complete Handbook of Profitable Marketing Research Techniques.* Englewood Cliffs, N.J.: Prentice-Hall, 1982. Forty basic marketing research techniques that are practical, productive, and economical for even the smallest organization. Includes applications, forms, checklists, and questionnaires.

## Consumer Behavior

Persons seeking to understand more of why people behave as they do, and how church marketers should take consumer behavior into account when formulating church communications, should read the following two books.

* James F. Engel, Roger D. Blackwell, and Paul Miniard. *Consumer Behavior.* Chicago: Dryden Press, 1990. Although the discussion and examples are largely for business marketers, this is considered one of the basic consumer behavior texts.

* James F. Engel. *Contemporary Christian Communications.* Nashville: Thomas Nelson Publishers, 1979. This book remains one of the major works of applying consumer behavior research to church communication strategy.

## Promotion

The low-budget marketer has scores of "how-to" guides to choose from in the area of promotion. Most are directed at small businesses, but have ideas useful to religious advertisers as well. Jean Herold's Information Sourcebook will help you find some of these books. The 3 we list below are good, relatively inexpensive books with some good ideas.

* Nancy Allen. *Phone 4 Growth* (a workbook). Re-creation Ministries, P. O. Box 408, Indianola, Iowa, 50125 (802) 484-1080.
* William K. Witcher. *How to Solve Your Small Business Advertising Problems.* Aptos, Calif.: Advertising Planners, Inc., 1986. This book and many others on advertising can be ordered from Adweek Books by calling 800-3-ADWEEK, or in New York 212-995-7208.
* Norman W. Whan. *The Phone's for You.* Church Growth Development International, 420 West Lambert, Suite E, Brea, CA (414/990-9551). The most used resource for tele-marketing.

## Demographics and Geodemographics

Listed below are several sources useful in helping you find and work with demographic and geodemographic data.

* Diane Crispell. *The Insider's Guide to Demographic Know-How.* Ithaca, N.Y.: American Demographic Press, 1990. Discusses how, when, and why to use demographics and what you can get from the 1990 census; federal government reports; private sources; academic, industrial, and non-profit sources; and state and local sources. Call 800-828-1133 to order.

The major sources of geodemographic data were discussed in chapter 6. All of these companies also supply extensive demographic data from United States census tapes, plus their own proprietary, demographic updating methods and desk-top computer mapping services.

* Donnelley Marketing Information Services, 70 Seaview Ave., P. O. Box 10250, Stamford, CT 06904; 800-866-2255.
* CACI Marketing Systems, 9302 Lee Highway, Fairfax, VA 22031.
* Church Information and Development Services, 151 Kalmus, Suite A-104, Costa Mesa, CA 92626; 714-957-1282.
* Claritas, 201 North Union Street Alexandria, VA 22314; 703-683-8300.
* National Decisions Systems, 539 Encinitas Blvd., Box 900, Encinatas, CA 92024-9007; 800-877-5560.

A good book to help you determine whether you should use computer mapping of your local area in developing a targeting strategy is Roberto Laserna and John Landis, *Desk-top Mapping for Planning and Strategic Decision-Making,* available from Marketing Tools Alert, Ithaca, NY; 800-828-1133. Although written to promote the software of Strategic Mapping, Inc., this book is valuable to anyone considering using a computer-mapping program to locate current new or total church membership, where visitors come from, high population areas, or high concentrations of population groups (e.g., Hispanics, 25–35 year olds, college educated, etc.), on a color-coded map of geographic area.

## Public Relations

Two good sources of information on pubic relations are:

* "The Practice of Public Relations in the Non-Profit Organization," in T. D. Connors, ed. *The Non-Profit Organization Handbook.* New York: McGraw-Hill, 1981. See pp. 5.1-5.141.
* *Promoting Issues and Ideas: A Guide for Public Relations for Non-Profit Organizations.* New York: The Foundation Center, 1987.

## Church Statistics

Several books with statistics of value to the church marketer are:

* George Gallup and Jim Castelli. *The People's Religion.* New York: Macmillan, 1989.
* George Gallup and Sarah Jones. *One-Hundred Questions and Answers: Religion in America.* Princeton, N.J.: Princeton Religion Research Center, 1989.
* Carol Ward. *Christian Sourcebook.* New York: Ballantine/ Epiphany, 1987.
* *Yearbook of American and Canadian Churches.* Nashville, Abingdon Press, published annually.

### Associations and Consulting Services

Pastors who desire professional help in tackling marketing problems may wish to contact an association or marketing consulting organization. In addition to the guides listed below, free or low-cost help may be found by contacting the marketing faculty at your local college, who sometimes look for student project opportunities. Consultants specializing in church-related marketing are:

Master Planning, Laguna Niguel, California
Management Development Associates, Wheaton, Illinois
The Ward Group, Washington, D. C.
George Barna, The Barna Group, Pasadena, California
Shawchuck and Associates, Chicago, Illinois

### Some Non-profit Associations That Can Locate Consultants to Help with Church Marketing

Christian Ministries Management Association
Diamond Bar, California
714- 861-8861
National Association for Church Management Consultants,
Raleigh, North Carolina
919-846-5944

The addresses and phone numbers for marketing consultants and associations can be found in the following directories, available at your local public or college library.

- * *Bradford's Directory of Marketing Research Agencies and Management Consultants in the United States and the World.* Annual. Fairfax, Va.: Bradford's Directory of Marketing Research Agencies. The more than 900 agencies and consultants included in this edition are arranged alphabetically by state or country. Indexed by type of marketing research, an alphabetical listing of agencies and key personnel, and a list of associations are provided.
- * *Dun's Consultants Directory.* Annual. Parsippany, N.J.: Dun's Marketing Service (4,038 pages). More than 25,000 U.S. consulting firms in 200 specialties are listed alphabetically by company name. The usual directory information also includes annual sales, date company started, business description, other locations, and officers for each agency. Indexes by geographic location for headquarters, branch offices, and business specialty are included.
- * *Green Book: International Directory of Marketing Research Houses and Services.* Annual. New York: American Marketing Association. The alphabetical arrangement of research organizations includes basic information and a description of the services offered. The 5 indexes provide access by company services, market/industry specialties, available computer programs, geographical arrangement of companies and names of principal personnel.
- * Katherine Gruber, *Encyclopedia of Associations.* 21st ed., 4 vols. Detroit: Gale Research Co. Volume 1, in 2 parts, is a comprehensive listing of national organizations classified by broad categories with 17 points of information for each entry. Part 2 is the expanded Name and Key Word Index, which also lists consultants, research, and information centers in other Gale reference publications. Volume 2 is a geographic and executive index. Volume 3, *New Associations and Projects,* supplies information on new organizations. Volume 4 lists nonprofit organizations with international memberships.

* *Handbook of Advertising and Marketing Services.* New York: Executive Communications. A directory of services, consultants, and experts in all areas of marketing. Includes advertising, broadcasting, and communications. Each entry concisely summarizes the service experience, expertise, type of clients, performance records, and contact persons of the company. A listing by major and subcategories is provided.

# Appendix B

# *Taking Stock of What We Have Accomplished*

## *Evaluation of Marketing*

In this appendix you will be introduced to a comprehensive evaluation paradigm (a pattern for doing something). You may choose not to do such evaluation on your own. Rather, you may invite a professional to carry out a full-scale evaluation of your ministries (which should be done about every 3 years). Nonetheless, we want you to know what good evaluation entails, so that whether you do it yourself or hire it done, you will know what is involved and thus will be equipped to communicate with your committees and the evaluator.

At a minimum, there are some things you can and should do:

1. If you are a pastor or rabbi, at least twice a month meet with a small group to evaluate the major worship service(s) *of that day.* The group should comprise those who presented the service and a cross-section of the worshipers. Each element of the worship experience should be examined with an eye toward doing it better—the sermon, readings, music, parking, greeting and ushering, printed materials, sound system, and so on. The worshipers offering the feedback should be about 50 percent who serve on the group for at least a year or more and 50 percent new each time. The sooner this evaluation is conducted after the service, the better.

2. Every 6 months, meet with each major committee and ministry task force and ask these questions: "What is the mission, and what are the goals of this ministry?" "What is working well, and why?" (The *why* is at least as important as the *what*.) "What needs doing?" "How do we get it done?"[1]

3. Every 3 years, conduct a full-scale evaluation of the committees and ministries of your organization, using the evaluation paradigm suggested below.

The following discussion of evaluation could have been appropriately included as the final step of the marketing planning process discussed in chapter 7, "Strategic Marketing Planning," since evaluation is an essential ingredient of marketing control. We have decided to place evaluation at the end of this book, however, because evaluation should be a part of everything the organization does, not merely its marketing planning. Evaluation speaks to the entire content of this book, not just the chapter on planning.

## Evaluation of Ministry

In Scripture is found this statement, "Test everything; hold fast to what is good" (1 Thess. 5:21). A great deal of work goes into planning and carrying out a program or ministry. Ministry is costly. A great deal of time, money, and volunteer energy is spent in any church or synagogue every year. It makes sense that the leaders would want to measure the results to see whether certain efforts should continue or be discontinued or whether some new programs should be started. It makes sense that leaders and congregations would want to evaluate their programs, as a matter of responsiveness to those who have planned, funded, and worked to carry them out. And so wisdom says, "Test everything; hold fast to what is good."

Why, then, is so little formal evaluation conducted by those responsible for the programs and ministries of congregations? The scarcity of evaluation is more a lack of nerve than a lack of skill. The majority of religious leaders know a good deal about how to evaluate, but many avoid it for fear of the consequences—some for good cause. In thousands of congregations across America, the only time evaluation is requested is when the ruling board wants to get rid of the pastor—and so they carry out something called evaluation, hoping to find something to support their already decided conclusion. In thousands of congregations, laypersons resist evaluation because of the idea that volunteers should not be accountable for results.

Perhaps evaluation is resisted because no one likes to be given a "grade" for his or her work. You pass! You fail! Such evaluation in organizations is almost always counterproductive.

Useful evaluation is never done to grade someone's effort. Evaluation is intended to provide leaders and workers with the information they need to make mid-course program corrections and to assist in future planning. The purpose of evaluation is to increase program effectiveness and aid in future planning.

Even though evaluation may be sparse in a congregation, the clergy and lay leaders frequently wish to try new ways of doing things, or they change the way they have been doing something, and want to know whether the change has made any difference. Any person who has defined a problem and constructed a solution for it wants to know whether the solution worked, and if so, how well and at what cost. In all these instances, an evaluation will provide a format for determining what difference has been made.

People who raise the following questions often have a need for evaluation:

1. Should we continue the program, and in the same way?
2. Did we use our resources wisely?
3. Should this same approach be used by others?
4. Is this new program worth the time, money, and effort we are putting into it?
5. Are we meeting our goals? Are these the right goals?
6. Who are we effecting, and to what degree?

Whenever possible, the evaluation should be planned and begun at the time of planning the event itself. Then the planners (or evaluators) can begin gathering data as soon as a new program is conceived, or as soon as the leaders decide what they want to learn from the evaluation. For example, if the planning effort is directed toward improving the quality of religious education in the primary department, the evaluators should immediately begin gathering data to determine the existing quality before any change or event is introduced.

*Every evaluation requires an event that is to be evaluated. An event may vary from a single, short-lived event (such as a one-time advertisement in a newspaper) to a multi-year program (such as drug abuse program offered by a church or synagogue). Or the event may be in the future; a congregation develops a new ministry outreach program. Whether the event is past, present, or future, an evaluator attempts to determine what happened as a result of the event.*

The leaders ane ruling committees and the evaluator need to share a common understanding of many common concepts, methods, and tasks.[2]

## *Types of Evaluation*

Three types of evaluation are possible: (1) Informal Use of Records, (2) After-the-Event Evaluation, (3) Before-the-Event Designed Evaluation.

Each has an appropriate role in organizations. Let us consider each of these.

*1. Informal Use of Records.* Data (bits of information, not yet assimilated) can be gathered from many sources that exist apart from the evaluation procedure. A good journal, diary, log book, minutes of past meetings, or set of financial records will allow you to partially reconstruct past events. Knowing what happened in the past allows you to evaluate an event in order to make better decisions for the future. This is one good reason that diaries should be kept by the major participants in the event and by the evaluation committee. In addition, correspondence, reports to agencies, or other official papers (covenants, guidelines, etc.) often provide evaluation data.

*2. After-the-Event Evaluation.* After an event has occurred, a leader or committee may want to ask the following questions: What happened? Why did it succeed or why did it fail? How well did it do? Was it a successful program? Have there been positive or negative *unexpected* effects? Is this project essential to the organization, or is this a benign activity that should be closed out? Answers to questions such as these often provide data for future planning after an event has been completed. The "report cards" idea for evaluating the present level of service quality, mentioned in chapter 10, is an example of this type of evaluation.

*3. Before-the-Event Designed Evaluation.* This type of evaluation occurs when one plans for the evaluation and starts the data gathering early in the history of the program. Evaluation designed before the event begins allows for evaluation to be made before, during, and after the event. If the event is running parallel to other events, before-the-event designed evaluation allows for comparisons and/or the use of control groups. For example, the evaluation might compare using billboards with telemarketing to see how well each produces the desired results. Measurements of before and after could be taken on both to determine what incremental results occurred. One may install a new program and compare its performance with an existing one.

Each type of evaluation serves different purposes. If you consider a variety of tasks—such as data gathering, developing procedures and management, devising organizational structures, implementing models, evaluating models, educating users, and measuring impact and benefits of a system—you may find one approach to evaluation to be more appropriate than the others. For example, given the interests, resources, and constraints of the organization, a before-the-event designed evaluation may not be feasible. However, keeping historical records, a diary of events, and a set of official minutes may allow for an informal use of records evaluation at a later time.

Whatever type of evaluation is used, certain basic steps need to be followed. They are described below.

## Evaluation Steps

Evaluation has 4 major steps: (1) Defining the mission of the organization, (2) evaluating the goals and objectives, (3) evaluating the program and activities carried out to achieve the goals and objectives, and (4) evaluating the evaluation's impact on the program.

**1. What is the mission of the program (or organization)?** The program's mission or "guiding principle" becomes the foundation against which evaluative measures will be made. Often the group or organization does not have a clearly defined, written mission. The evaluator will then work with the group to define its "assumed" mission. This is done by reviewing the group's major efforts and helping them to decide what core result or condition is the uniting principle of the several programs. The mission, if previously defined, may usually be found in the charter, constitution, and/or official minutes.

**2. Evaluation of goals and objectives.** What are the goals and objectives? Collect the documents that contain them (no evaluation can be carried out without a specific statement of goals and objectives). If written objectives do not exist, a set of objectives must be developed by looking at documentation (minutes, speeches, constitutions), interviewing persons to clarify what they are trying to accomplish, and so on.

It is possible to have more than one set of objectives. In that case, you could evaluate against any set of objectives. Two different groups may want to evaluate the same program against different objectives.

*a. Are the objectives and goals stated in measurable terms?* Not all aspects of each goal or objective must be measurable, but at least 1 or more measures must exist to have an acceptable objective or goal. Process measures are usable, but outcome measures are preferred. There must be a time-frame to every objective. A measure of a program may be that it relates to attracting 500 unchurched persons a year, or that a boiler must now be down for repair more than 3 times each winter.

*b. Are the goals and objectives consistent with an organization's mission/primary purpose?* You must look at the goals and objectives of the program in terms of the mission or purpose of your organization. The evaluative question is whether the objectives and goals are consistent with the organization's mission. For example, is a "goal to achieve 95 percent attendance at worship" consistent with a congregation whose primary purpose (mission) is to deepen the spirituality of its constituents?

After evaluating goals and objectives, you should then consider the programs and activities that are carried on to achieve the goals and objectives.

**3. Evaluation of programs and activities.** Is the program consistent with the goals and objectives? You must assess whether the program addresses the established goals and objectives. For example, if the stated goal is to improve the life of homeless persons, a program to increase their scriptural reading would be inconsistent.

*a. Is the program effective?* To what extent has the program achieved its goals and objectives? Clearly stated, measurable objectives must exist before program effectiveness can be evaluated. Only then can meaningful questions be asked regarding effectiveness.

*b. Is the program efficient?* What type and amount of resources were expended in the program? Two programs that have the same outcome may score very differently when compared in terms of their investment levels.

Another possible approach is to measure against a standard. The cost of teaching Hebrew at a seminary is $10,000 per student. We may want to compare it with a method of teaching Hebrew that costs $50 per student. In one method a full-time tutor is provided, while the other method merely provides each student with a book. The cost of the alternatives must be balanced against how well the students learn Hebrew.

Efficiency involves measuring both the effectiveness of the program and the resources used to achieve it (time, money, people, etc.). One can measure total expenditures and/or cost per output.

**4. Side-effects or Spill-overs.** *Side-effects* are unplanned, unanticipated events or conditions that result from the program. *Spill-overs* are unplanned, unanticipated effects the program had on other programs. In many instances, positive or negative side-effects and/or spill-overs may be more important than the original goal and objectives. For instance, an evaluation may discover that a Weight Watchers program in the church is having little or no effect on the participants' weight goals, but is proving a most popular place for persons to come for short-term crisis counseling or grief support.

A program may have sufficient positive side-effects/ spill-overs to make it worthwhile, even though it is not meeting its stated objectives. On the other hand, it may be causing sufficient negative side-effects/spill-overs to warrant its discontinuance even though its objectives are being met.

**5. What program changes or new programs should be added to improve goal achievement?** The evaluation will often point to the need for program change or the addition of new programs in order to achieve a goal or objective. For example, a congregation may have a visitation program to achieve a goal of increasing attendance. The evaluation may reveal that the goal is not being met. The visitation program may be changed to include more visitors, or a new advertising program may be added.

*Evaluation of the Evaluation*

**1. Is the evaluation a significant factor in achieving the goals or objectives?** Often the evaluation may be more significant in effecting desired change than the program itself. Having members of the congregation keep diaries of their activities may be a more powerful intervention than attending a religious education class which is being evaluated.

**2. Apply program evaluation steps regarding effectiveness and/or efficiency to the evaluation procedure.** Are the results of the evaluation sufficiently effective and efficient to warrant doing the evaluation? Issues such as data quality, data analysis, inference, and communication must be considered. (Are official records legible? Are the right statistics chosen? Are the computer programs correct? Are the conclusions correct? Is the report clearly written and disseminated?)

## Basic Evaluation Elements

Certain key elements are basic to all types of evaluation. These must be considered in the design and conduct of all evaluation.

1. *Data structures.* All evaluation records should include:
   a. date of writing;
   b. name of writer;
   c. location and time of the event about which data is being recorded;
   d. the data itself;
   e. where data will be/is being stored.

Other things to be collected include objectives, measurement techniques, frameworks or models to be used, computer and data processing techniques, file systems, and analytic procedures.

2. *Measurement techniques.* All evaluation involves some type of measurement of programs/activities against goals/objectives. Such measurement is often a difficult and/or technical problem. How does one measure achievement, behavior, or attitude? How does one measure the smile in a receptionist's voice? How does one measure the quality of a program or the level of service? Should one use ser-

vice per dollar and volunteer hour, return on investment of time and money, or total budget results?

A variety of measurements is generally available in doing an evaluation. For example, a telemarketing program may be measured by the number of addresses collected, the number of new attenders, the number of new members, and so on. The measures chosen depend on the specific evaluation design.

3. *Resources and constraints.* Any evaluation will require certain resources. The evaluation should, therefore, take into account the system's resources and constraints which impinge upon it, and it should be designed to function within the available resources.

4. *Environment.* The persons doing the evaluation should understand the organization and the environment in which the evaluation will be carried out. Is the program unique, or are there many like it? Does the program being evaluated encompass the entire organization, or only part of it?

5. *Framework or model.* Every evaluation will require an appropriate framework and/or model to measure the event against the goals/objectives and/or to compare it against other events. Should one use verbal, graphic, mathematical, or computer models? How can one measure and analyze the results from the model? How does one determine the extent to which the objectives are met? How does one discover unexpected events, side-effects, or consequences?

6. *Data gathering and storage.* Who should gather data? When and where should it be gathered? What data should be gathered? How and for how long should it be kept? Should the information be in machine-readable form and stored in a computer, or should it be in written form for storage in a file cabinet?

## Preparing an Evaluation Matrix

One method of designing an evaluation is to create a matrix of data sources versus the evaluation steps (the evaluation data wanted). An illustration of an evaluation matrix follows on page 403.

You will notice that an "X" is entered in each matrix cell, which indicates a data source that will be used to gather data for that particular evaluation step. For example, in Step 3, 1 data source will be used, while Step 5 will involve 7 data sources. Whenever 2 or more data sources for any step are used, they provide a validity check of the data gathered.

When 2 or more data sources exist for a particular evaluation step, the persons doing the evaluation may choose to use only 1 or 2, or it may be desirable to check all sources as a consistency or reliability test. If the same question is answered in each data source, but the information gathered is different, both data sources are important (i.e., information gathered in an interview may answer the same questions as information from a formal written report, but the interview may yield additional or more complete data than that contained in the written report).

Constructing the evaluation matrix serves several purposes:

1. It suggests where there are redundant sources of data; i.e., project files and minutes/documents (Step 1).
2. It identifies areas for which there is no data; i.e., Step 9.
3. Once completed, it becomes the basic data collection plan.

After the matrix has been completed, a remaining planning step is to determine who will gather the data from the data sources for each evaluation step. A single person or an evaluation team may be responsible for gathering all of the data. Or a person/sub-group may be assigned to gather data from 1 or more of the sources. When several persons/sub-groups gather discrete pieces of data, the evaluator or evaluation team collates the data and prepares the final evaluation report.

## Additional Evaluation Concerns

The person(s) or organization doing the evaluation may wish to consider other issues in designing and conducting the evaluation.

1. Is the evaluation intended to make a difference in one's performance? For example, if evaluation is being used in a Sunday school, can we eliminate the evaluation and still expect identical performance of teachers and students? The answer is not necessarily "yes," because the evaluation procedure itself may influence the behavior of teachers and students.

2. Are we doing a long-term analysis? Do we want to gather data for a current decision or for a decision a long time hence?
3. Are we being asked to create an ongoing evaluation system, or simply to provide data for decision-making here and now?
4. Is the present information system adequate to keep leaders up to date, or should we install a better one?
5. Are we to teach people how to make decisions, or merely to give them the data they need?
6. Who is the "client," the program committee whose program is being evaluated, the leadership team, the ruling board, and so on?

| EVALUATION STEPS | DATA SOURCES | | | | | | | | | | |
|---|---|---|---|---|---|---|---|---|---|---|---|
| (The evaluation data which is to be gathered) | Project Files and Material | Interventionist's Reports and Diaries | Evaluation Sessions | Evaluation Instruments | Official Minutes and Documents | On-site Observation | Personal Interviews with Leaders | Third-party Reports, Newspapers, etc. | Interviews with Clients | | |
| 1. Do written goals exist? | X (1) | | | | X (1) | | | | | | |
| 2. Are they measurable? | X | | | | X | | | | | | |
| 3. Are they coherent with the organization's purpose(s)? | | | | | X | | | | | | |
| 4. Is the program coherent with the goals? | X | | | | | X | X (5) | | | | |
| 5. Is the program efficient? | | X | X | X | X | X (7) | X | | X (7) | | |
| 6. Is the program effective? | X | | X | | X | X | X | | | | |
| 7. Are there side effects/spillovers? | | | | | | | X | X | X | | |
| 8. How is the evaluation interacting with the program? | X | X | | X | | X | | | | | |
| 9. Is the evaluation effective/efficient? | | | | | | | | | | | |

# Notes

## 1. Facing Change and Crisis in Congregations: The Role of Marketing

1. George Gallup, Jr., and Sarah Jones, *One Hundred Questions and Answers: Religion in America* (Princeton, N.J.: The Princeton Religion Research Center, 1989), p. 64.

2. Ibid., p. 102.

3. Ibid.

4. Ibid., p. 108.

5. For more information on the difference in religions by regions of the United States, see Samuel S. Hill, "Religion and Region in America," *Annals of the American Academy of Political and Social Sciences* 480 (July 1985): 132-41; Roger Stump, "Regional Divergence in Religious Affiliation in the United States," *Sociological Analysis* 45, 4 (Winter 1984); Roger Stump, "Regional Migration and Religious Commitment in the United States," *Journal for the Scientific Study of Religion* 23 (September 1984); and Roger Stump, "Regional Contrasts Within Black Protestantism: A Research Note," *Social Forces* 66 (1987): 143-51.

6. Gallup and Jones, *One Hundred Questions and Answers*, p. 131.

7. Ibid., p. 144.

8. Ibid., pp. 164-78.

9. The megachurch phenomenon has come to be observed and discussed by the *size* of the church and the *number* of persons attending. Consequently, the megachurch "model" is summarily dismissed by many who object to a congregation's numbering in the multiple thousands, or who feel their community could never spawn such a large congregation. A better way to view "megachurch" is not by size, but by a manner of thinking and doing ministry. In this respect, the megachurch model can be utilized by all congregations, large and small, urban and rural, even the small congregation can think expansively, and, perhaps, add at least one new ministry to meet the needs of some specific group. Megachurches deal not only with size, but more important with a new paradigm, a new way of thinking about the role of the congregation in the community.

10. Adapted from a talk by Dr. Gary A. Tobin, delivered at the 61st General Assembly of the Union of American Hebrew Congregations, Baltimore, Maryland, November 1, 1991. To be published under the title "Restructuring the Contemporary Synagague," *NASA Journal* (Winter 1991). Adapted by permission of the author.

11. We are indebted to Ric Olson, who was on the Northern Indiana United Methodist Conference staff, for this case. He is currently with the Iowa Conference, United Methodist Church.

12. See Thomas A. Stewart, "Turning Around the Lord's Business," *Fortune*, September 25, 1989, pp. 116-28.

13. For the Guthrie, Oklahoma, congregation, this was to ba a support system for the uneducated, distressed families in Guthrie; for McGrawsville United Methodist

Church, this was to provide an enjoyable and secure after-school program for children whose parents were at work; for Willow Creek, this was to provide persons with opportunities in exaltation, edification, evangelism, and extension.

14. The major critics in this connection are Vance Packard, *The Hidden Persuaders* (New York: Pocket Books, 1957); and John Kenneth Galbraith, *The Affluent Society* (Boston: Houghton Mifflin, 1958).

15. The American Marketing Association has published a Code of Ethics for Marketing Research. A good discussion of ethical perspectives and problems in marketing research is found in C. Merle Crawford, "Attitudes of Marketing Executives Toward Ethics in Marketing Research," *Journal of Marketing* (April 1970): 46-52.

16. Sidney J. Levy, "Marcology 101 or the Domain of Marketing," in *Marketing 1776-1976 and Beyond,* Kenneth Bernhardt, ed. (Chicago: American Marketing Association, 1976), pp. 577-81.

17. Ibid.

18. See Patrick E. Murphy and Richard A. McGarrity, "Marketing Universities: A Survey of Student Recruiting Activities," *College and University* (Spring 1978): 249-61.

19. Peter F. Drucker, *Management: Tasks, Responsibilities, Practices* (New York: Harper & Row, 1973), pp. 64-65.

20. See Kenneth Boulding, *A Primer on Social Dynamics* (New York: Free Press, 1970).

21. For a comparison of the managerial and social process definition of marketing, see Daniel J. Sweeney, "Marketing: Management Technology or Social Process?" *Journal of Marketing* (October 1972): 3-10.

22. This list of characteristics is based on Christopher H. Lovelock and Charles B. Weinberg *Public and Nonprofit Marketing,* 2nd ed. (Redwood City, Calif.: The Scientific Press, 1989), p. 15-20.

23. Cecily Cannan Selby, "Better Performance from Nonprofits," *Harvard Business Review* (September-October 1978): 93.

## 2. Approaching People in the Right Spirit: The Societal Marketing Concept

1. See John J. Gleason, "The Marketing of Pastoral Care and Counseling, Chaplaincy, and Clinical Pastoral Education," *Journal of Pastoral Care* (December 1984): 264-67. August G. Lageman, "Marketing Pastoral Counseling," *Journal of Pastoral Care* (December 1984): 274-80. Peter R. Peacock, "Applying Marketing Principles to Outreach Programs," *Managing Today's Church,* ed. by R. White (Valley Forge, Pa.: Judson Press, 1981). W. B. Lyon, "What Churches Can Learn from Marketing," quoted in Scot Jones, Bayard W. Lyons, and Lyle E. Schaller, "Churches Must Plan," *Christian Ministry* (September 1981): 5-16. Carnegie S. Calian, "Marketing the Church's Ministry," *Christian Ministry* (May 1983): 22-23. James F. Engel and H. Wilbert Norton, "Effective Evangelism: A Matter of Marketing," *Christianity Today,* April 15, 1977, pp. 12-15. J. Haskins, "Religion as a Marketing Problem and How Research Can Help," in Michael Reagen and Doris S. Chertow, *The Challenge of Modern Church—Public Relations* (Syracuse, N.Y.: Syracuse University, 1972). William C. Moncrief, Charles W. Lamb, Jr., and Sandra Hile Hart, "Marketing the Church," *Journal of Professional Services Marketing* 1, 4 (Summer

1986): 55-63. Geoffrey P. Lantos, "True Marketing Concept Is Based Upon the Biblical Philosophy of Life," *Marketing News* (December 20, 1985): 2.

2. See George Barna, *Marketing the Church* (Colorado Springs: NAV Press, 1988); Dan Day, *A Guide to Marketing Adventism* (Boise: Pacific Press Publishing Association, 1990).

3. The finding that a majority of pastors favor the use of marketing by the church has been duplicated several times. See Moncrief, Lamb, and Hart, "Marketing the Church"; Stephen W. McDaniel, "Marketing Communication in Techniques in a Church Setting: Views on Appropriateness," *Journal of Professional Services Marketing*, 1, 4 (Summer 1986): 39-54; and Gregory M. Gazda, Carlyn I. Anderson, and Donald Sciglimpaglia, "Marketing and Religion: An Assessment of the Clergy," *Proceedings of the Southern Marketing Association, 1984*. One of the findings from several of the studies quoted was that the public was less favorably inclined toward the use of marketing by churches than were the pastors. However, it is likely that "marketing" was perceived as "advertising," and therefore these opinions do not directly relate to marketing as we define it.

4. Lyle Schaller's book *It's A Different World!* (Nashville: Abingdon Press, 1987) describes some of the difficulties faced by contemporary pastors that were alien to previous generations.

5. See "A Guidebook to the Airlines," *Newsweek*, November 26, 1979, p. 88.

6. See Christopher G. Ellison, David A. Gay, and Thomas A. Glass, "Does Religious Commitment Contribute to Individual Life Satisfaction?" *Social Forces* 68, 1 (September 1989): 100-123.

7. Harold Kushner, *Who Needs God?* (New York: Summit Books, 1989).

## 3. Serving People Effectively: The Responsive Congregation

1. See Anthony Downs, *Inside Bureaucracy* (Boston: Little, Brown, 1967).

## 4. Traveling the Marketing Trail: Fundamental Marketing Concepts

1. When asked why he didn't ask this question of persons who attended church, Rick Warren's response was, "I wasn't interested in the opinions of Christians. You will never learn what non-Christians are thinking or feeling by asking Christians. If you want to reach non-Christians you have to learn how to talk to non-Christians. Jesus said 'the children of this world are wiser than the children of light,' which means the average McDonald's owner knows more about human behavior than the average pastor."

2. During our visit with Rick, he stated, "I was struck that none of the reasons people listed for not attending church were theological. They weren't having hang-ups with Jesus Christ. Gallup says 96 percent of Americans believe in God and 86 percent believe in the divinity of Jesus. What's the problem? The problem is that people don't like church. And most baby boomers say if they found a church that was culturally relevant and geared to the market of today, they would attend."

3. In the interview Rick said, "The person we are trying to reach is pro-God, pro-spirituality, but is anti-organized, institutional religion. So we say to them, "Fine, then come to Saddleback. We're disorganized religion."

4. The opening sentence of the letter was, "At last a new church for those who have given up on traditional church services."

5. The letter also stated that during a trial run of the service on the Sunday before Easter, sixty people came, five of whom committed their lives to Christ that day and joined the membership of the church.

6. When we visited the church offices for interviews, Pastor Warren greeted us wearing blue jeans and a blue sweat shirt. We asked about his style. "The key scripture for our church," he said, "is I Corinthians 9:19-23, where Paul said he became like Jews when he was with the Jews, and like Gentiles when he with them, in order to win all persons to Christ. We're in southern California, trying to win the baby-boomer generation, so we become like baby boomers in southern California. We dress this way because our image is we're casual, normal people, we have a family, we enjoy life. In reaching baby boomers here, you have to know what they're turned off to, and they're turned off to hype and can read an insincere person. What they're looking for is credibility, integrity, honesty, realness, genuineness."

7. Regarding their philosophy of ministry, Pastor Warren said, "Our philosophy is similar to Willow Creek, even though our style is very different. They use more drama, with the central and Eastern U.S. being more influenced by Europe, more formalized, a production. California is influenced by Mexico, with music and celebration. We party; we have fun. We sing a lot more than Willow Creek. People out here enjoy singing and music more than in Chicago. Everything we do on Sunday morning—prayers, songs, announcements—will make sense to the person walking in with no church background. So people aren't afraid to bring their friends."

8. We asked Pastor Warren how they managed to keep the individual from getting lost in such a large congregation. He said, "It's simple: you grow larger and smaller at the same time. You grow larger in your celebration (people know we're big and that there is something significant happening here) and smaller in your small groups. The average person in a church knows 67 people whether there are 60, 600, or 6,000 people in the church. A person doesn't have to know everyone to feel at home, to feel like this is his or her church, but the person does have to know a few very well. So you have to create structures that keep breaking the church down by cell division."

9. For further discussion of mission clarification in religious organizations, see Alvin Lindgren and Norman Shawchuck, *Management for Your Church* (Schaumburg, Ill.: Spiritual Growth Resources, 1985) and *Let My People Go: Empowering Laity for Ministry*; Lloyd Perry and Norman Shawchuck, *Revitalizing the 20th Century Church* (Chicago: Moody, 1986); and Peter F. Drucker, *The Nonprofit Drucker Tape Library*, vol. 1, "Mission and Leadership." All of the resources are available through Spiritual Growth Resources, Schaumburg, IL. (1-800-359-7363).

10. The sketch is adapted from Perry and Shawchuck, *Revitalizing the 20th Century Church*, pp. 13-30.

11. See Peter F. Drucker, *Management: Tasks, Responsibilities, Practices* (New York: Harper & Row, 1973), chap. 7.

12. See Derek F. Abell, *Defining the Business: The Starting Point of Strategic Planning* (Englewood Cliffs, N.J.: Prentice-Hall, 1980), chap. 2, esp. p. 17.

13. See C. Peter Wagner, *Your Church Can Grow* (Glendale, Calif.: G/L Publica-

tions, 1976), pp. 52-53. See also "Religion Inc.: Possibility Thinking—and Shrewd Marketing Pay Off for a Preacher," *The Wall Street Journal,* August 26, 1976, p. 1.

14. See David L. Sills, *The Volunteers: Means and Ends in a National Organization* (Glencoe, Ill.: Free Press, 1957). Also note that the National Center for Voluntary Action, 1785 Massachusetts Ave., N.W., Washington, D.C. 20036, researches, conducts seminars, and disseminates up-to-date information for managing volunteers.

15. See Drucker, *Management,* p. 61.

16. For additional discussion of the concept of exchange in marketing, see Richard P. Bagozzi, "Marketing as an Organized Behavioral System of Exchange," *Journal of Marketing* (October 1974): 77-81; and "Marketing as Exchange," *American Behavioral Scientist* (March–April 1978): 535-56.

17. Bagozzi, "Marketing as an Organized Behavioral System of Exchange," pp. 535-56.

18. See Robert S. Topor, *Institutional Image: How to Define, Improve, Market It* (Washington, D. C.: Council for the Advancement and Support of Education, 1986), vii.

19. Ibid, p. 1.

20. Topor's book gives many suggestions for image measurement.

21. C. E. Osgood, G. J. Suci, and P. H. Tannenbaum, *The Measurement of Meaning* (Urbanna: University of Illinois Press, 1957).

22. See Ralph E. Anderson, "Consumer Dissatisfaction: The Effect of Disconfirmed Expectancy on Perceived Product Performance," *Journal of Marketing Research* (February 1973): 38-44.

## 5. Finding Out What People Need and Want: Marketing Research

1. See Curtis Young, "Two Ministries Were Saved With Help From Research," *Marketing News,* January 3, 1986, p. 25; and Curtis Young, "Marketing in the Nonprofit Religious Sector," *Journal of Professional Services Marketing* 3, 1/2 (1987): 119-26.

2. This section is adapted from Alan R. Andreasen, "Cost Conscious Marketing Research," *Harvard Business Review* (July-August 1983): 74-77.

3. See, for example, James B. Higgenbotham and Keith K. Cox, eds., *Focus Group Interviews: A Reader* (Chicago: American Marketing Association, 1979).

4. See William Martin, "The Baptists Want You," *Texas Monthly,* February 1977, pp. 83-87, 149-57, as quoted in Christopher H. Lovelock and Charles B. Weinberg, *Public and Nonprofit Marketing,* 2nd. ed. (Redwood City, Calif.: The Scientific Press, 1989).

5. For an excellent reference to free or inexpensive secondary data, see Alan R. Andreasen, *Cheap But Good Marketing Research* (Homewood, Ill.: Dow Jones-Irwin, 1988), pp. 253-265. Also, see Appendix A for other books on conducting research on a tight budget.

6. A highly effective method of focus group interviewing is knows as the Nominal Group Technique (NGT). The NGT session can be conducted in 60 minutes, and it ensures that all participants will be fully involved in the discussion. For a most helpful resource on NGT, see Andre L. Delbecq et al., *Group Techniques for Program*

*Planning: A Guide to Nominal Group and Delphi Processes* (Middleton, Wis.: Green Briar Press, 1986. Another excellent reference on focus group interviewing is Alfred E. Goldman and Susan Schwartz McDonald, *The Group Depth Interview* (Englewood Cliffs, N.J.: Prentice-Hall, 1987).

7. For excellent suggestions on "sampling," see, Robert S. Topor, "Research Methods," *Your Personal Guide to Marketing a Nonprofit Organization* (Council for Advancement and Support of Education, 1988), pp. 40-44.

8. For more on experimental research, see Seymour Banks, *Experimentation in Marketing* (New York: McGraw-Hill, 1965). Also, most marketing research textbooks include a chapter on experimentation.

## 6. Ordering Your Priorities: Market Segmentation, Targeting, and Positioning

1. For an excellent study of the characteristics of each generation in American history, see William Strauss and Neil Howe, *Generations: The History of America's Future, 1584 to 2069* (New York: Willian Morrow & Co., 1991).

2. For a discussion of the religious attitudes and "shopping" behavior of the baby boomer, see "Rough Waters for Protestant Churches," *Progressions* 2, 1 (January 1990).

3. See James F. Engel, Roger D. Blackwell, and Paul W. Miniard, *Consumer Behavior,* 6th ed. (Chicago: Dryden Press, 1990), p. 30.

4. See Gilles Laurent and Jean-Noel Kapferer, "Measuring Consumer Involvement Profiles," *Journal of Marketing Research* 12 (February 1985): 41-53.

5. A basic review of the segmentation literature is found in Ronald E. Frank, William F. Massy, and Yoram Wind, *Market Segmentation* (Englewood Cliffs, N.J.: Prentice-Hall, 1972). See also Yoram Wind, "Issues and Advances in Segmentation Research," *Journal of Marketing Research* (August 1978): 317-37.

6. For another approach, see Patrick E. Murphy and William Staples, "A Modernized Family Life Cycle," *Journal of Consumer Research* (June 1979): 12-22.

7. See Stephen J. Miller, "Source of Income as a Market Descriptor," *Journal of Marketing Research* (February 1978): 129-31.

8. For an extensive discussion of denominational variations based on geography, social class, church attendance, education, and attitudinal, as well as denominational, switching patterns, see Robert Wuthnow, *The Restructuring of American Religion* (Princeton, N.J.: Princeton University Press, 1988), esp. pp. 83-91.

9. Arnold Mitchell, *The Nine American Lifestyles* (New York: Macmillan, 1983).

10. See W. Bruce Wrenn and Slimen J. Saliba, "New Approaches to Segmenting and Targeting for Religious Institutions," *Journal of Midwest Marketing* (Spring 1988): 229-35.

11. Several of these objectives were suggested by Dr. Ric Olson, Local Church Ministries Consultant, Iowa Conference, The United Methodist Church, in an interview with the authors.

12. See Wendell R. Smith, "Product Differentiation and Market Segmentation," *Business Horizons* (Fall 1961): 65-72.

13. Ibid.

14. Adapted from A Survey for the Register, by Facts Consolidated, Inc., 4/27/1982.

15. See Robert S. Topor, "Research Methods," *Your Personal Guide to Marketing a Nonprofit Organization* (Council for Advancement and Support of Education, 1988), p. 60.

16. Ibid.

17. For an excellent study of positioning and finding a niche in the market, see Trout and Reis, *Positioning: The Battle for Your Mind*.

18. See Patrick M. Baldasare, "True Believer Puts Its Faith in Marketing Research." *Marketing News* 24, 1 June 8, 1990, pp. 29, 31.

19. See C. Peter Wagner, *Your Church Can Grow: Seven Vital Signs of a Healthy Church* (Ventura, Calif.: Regal Books, 1976).

## 7. Capitalizing on Opportunities: Strategic Marketing Planning

1. See Randall Y. Odom and W. Randy Boxx, "Environment, Planning Processes, and Organizational Performance of Churches," *Strategic Management Journal* 9 (1988): 197-205.

2. Philip Kotler, *Marketing for Nonprofit Organizations* (New York: Prentice Hall, 1982), pp. 81-82.

3. Excerpted from Richard Phillips, "Silent 'Church of Good Cheer' Awaits Auctioneer's Gavel," *Chicago Tribune,* Thursday, July 20, 1978, Section 7, pp. 1-2. Copyright © Chicago Tribune. Used with permission.

4. "Spreading God's Word: Five Success Stories," *U. S. News and World Report,* Oct. 22, 1984, pp. 71-73.

5. Modified from James M. Carman and Eric Langeard, "Growth Strategies for Service Firms," *Strategic Marketing Management Journal* 1 (1980): 7-22.

6. See H. Richard Niebuhr, *The Social Sources of Denominationalism,* (The Shoe String Press, 1929).

7. See Odom and Boxx, "Environment, Planning Processes, and Organizational Performance of Churches, p. 202.

8. This section is adapted from William A. Cohen, *The Practice of Marketing Management* (New York: Macmillan, 1988), pp. 44-47.

9. See William A. Cohen, *Developing a Winning Marketing Plan,* (New York: John Wiley and Sons, 1987), pp. 2-6.

10. This mission statement is based on that of the Crossroads Community Church in Camarillo, California, as quoted in Michael T. Dibbert, *Spiritual Leadership, Responsible Management* (Grand Rapids, Mich.: Zondervan, 1989), p. 45. For more information on the development of a church's mission, see our chapter 4 and chapter 4 of Dibbert's book.

11. There are numerous instruments for measuring the spiritual gifts of a congregation. See *Spiritual Gifts and Church Growth: Modified Hauts,* Fuller Institute; D. W. Hoover and R. W. Leenerts, *Enlightened with His Gifts: A Bible Study on Spiritual Gifts* (St. Louis: Lutheran Growth, 1979); *Discover Your Gifts: Workbook* (Grand Rapids, Mich.: Christian Reformed Home Missions, 1981); *Trenton Spiritual Gifts Analysis,* Fuller Institute; and an empirically tested instrument, Roy C. Naden and Robert J. Cruise, *The Spiritual Gifts Inventory,* (Berrien Springs, Mich.: Institute of Church Ministry).

12. See E. Jerome McCarthy and William D. Perreault, *Basic Marketing*, 10th ed. (Homewood, Ill.: R. D. Irwin, 1990).

13. See William A. Cohen, *The Practice of Marketing Management* (New York: Macmillan, 1988), p. 55

14. For an excellent resource on planning and strategies, see Peter Drucker, "Planning and Strategies," *The Nonprofit Drucker*, Vol. 2 (Tyler, Texas: The Leadership Network, 1989). *The Nonprofit Drucker* is a 5-volume cassette tape library. Each volume contains 5 audio cassette tapes. Volume 2 of the library is devoted to marketing planning and strategies.

## 8. Designing Your Program Offerings: Product, Place, Price Decisions

1. For models of developing a mission statement, see Alvin Lindgren and Norman Shawchuck, *Management for Your Church* (Schaumburg, Ill.: Spiritual Growth Resources, 1977,); Lloyd Perry and Norman Shawchuck, *Revitalizing the 20th Century Church* (Chicago: Moody Press, 1982).

2. "Spreading God's Word: Five Success Stories," *U.S. News and World Report,* Oct. 22, 1984, pp. 71-73.

3. John Crompton, "Developing New Recreation and Park Programs," *Recreation Canada* July 1983, p. 29.

4. For a useful discussion of creativity techniques, see Sidney J. Parnes and Harold F. Harding, eds., *Source Book for Creative Thinking* (New York: Charles Scribner and Sons, 1962).

5. See Alex F. Osborn, *Applied Imagination,* 3rd. ed. (New York: Charles Scribner and Sons, 1962).

6. Ibid., p. 156.

7. See Everett M. Rogers and F. Floyd Shoemaker, *Communications of Innovation* (New York: Free Press, 1971).

8. For an example of developing new products see James L. Ginter and W. Wayne Talarzyk, "Applying the Marketing Concept to Design New Products," *Journal of Business Research* 6 (Jan. 1978): 51-66.

9. "Turning Around the Lord's Business," *Fortune,* September 25, 1989, p. 128.

10. For more details, see Philip Kotler, "Atmospherics as a Marketing Tool," *Journal of Retailing* (Winter 1973–74): 48-64.

## 9. Communicating with Key Publics: Advertising and Public Relations

1. See "Mighty Fortress: Megachurches Strive to Be All Things to All Parishioners," *The Wall Street Journal,* R. Gustav Niebuhr, Staff Reporter, May 13, 1991.

2. See "How Pope John Paul II and Other Religious Leaders View Advertising," *Madison Avenue,* 27, 9, Sept. 1985, pp. 18-28, 106.

3. See "Admen for Heaven," *Christianity Today,* September 18, 1987, pp. 12-13.

4. As quoted in Martin E. Marty, "Sunday Mass and the Media," *Across the Board* (May 1987): 55-57.

5. See "Advertising Your Church," *Christianity Today,* November 18, 1977, pp. 30-31.

6. See Chaim M. Ehrman, "Can Advertising Be Justified from a Talmudist's Point of View? Some New Insights," *1987 AMA Winter Educators' Conference Proceedings* (Chicago: American Marketing Association, 1987), pp. 78-80.

7. Marty, "Sunday Mass and the Media," p. 56.

8. See Stephen W. McDaniel, "Marketing Communication Techniques in a Church Setting: Views on Appropriateness," *Journal of Professional Services Marketing* 27, 9 (Summer 1986): 39-54.

9. These definitions, with the exception of the one for sales promotion, were taken from *Marketing Definitions: A Glossary of Marketing Terms* (Chicago: American Marketing Association, 1960).

10. There are several models of consumer readiness states. See, for example, Robert J. Lavidge and Gary A. Steiner, "A Model for Predictive Measurements of Advertising Effectiveness," *Journal of Marketing* (October 1961): 59-62. For another approach, see Geraldine Fennell, "Persuasion as Behavioral Science in Business and Nonbusiness Contexts," in Russell W. Belk, ed., *Advances in Nonprofit Marketing,* vol. 1 (Greenwich, Conn.: JAI Press, 1985), pp. 95-160. James Engel's well-known "Complete Spiritual Decision Process Model" is described on p. 83 of his book *Contemporary Christian Communications* (Nashville: Thomas Nelson, 1979).

11. See Russell H. Colley, *Defining Advertising Goals for Measuring Advertising Results* (New York: Association of National Advertisers, 1961.)

12. For good advice on using television as an ad medium, see William K. Witcher, *How to Solve Your Small Business Advertising Problems* (Aptos, Calif..: Advertising Planners, Inc., 1986).

13. See William D. Novelli, "Social Issues and Direct Marketing: What's the Connection?" Presentation to the Annual Conference of the Direct Mail/Marketing Association, Los Angeles, California, March 12, 1981.

14. See Belinda Hulin-Salkin, "Strategies of Charities," *Advertising Age,* January 19, 1981, p. 529.

15. Norman W. Whan, *The Phones's for You!* (Brea, Calif.: Church Growth Development International,). For more information write to Church Growth Development International, 420 West Lambert, Suite E, Brea, CA 9261, or call 414-990-9551.

16. From a personal conversation with Mr. Whan.

17. For an excellent resource on focus groups, see Andre Delbecq, *Group Techniques for Program Planning* (Middletown, Wis.: Greenbriar Press, 1986).

18. *Public Relations News,* October 27, 1947.

19. See Ben Ramsey, "Church Public Relations: A Check-off List," *Public Relations Quarterly* (Winter 1977): 17-21

20. To order these tapes, write to The Commission of Communications, The Evangelical Lutheran Church in America, 8765 West Higgins Road, Chicago, IL 60631, or call 1-800-638-3522.

21. See J. Donald Weinrauch and Nancy Croft Baker, *The Frugal Marketer* (New York: AMACOM, 1989); J. Donald Weinrauch, *The Marketing Problem Solver* (New York: John Wiley, 1987); Alec Benn, *The 27 Most Common Mistakes in Advertising* (New York: AMACOM, 1978); David Ogilvy, *Confessions of an Advertising Man* (New York: Dell, 1980); and Dan Danford, "Targeting Your Church Advertising," *Ministries Today* (May/June 1988): 50-53.

## 10. Energizing Members and Volunteers: Internal Marketing

1. See Chip R. Bell and Ron Zemke, "Service Breakdown: The Road to Recovery," *Management Review* (Oct.1987): 32-35; James L. Heskett, "Lessons in the Service Sector," *Harvard Business Review* (March-April 1987): 118-26; Stephen Koepp, "Pul-eeze! Will Somebody Help Me?" *Time,* February 2, 1987, pp. 48-56; Stew Leonard, "Love That Customer," *Management Review* (October, 1987): 36-39; "Making Service a Potent Marketing Tool," *Business Week,* June 11, 1984, pp. 164-70; Gregory L. Schultz, "Rediscovering the Customer," *Service Management* (July-August 1985): 22-26; Bro Uttal, "Companies That Serve You Best," *Fortune,* December 7, 1987, pp. 98-16; Anthony Czepiel, Michael R. Solomon, and Carol F. Suprenant, *The Service Encounter: Managing Employee/Customer Interaction in Service Businesses* (Lexington, Mass.: D. C. Heath, Lexington Books, 1985); Robert Desatnick, *Managing to Keep the Customer: How to Achieve and Maintain Superior Customer Service Throughout the Organization* (San Francisco: Jossey-Bass, 1987); Tom Peters, *Thriving on Chaos: Handbook for a Management Revolution* (New York: Alfred A Knopf, 1987).

2. The SAS story is taken from Karl Albrecht and Ron Zemke, *Service America!* (Homewood, IL: Dow-Jones-Irwin, 1985).

3. These key concepts were inspired by the SAS story and from several important books on customer service: Karl Albrecht and Ron Zemke, *Service America!* (Homewood, Ill.: Dow Jones-Irwin, 1985), pp. 20-26; Ron Zemke with Dick Schaaf, *The Service Edge* (New York: NAL Books, 1989); Karl Albrecht and Lawrence J. Bradford, *The Service Advantage* (Homewood, Ill.: Dow Jones-Irwin, 1990); Karl Albrecht, *At America's Service* (Homewood, Ill.: Dow Jones-Irwin, 1988).

4. Zemke and Schaaf, *The Service Edge,* p. 40.

5. "Spreading God's Work: Five Success Stories," *U.S. New and World Report,* October 22, 1984, p. 71.

6. Jan Carlzon, *Moments of Truth* (Cambridge, Mass.: Ballinger Publishing Co., 1987).

7. The experience cycle is based on the Cycle of Service discussed in Karl Albrecht, *At America's Service* (Homewood, Ill.: Dow Jones-Irwin, 1988), pp. 32-36.

8. Zemke and Schaaf, *The Service Edge,* p. 22.

9. Ibid., pp. 23-26.

10. The "one-minute manager" is discussed in a most creative series of 6 little books on management, which we heartily recommend. In the series, Blanchard recommends that compliments and criticisms should be as immediate as possible, specific and brief—one minute is long enough.

11. Zemke and Schaff, *The Service Edge,* pp. 23-25.

12. Ibid., p. 22.

13. See Albrecht and Zemke, *Service America,* pp. 170-80, and Albrecht, *At America's Service,* pp. 157-223.

14. Adapted from Albrecht, *At America's Service,* p. 178.

15. One of the best resources for learning to give on-the-spot compliments, or reprimands, is the "One-Minute Manager" series by Kenneth Blanchard.

16. See Peter F. Drucker, *The Temptation to Do Good* (New York: Harper-Collins, 1984).

17. See Eva Schindler-Rainman and Ronald Lippitt, *The Volunteer Community: Creative Use of Human Resources*, 2nd. ed. (La Jolla, Calif.: University Associates, 1977), pp. 21-45.

18. See Gordon Mauser and Rosemary H. Cass, *Volunteer at the Crossroads* (New York: Family Service Association of America, 1976); and John Vantil, "In Search of Voluntarism," *Volunteer Administration* 12, 2 (Summer 1979).

19. For a taped interview of Frances Hesselbein, see "People and Relationships," *The Nonprofit Drucker*, vol. 4 (Tyler, Texas: The Leadership Network, 1989). The interview discusses Mrs. Hesselbein's volunteer and marketing strategies.

20. Many of the books and papers by Lyle Schaller offer insights into voluntarism in the church.

21. Schindler-Rainman and Lippitt, *The Volunteer Community*, pp. 48-50.

22. For an in-depth discussion of this issue, see Norman Shawchuck, "The Local Church: Who Works for Whom?" *Leadership* 1, 1 (1980): 95-100. Leadership, Vol. XX, XX, 19XX, Leadership: Carol Stream, IL. and *Let My People Go: Empowering Laity for Ministry*, Alvin Lindgren and Norman Shawchuck (Schaumburg, Ill.: Spiritual Growth Resources).

## 11. Attracting Needed Resources: Fund Raising

1. We are aware there are some so-called religious organizations that receive substantial income through the sale of books, tapes, time share in resort facilities, and so on, largely under the cloak of "contributions." This chapter, however, deals not with such organizations, but with those that by-and-large operate without profits and rely on contributions in the purest sense of the word.

2. See, for example, George E. Brazell, *Dynamic Stewardship Strategies* (Grand Rapids, Mich.: Baker Book House, 1989); Manfred Holck, *Church Finance in a Complex Economy* (Nashville: Abingdon Press, 1983); Raymond B. Knudsen, *Stewardship Enlistment and Commitment* (Nashville: Abingdon Press, 1985); George W. Harrison, *Church Fund Raising* (Englewood Cliffs, N.J.: Prentice-Hall, 1964); W. A. Poovey, *How to Talk with Christians About Money* (Minneapolis: Augsburg, 1982); John H. MacNaughton, *Stewardship: Myth and Methods* (New York: The Seabury Press, 1975); Douglas W. Johnson, *The Tithe* (Nashville, Abingdon Press, 1984).

3. See *Giving U.S.A.* (New York: American Association of Fundraising Council Trust for Philanthropy, 1989), p. 8-9.

4. *The Charitable Behavior of Americans* (Yankelovich, Skelly, and White, Inc., 1988).

5. See Lanson Ross, "The Cross in Crisis," *Fund Raising Management* (July 1987): 70-74.

6. Adapted from ibid.; Dan Nicholas, "How to Get Cash Without Compromising Ethics," *Fund Raising Management* (July 1987): 31-34; and Carl F. H. Henry, "Heresies in Evangelical Fund Raising," *Fund Raising Management* (November 1988): 42-47.

7. Henry, "Heresies in Evangelical Fund Raising," p. 42.

8. It seems to the authors that across the nation can be heard a collective sigh of relief from the readers, timid souls fearing we were going to mention their "pet" money makers (barbecues in the South, Bingo in the East, car washes in the Mid-

west, surf board raffles in the West—or whatever). With the possible exception of Bingo, these activities are quite innocuous as money makers, and we won't worry about marketing them.

9. See chapter 7, "Strategic Market Planning," for an example of a pastor and congregation who learned this $500,000 lesson too late.

10. See Richard B. Cunningham, *Creative Stewardship* (Nashville: Abingdon Press, 1979).

11. An excellent book discussing why people contribute to religious organizations is Martin E. Carlson's *Why People Give* (New York: Council Press, National Council of Churches of Christ, 1968).

12. See Harold J. Seymour, *Designs for Fund Raising* (New York: McGraw-Hill, 1966).

13. See chapter 10, "Energizing Members and Volunteer: Internal Marketing," for an example of a local church that adopted this approach with a first-time visitor—and thereby converted him into an only-time visitor.

14. Useful books and articles on grantsmanship are Virginia P. White, *Grants: How to Find Out About Them and What to Do Next* (New York and London: Plenum Press, 1975); Lois DeBakey and Selma DeBakey, "The Art of Persuasion: Logic and Language in Proposal Writing," *Grants Magazine*, 1, 1, March 1978, pp. 43-60; F. Lee Jacquette and Barbara J. Jacquette, *What Makes a Good Proposal* (New York: Foundation Center, 1973); Robert A. Mayer, *What Will a Foundation Look for When You Submit a Grant Proposal?* (New York: Foundation Center, 1972). Some books specifically addressing grant proposals for churches are Raymond Knudsen, *New Models for Financing the Local Church* (Wilton, Conn.: Morehouse-Barlow Co., 1985) and Tom Emswiles, *Money for Your Campus Ministry, Church, or Other Non-profit Organization* (Norman, Ill.: The Wesley Foundation, 1981).

15. See Raymond B. Knudsen, *Stewardship Enlistment and Commitment* (Wilton, Conn.: Morehouse-Barlow, 1985).

16. The process, outlined above, is a way of doing strategic planning and market planning (see chap. 7). It is commonly called *Program Planning and Budgeting System* (PPBS) or *Program Planning, Budgeting, and Evaluation* (PPBE).

17. For several examples, see Suzanne Seixas, "Getting More from Givers," *Money*, September 1976, pp. 79-82.

18. In a study by Freedman and Fraser, the experimenters asked subjects to comply with a small initial request. Two weeks later, they were contacted and asked to comply with a large request. It was found that 76 percent of the experimental participants agreed to comply with the large request, compared to a 17 percent compliance rate by those subjects approached with only the large request. See J. L. Freedman and S. Fraser, "Compliance Without Pressure: The Foot-in-the-Door Technique," *Journal of Personality and Social Psychology* 4 (1966): 195-202.

19. See Joel Brockner, Beth Guzzi, Julie Kane, Ellen Levine, and Kate Shaplen, "Organizational Fundraising: Further Evidence of the Effect of Legitimizing Small Donations," *Journal of Consumer Research* (June 1984): 611-13.

20. See Peter H. Reingen, "On Inducing Compliance with Requests," *Journal of Consumer Research* (September 1978): 96-102; Robert B. Cialdini and David A. Schroeder, "Increasing Compliance by Legitimizing Paltry Contributions: When Even a Penny Helps," *Journal of Personality and Social Psychology* (October 1976): 599-604.

21. See Knudsen, *New Models for Financing the Local Church*, pp. 108-9; also see chapter 12 of his book for details on how to start electronic fund transfer programs, like AUTOGIVE, or the use of bank-cards for donation purposes in a church.

## 12. Marketing Is Not Enough: Vision, Spirit, Integrity, and Discernment

1. Leadership Network is a private foundation that uses a major amount of its resources to network and train pastors of large (800+ in Sunday attendance) and growing churches.

2. Copies of the Better Preparation for Ministry report are available for review at the Center for Church Organizational Behavior, McCormick Theological Seminary, Chicago, Illinois. The full report may be purchased through the school's office of the academic dean at the price of $30.00.

3. Bill Hybels *Too Busy Not to Pray: Slowing Down to Be with God* (Downers Grove, Ill.: InterVarsity Press, 1988).

4. For the story of one congregation that moved to discernment as its preferred decision-making model, see Bob Slosser, *Miracle in Darien* (Plainfield, N.J..: Logos International, 1979).

## Appendix B. Taking Stock of What We Have Accomplished: Evaluation of Marketing

1. These questions were first suggested to the authors by Peter F. Drucker, in a seminar for pastors and parachurch organization leaders.

2. Benjamin S. Bloom, J. Thomas Hastings, and George F. Madaus, *Handbook on Formative and Summative Evaluation of Student Learning* (New York: McGraw-Hill, 1971). See also John Van Maanen, *The Process of Program Evaluation* (Washington, D.C.: National Training and Development Service Press, 1973).

# INDEX